PASCAL

PASCAL

Charles H. Goldberg
Trenton State College

Walter S. Brainerd
University of New Mexico

Jonathan L. Gross
Columbia University

BOYD & FRASER PUBLISHING COMPANY
BOSTON

Credits:

Editor: Tom Walker
Production supervisor: Joan H. Parsons
Development editor: Sharon Cogdill
Artwork: Marilyn Hill
Typesetting: UNICOMP
Printer: R. R. Donnelley & Sons

Library of Congress Cataloging in Publication Data

Goldberg, Charles E.
    Pascal.

    Includes index.
    1. PASCAL (Computer program language)   I. Brainerd, Walter S.   II. Gross,
Jonathan L.   III. Title.
QA76.73.P2G65   1984   001.64′24   83-25810
ISBN 0-87835-140-X

Cover photo: Detail of a red laser beam reflecting off a spinning video disk. © Jon Goell.

CONTENTS

DEDICATION

To Rosalyn, Betty, and Susan

PREFACE

Our book was designed for students taking an introductory course in computer science. We agree with the recommendations of the ACM Curriculum Committee, and have prepared this text with the objectives of Curriculum 78 (course number CS 1, Computer Programming) in mind.

We feel that the primary objectives of such a course are twofold: students should develop skills in analyzing and solving problems in their original context; and students should also become proficient in designing, coding, debugging, and documenting programs to solve these problems, using good programming style in a high-level programming language. Analyzing a problem is pretty much the same, no matter what computer language is used to write the program. However, writing instructions the computer will follow can be made much easier by choosing a suitable programming language. Pascal is both simple and powerful, and is therefore an ideal language to introduce the major concepts in computer programming.

As experienced instructors of introductory programming courses, we recognize the value and importance of accuracy in a textbook with respect to the presentation of the language itself as well as its implementation. Nothing in a text is more unsettling for students or instructors than example programs that contain errors. In addition to the over 150 complete, tested programs and their executions, the entire text of this book was typeset by one of the authors, Walter Brainerd, at Unicomp, using a DEC PDP 11/34 with a UNIX operating system.* We believe this process contributed greatly to the production of a book which complies with our own rigid standards of accuracy.

Our book is designed to be used in a one-semester course in Pascal programming. No previous experience with a computer is assumed, and no mathematics beyond the high-school level is required.

Major emphasis on problem-solving techniques and structured programming concepts requires students to develop good programming practices from the beginning. Discussions of procedures and modularity start as early as Chapter 3, to familiarize students with the concepts of structured design.

---

*UNIX is a registered trademark of Bell Laboratories.

This important topic, as well as others like testing and debugging, are introduced early and discussed consistently throughout the book.

A typical chapter contains about the amount of material that a student can master in a week. Each chapter is divided into sections, which begin with a Section Preview. Consistent with our top-down philosophy of programming, the Section Preview describes in condensed form the major syntactic structures and concepts introduced in that section. Each section ends with a list of Self-Test Questions (answers are provided in the Answer section at the end of the book). This enables students to individually assess their own understanding of the material. Also at the end of each section are interesting exercises encouraging students to apply their knowledge of programming and Pascal. Together, there are over 500 exercises in the book, ranging in difficulty from routine to challenging. There are also additional exercises designed for the more advanced or curious students, offering them numerous stimulating problems with which to test their knowledge of mathematics and their skills in problem-solving.

A succinct, list-formatted chapter review, entitled "What You Should Know," appears at the end of each chapter, reinforcing key concepts, good programming practices, and the major vocabulary of Pascal and programming.

Learning Pascal programming requires that students also master the vocabulary of computer science. Major vocabulary items are printed in boldface when they first appear and are defined in the text. These boldface words are alphabetized and defined again in a separate section at the end of the book, called "The Vocabulary."

In addition to our careful, consistent emphasis on programming fundamentals and style, we have included numerous discussions of program efficiency. We consider these discussions valuable not only for students of computer science, but for anyone interested in computer applications. Program efficiency is central to the writing of cost-effective programs.

A complete Instructor's Manual and Answer Book is available to instructors upon request from our publisher, Boyd and Fraser. It includes:
- chapter-by-chapter objectives
- solutions to programming exercises
- chapter-by-chapter vocabulary lists
- transparency masters from each chapter
- Quick-Test masters—with true/false, short answer, fill in the blank, multiple choice and programming exercises.

Pascal has been written for the student. We have tested this material with great success and trust that others will find it to be equally successful. We would appreciate hearing from both students and instructors who might have any comments or suggestions regarding this book. Write us in care of our publisher, Boyd and Fraser, 286 Congress Street, Boston, Massachusetts 02210.

Charles H. Goldberg
Walter S. Brainerd
Jonathan L. Gross

ACKNOWLEDGMENTS

We would like to express our sincere appreciation to those individuals who contributed in a variety of ways to the quality and success of this book. We are grateful to the many reviewers of the various drafts of this work for their valuable comments and suggestions.

Professor Kent Bimson, Department of Computer Science at California State University, Sacramento, and Professor David Kay, Department of Computer Science at U.C.L.A., deserve our special thanks for their contributions.

Robert Holloway, Computer Science Department, University of Wisconsin, Madison, should be singled out for his help with this project when we were faced with some very tight deadlines.

We would like to thank Tom Walker, Senior Editor at Boyd and Fraser. Tom's insights contributed substantially to this book's organization, scope, level and design.

There is no question that this book was greatly improved by Sharon Cogdill, our Development Editor at Boyd and Fraser. Her editorial talents and sensitivity to students' needs merit special praise.

Finally Joan Parsons, Production Supervisor at Boyd and Fraser, is deserving of our gratitude for seeing this book through the various stages of production.

NOTES

1. The Section Previews, highlighted in blue, describe in condensed form the major syntactic structures and concepts introduced in that section.

2. Pascal and programming terms are printed in **boldface** when they first appear. These terms are defined in "The Vocabulary" section at the end of the book.

3. Answers to all Self-Test Questions are provided in the Answer section at the end of the book.

4. The Appendices are a valuable reference tool. They provide a complete, succinct review of the Pascal syntax.

COMPUTERS AND PROGRAMMING 1

A **computer** is a device for processing information in a wide variety of ways, both simple and complex. It can perform arithmetic and read, remember, transcribe, modify, and print information with speed and accuracy. In fact, some computers can do more arithmetic in one second than a person can do in a lifetime, even if the person were to work 12 hours a day, every day, from birth to the age of 100. Moreover, the computer is unlikely to make even a single mistake in the process.

Computers are versatile, general purpose machines. The same computer that prepares a payroll one minute can also perform a scientific calculation or alphabetize a list of names the next minute. Computers are versatile because they combine relatively simple basic operations like reading, writing, and arithmetic into meaningful sequences, called **programs**. The more programs there are for a computer, the more different things it can do.

This book is an introduction to **computer programming**, the writing of computer programs, and to the computer programming language Pascal, which is rapidly becoming the language of choice in Computer Science programs. All of the features of the standard Pascal language are introduced in this book, with typical applications showing what a computer can do. Complete programs and sample executions are given throughout.

Learning a computer language is like learning a natural language in the sense that it is not necessary to know the entire unabridged dictionary before anything meaningful can be said. In fact, using only a few dozen different words, it is possible to communicate quite well with a computer in Pascal.

We believe you should start reading and writing programs as soon as possible. After a brief discussion of the history and nature of computers in this chapter, Chapter 2 shows that it is possible to read, write, and run meaningful programs with a minimum of fuss and bother.

This book assumes no prior knowledge of computers or of computer programming. However, some readers already may know another programming language or may know some Pascal constructions.

Each section begins with a Section Preview, which condenses the major syntactic structures and concepts presented in the section. If you are already familiar with a programming construct and know how to program it in another computer language, then the Section Preview will give you the Pascal syntax for the construct in condensed form and you probably will be able to skip the section. The same holds true if you already know some Pascal. The Section Preview provides a quick review of the topics covered.

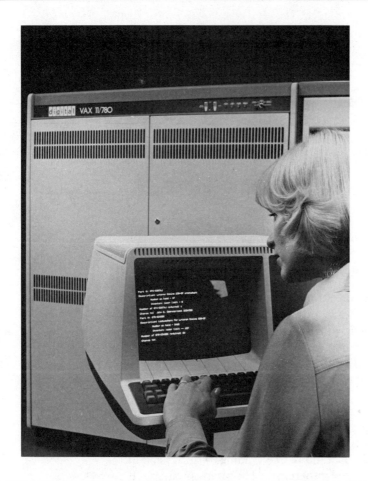

Figure 1.1   DEC VAX 11/780, a medium-scale computer system with interactive
processing capability.   *Courtesy Digital Equipment Corporation.*

1.1   What is a computer?

These days, a great many devices are called computers, either by their manufac-
turers or by the general public. Since the kinds of computers discussed in this
book are widely acclaimed as models of technological achievement, it is not
surprising to find that many of the near and distant relatives are also called
"computers" in order to claim their kinship. This section describes some computers and discusses the characteristic attributes and capabilities they share.

Section Preview

The first computer was Charles Babbage's Analytical Engine,
which was designed in 1834 but never built. The second computer was Howard Aiken's Mark I, built in 1939-44.

A computer is a device with the following capabilities.
Some computers have additional capabilities, but all computers
have the ones listed below. A computer can

Figure 1.2 IBM Personal Computer. *Courtesy International Business Machines Corporation.*

1. Operate automatically without step-by-step human control
2. Perform arithmetic calculations
3. Accept input data
4. Send output data to the user
5. Save data in its memory and later retrieve the data
6. Move data from place to place in its memory
7. Be **programmed** to execute any meaningful sequence of its built-in operations
8. Choose between programmed alternatives while operating automatically
9. Access its memory in a flexible manner
10. Store its program in the same memory cells that can at other times store data

Ancient History

At one time, a computer was a person who performed arithmetic computations. In the eighteenth and nineteenth centuries, when knowledge of the basic arithmetic operations was far from universal, and proficiency in the more difficult operations of multiplication and division was quite rare, these human computers were in some demand, especially for computing the astronomical tables essential to navigation and the tables used in trade and insurance.

Unfortunately, it is not humanly possible to manipulate great volumes of numbers without error, and consequently the mathematical, astronomical, and navigational tables until relatively recently contained a profusion of errors. Even the most carefully prepared and edited tables might average one error per page, while less carefully prepared tables might have many more. Some of the errors were due to the human computers, but others entered later in the process, for instance in recopying the table for the printer, in typesetting, and even in the printing process itself.

One remarkable error originated in Vlacq's table of logarithms, printed in Gouda in 1628. Two digits, one above the other on successive lines of the table, were interchanged. It seems probable that this error occurred when two adjacent pieces of type came loose from the printing matrix at the same time during the printing of the table and were replaced by the pressman in the wrong positions. All subsequent copies of this table, which was reprinted for over 300 years, contained this error, clearly not the result of an arithmetic mistake.

The First Modern Computer

The first modern computer was Charles Babbage's Analytical Engine, designed in 1834 to eliminate these sources of error and to produce perfectly accurate tables. Even though Babbage's machine was never built in its entirety, its design is remarkable because it was so innovative. Only one of its features had ever been incorporated into a computational device: its arithmetic capability. In 1671 Baron Gottfried Wilhelm von Leibniz designed a calculating machine that could add, subtract, multiply, and divide, but Babbage's machine was completely automatic. Leibniz's machine required additional human assistance in division because the carry mechanism worked incompletely in reverse. One original model of Leibniz's machine may be found in a library in Hannover, Germany.

Babbage was unable to construct his "engine" because of the state of the art of machining in his day. He was trying to construct a machine with thousands of gears at a time when even the gears of most clocks had to be hand-fitted to mesh properly. He contributed greatly to the art of machining, devised a system of mechanical notation for representing moving machinery, and wrote a pioneer work in a field now called operations research. He devised a method for dating archeological sites using sequences of growth rings of trees that was later rediscovered and used extensively in the archeology of the American Southwest. He published an excellent table of logarithms, hand-computed and edited, and is credited with many inventions. His life and works make interesting reading.

The first operational computer, the Mark I, was designed by Howard Aiken at Harvard from 1939 to 1944, over 100 years after Babbage designed his Analytical Engine. In design, the Mark I is fundamentally the same as Babbage's machine, with improved flexibility in accessing its memory. The difference is in the hardware, which consists of electrical circuits instead of gears.

Characteristics of a Computer

Computers, from Babbage's Analytical Engine to the most modern computer, have a great deal in common. Improvements in technology have continually changed their size, speed, and physical appearance, but the fundamental principles on which they are based have changed little. The remainder of this section describes ten attributes of computers that enable them to perform the applications of this book.

Figure 1.3   CRAY X-MP computer system, a supercomputer. *Courtesy Cray Research, Inc.*

Computer Attribute 1: Automatic Operation

The most fundamental principle in computer design from Babbage's time to the present is **automatic operation**, that is, the ability of a computer to operate as much as possible without human direction or assistance. According to Babbage's own account, the idea of performing repetitive computations by machine first came to him in the following way. On one occasion, his longtime friend, the scientist John Hershel, brought in some calculations done for the Astronomical Society by a (human) computer. In the course of their tedious checking, Hershel and Babbage found a number of errors, and at one point Babbage said, "I wish to God these calculations were executed by steam", by which he meant "automatically". If Babbage's metaphor seems strange to modern ears, it is because now, more than a century and a half later, steam power is no longer the new and innovative source of energy for industry and commerce it was then. Had he lived to see the invention of the vacuum tube, the transistor, and the integrated circuit, Babbage might well have wished the calculations were executed by electronics, as indeed they are today.

The principle of requiring as little human assistance and direction as possible can be found in every aspect of computer design. In most instances, not only does accuracy improve with the elimination of unnecessary human intervention, but speed increases as well.

Computer Attribute 2: Arithmetic Calculations

The heart of Babbage's Analytical Engine, an apparatus called the "mill", is capable of performing the four basic arithmetic operations without human intervention once the numbers have been entered. Other automatic devices had

been built earlier, notably a device built by Blaise Pascal, after whom the programming language used in this book was named. Also, before building the
Analytical Engine, Babbage had built a Difference Engine, which was used to
calculate mathematical tables. However, only Leibniz's machine could perform
multiplication without human assistance, and none previously had been
invented to perform division automatically. Modern computers still rely on the
four arithmetic operations as the basis for numeric computing.

A working model of Babbage's mill was constructed from his drawings by
his son, Henry P. Babbage. It worked as well as Babbage had anticipated. With
the main axis turning approximately once per second, the addition or subtraction of two 29-digit numbers takes approximately 1 second. Multiplication or
division of 29-digit numbers requires up to 3 minutes, depending on the sum of
the digits in the multiplier or quotient. The original mill, which still works, is
in the Science Museum, London.

Today, a battery-powered electronic hand calculator that performs these
four basic arithmetic operations in fractions of a second can be purchased for
less than the price of a book, but until recently a mechanical desk calculator
with the same capabilities was at least as large as a typewriter, weighed twice as
much, and cost several hundred dollars.

Computer Attribute 3: Input

A computer or calculator must have some means of receiving information, the
data of the problem, from its human operators. All operations supplying a
computer with information are **input**. Babbage's Analytical Engine had
"number cards" for receiving information, an adaption of the pattern cards
used by Jacquard in his automatic loom for weaving brocaded silk cloth. As
shown in Figure 1.4 each column of a pasteboard number card had nine positions; no holes were punched for the digit 0, one hole for the digit 1, two holes
for the digit 2, and so on. Thus each digit required a full column of the card
for its representation in holes, and the number of digits encoded on a number
card corresponded exactly to the number of columns on the card.

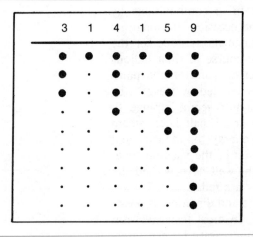

Figure 1.4 A number card for Babbage's Analytical Engine.

The modern computer **punchcard** is very much the same as Babbage's
number cards (see Figure 1.5). In the most commonly used punchcard code,
named for its inventor, Herman Hollerith, each column still represents 1 digit
of input information. In the Hollerith code, each digit from 0 to 9 is encoded

as a single punch in an appropriate position in the column. Alphabetic characters, requiring two holes per column, and other special characters like punctuation marks, dollar signs, and arithmetic symbols, requiring up to three holes per column are added to augment the simple numeric code. Containing 80 columns, a standard Hollerith card is capable of encoding up to 80 digits, letters, or other characters of input information. Punchcards are still used at some computer installations to supply information to a computer. A typical punchcard reader can read 500 Hollerith punchcards per minute.

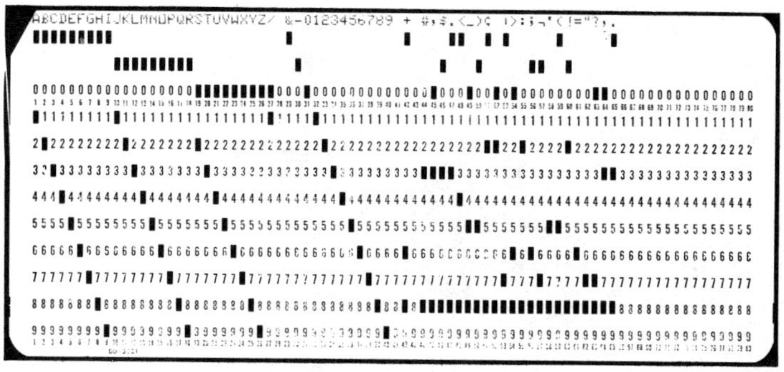

Figure 1.5 A computer punchcard, punched with the complete Hollerith code.

In contrast, input is accomplished by means of the entry keys in most hand or desk calculators. If two numbers are to be multiplied, each is entered into the machine by way of the entry keys before multiplication can begin.

Today, the primary means of supplying input information to a computer is a typewriterlike **computer terminal**. Basically, this is an electric typewriter equipped to encode electronically the letters and numbers that are typed and to transmit the encoded information directly to a computer. Like calculator keyboards, a computer terminal can supply input information only as fast as a person can press the keys.

Much greater input speeds are possible using **magnetic tapes** and **magnetic disks**. Many efficient operating systems accept input information entered from cards or terminals at whatever speeds these devices can manage and then recopy the input information onto magnetic disk or tape files for faster availability when the information is needed. Many computer systems now support direct creation and editing of disk files from an interactive terminal, providing great flexibility and convenience in the preparation of high speed input files. Similarly, calculated results that are to be reread at a later time as input data are written on magnetic disks and tapes, because of the higher reading and writing speeds of these devices.

A wide variety of other computer input devices are used at the present time, though they are much less common than punchcards and computer terminals. For example, optical scanners can read carefully printed block letters and numerals; magnetic ink scanners are used to read account numbers on bank checks. Television cameras are used as input devices to analyze pictures transmitted from Mars and Jupiter and to produce portraits on a printer. Thermocouples and other measuring instruments are used as input devices when a computer directly controls industrial processes. In fact, nearly any device capable of producing numeric or alphabetic information can probably be connected to a computer if there is good reason to do so.

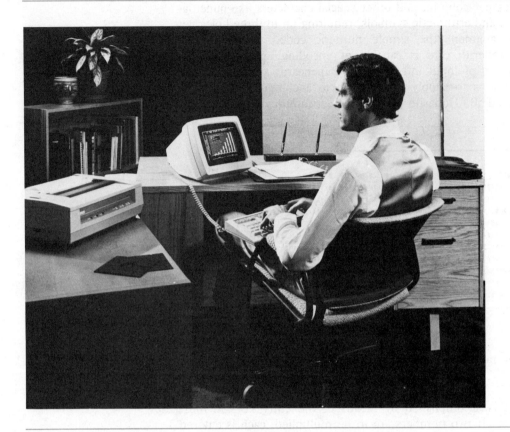

Figure 1.6   DEC Rainbow personal computer. *Courtesy Digital Equipment Corporation.*

Computer Attribute 4: Output

A computer must be able to communicate its answers back to the proposer of the problem. Omitting a statement instructing the computer to print the answer is a mistake often made by beginners in their first programs. Since a computer does exactly what it is told, the computer may compute the answer when such a program is run, but it will never tell anyone what the answer is.

Any means of transcribing information held within a computer into a form external to the computer is **output**. Programmers usually speak of **writing** output, regardless of whether the result is printed, typed, displayed on a television screen, plotted, or encoded as magnetic spots on a tape or disk.

Babbage was especially careful in designing the output for his Analytical Engine, because so many of the errors in the tables of his day were introduced after the computation. He provided for three types of output, a printing device capable of printing one or two copies of the results, a means for producing a stereotype mold from which printing plates for the tables could be made directly, and a mechanism for punching the numerical results of its computations into blank pasteboard cards for error-free rereading by the Analytical Engine. Great pains were taken in the design of these output features to ensure that no human error could intervene between the correct computation of the results and the final printing of the table.

At a modern computer installation, a principal form of output for human consumption is still the printed page. Direct computer typesetting has made a comeback in recent years with the complete computerization of the printing of

Figure 1.7 IBM 3084, a large-scale computer system. *Courtesy International Business Machines Corporation.*

several major newspapers. However, using modern photographic reproduction and printing processes, a computer text editing system that produces clean printed copy also eliminates errors in printing. The text of this book was produced this way.

Another form of computer output that dates back to Babbage is the punchcard. Babbage wanted his computer to be able to punch cards so that results calculated by the machine could later be reentered into the machine without the consequent opportunities for error. This technique is still in use for bills sent through the mails. Customers are requested to return their prepunched billing card with their payment to minimize errors in crediting the payment. Most of the programs in this book were put in disk files, run, and then the program and output files were edited directly into the text to eliminate copying errors.

Most desk calculators, especially those of the hand-held electronic variety, have only one form of output, visual display. A numerical answer is displayed in lights or other readable form, and the user must copy it onto paper if a more permanent record is desired. Persons who have had occasion to copy quantities of numbers, or even to copy notes from the blackboard in a technical course, know that this process introduces many opportunites for error. Because there is a practical limit to how many figures can be copied without making a mistake, desk calculators become progressively less suitable as the volume of output information increases. Most adding machines and a few desk calculators provide a printed record of their calculations.

Many modern computers also have a provision for visual display. A television-type screen can be used to display several dozen lines of printing at the same time, or it can be used to produce other shapes for viewing. Used as an alternative to printing, this type of output can reduce substantially the amount of **hard copy** needed at a computer installation, an important conservation role. Graphic display is also important when computers are used to teach languages like Japanese, Hebrew, Russian, and graphic arts like architectural drawing, all of which require shapes and characters not found in the usual English alphabet and consequently not available on standard printers. Graphic displays, including diagrams, line drawings, and computer-generated cartoons can be produced in this way, and the result photographed for a more permanent record.

Other specialized output devices include plotters and electronic sound synthesizers for producing computer-generated or computer-processed music. For direct control of other machinery, output can be in the form of control impulses to that machinery, as is the case in airplane guidance systems, numerically controlled milling machines, and forms of industrial process control.

Computer Attribute 5: Memory

In a computer or calculator, **memory** is the capacity to retain information and to recall that information later. Many simple hand calculators have no memory capacity beyond what is required to retain the two numbers being added, subtracted, multiplied, or divided, and to produce the answer. Unless they are used in the very next step, intermediate results must be copied on paper and reentered later in the calculation on simple calculators. Thus, the calculation

$$(2 \times 3) / 4 = 6 / 4 = 1.5$$

can be performed without recording the intermediate result 6, but the calculation of the expression

$$(2 + 3) / (4 + 5)$$

requires the recording of at least one intermediate result. Writing intermediate results on paper is jokingly called using the calculator's "paper memory", because this memory is a feature of the user and not of the calculator.

The most straightforward way to perform the intended calculation is to compute

$2 + 3 = 5$ which is recorded on paper
or stored in the calculator

$4 + 5 = 9$ which is recorded on paper
or stored in the calculator

and finally

$5 / 9 = 0.5555555556$ which is the answer

A standard trick, known to experienced users of desk calculators, is to compute and record the denominator first. Then the numerator does not have to be recorded, because it is used in the very next step when it is divided by the already calculated denominator to produce the answer. This trick also is used in efficient machine language programming of a computer.

In principle, the calculation

$$(2.345678 + 3.456789) / (4.567890 + 5.678901)$$

is similar to the previous example, because it involves the same sequence of arithmetic operations, but the penalty for having to copy and reenter a number and the probability of making a mistake are both increased by the larger number of digits in the intermediate results for the numerator and denominator. A large number of desk calculations can be made significantly easier by the addition of a small number of **memory cells**. For example, Table 1.1 shows the steps a person might follow to perform the harder calculations using a hand calculator that has an additional memory cell. The error-prone process of copying and reentering a number is replaced by use of the relatively error-free features called something like **store** and **recall** on programmable calculators.

Table 1.1   A hand calculation that uses memory.

STEP	USER ACTION	DISPLAYED NUMBER
1	Enter 4.567890	4.56789
2	Add	
3	Enter 5.678901	5.678901
4	Equals	10.246791
5	Store displayed number	
6	Enter 2.345678	2.345678
7	Add	
8	Enter 3.456789	3.456789
9	Equals	5.802467
10	Divided by	
11	Recall stored number	10.246791
12	Equals	0.5662716259

Among typical desk calculators can be found simple machines with no additional memory, more powerful calculators with 1 to 3 memory cells, calculators designed for statistical or financial use with 6 to 10 memory cells, and even calculators with several dozen memory cells, each capable of storing one piece of data with the same number of digits as handled by the rest of the calculator. For his Analytical Engine, Babbage wanted 1000 memory locations in what he called the "store", but this part of his computer was never built. Modern computers have thousands, and sometimes millions, of memory locations. With recent technological advances, the cost of manufacturing and operating large memories is dropping rapidly, and they are becoming more common.

The ease and speed with which a piece of information can be stored and recalled from a memory location may be different for different parts of a computer's memory. Many computers have a variety of different types and speeds of memory. At the slow end of the scale, the distinction between a computer storing a piece of information in a memory location and a computer preserving the same piece of information by writing it on an output device like a magnetic disk for eventual recall as input data is almost imperceptible.

In a Pascal program, each memory location is given a name that reminds the programmer what the values stored in that location represent. These names for memory locations, called **variable names**, usually are taken from the original problem statement and are easier to remember than the numeric **addresses** used in hand calculators and machine languages.

Computer Attribute 6: Data Transfers

Many data processing tasks require rearranging the input data during the processing. **Sorting**, the arranging of data in alphabetic or numeric order, is such a task commonly performed by computers.

In most computer systems, all input data, regardless of their ultimate destination in the computer's memory, are read first into a set of fixed locations called the **input buffer**. Then, they are transferred from the input buffer to other parts of the memory. Output data usually follow a similar path, but in reverse. All output data are transferred first to an **output buffer**, from which they are written onto an output device.

On a hand calculator with more than one memory cell, the following sequence of operations might copy a value from memory cell 7 to memory cell 10.

Recall from memory cell 7
Store in memory cell 10

The **data transfer** takes place in two stages. First, the value in memory cell 7 is copied to the display register by the recall operation. Then the value in the display register is copied to memory cell 10 by the store operation. As a result, the old value from memory cell 7 now appears in both cells as well as the display register.

All computers have similar sequences of operations for moving a single piece of data. Many computer also have more powerful operations for moving whole blocks of data at one time.

In Pascal, the transfer of information from a memory cell named a to a memory cell named b is done by an **assignment statement**

    b := a

which is read "b is assigned the value of a".

Computer Attribute 7: Programmability

Every hand or desk calculator has a set of basic operations which may be used individually or in meaningful combination to accomplish a desired computation. Typical basic operations include the four arithmetic operations—addition, subtraction, multiplication, and division—and the input operation of keying in a number. If a calculator has memory, the store and recall operations also are included. Many hand calculators also have more complex basic operations, like reciprocal ($1/x$), square root, logarithms, and trigonometric functions. With simpler hand calculators, human direction is required to initiate all basic operations, although they are completed automatically.

A calculator is **programmable** if meaningful sequences of basic operations can be selected in advance and an entire preselected sequence of operations executed automatically. Usually, the entire preselected sequence of operations

Table 1.2 Raising 1.06 to the fifth power on a hand calculator.

STEP	USER ACTION	DISPLAYED NUMBER
1	Enter 1.06	1.06
2	Store displayed number	
3	Multiply by	
4	Recall store number	1.06
5	Equals	1.1236
6	Multiply by	
7	Recall stored number	1.06
8	Equals	1.191016
9	Multiply by	
10	Recall stored number	1.06
11	Equals	1.26247696
12	Multiply by	
13	Recall stored number	1.06
14	Equals	1.3382255776

is stored in a special **program memory** so that the sequence can be rerun easily, perhaps using different input data. Of course, input operations cannot be completely automatic if the only available form of input is a person using the entry keys.

For example, the operation of raising a number to the fifth power is useful in finding compound interest over a 5-year period, but it is not a basic operation on many hand calculators. On these hand calculators, a number may be raised to the fifth power by multiplying it by itself five times. To raise 1.06 to the fifth power, the user might perform the sequence of basic operations shown in Table 1.2.

If it is also desired to raise 1.0625 to the fifth power on a nonprogrammable calculator, the same 14 steps shown in Table 1.2 must be repeated by the user, this time with the number 1.0625 entered in step 1. However, if the calculator is programmable, this sequence of basic operations can be made into a program by replacing the specific first step, "Enter 1.06", with a more general input request to enter any number. A program like that in Table 1.3 can be stored in the program memory of a programmable hand calculator and easily run to raise any desired number to the fifth power.

Table 1.3 A program for raising any number to the fifth power.

PROGRAM STEP	BASIC OPERATION
1	Halt for input (user must enter a number and resume program execution to complete this step)
2	Store displayed number
3	Multiply by
4	Recall stored number
5	Equals
6	Multiply by
7	Recall stored number
8	Equals
9	Multiply by
10	Recall stored number
11	Equals
12	Multiply by
13	Recall stored number
14	Equals
15	Halt so user can read the result

Once this program has been entered and stored in the calculator's program memory, both of the desired calculations, raising 1.06 and 1.0625 to the fifth power, can be obtained as shown in Table 1.4.

Computers are programmable. The set of basic operations available on a computer is that computer's **machine language**. A large number of the machine language instructions for most computers are variants of the basic arithmetic operations, the input and output operations, and the store and recall operations.

If the computer is powerful enough to support a **compiler**, the programs do not have to be written in machine language, because the compiler automatically translates from Pascal to machine language. The following program steps written in Pascal are equivalent to the machine language program for raising an input number to the fifth power.

Table 1.4 Using a program twice on a programmable hand calculator.

STEP	USER ACTION	DISPLAYED NUMBER
1	Start program	
2	Enter 1.06 and resume execution	1.06
		1.06
		1.1236
		1.06
		1.191016
		1.06
		1.26247696
		1.06
		1.3382255776
3	Start program	
4	Enter 1.0625 and resume execution	1.0625
		1.0625
		1.12890625
		1.0625
		1.199462891
		1.0625
		1.274429321
		1.0625
		1.354081154

```
begin
read (value);
answer := value * value * value * value * value;
writeln (answer);
end.
```

The asterisk (*) is the symbol for multiplication in Pascal and the abbreviated keyword "writeln" means "write output and move to the beginning of a new line". Everything else is more or less self-explanatory.

Both the modern computer and Babbage's Analytical Engine are designed to allow the user to specify that nearly any sequence of basic operations be performed. Of course, this transfers the responsibility for ensuring that the sequence of computational steps produces a meaningful result from the designer of the machine to the designer of the program, the programmer. This is what computer programming is all about: how to design sequences of computational steps to produce meaningful and useful results.

Probably the first computer programmer, aside from Babbage himself, was his longtime supporter, Augusta Ada, Countess of Lovelace, a knowledgeable mathematician in her own right. Her mother, Annabella Milbanke, also was interested in mathematics and her father was Lord Byron, the poet. The programming language Ada, developed by the Department of Defense, was named after her.* She translated into English the first published description of the Analytical Engine, adding a set of translator's notes more than twice the length of the original article, in which she gave several computer programs for the Analytical Engine. These programs are equivalent to machine language programs for a modern computer or programmable hand calculator.

*Ada is a trademark of the United States Department of Defense (Ada Joint Program Office).

Computer Attribute 8: Decisions

While operating automatically, that is, not under direct step-by-step human control, a computer can "choose" what to do next based on computed values or input data. The **decision** is made automatically, but the programmer must first indicate in the program exactly when the decision is to be made, what test is to be applied, and what step is to be executed next for every possible result of the test.

Two important programming techniques, loops and alternative computations, rely on the ability of a computer to decide. It is a rare and straightforward computer program that does not use one or the other of these techniques.

A **loop** is a sequence of program steps that may be repeated more than once during a single running of a program. For example, if the same computations are to be performed on the data for each student in a class or each worker in a factory, it is a dreadfully inefficient use of both the programmer's time and the computer's memory to write the computational steps out in full as many times as they are needed. A loop is written instead.

The decision step in a loop can almost always be based on the answer to the questions, "Are we done?" or "Have the computational steps in the loop been executed a sufficient number of times?" or a more specific inquiry of the same sort. If the computational steps in the loop have not been executed a sufficient number of times, the next thing the computer should do is to repeat them. If they have been executed the correct number of times, the computer should not repeat but go on to the next instruction after the loop, perhaps to compute an average or to print summary totals, or even to stop if nothing else needs to be done by the program.

Alternative computational procedures use the same decision capability of a computer, but for a different purpose. Here the choice is not whether to repeat, but which computational procedure is to be performed next. This technique allows overtime pay to be calculated by a different formula than nonovertime pay and deposits to be handled differently from withdrawals.

Both Babbage's Analytical Engine and the modern computer or desk calculator can make these kinds of decisions. Some relatively simple devices also can make decisions. For example, a digital alarm clock "decides" each minute whether to start its alarm or not and "decides" again several minutes later whether to turn the alarm off, in case no one has done so in the meanwhile.

Computer Attribute 9: Flexible Memory Access

In a modern computer, individual operations like store and recall operations need not be tied permanently to a specific memory cell at the time the program is written. The computer can calculate during automatic operation which memory cell will supply data for the operation or receive the results of the operations.

To be more specific, the hand calculator operations

Recall the contents of memory cell 7
Store in memory cell 10

are tied to specific memory cells. The former can only retrieve a value from memory cell 7, and the latter can only store a value in memory cell 10. Some programmable hand calculators and many computers have an operation similar to the following operation.

Look in memory cell 10;
the value you find there will tell you which memory cell
    to store the answer in.

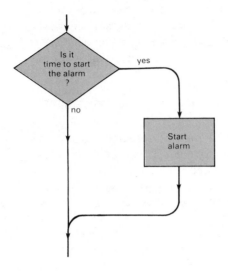

Figure 1.8 Flowchart for an alarm program on a digital watch.

For example, if memory cell 10 contains the value 3, this operation has the same effect as the operation

>   Store in memory cell 3

However, if memory cell 10 contains the value 5, this operation has a different effect, namely the same as the operation

>   Store in memory cell 5

This two-step specification of which memory cell is intended is **indirect addressing**. Since the contents of memory cell 10 may be the result of a previous calculation, the access this operation provides to memory is very flexible.

Computer Attribute 10: Stored Program

In most computers, the program is stored in the computer's memory in exactly the same memory cells that at other times could store data. In order to run its programs rapidly and efficiently, a programmable calculator or computer must be able to locate and read its next instruction about as fast as a typical instruction is executed. Usually this means that a program, or as much of one as will fit, is stored in memory cells of the same general accessibility and speed as those used to store data.

In most programmable calculators, the program memory is distinct from the data memory. Many computers allow the same memory cells to be used for either data or program steps, however, and there are advantages to this. First, the computer's design is simplified because certain parts of the circuitry do not have to be duplicated for separate program and data memories. Second, short programs with a great deal of data and long programs with comparatively little data both can be run on the same computer without wasting valuable memory capacity.

These ideas, called the stored program concept, are attributed to John von Neumann, one of the greatest mathematicians of the century and a pioneer in the early development of computers. They first appeared in print in a 1946 paper written by Arthur Burks, Herman Goldstine, and von Neumann. A side effect of program and data sharing the same memory is that a program can act on its own instructions as data, changing itself as it runs. This idea has spurred much research in artificial intelligence, but it is not ordinarily used outside that field. Babbage imagined this process as a computer eating its tail.

Self-Test Questions

Which of the ten characteristic attributes of a computer are possessed by the following devices? You may need to refer to sources outside this book for sufficient information to help you make your decisions.

1. A clock radio
2. A digital clock radio
3. A desk calculator or hand calculator. Use the one you are most familiar with, if any.
4. A programmable hand calculator
5. Babbage's Analytical Engine
6. A computer you have seen, or are using in conjunction with this book
7. A player piano or music box
8. A multichanger record player, that is, one that accepts more than one record at a time
9. The automatic speed control mechanism in an automobile ("cruise control")
10. A Jacquard loom for weaving brocades

1.2 What You Should Know

1. A computer is a device for processing information in a wide variety of ways, both simple and complex.
2. The first computer was the Analytical Engine, designed by Charles Babbage in the 1830s.
3. The first operational computer, the Mark I, was built in the 1940s.
4. The most fundamental principle in computer design from Babbage's time to the present is automatic operation, that is, the ability of a computer to operate as much as possible without human direction or assistance.
5. Modern computers rely on the four arithmetic operations as the basis for numeric computing.
6. Computers can receive input data from many sources, including terminals, magnetic disks, punchcards, and other computers.
7. Computers write output in many forms, including printed output, video display, plotted graphic output, and disks, tapes, and punchcards.
8. Regardless of what the actual medium is, computer scientists speak of reading all input and writing all output.
9. In its memory, a computer can save information and retrieve it later.
10. In a Pascal program, each memory location is referenced by a variable name that reminds the programmer what the values stored in that location represent.
11. A computer can move data around in its memory.
12. A computer is a general-purpose machine that can perform a specific task only if it has been programmed.
13. The instructions to a computer are not always executed in sequence. The computer's instruction set includes instructions to change the sequence on the basis of computed results.

14.   A loop is a sequence of program steps that may be repeated more than once during a single execution of a program.

15.   The computer can choose between computational alternatives on the basis of a calculated selector variable or expression.

16.   In most computers, the program is stored in the computer's memory in exactly the same memory cells that at other times could store data.

PROBLEM-SOLVING AND PROGRAMMING IN PASCAL 2

A computer "solves" problems by executing a planned sequence of instructions. The computer's considerable success in "solving" problems is built on advances in two areas of computer science. First, in an area not treated in this book, it is built on major achievements in designing electronic circuits that perform with speed, reliability, and at increasingly low cost. Second, much is now known about how to analyze problems for computer solution and how to write reliable computer programs to solve the problems.

Analyzing a problem is pretty much the same no matter what computer language is used to write the program. However, writing the instructions the computer will follow can be made much easier by a suitable choice of programming language. The language Pascal is both simple and powerful, and it is an ideal language to introduce the major concepts in computer programming.

The vocabulary of Pascal is not large. Moreover, you can begin writing meaningful programs to solve real problems as soon as you know just a few words of Pascal. Section 2.1 shows how to write Pascal programs to perform standard arithmetic calculations, and the rest of Chapter 2 shows how to write programs to do more complex calculations and how to run these programs on a computer.

We believe you should start reading and writing programs immediately. If a computer is available, begin to write and **run** programs modelled on our sample programs. A short set of directions from the instructor or computer center or, better yet, a brief demonstration using the computer will show you how to enter and run a program at your local installation.

2.1 Programs That Calculate

Since computers are very good at arithmetic, one reasonable thing to learn first about computer programming is how to tell a computer to do the sort of arithmetic that otherwise might be done by hand or with the aid of a hand calculator. This section describes how to write programs to calculate and to print.

Section Preview

General form of a Pascal program:

```
program program name ( list of files );
  begin
  ...;
  Pascal statements ;
  ...;
  end.
```

Example:

```
program calculation1 (output);
  begin
  writeln (84 + 13);
  end.
```

Writeln statement (write with following linefeed):

```
writeln ( list of expressions to be printed )
```

Example:

```
writeln ('The answer is ', (84 + 13) / 2)
```

Simple Calculations

The first example is a program that prints the result of an addition:

```
program calculation1 (output);
  begin
  writeln (84 + 13);
  end.
```

The program calculation1 tells the computer to add the numbers 84 and 13 and then to write the sum, which is 97. When the computer is told to run calculation1, it does precisely that: it adds the two numbers and writes their sum. The execution printout will look something like this, with only minor variations from computer to computer:

```
run calculation1

      97
```

A printed copy of a program is a **program listing**. The display above of the four-line program calculation1 is a program listing.

Five questions of immediate relevance are brought up by this example. Their answers will occupy the rest of this chapter.

1. How does the computer know that it is supposed to write the sum 97, and not the statement of the problem "84 + 13" instead?
2. What kinds of expressions may be written inside of the parentheses after the word "writeln"? "Writeln" is an abbreviation for "write line".
3. Just how much English is incorporated into the Pascal programming language? For example, are there any acceptable synonyms for "begin", "end", and "program", and the command "writeln"?
4. What is the meaning of the program name "calculation1"? Does it have to start with "calculation" to work properly?
5. How is a computer told what the program is and when to run it?

Printing Messages

If you want the computer to print the exact typographic characters that you specify, you enclose them in apostrophes (or single quotes), as illustrated by the program printcharacters. The apostrophes are not printed in the output.

```
program printcharacters (output);
  begin
  writeln ('84 + 13');
  end.
run printcharacters

84 + 13
```

In a Pascal program, a sequence of typographic characters enclosed in apostrophes represents a **character string**. A character string may contain alphabetic characters as well as numeric characters and other special characters such as punctuation marks and arithmetic symbols. For example, the program hello prints a largely alphabetic character string.

```
program hello (output);
  begin
  writeln ('Hello, I am a computer.');
  end.
run hello

Hello, I am a computer.
```

Printing both exact literal characters and a computed value produces the following easy-to-read output.

```
program calc1version2 (output);
  begin
  writeln ('84 + 13 = ', 84 + 13);
  end.
run calc1version2

84 + 13 =          97
```

In the program calc1version2 (calculation1 version 2), there are two items in the list, a **character constant** '84 + 13 = ' to be printed exactly as written, and an arithmetic expression whose value is first calculated and then printed. Although the two items may look identical, they are not. Enclosing the character string in apostrophes means that it is to be transcribed *character for character*, including the four blank characters (spaces, in ordinary typing), while the same expression written without apostrophes is to be evaluated so that the sum can be printed. Commas are used to separate the items in a write list.

Constants: Character String, Real, and Integer

All of the numbers and character strings in the programs in this section are examples of constants. There are several **types** of constants. A **character string constant** is a character string enclosed in apostrophes. A **real constant** is a string of digits followed by a period, used as a decimal point, followed by another string of digits. The following are real constants.

```
13.5   0.1234567   123.45678   3.0   00.30
```

The following are not real constants in Pascal because there must be at least one digit before and at least one digit after the decimal point.

    .1234567   3.   12345.   .0

An **integer constant** is a string consisting only of the digits 0 to 9. The following are examples of integer constants.

    23   0   1234567

In Pascal, the distinction between **integer type** and **real type constants** is a matter of the appearance of a decimal point, not whether the number is whole or has a non-zero fractional part. There are some places in a Pascal program where an integer may and a real number must not be used. For instance, it would make no sense to have a Pascal statement that says to repeat something 5.17 times. However, an integer may be used any place that a real number may be used.

A **number** is a real constant or an integer constant. A **signed number** is a number, or a number preceded by a plus (+) or a minus sign (−). The following are examples of signed numbers.

    −23.7955   −6   +7.42   +3453   0.7   1

Exponential Notation Versus Positional Notation

The usual way of writing real numbers, like 32.17, 0.0021, or 384.41, is called **positional notation** because the place value of each digit is determined by its position relative to the decimal point. Since computers ordinarily store only a limited number of significant digits, there is another common representation of numbers to allow for very large or very small numbers.

A real or integer constant may be followed by the letter "e" and an integer to form a real constant written in exponential notation. The letter "e" is read as "times ten to the power" and the integer following the "e" is a power of ten to be multiplied by the number preceding the "e". This form, called the **exponential notation** is useful for writing very large or very small numbers. For example, 2.3e5 is 2.3 times ten to the power 5, or $2.3 \times 100000 = 230000$. The integer power may have a minus or plus sign preceding it, as in the real constant 2.3e−5, which is 2.3×10^{-5} or $2.3 \times 0.00001 = 0.000023$. Two more examples are 1e9, which is one billion, and 1e−3, which is one one-thousandth. Do not put a blank before the "e"; blanks must never be written in a Pascal number.

Real values written as output appear in the exponential form unless the precision is specified using the decimals indicator, as described in Section 2.3.

Arithmetic Expressions

Just about any arithmetic expression may appear within the parentheses of a writeln statement, and the computer will evaluate it and print the result. The Pascal notation for arithmetic operations conforms generally to ordinary notation, except in cases where the ordinary notation is difficult or impossible to type on standard computer input devices. Even when the notation is modified, as in calculation2, the evaluation is the usual one:

```
program calculation2 (output);
  begin
  writeln (8 * (12 * 3 − 143 / 11));
  end.

run calculation2
```

    1.84000000000000e+02

Two modifications of ordinary notation used in the program calculation2 are the asterisk (∗) which means multiplication, and the slash (/) which means division. The number 8 is to be multiplied by the expression in parentheses. Within the parentheses, the number 12 is multiplied by 3 to give 36. The term 143 / 11, which is written all on one line because typing the numerator over the denominator is typographically more difficult. 143 / 11 has the value 13. Therefore the expression in parentheses has the value 36 − 13, which is 23. The product of 8 and 23 is 184, the answer. The answer is printed as a real number because the result of a division (/) is always real, even if both operands are type integer.

Warning: The asterisk denoting multiplication of the 8 by the expression in parentheses cannot be omitted, even though it may be omitted in ordinary algebraic notation. On the other hand, the use of spacing around the values or the operators is unrestricted and improves the readability of the expression. Spaces must not be inserted within a number, however.

Pascal does not have an operator designating exponentiation. It must be programmed as a combination of simpler operations.

As in ordinary algebra, the evaluation of a complicated expression with many parentheses begins with evaluation of a subexpression enclosed by an innermost pair of parentheses. In Pascal, as in algebra, multiplication and division are performed before addition or subtraction. It is always permissible, and often advisable, to insert parentheses to clarify the meaning of an arithmetic expression. The precedence rules as they apply in the absence of overriding parentheses are illustrated in the following example.

```
  4 + 12 / 2 − 1 + 5 ∗ 9
= 4 + 6 − 1 + 5 ∗ 9        first multiplications and divisions,
= 4 + 6 − 1 + 45              going from left to right
= 10 − 1 + 45             then additions and subtractions,
= 9 + 45                     going from left to right
= 54
```

Expressions involving repeated divisions are evaluated from left to right, as shown below:

```
  432 / 12 / 6 / 3
= 36 / 6 / 3        leftmost division first
= 6 / 3            leftmost remaining division next
= 2
```

As in algebra, it is a good practice to insert parentheses to distinguish this meaning more clearly from such other possible interpretations as

(432 / 12) / (6 / 3)   and   432 / (12 / (6 / 3))

which have different values. Similarly, expressions involving a mixture of multiplications and divisions are evaluated from left to right. Thus

```
  12 / 6 ∗ 2
= 2 ∗ 2        leftmost operation first
= 4
```

When the calculated expression 12 / (6 ∗ 2) is desired, the parentheses must not be omitted.

Does A Computer Understand English?

A computer understands only as much English as it is programmed to understand. The similarity between English and a programming language represents a compromise between what is convenient for English-speaking programmers and the computer, which "speaks" machine language. In general, the more the properties possessed by a programming language are like English, the more computational time and power are required to translate a program into machine language for execution, so the more it costs to operate. Pascal is not much like English, but instead borrows much of its notation from mathematics.

Keywords

The instructions given to a computer must be precise, unambiguous, and complete. When English words are used in Pascal, they acquire a precise, unambiguous, technical meaning. For example, "program" means: "This is the beginning of a Pascal program" and "end" followed by a period means: "This is the end of a Pascal program".

An English word like "program", "begin", or "end" used in a program for its precise, technical meaning is a **keyword**. Program steps that use a keyword make sense on two different levels. First, using the technical meaning, they are precise and unambiguous directions to a computer. Second, using the ordinary meaning of the English word, they are understandable by people who speak English. It is a great convenience to programmers and an incalculable aid to clear thinking if the technical meaning of a keyword is consistent with the ordinary meaning. Every Pascal statement begins with a keyword except an assignment statement (described in Section 2.2) and a request for execution of a procedure.

The characters "writeln" do not form a Pascal keyword. Instead, the statements that have used this word are requests to execute a built-in procedure whose name is **writeln**. For the same reasons that it is helpful to have keywords that correspond to their English meaning, it is helpful to pick names for procedures and programs that reflect their function.

The Program Heading

Each Pascal program begins with a **program heading**. It consists of the keyword "program" followed by a **program name** of the programmer's choosing. The name must start with a letter and consist of letters and digits. The program name "calculation1" does not mean anything to the computer. Any other name following the rules would work just as well. However, the first calculation program in this book is named "calculation1" for the benefit of its human readers.

Following the program name is a list of the names of the **files** used by the program. All a beginner needs to know about files is that any Pascal program that produces printed or displayed output using the procedures write or writeln must list the special output file named **output**, and any program that accepts execution-time input from the standard input file (card reader, terminal, or prepared disk file) must list the special input file named **input**. At a more advanced level, other files may be specified by the programmer.

The file names are separated by commas and enclosed in parentheses. The file names input and output are special in Pascal in that any read operation that does not name a file uses the file name input. Similarly, any write operation that does not name a file uses the file named output. Unless the programmer indicates differently when the program is run, the files named input and output refer to a standard input or output device, like a card reader, terminal, or printer.

The Keywords Begin and End

The keywords "begin" and "end" are used to delimit a sequence of statements that belong together. Such a sequence of statements is a **compound statement**. All of the statements of a program are preceded by the keyword begin and are terminated by the keyword end, which makes them one compound statement.

The entire program is terminated with a period.   There are no acceptable synonyms for the keywords begin or end, or for any keywords in Pascal.

Running a Program

How to tell a computer to run a program depends very much on the computer being used.   It also may depend on the type of device that is used to enter the program into the computer.   This is discussed further in Section 2.5, but you should get instructions specific to the computer you will be using from your instructor or computer center.   The simplest example is given by the program executions already shown.   Once the program named "xxx" has been typed in at a terminal on the computer used to run the programs in this book, typing "run xxx" causes the program to run.

   In order to run a Pascal program, you must present it to the computer in a form the computer can accept.   The two most common media for transmitting a program to a computer are terminals and punched cards.   In addition to the Pascal program itself, other information must be presented with the program indicating such things as the name of the programmer and the programming language being used.   The form required for this information varies widely from one computer installation to the next.   At this point, learn how to submit a program to the computer system that is available and run at least one demonstration program to verify the procedures.   Detailed instructions are available from an instructor, computer manuals, or computer center memoranda.

   Regardless of the computer used or the media used to input the program to the computer, the form of a Pascal program is always the same.   The entire program is considered to be one long string of characters.   The parts of the program may be placed on lines in any way the programmer chooses, as long as a new line is started only at a place in the program where a space may occur. However, it is usually considered good programming practice to begin each statement on a new line.   If all of a statement will not fit on one line, then the statement may be continued on the next line.

Calculating an Average of Four Numbers

To further demonstrate the convenience of doing routine calculations on a computer using Pascal, this section closes with the program calculation3 for computing the average of four numbers.

```
program calculation3 (output);
  begin
  writeln ((92 + 72 + 83 + 89) / 4);
  end.
run calculation3

 8.40000000000000e+01
```

A second version of this program is named calc3version2.   It identifies the answer by specifying a character string to be printed along with the computed answer.

```
program calc3version2 (output);
  begin
  writeln ('The average is ', (92 + 72 + 83 + 89) / 4);
  end.
```

```
run calculation3version2

The average is    8.400000000000000e+01
```

Self-Test Questions

1. For each line of the following program, tell whether it is correct Pascal or
    not.

    ```
    program division (output);
      begin
      writeln 243 / 11;
      end
    ```

2. Correct the errors in the Pascal program in Self-Test Question 1.
3. Which lines of the following Pascal program are correct?

    ```
    program multiplication (output);
      begin.
      writeln ( * 2 * 3 * 4 * 5);
      end;
    ```

4. Write correct versions of the incorrect lines in the program multiplication.
5. Is the following a compound statement?

    ```
    writeln (a + b, c − d, e * f);
    ```

6. What is the command to run a program?
7. True/false:

    a. The symbol for division is /.
    b. The symbol for multiplication is ×.
    c. The symbol for raising to a power is ˆ.

Exercises

1. What computer output might be expected when the following program is
    run?

    ```
    program calculation4 (output);
      begin
      writeln ((201 + 55) * 4 − 2 * 10);
      end.
    ```

2. The program calculation5 uses a confusing sequence of arithmetic opera-
    tions whose meaning would be clearer if written with parentheses. What
    computer output might be expected when it is run? Insert parentheses in
    the writeln statement in a way that does not change the value printed, but
    makes it easier to understand.

    ```
    program calculation5 (output);
      begin
      writeln (343 / 7 / 7 * 2);
      end.
    ```

3. What computer output might be expected when calculation6 is run?

    ```
    program calculation6 (output);
      begin
      writeln (2 * (3 * (5 − 3)));
      end.
    ```

4. Some computer programs have nothing to do with numerical computation.
    What computer output might be expected when the program wheeee is
    run?

```
program wheeee (output);
  begin
  writeln ('It is easy to do calculations on a computer.');
  end.
```

5.   What computer output might be expected when the program powerof2 is run?

```
program powerof2 (output);
  begin
  writeln (2 * 2 * 2 * 2 * 2 * 2 * 2 * 2 * 2 * 2);
  end.
```

6.   What computer output might be expected when the following program is run?

```
program simpleadd (output);
  begin
  writeln (1, ' and ', 1, ' makes ', 1 + 1);
  end.
```

7.   Write a program to divide 125 by 16.
8.   Write a program to add 5 squared and 12 squared.
9.   Write a program to add the numbers 1, 2, 3, ..., 7.
10. Write a program to find the average of the numbers 1, 2, 3, ..., 10.
11. Write a program to print your name.
12. Write a program to compute how many seconds there are in a year.
13. Write a program to calculate the number of seconds in a year and to print the answer with appropriate alphabetic identifying information.
14. Write a program to print the division problem "16,384 divided by 256" and the answer to the problem.
15. Write a program to print your telephone number.
16. Write a program to print your address.
17. Write a program to print the Gettysburg address.
18. Convert the following type real numbers from positional notation to exponential notation.

> 48.2613   −0.00241   38499.0
> 0.2717   −55.0   7.000001

19. Convert the following type real numbers from exponential notation to positional notation.

> 9.503e2   4.1679e+10   2.881e−5
> −4.421e2   −5.81e−2   7.000001e0

2.2   Variables, Input, and Output

One benefit of writing a computer program for doing a calculation rather than obtaining the answer using pencil and paper or a hand calculator is that when the same sort of problem arises again, the program already written can be applied to it. While this is not true of the programs in Section 2.1, this section tells how the use of **variables** gives the program the flexibility needed for such reuse.

Section Preview

Variables:

Variables hold values during execution.

Variable names start with a letter followed by any mixture of letters and digits.

Three intrinsic variable types are introduced: integer, real, and char.

Constants:

Constants have names like variables, but have values that cannot change.

Declarations:

The type of every variable and the value of every constant must be declared.

Example:

```
program example1 (input, output);
  const
    dozen = 12;
    pi = 3.14159;
    exclamation = '!';
  var
    first, last, next : integer;
    x, y, area, d2ydx2 : real;
    alpha, letter, symbol : char;
  begin
    ...;
  end.
```

Assignment statement:

General form:

variable := *expression*

Example:

```
average := (a + b) / 2
```

Read statements:

General form:

read (*list of variables*)

Example:

```
read(this, that, theotherthing)
```

Variables

The program add2 uses two **variables** named x and y. The first sample run shows how this new program could be used to add the numbers 84 and 13 instead of the program calculation2 in Section 2.1.

```
program add2 (input, output);
  var
    x, y : integer;
  begin
    read (x);
    writeln ('Input data  x: ', x);
```

```
    read (y);
    writeln ('Input data  y: ', y);
    writeln ('x + y = ', x + y);
   end.
 run add2

 Input data  x:          84
 Input data  y:          13
 x + y =          97
```

The program add2 tells the computer to read a number from an input device and call it x, then to read another number and call it y, and finally to print the value of x + y, identified as such. Two additional writeln statements that "echo" the values of the input data complete the program add2. During the execution of this program, the two numbers which are the values for x and y must be supplied to the computer, or the computer cannot complete the run.

The method used to provide input to the computer varies widely from one computer system to the next and, like the method of providing the program, can depend upon the type of input device being used. Most of the example programs in this book get their input from a file that is prepared before the program is run. However, other Pascal systems allow the user to enter the input data during execution of a program. Your instructor will tell you what kind of system you have and how your programs are to be run.

Declarations of Variables

Every variable that is used in a Pascal program must be listed in a **variable declaration** that appears between the program heading and the keyword begin at the beginning of the executable part of the program. Variable declarations follow the keyword var (short for variable). A variable declaration consists of a list of variable names separated by commas, followed by a colon, and then by a type. The only types that have been discussed so far are real and integer. For example, if the variables q, t, and k are to be real variables in a program and the variables n and b are to be integer variables, then the following lines contain the necessary declarations.

```
var
   q, t, k : real;
   n, b : integer;
```

Semicolons separate variable declarations from each other and from the rest of the program.

Echo of Input Data

In Pascal, as well as most other programming languages, it is a good programming practice for the user to provide an **echo** of the input data using writeln statements, so that the output contains a record of the values used in the computation.

Rerunning a Program With Different Data

The program **add2** contains echoes, whose importance is demonstrated as soon as the program is rerun using different input data. The echoes of input data help identify which answer goes with which problem. Other important uses of input echoes will appear later. In showing another sample run of the program add2, this time adding two different numbers, it is not necessary to repeat the program listing. The program does not change; only the input data change.

```
run add2
```

```
Input data  x:          4
Input data  y:          7
x + y =            11
```

The final writeln command of add2 refers to the variables x and y. As the execution printout for the two sample runs shows, what actually is printed is the value of the character string constant 'x + y = ' followed by the value of the expression x + y at the moment the writeln command is executed.

The program add2reals is obtained from the program add2 simply by changing the keyword integer to the keyword real, which causes the type of the variables x and y to be real. The program add2reals can be used to add two quantities that are not necessarily whole numbers. This execution of the program also illustrates that the input data values may be negative.

```
program add2reals (input, output);
  var
    x, y : real;
  begin
  read (x);
  writeln ('Input data  x: ', x);
  read (y);
  writeln ('Input data  y: ', y);
  writeln ('x + y = ', x + y );
  end.
```

```
run add2reals
```

```
Input data  x:    9.76000000000000e+01
Input data  y:   -1.29000000000000e+01
x + y =    8.47000000000000e+01
```

Roundoff

Real quantities sometimes differ from their intended values by a small amount in the least significant digit. Perhaps you have already seen this in your own output. Often, the first hint that this has happened is a tell-tale sequence of 9s in the last decimal digits printed. For example, using the same program add2reals, the same input data, 97.6 and −12.9, and a different computer, the following output resulted:

```
run add2reals
```

```
Input data  x:    9.759999e+01
Input data  y:   -1.289999e+01
x + y =    8.469999e+01
```

The value of the variable x prints as 9.759999e+01 = 97.59999 although the value supplied in the input file is 97.6. The difference between the intended and calculated values, −0.00001 in this case, is **roundoff** or **roundoff error**. It is normally of no consequence in practical calculations because virtually no measuring device is capable of distinguishing between such nearly equal values as 97.59999 and 97.6.

Similarly, the printed value of the variable y is 0.00001 too large at −12.89999 instead of −12.9. The printed value of x + y is 84.69999, differing by 0.00001 from both the sum of the intended values and the sum of the printed values of x and y, a hint to the expert that the computer being used probably does not use decimal arithmetic for its internal calculations.

Roundoff shows up when more decimal digits are printed than are accurately calculated or represented in the computer. If the echoes of input data and the answer are rounded to 4 decimal places before printing, the calculated results will appear precisely as expected: $97.6000 + -12.9000 = 84.7000$. On many computer systems, you rarely see any trace of roundoff, while on others, roundoff shows up in the first few calculations with reals. We mention roundoff at this point only to forewarn the beginner who sees it in output that roundoff is not a malfunction of the computer's hardware but a fact of life of real arithmetic on computers. If this presents a problem, it can be solved by rounding printed answers; a full discussion of this is presented in Appendix E.

Reading Several Values

The **read** command may be used to obtain values for several variables at a time, as shown in the program averageof4, which calculates the average of any four numbers supplied as data.

```
program averageof4 (input, output);
   var
      a, b, c, d : real;
   begin
   read (a, b, c, d);
   writeln ('Input data  a: ', a);
   writeln ('            b: ', b);
   writeln ('            c: ', c);
   writeln ('            d: ', d);
   writeln ('Average = ', (a + b + c + d) / 4)
   end.
run averageof4

Input data  a:    5.85000000000000e+01
            b:    6.00000000000000e+01
            c:    6.13000000000000e+01
            d:    5.70000000000000e+01
Average  =    5.92000000000000e+01
```

As shown in the sample execution, the data are supplied to the variables in the order they are listed in the read command. Note that the four variables in the read statement are separated by commas. Although it is not required by Pascal, it is often desirable to put all input data for a read command on one line in the input file, creating a correspondence between read commands and data lines. Execution of each read command reads data from the point in the input file where the previous read command finished. Four separate read commands also could be used to read the variables a, b, c, and d, even if they were all on one input line.

Pascal has another built-in procedure **readln** that causes one complete line of input data to be read, even if there is more data on the line than required to determine values for the variables in the readln command. Four separate readln commands can be used only for reading data presented on four separate input lines.

Rules for Naming Variables

The **variable names** x and y are used in the program add2, and the variable names a, b, c, and d are used in averageof4. Single letters of the alphabet are acceptable variable names in Pascal. However, greater variety is desirable, both to improve the readability of programs and to provide for programs with more than 26 variables. Pascal has the following rules for naming variables:

1.   The first character of any variable name must be a letter.
2.   The remaining characters may be any mixture of letters or digits.
3.   The name must not be a keyword. See Appendix A for a list of keywords.

These rules allow ordinary names like lisa, pamela, and julie to be used as variable names. They also allow ordinary English words like sum, serendipity, and brains and more technical-looking names like x3j9 and w3kt as variable names.

Blanks are important in Pascal programs. They must not appear in the middle of a Pascal variable name. Thus, "box top" is not a legal Pascal name, but "boxtop" is.

The rules for naming variables are the same as the rules for naming anything else in a Pascal program. Other things that have names are constants, types, procedures, functions, and files.

Implicit in the first two rules for naming variables is that characters other than letters and digits are not allowed in Pascal names. Arithmetic symbols must be excluded to prevent ambiguity. For example, if minus signs were allowed in variable names, there would be no way to decide whether a−1 was a single variable "a−one" or the result of subtracting the number 1 from the value of the variable a. Although some of the other characters available on computer input devices often could be allowed in names without causing ambiguity, some characters like the comma or decimal point have specific meaning, and it is simpler to exclude them all, since sufficient variety is already available. Tables 2.1 and 2.2 summarize what is and is not allowed in a name in Pascal.

Table 2.1 Acceptable Variable Names in Pascal.

lisa, pamela, julie	usual names
answer, number, nextvalue	English words
sitzmark, espirit, mucho	foreign words
x3j9, w3kt, yhvvqzt93x, expo67	mixed alphabetic and numeric

Table 2.2 Unacceptable Variable Names in Pascal.

6au8, 14u2	starting with a digit
e/l/o, many%, a−1	characters other than letters or digits
i o u, go home	blanks not allowed
begin, do, then	keywords

In theory, a name may be any length, but some Pascal systems do not distinguish between different names if they have the same first eight characters. Therefore, it is unwise to use two different names whose first eight characters are the same.

Assignment Statements

An **assignment statement** provides another way to give a variable a value besides reading that value as input. The program costofsandwich illustrates the use of assignment statements.

```
program costofsandwich (output);
{ computes the cost of a peanut butter and jelly
    sandwich using two slices of bread, 0.0625 jars
    of peanut butter, and 0.03125 jars of jelly  }

  const
    loafofbread = 0.59;
    jarofpeanutbutter = 1.65;
    jarofjelly = 1.29;
    slicesperloaf = 16;

  var
    sliceofbread, sandwich : real;

  begin
    sliceofbread := loafofbread / slicesperloaf;
    sandwich := 2 * sliceofbread +
        0.0625 * jarofpeanutbutter +
        0.03125 * jarofjelly;
    writeln ('A peanut butter and jelly sandwich costs $',
        sandwich);
    writeln ('Prices are subject to change at any time');
    writeln ('    without prior written notice.');
  end.
run costofsandwich

A peanut butter and jelly sandwich costs $  2.17187500000000e-01
Prices are subject to change at any time
    without prior written notice.
```

The first statement in the executable part of the program costofsandwich is an assignment statement that assigns to the variable sliceofbread the cost of one slice of bread, obtained by dividing the cost of a loaf of bread by the number of slices of bread in the loaf. The next statement is also an assignment statement; it assigns to the variable sandwich the cost of a peanut butter and jelly sandwich. **Arithmetic expressions** can be assigned as the value of a variable.

In Pascal the **assignment operator** is a colon followed by an equal sign (:=). This combination of symbols was chosen to suggest a left-pointing arrow, indicating that the value of the expression on the right is assigned to the variable on the left.

The program concludes with three separate writeln commands in order to produce three lines of output. The value printed represents a cost of approximately 22 cents (0.22 expressed in exponential notation). Methods of avoiding exponential notation in output are described in the next section.

Constant Declarations

The program costofsandwich illustrates another new feature, the **constant declaration**. A quantity whose value will not change during the entire execution of the program is a **constant**. A constant is declared and given its value in a constant declaration that appears in a program after the program heading and before all variable declarations. Constant declarations begin with the keyword const (for constant) and consist of a constant name, followed by an equal sign, followed by the value of the constant, and ending with a semicolon. The name of the constant then may be used any place in the program that the constant value itself could be used. A constant may be a real number, an integer, or a character string. Note that the equal sign is used in constant declarations, the colon is used in variable declarations, and a combination of the two (:=) is used in assignment statements.

There are two major differences between constant declarations and assignment statements. First, the value in a constant declaration must be a simple constant without arithmetic operations or other calculations implied, except that if the constant is real or integer, the constant may be preceded by a plus or minus sign. The integer value 16 for the constant slicesperloaf and the real value 0.58 for the constant loafofbread are examples. In the program costofsandwich, the values of the quantities sliceofbread and sandwich also never change, but it is not possible to give them values in constant declarations because arithmetic operations are used to compute their values. Second, the value of a constant is fixed by its declaration for the entire execution of the program. However, the value of a variable may change. This ability of variables to assume different values during an execution becomes important in programs that use loops.

It is good programming practice to declare quantities to be constants whenever possible. It allows the reader of the program to learn that the value corresponding to that name will never change when the program is running. It also allows the computer to provide a diagnostic message if the programmer inadvertently tries to change the value of the quantity using a read or assignment statement.

Perhaps the most important reason for using a constant declaration is that the program can be modified very easily if the particular value represented by the constant name needs to be changed. This will happen in the program costofsandwich when the price of any of the ingredients changes. When, for example, the price of a loaf of bread changes, the program can be updated by changing one single number in the program. The programmer can then be sure that the constant will be correct whenever it is used throughout the program.

Descriptive Names for Variables

The name of a variable should be chosen so that it describes what the value of the variable represents. The use of appropriate variable and constant names helps make the program costofsandwich almost completely self-explanatory. Some of the names might make their meaning even clearer if they were longer, such as costofajarofjelly in place of jarofjelly, but in a larger program in which the names were used often, one would quickly tire of writing such names.

Comments

An additional feature that also helps clarify a program for the reader is the use of **comments**. Any left brace ({) that occurs in a Pascal program, except one inside a character string, begins a comment. The comment is terminated by the next right brace (}). All characters that appear between the braces form the text of the comment. The explanations given in comments are reproduced every time a program is listed, but have absolutely no effect on the execution of the program. The comments in the program costofsandwich describe exactly what the program is supposed to do. This description makes it even easier for the reader to follow the rest of the program.

Important Rules About Assignment Statements

The Pascal statement

        a := b

(pronounced "a is set equal to b") means "Set the value of the variable a to whatever the value of the variable b is". It changes the value of a while leaving the value of the variable b fixed. It does not mean the same thing as

        b := a

whose execution changes the value of b while leaving the value of the variable a fixed. A statement such as

        4.7 := a

is absurd and unacceptable, because its left-hand side is a constant, whose value must not be changed.

The left-hand side of an assignment statement must be a variable (or as we will see later, an array element), and the right-hand side must be something whose value can be assigned to that variable. The right-hand side may involve the same variable that appears on the left-hand side.

The Statement Separator

A semicolon (;) is used to *separate* two consecutive statements. The keywords begin and end are not statements and thus do not need to be separated from the statements that occur between them. No semicolon is required after the keyword begin or before the keyword end. The semicolon also is used to separate the declarative parts of a program. It must occur between the program heading and the declarations, and it is used to separate constant and variable declarations.

Since separate statements usually go on separate lines, most semicolons appear at the ends of lines, but not every line should be terminated with a semicolon. The semicolon should appear only if what follows is another statement.

The Empty Statement

One of the legal Pascal statements consists of no characters at all. This statement has no effect on the execution of the program, but allows a semicolon to appear in places where the rule given above might indicate that it should not. For example, a semicolon may always be put between any statement and a following keyword end. Since the semicolon is a statement separator and end is not a statement, the Pascal compiler assumes that the semicolon before the keyword end is separating your last statement from an empty statement.

There are, however, some places where a semicolon must not appear. A semicolon must never appear any place except at the end of a statement. This means, for example, that one must never appear just before the keyword else or just after the keywords do or then.

This book follows the style of putting a semicolon after each statement unless it is not allowed. Two benefits result. The first is that it is easier to put in a semicolon in all cases except those few that specifically forbid it. The second is that putting a semicolon after each statement makes it much easier to add another statement after the semicolon. If the semicolon were not there, then two lines would have to be changed—the one containing the new statement, and the previous one to add the semicolon. Adopting the style of terminating most statements with a semicolon also usually makes it easier to delete a statement. In the program costofsandwich, the last writeln command could be removed by simply removing one line, leaving the semicolon on the previous line. If it were necessary to add another writeln command at the end of the program, this also could be done without changing any lines already there.

Converting Meters to Inches

The program meterstoinches, which converts a length in meters to the same length expressed in inches, illustrates again how an appropriate choice of variable and constant names can enhance the readability of a program.

```
program meterstoinches (input, output);
{ converts length in meters to length in inches }

    const
      inchespermeter = 39.37;
    var
      meters, inches : real;

    begin
    read (meters);
    inches := meters*inchespermeter;
    writeln (meters, ' meters = ', inches, ' inches');
    end.

run meterstoinches

    2.00000000000000e+00 meters =    7.87400000000000e+01 inches
```

The assignment statement of the program meterstoinches tells the computer to assign to the variable inches the value obtained by multiplying the value of the variable meters by the constant named inchespermeter with value 39.37, the conversion factor rounded to two decimal places. An extra space is inserted at the beginning and end of the messages in quotes to provide separation between the character strings and the numbers that precede or follow them.

The program meterstoinches also gives some indication why the rules for naming variables are not more flexible. If just any combination of characters were allowed as a variable name, then the assignment statement in meterstoinches might mean that the variable inches should be assigned the value of a variable called meters*inchespermeter. While it is clear to many persons that the context calls for multiplication of the variable meters by the conversion factor, it is extremely difficult to design a workable computer language with even this much sensitivity to the context of human experience. A computer language must be unmambiguous. Thus, variable names that look like arithmetic expressions cannot be allowed.

Character Data Type

In addition to the data types integer and real, there is a character data type denoted by the keyword char. A variable may be declared to be **type character** as illustrated in the following declaration.

```
    var
      q23, keystroke, initial : char;
```

A variable of type character must have as its value *one single character*. Character constants may also be declared by enclosing their single-character values in apostrophes. The following examples are typical.

```
const
  percent = '%';
  bee = 'b';
  blank = ' ';
```

Self-Test Questions

1. True/false:

   a. Any correct variable name is also a correct name for a constant.
   b. Every variable has a type.
   c. Every constant has a type.
   d. A constant may be used in place of a variable in any valid Pascal statement.

2. Which of the following are valid names for variables?

name	address	phone#	phoney	real
iou	iou2	4gotten	packet	laurie

3. Which of the following constant declarations are correct?

```
const
  x = 12;
  n : integer;
  equalsign = '=';
  number = integer;
  baseofnaturallogarithms : 2.718281828459045;
```

4. Which of the following variable declarations are correct?

```
var
  x = 12;
  n : integer;
  letter : character;
  number = integer;
  e : real;
```

5. Which of the following assignment statements are correct?

```
average := (a + b) / 2
sum = a + b + c + d + e + f
rate * time = distance
n := 6.25
```

Exercises

1. Using the data given in the comments as input, what is the output produced when the following program is run?

```
program subtract (input, output);
  var
    a, b : real;              { data for Exercise 1 }
  begin                       { a = 27.93, b = 14.65 }
  read (a);
  writeln ('Input data  a: ', a :1:2);
  read (b);
  writeln ('Input data  b: ', b :1:2);
  writeln (a − b :1:2);
  end.
```

2. What does the printout for the following computational program look like? The data are in the comments.

```
program productof3 (input, output);
   var
      x, y, z : integer;              { data for Exercise 2 }
   begin                             { x = 3, y = 5, z = 7 }
   read (x, y, z);
   writeln ('Input data  x: ', x :1);
   writeln ('              y: ', y :1);
   writeln ('              z: ', z :1);
   writeln (x * y * z :1);
   end.
```

3. The program inchestofeet is similar to the program meterstoinches described in this section. What output is produced when inchestofeet is run using 110 inches as the input value?

```
program inchestofeet (input, output);
   const
      inchesperfoot = 12.0;           { data for Exercise 3 }
   var                               { inches = 110 }
      inches, feet : real;
   begin
   read (inches);
   feet := inches / inchesperfoot;
   writeln (inches :1:2, ' inches = ', feet :1:2, ' feet');
   end.
```

4. Write a program that reads two numbers, divides the first by the second, and then prints the result.

5. Near the surface of the earth, 453.6 grams weigh a pound and there are 1000 grams in a kilogram. Write a program that converts a weight in pounds into kilograms.

6. From each of the following groups, pick out which combinations of characters are and which are not permissible names in Pascal. For those that are not permissible, tell which rule is violated.

7eleven	svn 11	svn−11	seven11
two+2	six ft two	6ft2	
firstnumber	second number	3rdnumber	
john's	marysage	his/her	
1stname	last name	middleinitial	
time	minutes	seconds	hr:min

7. Which of the following are permissible names for variables in Pascal? Explain your answers.

> ph   phd   ph.d.   doctor of philosophy

8. Both the variables in the program rhyme are assigned their values by constant declarations in the program. What does a computer print when this program is run?

```
program rhyme (output);
   const
      jack = 1;
      jill = 2;
   begin
   writeln (jack + jill, ' went up the hill.');
   end.
```

9. Discuss the syntactic correctness of program rhyme in Exercise 8. Does the choice of constant names distract the reader of the program with extraneous connotations?

10. Modify the program costofsandwich to compute the cost using the current prices of the ingredients.

11. Write a program to compute and print the percent change in the cost of a peanut butter and jelly sandwich since this book was written. Also, have this program compute and print the percent increases in each of the ingredients.

12. Write a program to compute the average of any two numbers supplied as input data. The program should also identify the answer with an appropriate message.

13. What does the following program print? Its style is *not* recommended.

```
program
                              ugh  (
           output                        )
                                ;
                                               begin
       writeln
   (
                        12.0
                                                     +

   34.6)end
                                     .
```

2.3 Formatting

The format of the output produced so far using the write and writeln commands has not always been satisfactory. For example, when a quantity of dollars is printed, usually it is not necessary to print decimal places past the pennies, and it is undesirable to print it in exponential form. Another problem is that values such as x = 1.0 and y = 2.5 might be printed as

    1.00000000000000e+00   2.49999999999999e+00

This section tells what to do if you are not satisfied with output in this form. A programmer may control the form of printed numerical values by using a columns indicator or a decimals indicator.

Section Preview

Columns indicator:

   The columns indicator specifies the minimum number of columns to be printed for a real value.

Decimals indicator:

   The decimals indicator specifies the number of decimal places to be printed for a real value. Answers are rounded for printing.

   Example:

```
writeln (price :8 :2, quantity :4, largevalue :1)
```

The Columns Indicator

In a write or writeln command, a numeric or character value to be printed may be followed by a colon and an integer expression that determines the number of columns used to print the value. If a *numeric* value requires more columns than are specified in the program, then the computer uses extra columns to print the value. If a *character* value exceeds the specifications, the field is not expanded, and only the specified number of characters is printed, starting with the left most character.*

The following program shows how various values will appear when printed using different **columns indicators**. The columns used to print the values are separated by a vertical bar.

```
program format1 (output);
  const
    bar = '|';
    n = -999;
    x = 4.56;
    s = 'abcd';
  begin
  writeln (bar, n :1, bar, n :4, bar, n :5, bar, n :8, bar);
  writeln (bar, x :1, bar, x :4, bar, x :5, bar, x :8, bar);
  writeln (bar, s :1, bar, s :4, bar, s :5, bar, s :8, bar);
  end.

run format1

|-999|-999| -999|    -999|
| 4.6e+00| 4.6e+00| 4.6e+00| 4.6e+00|
|a|abcd| abcd|    abcd|
```

The Decimals Indicator

For real values, the number of decimal places to be printed is indicated with a **decimals indicator**. The decimals indicator, which is an integer-valued expression, must be written after a columns indicator with a colon between the two indicators. Another effect of using a decimals indicator is that a real value will be printed using positional notation instead of exponential notation. For example, the statement

```
write ('|', 1.234567e2 :9 :2, '|')
```

will produce the output

```
|   123.46|
```

which is the value of 1.234567e2 expressed in positional notation and rounded to two decimal digits after the decimal point.

The program format2 shows how this same value will appear using different combinations of columns and decimals indicators.

```
program format2 (output);
  const
    bar = '|';
    x = 1.234567e2;
```

---

*Boolean values follow the same rules as character values.

```
begin
writeln (bar, x :1:1, bar, x :6:1, bar);
writeln (bar, x :1:3, bar, x :9:3, bar);
end.
```
run format2

```
| 123.5| 123.5|
| 123.457|   123.457|
```

Self-Test Questions

1. If the variable x has value 2.5, what does the output for the following statement look like? Show blank columns with a "b".

    ```
    writeln (x :6 :3, x * x :7 :1)
    ```

2. What are the largest and smallest values that can be printed by the statement

    ```
    writeln (value :8 :3)
    ```

3. Suppose the value of x is 1000. How many columns are printed by the statement

    ```
    writeln (x :3 :1)
    ```

    What will the printed output look like?

4. What does the following statement print? Use "b" for blank columns.

    ```
    writeln ('|', 1/3 :1 :5, '|')
    ```

Exercises

1. If gold sells for $475 per ounce, write a program to calculate how much 1/3 ounce of gold is worth, and to print the answer rounded to the nearest penny.

2. Write a program to calculate how much $10,000 grows to in one year at a simple interest rate of 9.75%. Print the answer with no blanks between the dollar sign and the first digit.

3. Modify the program costofsandwich in Section 2.2 to print the final answer as an ordinary dollars and cents amount $0.22 rounded to the nearest penny, eliminating the objectionable exponential form of the output.

2.4 Built-In Arithmetic Functions

Built-in operations, functions, and procedures increase the power of the language Pascal. They are supplied with every Pascal system and should be considered part of the language. This section describes the standard arithmetic built-in features that can be used in more complex calculations.

Section Preview

The following built-in operations, functions, and procedures are described:

1	div	integer quotient
2	mod	remainder
3	round	nearest integer
4	trunc	integer part
5	abs	absolute value
6	sqr	square
7	sqrt	square root
8	ln	natural logarithm
9	exp	e to the power
10	sin	sine
11	cos	cosine
12	arctan	inverse tangent
13	odd	odd/even parity testing
14	read, readln	input procedures
15	write, writeln	output procedures

The Integer Operators Div and Mod

When working with integers, it is sometimes inconvenient that the quotient of two integers is not an integer. For example, when the net weight of a 50 ounce jar of apple sauce is quoted in other units, it is not listed as 50 / 16 = 3.125 pounds, but as 3 pounds 2 ounces. The integer operators **div** and **mod** provide a simple and convenient way to calculate these quantities, as shown in the program ouncestopounds. The number 16 in this program is assigned as the value of the constant ouncesinapound.

```
program ouncestopounds (input, output);

   const
      ouncesinapound = 16;

   var
      totalounces, pounds, ounces : integer;

   begin
   read (totalounces);
   pounds := totalounces div ouncesinapound;
   ounces := totalounces mod ouncesinapound;
   writeln (totalounces :1, ' oz = ',
       pounds :1, ' lb(s) ',
       ounces :1, ' oz.');
   end.

run ouncestopounds

50 oz = 3 lb(s) 2 oz.
```

The value of the expression 50 div 16 is 3 (pounds), the integer part of the exact quotient 50 / 16 = 3.125 pounds. The value of the expression 50 mod 16 is 2 (ounces), the remainder after 48 of the 50 ounces have been accounted for to make the 3 pounds. In general, the value of the expression n div d is the integer part of the quotient n / d, and the remainder n mod d is given by the formula

n mod d = n − d ∗ (n div d)

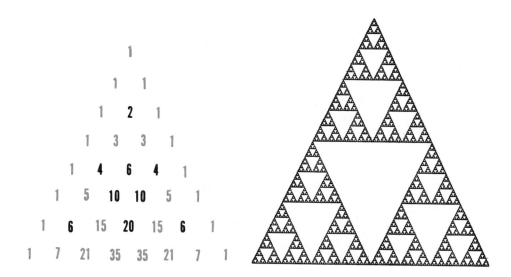

```
            1

          1   1

        1   2   1

      1   3   3   1

    1   4   6   4   1

  1   5  10  10   5   1

 1   6  15  20  15   6   1

1   7  21  35  35  21   7   1
```

Figure 2.1 The binomial coefficients may be calculated using a triangle, invented by Pascal, in which each number is the sum of the two numbers diagonally above it, except the first number, 1. The program to produce this display uses the built-in function odd or the integer operator mod. Each odd number in the numeric triangle is replaced by a black square and each even number is left blank.

Built-In Functions

Built-in functions are used in arithmetic expressions in much the same way as the standard arithmetic operations ($+$, $-$, $*$, and $/$) or the integer operators div and mod. The only difference is that a function evaluation uses a mathematical notation in which the value to be operated on is enclosed in parentheses. For example, the statement

        y := sin (x) + cos (x)

calculates a value for the variable y by adding the (trigonometric) sine of the angle x to the cosine of the angle x. The standard arithmetic built-in functions are described in this section. Nonarithmetic built-in functions are described later.

Rounding

The familiar process of rounding a number to the nearest integer is performed by the built-in function **round**. The value to be rounded must be type real and the result is type integer. For example,

        round (1.234) = 1
        round (1.543) = 2
        round (−2.76) = −3
        round (0.000) = 0

The built-in function round can be used to perform rounding to any arbitrary precision. For example, the value of the following expression is x rounded to the nearest 1/100.

```
round (x / 0.01) * 0.01
```

Minor peculiarities with rounding can be expected when the computer representation of the precision is not exact. For example, the value assigned to x by the statements

```
onethird := 1/3;
x := round (1.0  / onethird) * onethird
```

is often calculated as 0.9999999 instead of 1.000000, because 1/3 is best represented by 0.3333333 and three times 0.3333333 is 0.9999999 and not 1.000000.

You would not expect there to be roundoff error when rounding to the nearest tenth or hundredth, because these precisions have the exact decimal representations 0.1 and 0.01, but there sometimes is.

Although all computers that run Pascal communicate with the user using numbers in the ordinary decimal (base 10) number system, most computers are **binary computers**, which means that they do their internal arithmetic in a **binary number system** (based on the number 2).

Neither 0.1 nor 0.01 has an exact binary representation, so a small amount of roundoff is inevitable. Whether this roundoff shows up in printed answers depends on how good the Pascal system is at conceding small roundoff errors.

The Integer Part of a Number

The integer part of a real number is obtained by **truncation**, that is, eliminating the fraction, if any. The integer part of a whole number is that number itself. The Pascal built-in function **trunc** produces a type integer value that is the integer part of its real argument. For instance,

```
trunc (4.73) = 4
trunc (3.14159) = 3
trunc (17.0) = 17
trunc (-5.6) = -5
trunc (2/3) = 0
```

For positive numbers that are not whole numbers, the integer part of the number is less than the number, but for negative numbers that are not whole numbers, as the fourth example shows, the integer part is algebraically greater than the number.

Absolute Value

The **absolute value** of a number x is the number x itself if x is positive or zero, but the absolute value of a negative number x results from changing the sign of x to positive. Algebraically, this means that the absolute value of a negative number x is equal to the positive number $-x$. The built-in function **abs** is used to obtain absolute values in Pascal. The argument of the function must be either integer or real and the result will be the same type as that of the argument. For example,

```
abs (6.75) = 6.75
abs (0) = 0
abs (-13.8) = 13.8
abs (-9) = 9
```

Square and Square Root

The square of a number x is x multiplied by itself, that is, $x \times x$. The Pascal built-in function **sqr** computes the square of an integer or a real number. The result has the same type as the argument. For example,

```
sqr (4) = 16
sqr (-3.2) = 10.24
```

The square root of a nonnegative number x is the unique nonnegative number y such that $y^2 = x$. However, computer language square root functions are burdened with the problem that for most computer-representable numbers x, including integers, there is no computer-representable number y whose square is exactly equal to x. For example, the best possible seven-significant-digit decimal approximation to the square root of 2 is the number 1.414214, but the square of 1.414214 is equal to 2.000001237796, which is represented in seven significant decimal digits as 2.000001 and not 2. This phenomenon is not restricted to seven-digit computers nor to decimal computers. Even if a computer were to permit more digits of precision, roundoff error would still cause minor inconsistencies in a computer square root function.

The built-in Pascal function **sqrt** assigns the best possible approximate square root to a nonnegative number. For example, on a decimal computer with a precision of seven significant digits,

```
sqrt (2) = 1.414214
```

The programmer should be prepared for an error message and possible program termination if the square root of a negative number is called for. The argument of the function sqrt must be integer or real, and the result is always real. In this regard, sqrt behaves like the division operator (/).

Scientific Functions

Table 2.3 lists the standard scientific functions available as Pascal built-in functions. Each of these functions has one argument that must be type integer or real. The result is always real.

Table 2.3   Some scientific built-in functions.

Pascal name	Description
ln	natural logarithm
exp	exponential (e to a power)
sin	sine
cos	cosine
arctan	arctangent

Exponentiation

It is possible to use the fact that x^p is mathematically equivalent to the Pascal expression exp (p * ln (x)) to raise any positive quantity to any power. The program raise shows some examples of calculating exponentiations in this manner.

```
program raise (output);
   begin
   writeln ('2 to the 10th power = ',
       round (exp (10 * ln (2))) :1);
   writeln ('14.7 to the-7.2 power = ',
       exp (-7.2 * ln (14.7)) :10);
   writeln ('The population of NJ in 2590 will be ',
       6066782.0 * exp (63 * ln (1 + 0.181543)) :10);
   end.

run raise


2 to the 10th power = 1024
14.7 to the -7.2 power =    3.94e-09
The population of NJ in 2590 will be    2.22e+11
```

Parity of an Integer

An integer can have either odd or even parity. Pascal has a built-in function, odd, that tests the parity of an integer. For example,

```
odd (33) = true
odd (0) = false
odd (2 * trunc (x)) = false
```

The values of the built-in function odd are of **boolean** type—that is, the only possible values of odd are **true** and **false**. The type boolean is named after the mathematical logician George Boole, whose book *Laws of Thought*, was the first arithmetic treatment of logic.

Other Built-In Functions

The other standard Pascal built-in functions are ord (ordinal position), chr (character with ordinal position), succ (successor), pred (predecessor), eoln (end of line), and eof (end of file). These are used with character data, programmer-defined data types, and files of characters. They are described in Sections 4.4, 7.2, and 7.7.

Built-In Procedures

Pascal has two built-in procedures for input, read and readln, and two built-in procedures for output, write and writeln. The built-in procedure **readln** is exactly like the built-in procedure read except that after all of the data requested in its list have been read, the computer moves its input cursor to the beginning of a new line. The procedure **write** is exactly like the procedure writeln except that the output cursor does not move to a new line after the specified output is completed.

The two procedures reset and rewrite are used with files. **Reset** prepares a file to be read and **rewrite** prepares a file to be written into. They are discussed in Sections 2.5 and 11.1. There are also two built-in procedures for the dynamic allocation of storage or data structures. These procedures are named **new** and **dispose** and are discussed in Section 12.2.

The Purpose of Built-In Functions and Procedures

Built-in functions and procedures are augmentations of a computer language to improve its convenience to users. Some functions and procedures are built into the language by the designer of the compiler for that language. Others might be added by a local computer center. It makes no difference who builds a particular function or procedure into a language, except that the programmer can rely on the standard ones being available with any Pascal system. All a programmer needs to know to use a built-in function or procedure is its name and what it is supposed to do.

Built-in functions can be used to improve the readability of programs, even though other means exist for writing equivalent expressions. For example, the expression sqr $(2 * x + 1)$ might be used instead of the mathematically equivalent expression $(2 * x + 1) * (2 * x + 1)$ to make a program easier to write and easier to read.

Self-Test Questions

1. Write an expression that rounds the value of the variable x to the nearest tenth.
2. Which is larger, 123 / 10 or 123 div 10?
3. When is x / y equal to x div y?
4. What are the values of the following expressions?

    ```
    abs (5.3)
    sqr (4)
    trunc (-123.456)
    abs (-123.456)
    sqrt (1.21)
    ```

5. What is the difference between the built-in procedures write and writeln?

Exercises

1. Which of the following relationships is always true?

    sqrt (sqr (x)) = x for all x
    sqr (sqrt (x)) = x for all x $\geqslant$ 0

2. Rewrite the following expression using the integer operator mod. Assume n is type integer.

    ```
    n - (n div 100) * 100
    ```

3. Write an expression using the built-in function odd that is true if the value of the variable n is even and is false if n is odd.
4. Write an expression using the built-in operator mod that has the value 1 when n is odd and 0 when n is even.
5. Using five separate Pascal statements, print the values of the five variables a, b, c, d, and e all on one line. Write a single Pascal statement that does the same thing.
6. Write a Pascal program to read a real number and to print that number rounded to three decimal places. Do it two ways, once using the built-in function round and once using the decimals indicator.

2.5   Running a Program

There are two fundamentally different ways of running a program. In **batch mode**, all the input data is prepared in advance of the program execution. In **interactive mode** input data is entered into the computer *during* the program execution. Some Pascal systems support batch execution, some support interactive execution, and some support both.

Section Preview

Batch systems:

Program and data are prepared in advance and submitted together. Execution takes place at the central computer's convenience, often after a wait for the program's turn.

Interactive:

The computer responds relatively quickly to user requests.

Interactive execution:

The user is at a terminal when the program executes. The user may receive ouptut at the terminal screen or printer, and may enter input data for the program execution during the program execution.

Interactive editing of programs and input data:

The computer maintains a copy of the text and modifies it under direction of the user. Some systems have interactive editing but batch execution, while other systems have both interactive editing and interactive execution.

Timesharing:

When many users share a central computer, timesharing is a way to make it seem as though each user has his or her own central computer.

Echo of input data:

When execution is in batch mode, input data are "echoed" to the printer or output file as soon as they are read. Echoes of input data are very useful in debugging.

Input prompts:

When execution is interactive, the user is "prompted" with a message describing what input data are expected before each read or readln statement.

Batch Execution

All the sample executions shown so far have been in batch mode. Before running the program, we entered all the input data for the program into a computer data file. During execution there is no appreciable delay when a read statement is executed because the input data for that read statement is available in the input file.

In programs written for batch execution, we customarily echo all input data to the output file, which otherwise would have no record of this information.

Batch execution has one major advantage: executing a program in batch mode does not destroy the input file. Since most programs are run many times before they are finally correct, we benefit from the fact that the input data, which may be extensive, have to be entered only once.

At large computer centers, more effeicient use often can be made of the central computer if several programs in the same computer language are read consecutively. These programs are batched together so they can run together. Input files, of course, must be prepared in advance or the benefits of batching would not be realized. This kind of batching has the disadvantage that the programs often are run at the computer's and not at the programmer's convenience.

The term **batch execution** means that input files are prepared and entered in advance, whether or not several jobs are grouped together. It is even applied to execution on a single-user, single-job microcomputer, as long as input comes from a prepared file.

Preparing and Specifying the Input File

It is easiest to prepare an input file with an editor, if one is available on your system. There are so many different editors that you will have to get instructions specific to the one you have available. It is no paradox that editing is interactive while the eventual execution of your program will be in batch mode.

Another way to prepare an input file is to punch it in cards. Some systems copy this card file to a disk file before execution, while others read directly from the card file during execution. Also, the output files of one program can be used as input files to another program.

A computer system ordinarily has many files saved. The computer must be told which file to use as input and which file to use as output when a program is run. Methods vary among systems, so you must inquire locally to find out which method works on your computer. Some of the possibilities include additional information in the run command, default names for the input and output files related to the name of the program file, and specifying the file names in various ways inside the program.

Interactive Execution

When a program is run **interactively**, input data may be supplied to the program by a person as the program is running. This is usually done using a terminal. Whenever a read command is executed in the program, the user is expected to type some input data at the terminal. Whenever a write command is executed, the data are written to the terminal. This mode of running a program is **interactive execution**.

When input data are expected from a terminal during an interactive execution of a program, it is a good programming practice to have the program send a **prompt**, an output message, giving the user at the terminal a clue as to what is supposed to be entered. A good way to provide such a prompt is to replace the write command that occurs in batch programs after each read statement to provide the echo of input data with a prompt that occurs just before each read statement. This is illustrated in the program sub2.

```
program sub2 (input, output);
  var
    x, y : integer;
  begin
  writeln ('Input data  x: ', x);
  read (x);
```

```
     writeln ('Input data  y:  ', y);
     read (y);
     writeln ('x - y = ',  x - y);
     end.
  run sub2

  Input data  x:          83
  Input data  y:          67
  x - y =             16
```

What happens during interactive execution of the program sub2 is as follows. The computer types "Input data x: " as directed by the first write statement and then pauses in the middle of the line to wait for the user to supply a value for x to complete execution of the read (x) statement. When the user types a value, 83, followed by the carriage return, execution resumes, the computer types "Input data y: " and pauses until the user supplies an input value to complete the read (y) statement. When a value, 67, and a carriage return are typed by the user, execution resumes again and the answer, x − y = 16, is written by the computer.

For interactive execution no input file is prepared prior to execution and the output file is written on the terminal. If the program is run again, the input data must be retyped. While this is not a serious problem with only two input values, its severity increases with the number of input values.

The advantages of interactive execution are that output is available to the user as soon as the statements that produce it are executed and that the user does not have to decide in advance what values are to be supplied as input. If the value that the user types as input depends on previous output, the user and computer interact during exeuction. Some applications, like editing and computer-assisted instruction, make sense only if executed interactively.

Operating Systems

Once the program is prepared, either by using an editor or by punching the program on cards, commands must be given to indicate that the program is to be run. These commands are actually instructions to the computer's **operating system**. The operating system is a complex program that controls the flow of information through the computer and schedules the use of the computer's hardware components. Different computer installations, even if they have exactly the same model of the same computer produced by the same manufacturer, may use different operating systems and consequently may require different commands. Upon arriving at a new installation, one of the first things a programmer needs to learn is a small amount of the command language used.

The Good Old Days of Computer Programming

There are programmers who can remember the good old days of personally reserving a whole computer, perhaps some time in the evening or after midnight. As recently as the early 1960s, it was common practice for programmers to place their cards in the card reader, put their feet up on the console, and sit back and watch the program run. Programmers shut the machine off during dinner or a coffee break and turned the power back on after returning. They could stop the execution of a program to see what was happening, or step through a program one instruction at a time. They could examine any location in memory and make corrections from the console. In those days, programmers dealt directly with the computer and spoke the machine's own language. At least some of these programmers are happy that the recent trend toward

Figure 2.2 Mark I computer. *Courtesy International Business Machines
Corporation.*

minicomputers and microcomputers is bringing back the good old days.

People who had the opportunity to work so intimately with a computer did not soon forget the experience, but the environment has evolved to the point that a programmer might never see an actual computer. Advances in electronic technology have made this change desirable. Although earlier machines were still much faster than desk calculators or other computational devices, their computational speeds were slow enough that it was reasonable for a programmer to stop the machine, open up a program listing, try to locate what needed changing, and enter a correction or change before resuming execution of the program.

As computational speeds increased by more than several thousand-fold, however, there was no comparable increase in efficiency of programmers to locate errors. It was no longer economically feasible for the computer to halt while the programmer monitored the execution of a program or made corrections from the console. A dozen complete programs could have been run while the computer was waiting for a programmer to make one correction. Machine operators took over the job of shuttling the cards, printouts, and other data into and out of the machine as efficiently as possible. Computer programmers from the good old days welcomed the improvements in computer speed and power, but they began to feel that computer programming was becoming depersonalized.

Even certain machine operations suffered a similar fate. The input and output operations, which are partly mechanical in nature, still could not keep pace with the increases in electronic computational speeds even though they were speeded up substantially. It became inefficient for the central processing unit, which performs the arithmetic and logical computations, to halt its operations while a card, or even a magnetic tape, was being read. The input and output operations were farmed out to satellite computers of limited computational ability, which signalled the central processing unit when the reading or writing was completed. This enabled the central processing unit to continue computing at the same time that data was being read or written.

Figure 2.3 Apple IIe personal computer. *Courtesy Apple, Inc.*

Timesharing

The increased speed of computation which brought about separation of the computer programmer from the computer also can be used, paradoxically, to simulate the effect of giving each programmer a complete machine, by a process called **timesharing**. Imagine dining at a very well-run restaurant. You are met at the door and escorted immediately to a private booth from which no other diners can be seen. The waiter arrives with rolls and butter and fills the water glasses. He returns immediately with the menu and retires from sight to let you choose your dinner. When you are ready to order, he reappears to take your order. After a sufficient time for the preparation of each dish, the waiter returns to serve it. When the main course has been eaten, he returns in time to take dessert orders. When the service is good enough (remember that no other tables can be seen), it is impossible to determine whether there are any other diners in the restaurant. It doesn't matter if the waiter takes menus to another table on his way to the kitchen, or takes orders from a third table while your dinner is being cooked. As long as the waiter responds relatively quickly whenever you need his services, for all intents and purposes you have his undivided attention.

   In timesharing, many users are connected simultaneously to a computer by means of relatively inexpensive input/output terminals. If the computational speeds of the central computer are fast enough so that no user needs all the computer's capabilities for very long, then all users have use of the computer almost as soon as they want it. All users have the illusion of being the only user and can program and operate from a terminal as though the computer were all their own. In addition, the capabilities of a much larger computer than could be reserved reasonably for one person's use are available when needed.

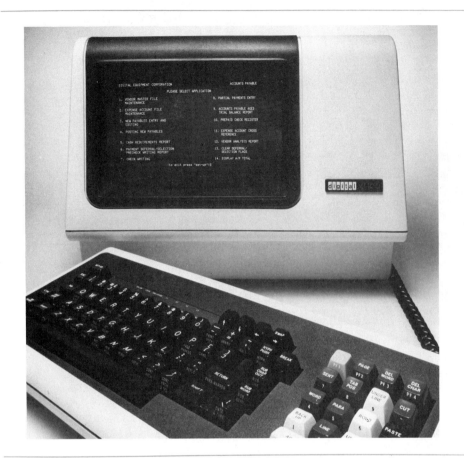

Figure 2.4 DEC VT100, a visual display terminal. *Courtesy Digital Equipment Corporation.*

Operating Systems for Timesharing

With many users simultaneously connected to the computer, the operating system must be more complicated. It must handle many kinds of requests, from editing one line of a program to running a compiler or processing an input/output request from a running program. In scheduling these requests, the operating system must decide how long a wait is tolerable for each kind of request.

Scheduling Algorithms

An operating system serving several users may receive requests requiring as little as several millionths of a second or as much as several hours of processing time. The design of a satisfactory scheduling procedure is a complex task, very much the subject of active research and experimentation among computer scientists. In general, most **scheduling algorithms** provide for very short waiting times for requests demanding only a few central processing unit (CPU) cycles, and progressively longer waiting times for requests for greater usage. A request to enter a single line of a program from a terminal may be processed almost immediately, while a request to run a program may wait from several seconds to several minutes, and a request for a solid hour of computational time may have to wait until the end of the day or the end of the week.

Figure 2.5 DEC Correspondent, a hardcopy terminal with built-in modem.
Courtesy Digital Equipment Corporation.

Other factors are also taken into account. If a programmer is waiting at a terminal for the request to be completed, the priority may be higher than that given to a similar request when the programmer is not waiting. It is ordinarily more efficient for a computer to run several consecutive programs written in the same computer programming language than to skip from one language to another. Some operating systems collect short jobs in the most popular programming languages over a period of perhaps 20 minutes and run the entire group at the end of the collection period. Such batch processing ordinarily is unacceptable if the user is waiting at a terminal. Another consideration is how long a request has been waiting for action. A sophisticated scheduling algorithm may permit a lower-priority request that has been waiting a relatively long time to be run ahead of higher-priority requests that have not been waiting nearly as long.

Requests specifying computer facilities that are already in use for another purpose or job must be delayed, although the importance of the job must be taken into account. A business might want to be sure that its payroll program is run by Friday afternoon. A student program may or may not be given priority over an accounting or record-keeping program, depending on whether the installation views its primary function as teaching programming or keeping records. Priorities may also vary with the time of day. Often shorter programs are given higher priority during the day, and longer programs are given elevated priority at night.

Self-Test Questions

1.   True/False:

a. Timesharing is the same as interactive editing.
b. In a batch system the program and input data must be on cards.
c. In batch execution, input data must be prepared in advance.

    d. You can't have interactive editing without interactive execution.

    e. Interactive editing and execution require timesharing.

    f. Operating systems for large computers generally use timesharing.

2. True/false: which of the following are reasons for echoing input data?

    a. They are useful in debugging.

    b. Echoes keep input data from getting lost.

    c. They provide a record of which input data were used in a given execution.

    d. They provide a check that the right input data were read at the right time and assigned to the right variables.

    e. Input echoes are a good programming practice.

    f. Your instructor insists on them in all your programming projects.

Exercises

1. What are the major differences between running a program from a terminal using prepared input files and running the same program from a terminal interactively?

2. a. When a program is run interactively, why is it desirable to have a prompting message printed before the user types each item of input data?

    b. What difficulties might occur if a computer program with a large number of read statements did not give sufficient information to the user in its prompting messages or did not provide prompting messages at all?

3. a. When running a program interactively, is an echo of input data desirable after the user has entered a piece of data in response to an input prompting message?

    b. Why are prompting messages superfluous when running a program from cards or from a terminal using prepared input files?

    c. Why is an echo of input data desirable when running a program in batch mode?

2.6 What You Should Know

1. A printed copy of a program is the program listing.
2. To get the computer to print the exact typographic characters specified, enclose them in apostrophes.
3. A sequence of typographic characters in apostrophes is a character string.
4. A real constant is a string of digits followed by a period, followed by another string of digits.
5. An integer constant is a string consisting only of the digits 0 to 9.
6. Exponential notation is the equivalent of scientific notation in a computer. For example, 2.3e5 means 2.3×10^5.
7. The symbols for the four arithmetic operations are $+$, $-$, $*$, and $/$.
8. "Program", "begin", and "end" are Pascal keywords. No substitutions are allowed.
9. A compound statement is a sequence of statements beginning with the keyword begin and ending with the keyword end.
10. Statements are separated by semicolons.
11. Variable names start with a letter followed by any mixture of letters and digits.
12. Every variable has a type describing what type of data is stored in it. Its type is declared following the keyword var.

13. The three most common intrinsic types are integer, real, and char.
14. Constants may be named following the keyword const.
15. It is good programming practice to provide an echo of the input data, so that the output contains a record of the values used in the computation.
16. For interactive execution, it is good programming practice to give the user an input prompt indicating what kind of data is expected.
17. The computer stores a fixed number of significant digits for each real value. All values are rounded to that number of digits.
18. The built-in procedure readln works the same way as the procedure read until it satisfies its input list. Then it skips to the beginning of the next line.
20. The built-in procedure write writes a list of values to an output device.
21. The built-in procedure writeln is exactly the same, except that it skips to a new line when it is done.
22. An assignment statement is another way to give a variable a value besides reading that value as input.
23. Constants, variables, and arithmetic expressions can be assigned as the values of a variable.
24. In Pascal, the assignment operator is a colon followed by and equal sign (:=).
25. The name of a variable should be chosen so that it describes what the value of the variable represents.
26. Comments are placed in a program as explanation to a human reader of a program. Comments are delimited by braces ({}).
27. The empty statement consists of no characters at all.
28. The columns indicator specifies the *minimum* number of columns to be used to print a value. If a numeric value doesn't fit, extra columns are used. If a string value doesn't fit, characters are dropped.
29. The decimals indicator specifies the number of decimal places to be printed for a real value. Answers are rounded for printing.
30. The integer operator div calculates the integer part of a quotient.
31. The integer operator mod calculates the remainder in integer division.
32. Built-in operations, functions, and procedures increase the power of Pascal:

    a. round rounds a real value to the nearest integer.
    b. trunc takes the integer part of a real value.
    c. abs is the absolute value function.
    d. sqr squares a number.
    e. sqrt extracts the square root of a number.
    f. ln is the natural logarithm function.
    g. exp means "*e* raised to the power".
    h. sin, cos, and arctan are trigonometric functions.
    i. odd is true if an integer is odd.

33. In batch mode, all the input data are prepared in advance of the program execution.
34. In interactive mode, input data are entered into the computer *during* the program execution.

PROGRAMMER-DEFINED PROCEDURES AND TOP-DOWN DESIGN 3

If your experience at computer problem-solving is limited to reading programs that do the necessary jobs, it might look as if solutions grow on trees. This chapter introduces you to a methodology known as **top-down design** that enables you to analyze hard problems yourself.

Top-down design is fundamentally a common sense way to construct a solution to any difficult problem. It means you begin with strategic planning and gradually become more specific. If the first attempt to break the problem down does not reveal how the available tools and methods can solve the problem, you **refine** the steps into simpler steps. You continue with this **stepwise refinement** until the tactics are clear throughout your plan.

In developing computer solutions, the final step in a top-down design process is to write the solution as an executable Pascal program. However, there is more to the goal than the executable program itself. For a number of reasons, it is desirable also to retain a record of the stepwise analysis of the problem.

In structured Pascal programming, the reasoning that leads to the executable program is retained by organizing the instructions in that program into into groups called **programmer-defined procedures**. Each such procedure is a well-defined subtask that contributes to the solution of the original problem. The organization of programs into programmer-defined procedures is what lends human sense to the details of the Pascal code.

3.1 Stepwise Refinement

Let's suppose you have a goal to become a millionaire by 1990. It's all very well to say you will work hard every day until it happens, but most people who work hard don't make a million. Here is the question: you will work hard at doing what? Will you carry grains of sand one at a time from the beach to the top of the mountain? That can be very hard work.

Section Preview

Top-Down Design:

A method of analyzing problems in which the solution is attempted first at the highest possible conceptual level, in terms closest to the problem statement. Then, details are added to each step of the proposed solution until a fully implemented solution results.

Successive Refinement:

The process of adding detail to a step of a problem solution to make it more specific is refinement. If a refined step is still not perfectly clear and unambiguous, each of its substeps is refined again. Successive stages of refinement continue until each step of the solution is clear and unambiguous. If the solution is to be expressed as a computer program, refinement continues until each step is an executable Pascal statement.

An Initial Version of the Solution

Perhaps you finally have an inspiration that a way to make money is to sell people what they want. As obvious as this sounds, it is great progress, because it transforms a vague problem of making a million into a more concrete problem of selling people what they want. This inspiration is rendered as a flow diagram in Figure 3.1.

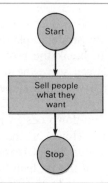

Figure 3.1 How to make a million: the initial inspiration.

Wanting to put a person on the moon is another general goal. Using a rocket, rather than jumping, is an inspired idea for a method. It narrows down what you have to do next. In this case, it lets you work on rocket engineering rather than on improved nutrition and athletic training.

Once you have the main inspiration of how you will achieve you goal, the analytic process becomes more systematic. Think of your fundamental inspiration as a first refinement or a restatement of the problem into a statement of the solution. If the fundamental inspiration is not itself a detailed solution, you will break it down into smaller steps. You will do this over and over again, until the resulting steps are small enough for the purposes of implementation.

Often there is more than one way to do the breakdown at each stage. This is more common sense. After all, there are many ways to solve a problem. This certainly applies to the problem of making a million.

A First Refinement

One possible refinement of the basic strategy of selling people what they want assumes that you will have a product to sell. This refinement is shown in Figure 3.2.

Figure 3.2 This refinement of the initial inspiration to sell something assumes that you will sell a product.

A second refinement might suppose that you will sell a professional service. Other alternatives might be in entertainment or athletics.

If you can think of more than one way to refine a problem into steps, pick one and pursue it. You can always return to one of the others if the first way doesn't work out. The one you pursue first should be the one that seems the best to you.

One way might be the fastest to construct. Another way might be more expensive to construct, but cheaper to use after it is built. A third way might be the most resistant to error. It is an unusual problem if a single approach exists that is the best in all regards. Good judgement is needed in the choice of an approach.

In order to continue the example, we shall exercise our good judgement and proceed with the selling of a product. We shall make further refinements of our program in that direction. If we happened to encounter an insurmountable obstacle along a particular direction, we could backtrack and pursue one of the other directions.

A Second Refinement

There is still a long way to go from the flow diagram in Figure 3.2 to an executable plan to get rich. To stock what people want, you have to find out what they want and then acquire a supply. To market what people want, you have to find the people who want whatever it is you are stocking, let them know you have it, take orders for it, deliver it, and collect the money. Figure 3.3 incorporates this level of detail.

Overview of the Refinement Process

Figures 3.1 and 3.3 show how a large problem, when viewed in increasing detail, breaks up into a sequence of smaller problems. Figure 3.4 shows the refinement process from a different point of view. It shows the dependence of each subproblem on the larger problem it helps solve.

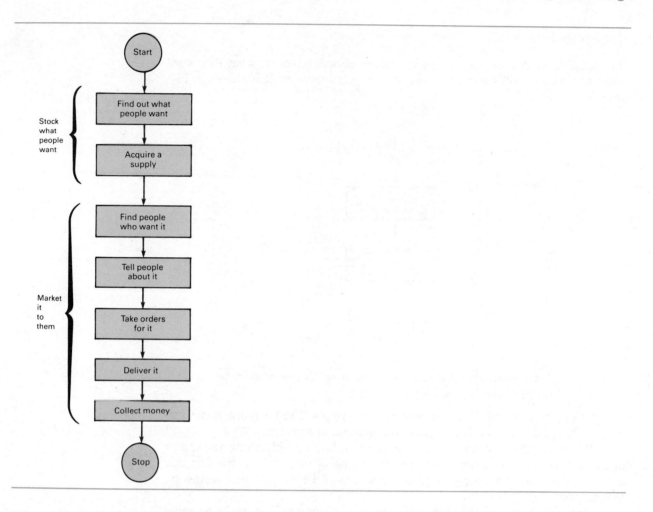

Figure 3.3 A deeper level of refinement.

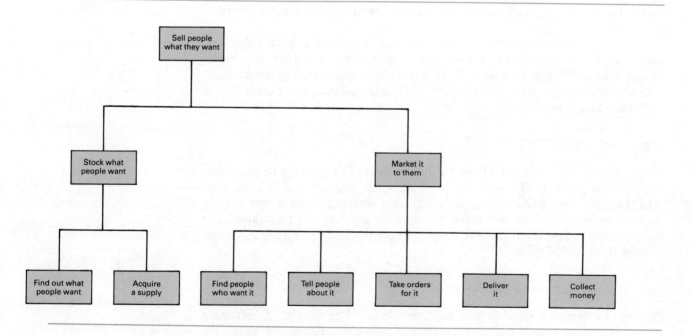

Figure 3.4 Hierarchical organization of subproblems in the task of becoming a millionaire.

Self-Test Questions

1.   True/false:

   a. You should discipline yourself so that when you want to solve a problem, you begin writing Pascal code immediately.

   b. Stepwise refinement means deepening the level of detail of a proposed solution.

   c. What distinguishes outstanding programmers from others is that the outstanding ones invariably can find the best all-around way to solve a problem.

3.2 Modularity and Procedures

Section Preview

Modules:

> A module is a coherent set of instructions that serve a specific and well-defined purpose in the solution of a problem. Each step in a high-level breakdown of the solution to a problem is often a module.

Procedures:

> When the solution to a problem is expressed as a computer program, each module becomes a programmer-defined procedure.

Order of Refining Modules:

> In general, this order depends on the individual nature of the problem. However, when the modules are relatively independent, refinement may proceed in any order. Modules may even be refined in parallel by different programmers at the same time.

Initialization Steps:

> The first module executed is rarely the first module refined. Such modules are often initialization modules, executed in preparation for more important steps that are executed later, but must be refined sooner.

Continuing the Refinement Process

The refinement process must continue until you have written the steps precisely and unambiguously, so that they may be executed by whomever or whatever will carry them out. Ultimately, you will need to break the solution down, at least to a level with steps like this:

> Send Jodi to Chicago in mid-November with a list of all the retail outlets there.

More likely, you will need even more minute detail, such as the name of the airline, the hotel where your sales representative will stay, and her exact agenda in Chicago.

By the time you have refined the program down to an executable level, there might be hundreds, thousands, or even tens of thousands of steps. This section explains how to modularize your program so that a reader won't get lost in the details.

Two sequences of steps have been bracketed according to the higher level of design illustrated in Figure 3.2. With programmer-defined procedures, Pascal and other structured programming languages provide a natural way to represent this bracketing. by means of programmer-defined procedures.

In this example of getting rich, the first two steps of Figure 3.3 are the body of the first procedure, whose name is "Stock what people want". The last five steps of Figure 3.3 are the body of the second procedure, whose name is "Market it to them". The program for getting rich would look like this when it is organized into procedures.

```
Program:  Make a Million
   Stock What People Want
   Market It To Them
   end

Procedure:  Stock What People Want
   Find out what people want
   Acquire a supply
   end

Procedure:  Market It To Them
   Find people who want it
   Tell people about it
   Take orders for it
   Deliver it
   Collect money
   end
```

There is a **main program** that contains two major steps. Each step is regarded as a **module** that can be called upon to do its job. Below the main program, both of the procedure modules are broken down into steps. The last step of each procedure is to return to the **calling program** so that it may continue with the steps that come after the **procedure call**.

One benefit of decomposing the problem into modules is that it often enables us to analyze and refine each module independently of the others. We might even want to parcel out separate modules to a group of programmers who work as a team.

If we were to continue the refinement process, we might represent each of the steps of the procedure as a procedure, so that high-level procedures would call lower-level procedures. There would be a hierarchy, rather like a big business. The president delegates work to the vice presidents. The vice presidents delegate work to the department heads. The department heads parcel out work to the supervisors. Finally, the supervisors assign well-defined tasks to the persons who carry them out.

Order of Refining Modules

Sometimes the order in which you refine the modules depends on the problem itself. As a second example, let's consider planning a vacation. What follows is a top-level breakdown of the solution of the vacation problem:

```
Program:  Vacation
   Make reservations
   Pack luggage
   Travel there
   Do vacation things
   Travel home
   end
```

The crucial factor in deciding everything else is likely to be what things you want to do on your vacation, because that will allow you to pick a place where such things can be done. Thus, the first statement to be refined is likely to be

    `Do vacation things`

Once you have that straight, you can choose where to do them, which will enable you to refine the statements

    `Travel there`

and

    `Travel home`

The last statements you will refine are the initialization statements

    `Make reservations`

and

    `Pack luggage`

What often happens in life, as well as computer programming, is that the part of your program that is to be executed first is the very last that can be planned in detail.

Planning a vacation is an example of a program in which the top-level steps could not be delegated to separate analysts at the outset. In fact, considerable refinement might be necessary before independent analysis would be possible. For instance, the choice of a hotel might depend on what you want to do.

Self-Test Questions

1. Why don't you have to refine a program all the way down to machine language? (See if you know this one, even though the text does not tell you the answer explicitly.)
2. True/false:

    a. The body of a main program might consist of nothing but calls to programmer-defined procedures.

    b. The systematic way to refine a program is to refine the individual steps in the sequential order in which they appear in the program.

3.3 Testing and Documentation

Section Preview

Testing:

A program designed top-down may be debugged bottom-up. This means that the lowest-level procedures are tested first. When they are know to be error-free, they are put together to form the next higher level procedures, which are tested, and so on up the tree until the highest-level procedure, the main program that solves the problem, is debugged.

Documentation:

> Documentation is material that explains, describes, anno-
> tates, clarifies, or elucidates the nature of the problem,
> the plan for its solution, the organization of the modules,
> the details of the solution, or which describes how to use
> the program, when to use the program, when not to use
> the program, etc.

Top-Down Design and Documentation:

> The hierarcical organization of a program designed top-
> down provides a natural and effective framework for
> documenting a program.

Bugs and Debugging:

> A mistake in a computer program is called a bug.
> Removing bugs from a program is called debugging. It is
> much easier to debug a well-organized and well-
> documented program than to debug a program which falls
> short on either account.

Bottom-up Testing

Another benefit of modularizing your program into procedures will become
apparent when it is time to test it to see if it works. You can test from the bottom level up. Once you have determined that an individual low-level procedure works, you can assume that any problems that arise must be due to
something else.

The principle in operation here is that once you establish that the individual components of a system work correctly, all that remains to be tested is
whether they are assembled correctly into the higher-level units.

Of course, when you test a procedure, you have to make sure that it
operates correctly under every possible combination of conditions. After all,
you wouldn't want a distributor in you car that doesn't work on rainy days.

Yet another benefit of top-down design is that your program becomes
self-documenting. That is, it explains itself to people reading the program.
The level-by-level breakdown into procedures is organized to coincide with
human experience, so that human readers can interpret higher-level modules of
the program from their own context, instead of having to simulate a computer
to understand the lower-level details.

From time to time, a programmer must compromise somewhat in order to
make use of the efficiency of the computer. When you do this, make a comment in the Pascal code so that readers will know the purpose of obscure-
looking instructions.

Why Document A Program

Beginners often ask why it is necessary to worry about stylistic matters like
documentation, when the program is to be read only by a computer. Here are
some reasons.

Even when you write a program strictly for your own purposes, you might
come back to it months later even if no one else ever reads it. For instance,
you might need to run it on some different input. Suppose there was
apparently an error the second time around and you could not remember what

you had in mind when you wrote the program the messy way. How would you debug it? You might have to start over.

Well, what if you knew that the program would be run exactly once, and then never again. Would there be any point to designing it top down and to modularize it with programmer-defined procedures? The answer is still yes, but most programmers have to learn this by experience. What often happens is that the first attempt at a complete program simply does not run correctly. It is much harder to locate and correct the flaws in a program that is not segmented into modules.

Flaws in computer programs are **bugs** and correcting them is **debugging**. Searching for problems procedure by procedure is much easier than line by line.

The temptation to plunge right in and get the job done is so great that nearly every programmer succumbs to it from time to time. Writing lines of Pascal code seems like progress, but doing so before you plan your program carefully may not be progress at all.

Would you want to live in a house that was built without plans or to drive a car that was manufactured without a design? Do you think houses or cars could be built faster without plans? Even if the house stands or the car runs, remember that it is the plan that enables someone to fix it when something goes wrong.

Self-Test Questions

1.   True/false:

   a.   When you test a program, you should test all cases equally, with no special stress on the cases most likely to occur.
   b.   Good documentation means frequent comments throughout a program.
   c.   The purpose of organizing a program into procedures is so that someone else can read it.

3.4   What You Should Know

1.   Top-down design means beginning with strategic planning and gradually becoming more specific.
2.   A step in the solution of a problem is refined when it is rewritten in greater detail.
3.   The refinement process continues until the steps are precise and unambiguous. For our purposes, this means an executable Pascal program.
4.   A module is a more or less self-contained part of the program. Modules are often refined as programmer-defined procedures.
5.   One benefit of decomposing the problem into modules is that it often enables us to analyze and refine each module independently of the others.
6.   The organization of a program that has been designed from the top down is hierarchical. The main program calls lower-level procedures to perform its subtasks. The procedures in turn call lower-level procedures to perform their subtasks.
7.   Modules rarely are refined in the order in which they are executed.
8.   Documentation helps readers of the program understand what it does.
9.   The structure of a program that has been well-organized from the top down is self-documenting.

10. Bugs are flaws in computer programs; debugging is finding and removing bugs.
11. It is unwise to rush into writing executable code until the structure of the solution has been thoroughly planned and verified.

DECISION STRUCTURES 4

The sequence of steps a computer follows in executing a program does not have to be the same every time the program is run. The computer is capable of choosing one of several computational alternatives. A company payroll is a situation in which such a choice is necessary to handle the possibility that some of the employees work overtime, for which they are paid time and a half instead of straight time. Calculating a graduated income tax also requires a choice among alternative computational procedures because the percentage of income paid as tax depends on the amount of taxable income.

In this chapter, compound statements are introduced and used as parts of an if-statement to describe alternative sequences of instructions. The computer chooses one of the sequences depending on the results of a test or comparison. The form of the if-statement shows clearly the parallel sequences of steps the computer might take. In some circumstances, a selection may be made from among several alternative computational sequences using **the case statement**. Case statements are described in Section 4.2.

Sometimes a single test is not enough to determine which course of action the computer should follow. Section 4.3 shows examples where if-statements are "nested" within other if-statements to implement multi-stage decisions. Section 4.4 discusses character strings and comparisons involving character string variables and constants.

4.1 If-Statements

The if-statement is the simplest decision statement in Pascal. In may ways, it is also the most powerful. This section introduces the if-statement and uses it in programs both with and without the optional else-clause.

Section Preview

General forms of an **If-Statement:**

    if *expression* then
        statement 1
    else
        statement 2

67

Examples:

```
if a >= b then
  begin
  temp := a;
  a  := b;
  b  := temp;
  end
else
  writeln ('b was bigger');

if a = b then
  begin
  c  := a;
  writeln (c);
  end;
```

Cautions:

Beware of inserting extra semicolons near "then" or "else". The results are often disastrous. (See Self-Test Questions.)

The comparison operator (=) is not the same as the assignment operator (:=).

Syntax Charts are another way of describing Pascal syntax.

Example:

```
<IF_STATEMENT>:

─→if─→<EXPRESSION>─→then─→<STATEMENT>─┐
                                       │
   ┌─else ─→<STATEMENT>────────────────┘
```

General form of a **compound statement**:

```
begin
  statement 1;
  statement 2;
  ... ;
  statement n;
```

Example:

```
begin
  read (x);
  writeln ('Input data  x: ', x);
  sum := 357 + x
  end
```

Semicolons are used to separate statements, not to terminate statements. The three statements of the compound statement above require only two semicolons to separate them.

The **empty statement** consists of no characters.

If a semicolon immediately precedes the keyword "end", a harmless empty statement is assumed to follow the semicolon. If, however, a semicolon follows the keyword "then" in an if-statement , the if-statement is concluded with an empty then-clause, and no else-clause is permitted.

Payroll Without Provision for Overtime

The program payroll1 computes the gross pay of a single hourly worker in the simplest possible way, as the product of the hourly rate and the number of hours worked.

```
program payroll1 (input, output);

   var
     hourlyrate, hoursworked, grosspay : real;

   begin
   read (hourlyrate, hoursworked);
   writeln ('Input data  hourlyrate: ', hourlyrate :1:2);
   writeln ('              hoursworked: ', hoursworked :1:2);
   grosspay := hourlyrate * hoursworked;
   writeln ('Gross pay = $', grosspay :1:2);
   end.
run payroll1

Input data  hourlyrate:  4.75
              hoursworked:  37.00
Gross pay = $ 175.75
```

The hourly rate of $4.75 must not be entered with a dollar sign, but as the number 4.75. The dollar sign appears in the printed output line for gross pay only because it is part of the message within the apostrophes in the writeln command.

Payroll With Provision for Overtime

Among its many oversimplifications, the program payroll1 does not take into account the fact that hourly workers are usually paid at a higher rate for over-time hours. The program payroll2 provides for this possibility, calculating the gross pay by a simple formula if the number of hours worked is 40 or fewer, but calculating gross pay by a slightly more complicated overtime pay procedure whenever the number of hours worked exceeds 40 hours. In a common over-time pay formula, the first 40 hours are paid at the worker's usual hourly rate, but the hours worked in excess of 40 hours are paid at 1½ times the worker's rate. As good programming practice, the value 40 is assigned to a constant so that if the traditional 40-hour work week is shortened to a 30-hour work week, this program can be modified easily to take this change into account. For similar reasons, the overtime pay factor 1.5 is also given a name.

```
program payroll2 (input, output);   { initial version }

   const
     regularhours = 40;
     otfactor = 1.5;

   var
     hourlyrate, hoursworked,
     grosspay : real;

   begin
   read and echo the input data;
```

```
if hoursworked > regularhours then
   compute grosspay by the overtime formula
else
   compute grosspay by the regular formula;
writeln ('Gross pay = $', grosspay :1:2);
end.
```

The If-Statement

The alternatives in the program payroll2 are contained in the four-line if-statement that begins with the keyword "if" and ends with the semicolon just preceding the next writeln statement. The form of the if-statement is shown in the syntax chart of Figure 4.1. The chart shows that, like the for-statement, the if-statement is built using other statements. It is also possible to see from the syntax chart for the if-statement that the else-clause may be omitted, as will be discussed later in this section.

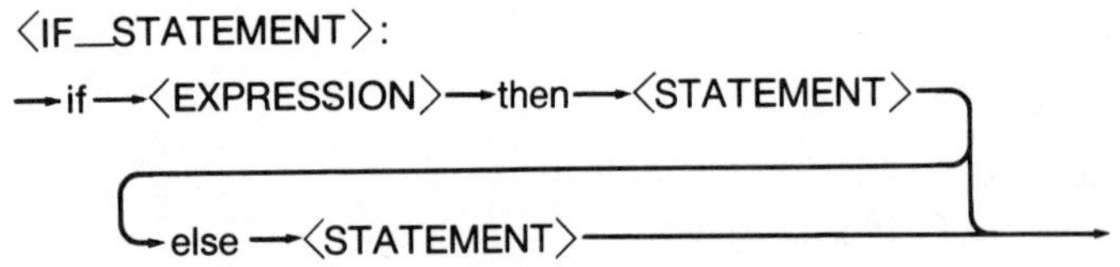

⟨IF__STATEMENT⟩:

→ if → ⟨EXPRESSION⟩ → then → ⟨STATEMENT⟩

                          └ else → ⟨STATEMENT⟩ ──────────→

Figure 4.1 If-statement syntax chart.

Recall that a statement may be a compound statement, so that there may be many statements between the keywords "then" and "else" or after "else", provided they are bracketed by "begin" and "end". It is imperative that no semicolon be placed on the statement preceding "else", because a semicolon in this position would terminate the whole if-statement and indicate that there should be no else-clause following.

When the program payroll2 is executed, there are two possibilities. Either the computer executes a sequence of steps corresponding to the English language statement

```
compute grosspay by the overtime formula
```

or it executes a sequence of steps corresponding to the English language statement

```
compute grosspay by the regular formula
```

The first alternative is taken if the number of hours worked by the employee is more than 40, the number of regular hours; otherwise, the second alternative is taken. The flowchart in Figure 4.2 is another way of illustrating the execution sequence in an if-statement.

The if-statement is terminated by the end of the statement that follows "else". In this case, the statement

```
compute grosspay by the regular formula
```

is part of the if-statement, but the statement

```
writeln ('Gross pay = $', grosspay :1:2)
```

is not part of the if-statement. It is the first statement to be executed after completion of whichever alternative is taken in the if-statement. Thus, when an employee works more than 40 hours, the gross pay is computed by the overtime formula and then printed as output. When the employee works 40 or fewer hours, the gross pay is computed by the regular formula and then printed as output. In other words, the gross pay is printed whether or not the employee works overtime.

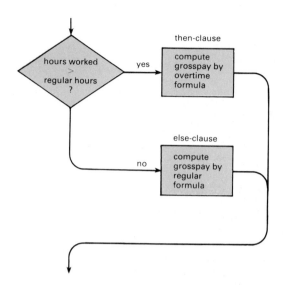

Figure 4.2 Flowchart for an if-statement with an else-clause.

Indenting the Parts of an If-Statement

The statement

    compute grosspay by the overtime formula

is executed only if the condition hoursworked > regularhours is satisfied. This is emphasized visually by indenting it under the if-statement heading which starts with "if". The alternative calculation

    compute grosspay by the regular formula

is indented under "else". The fact that the statement

    writeln ('Gross pay = $', grosspay :1:2)

is not part of the if-statement is reinforced visually by the absence of indentation.

The entire if-statement is the complete thought that starts with "if". The if-statement is more fully described as an if-then-else-statement. A complete if-statement tells a computer, "If some condition is satisfied, then do one thing, otherwise do the other thing".

Arithmetic Comparisons

It is reasonable to ask at this point what sort of expressions are allowed as the condition following the keyword "if" in an if-statement. Technically, the condition is a boolean expression. For now, it is enough to imitate the types of boolean expressions shown in the examples in this book.

In the program payroll2, the if-test is a simple **arithmetic comparison**.

    if hoursworked > regularhours then

The current value of the variable hoursworked is compared to the constant regularhours (which has the value 40) and the appropriate alternative is performed depending on the outcome of the comparison. There are five other arithmetic comparisons that may be used as well. Table 4.1 gives the Pascal symbol and the appropriate English phrase for each comparison.

Table 4.1 Arithmetic comparison symbols and their English equivalents.

>	is greater than
<	is less than
=	is equal to
>=	is greater than or equal to
<=	is less than or equal to
<>	is not equal to

For example, the if-test

```
if count = 100 then
```

is read: "If the value of the variable count is equal to 100, then ...".

There is no reason why one side of the comparison must be a constant. Both sides are allowed to be variables.

```
if x < y then
```

is permissible, and the instructions immediately following this if-test are to be executed if the current value of the variable x is less than the current value of the variable y. When the comparison is changed to

```
if x <= y then
```

the instructions executed immediately following the if-test are performed not only when the value of x is less than the value of the variable y, but also when the value of x is equal to the value of y.

Arithmetic expressions also may be used in place of simple variables or numbers in the comparisons. Thus

```
if a + b < 10 then
if a + b < c + d then
if price * quantity > 75 then
if (first + last) / 2 = middle then
```

are all valid if-tests. Any expression that may be used in an arithmetic assignment statement also may be used in a comparison, but long and complicated if-tests, which tend to be confusing, are rarely necessary or desirable.

Refining a Program

In the program payroll2, informal use of English in the three statements

```
read and echo the input data
compute grosspay by the overtime formula
compute grosspay by the regular formula
```

makes it easy to see what the program does. Unfortunately, a computer cannot understand this informal usage. These two statements must be **refined** into Pascal: they are replaced by instructions in Pascal that direct a computer to do what these English language statements say to do. When we make this replacement, we often keep the informal English as a comment.

The first of these informal statements can be replaced with the Pascal statements:

```
{ read and echo the input data }
read (hourlyrate, hoursworked);
writeln ('Input data  hourlyrate: ', hourlyrate);
writeln ('             hoursworked: ', hoursworked);
```

The formula for computing gross pay when there is overtime is based on the worker's usual hourly rate for the first 40 hours, but 1.5 times the usual hourly rate for overtime hours worked in excess of 40 hours. The English phrase

```
compute grosspay by the overtime formula
```

may be refined to the following Pascal compound statement:

```
begin  { compute the gross pay by the overtime formula }
regularpay := hourlyrate * regularhours;
otworked := hoursworked − regularhours;
otpay := otfactor * hourlyrate * otworked;
grosspay := regularpay + otpay;
end
```

It is perfectly reasonable for a single English sentence to be refined to several Pascal statements. The English sentence was used in the first place to postpone consideration of a mess of details.

It is also possible to refine the same English sentence to a single assignment statement:

```
grosspay := (hourlyrate * regularhours)
      + otfactor * hourlyrate * (hoursworked − regularhours)
```

Both refinements specify the same computation, performed in the same way, but the six-line computation introducing "otworked" and "otpay" is more self-explanatory than the longer algebraic formula.

Payroll2 is refined by substituting the details just worked out for the English phrases in the first version of the program. The program needs no further refinement because all statements are in Pascal. The regular gross pay formula is identical to the one in the program payroll1. To improve the appearance of the output, columns and decimal indicator indicators have been used. Since the refined program is really the same program with more of the details spelled out, the same program name is used before and after refinement.

Because of the presence of the else-clause, a semicolon must not follow the keyword "end" of the compound statement that forms the then-clause, nor may one follow "then" or "else".

```
program payroll2 (input, output);  { final version }

  const
    regularhours = 40;
    otfactor = 1.5;

  var
    hourlyrate, hoursworked,
        regularpay, otworked,
        otpay, grosspay : real;

  begin
  { read and echo the input data }
  read (hourlyrate, hoursworked);
  writeln ('Input data  hourlyrate: ', hourlyrate :1:2);
  writeln ('            hoursworked: ', hoursworked :1:2);
  if hoursworked > regularhours then
    { compute grosspay by the overtime formula }
    begin
    regularpay := hourlyrate * regularhours;
    otworked := hoursworked − regularhours;
```

```
        otpay := otfactor * hourlyrate * otworked;
        grosspay := regularpay + otpay;
        end
    else
        { compute grosspay by the regular formula }
        grosspay := hourlyrate * hoursworked;
    writeln ('Gross pay = $', grosspay :1:2);
    end.
run payroll2

Input data  hourlyrate:  4.75
            hoursworked:   46.00
Gross pay = $ 232.75
run payroll2

Input data  hourlyrate:  4.75
            hoursworked:   37.00
Gross pay = $ 175.75
```

Two sample executions are shown for payroll2, one for each alternative way of computing the gross pay. In the first sample execution, the input value for hoursworked is 46, which means that the overtime pay computation formula is used. In that formula, the hourly rate $4.75 is multiplied by the first 40 hours to obtain $190.00, the gross pay for the first 40 hours. To this is added the overtime pay for the last 6 hours, computed as 1.5 times the hourly rate times the number of hours in excess of 40. Since 1.5 times $4.75 per hour times 6 hours is $42.75, the overtime pay, the computed gross pay is $190.00 + $42.75 = $232.75, the printed answer.

The only interest in the second sample run is to show that, if the number of hours worked is less than 40, the program payroll2 computes the same gross pay as the simpler program payroll1. This is not surprising, since the assignment that computes the overtime is exactly the same assignment statement used to compute the gross pay all the time in the program payroll1.

Compound Statements

Except for the compound statements that comprise the complete executable portion of every Pascal program, the if-statement in the program payroll2 contains our first example of the use of a **compound statement**. Starting with "begin" and extending to "end", it forms the refined then-clause of the if-statement. This compound statement is executed only if there is overtime. The form of a compound statement is

```
begin
statement;
statement;
 .

 .

statement
end
```

which means that as many statements as are needed may be included between "begin" and "end" as long as they are separated by semicolons. Because an invisible empty statement may be considered to follow a semicolon after the last statement before "end", the use of a semicolon there is optional.

A compound statement itself is one kind of statement. This means that any of the statements in a compound statement may be compound: statements may be used to construct more complex statements, and these more complex statements, in turn, may be used to build even more complex statements, and so on. In fact, the entire executable section of this and every other Pascal program is a compound statement.

Syntax Charts

The correct form of Pascal programs can be described using **syntax charts**. The syntax chart for a compound statement is shown in Figure 4.3.

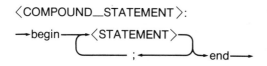

⟨COMPOUND_STATEMENT⟩:

Figure 4.3 Compound statement syntax chart.

Such a chart is sometimes called a **railroad syntax chart** because each correctly formed compound statement can be constructed by following a path through the chart. Backing up is not permitted. Characters not enclosed in angle brackets (< >) must appear as written. Each name in angle brackets in the chart represents a syntactic construct whose form must be determined by examining another chart. For example, in order to understand from Figure 4.3 what a compound statement is in Pascal, it is necessary to look at the syntax chart that describes a Pascal statement. This chart is shown in Figure 4.4.

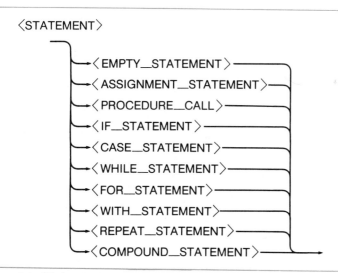

Figure 4.4 Statement syntax chart.

A syntactically correct Pascal statement can be formed in many ways. The empty statement is represented by the top path through the statement chart. One of the possible statements is a compound statement, and one of the parts of a compound statement is a statement. This just means that statements can be grouped together to form compound statements, and that compound statements, in turn, can be used to build more complicated statements.

The precise definition of the correct form of each Pascal language construct is found in the set of syntax charts in Appendix B.

Omitting the Else-Clause

The if-statement of payroll2 is an example of a two-alternative decision. The computer is directed to calculate overtime pay if there is overtime, or to calculate regular pay if there is not. Decisions with two alternatives are the type most often encountered in programming.

Sometimes, no programming steps are required in one of the two alternatives of an if-statement. In the next program makexpositive, no action is needed if x is already positive. In this case, the else-clause of the if-statement may be omitted (see Figure 4.5).

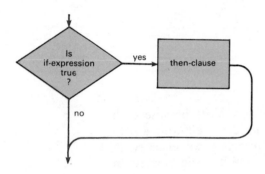

Figure 4.5 Flowchart for an if-statement with no else-clause.

```
program makexpositive (input, output);

  var
    x : integer;

  begin
  read (x);
  writeln ('Input data  x: ', x :1);
  if x < 0 then
    x := -x;
  writeln ('Absolute value = ', x :1);
  end.
run makexpositive

Input data  x: -5
Absolute value = 5
run makexpositive

Input data  x: 7
Absolute value = 7
```

These executions are easy to follow if you remember that $-(-5) = 5$. When x is negative, $-x$ is positive, which is what x is changed to before printing.

Self-Test Questions

1. Which of the following if-statements are syntactically incorrect? Which are syntactically correct, but probably meaningless?

a.
```
if hour > 12 then
   writeln ('It is late')
```

b.
```
if (hour > 24) then
   writeln ('It is very late')
```

c.
```
if x = y then
   begin
   writeln (x);
   z := x;
else
   z := 5;
   end
```

d.
```
if 5 = 5 then
   x := 6
```

e.
```
if a >= 0 then b := a else b := -a
```

f.
```
if a >= 0 then b := a;
else b := -a;
```

g.
```
if you = me then;
   we := 'yes';
```

h.
```
if x + 1 := y - 1 then
   begin
   z := x;
   writeln (y - 1);
   end
```

2. Correct the if-statements in Question 1 that are either syntactically incorrect or probably meaningless.

Exercises

1. On the first $25,900 of annual earnings an employee must pay 6.13 percent FICA tax (Social Security). Earnings beyond $25,900 are not subject to this tax. Write a program that computes the total FICA tax an employee must pay in a year, based on the amount of gross earnings supplied as input.

2. If a person works for two or more employers, each employer deducts 6.13 percent FICA tax. If a person earns a total of more than $25,900, it is possible that the total of all the FICA tax deductions by all employees will exceed $1,587.67 (which is 6.13 percent of $25,900). The government then gives the person a tax credit equal to the difference between the total FICA deductions and $1,587.67. Write a program that accepts as input the gross earnings from each employer, computes the total FICA tax deducted, and computes the amount of the tax credit.

3. Write a bank account program that accepts as input a starting balance and then either a deposit (positive number) or a withdrawal (negative number). It prints the resulting balance if the second supplied number is either a positive number (a deposit) or a negative number (a withdrawal) that would not reduce the balance below zero. If the balance would be reduced below zero, the program prints the word "overdraft".

4. The Old Fashioned Department Store offers its cash customers a 7 percent discount but makes charge customers pay full price. Write a program that accepts as input a price and a mode of payment that is either "C" for cash or "P" for charge (plastic) and prints the price the customer will be asked to pay.

5. Modify the program written for Exercise 6 so that, if the mode of payment is neither "C" for cash nor "P" for charge, the program prints out "Mode of payment undecipherable, please reenter information".

6. Write a program that reads 25 numbers but prints only the numbers greater than 100.

4.2   Multiple Alternatives, Case-Statement

This section begins the discussion of more complex decision processes. When a decision involves more than two alternatives, there are several ways it can be programmed. If the alternatives are mutually exclusive, it is possible to write mutually exclusive boolean conditions to distinguish between them. In a sequence of if-statements with these conditions as tests, only one condition will be true and only one then-clause will be executed.

The decision may be programmed as a case-statement in the special case that the alternatives can be distinguished by a single selector variable or expression that takes on a limited number of possible values.

Section Preview

Decisions involving more than two alternatives are handled

1. by a sequence of if-statements with mutually exclusive if-tests

or

2. by a case-statement when selection can be made on the basis of lists of values of a selector variable or expression

The **boolean operators** and, or, and not are used to formulate more complex conditions for if-tests.

The **case-statement:**

General form:

```
case expression of
  constant, constant, ..., constant :
    statement ;
  constant, constant, ..., constant :
              .
              .
              .
    statement ;
  constant, constant, ..., constant :
    statement ;
  end
```

Example:

```
case diceroll of
  2, 3, 12:
    writeln ('You lose!');
  7, 11:
```

```
      writeln ('You win!');
4, 5,6, 8, 9, 10:
   begin
   writeln ('You have to keep rolling until you get');
   writeln ('either a 7 or a ', diceroll) ;
   end;
end { of case statement }
```

Notes:

To use a case-statement, it must be possible to enumerate (i. e., list) the cases for each alternative.

There is no "else" clause in the case-statement in standard Pascal.

Multiple Alternatives, Income Tax

In the next example, a program incometax1 is written to compute the federal income tax for a single taxpayer according to Tax Rate Schedule X which applies to such taxpayers. The input is the person's taxable income, after all deductions and adjustments, and the output is both the tax due on that taxable income and the person's tax bracket, that is, the rate at which the last dollar earned is taxed. To avoid a very long program, only part of the complete Tax Rate Schedule X is incorporated into the program incometax1. This program cannot be used to compute the tax on incomes over $10,000. However, it is not difficult to continue the pattern of program steps to incorporate all of Tax Rate Schedule X, and avoid the limitation on applicable taxable incomes.

```
program incometax1 (input, output);

var
   income, tax : real;
   bracket : integer;

begin
read (income);
{ find appropriate range and compute tax }
if income = 0 then
   begin
   tax := 0;  bracket := 0;
   end;
if (income > 0) and (income <= 500) then
   begin
   tax := 0.14 * income;  bracket := 14;
   end;
if (income > 500) and (income <= 1000) then
   begin
   tax := 70 + 0.15 * (income — 500);  bracket := 15;
   end;
if (income > 1000) and (income <= 1500) then
   begin
   tax := 145 + 0.16 * (income — 1000);  bracket := 16;
   end;
```

```
 if (income > 1500) and (income <= 2000) then
   begin
   tax := 225 + 0.17 * (income - 1500);   bracket := 17;
   end;
 if (income > 2000) and (income <= 4000) then
   begin
   tax := 310 + 0.19 * (income - 2000);   bracket := 19;
   end;
 if (income > 4000) and (income <= 6000) then
   begin
   tax := 690 + 0.21 * (income - 4000);   bracket := 21;
   end;
 if (income > 6000) and (income <= 8000) then
   begin
   tax := 1110 + 0.24 * (income - 6000);   bracket := 24;
   end;
 if (income > 8000) and (income <= 10000) then
   begin
   tax := 1590 + 0.25 * (income - 8000);   bracket := 25;
   end;
 { end of tax computation section }

 if income <= 10000 then
   begin
   writeln ('The tax on $', income :1:2, ' is $', tax :1:2);
   writeln ('This income is in the ', bracket :1, '% tax bracket.');
   end
 else
   begin
   writeln ('Input data  income:', income :1:2);
   writeln ('Taxable income too high for this program');
   end;
 end.
```

None of the if-statements in the tax computation section has an else-clause. If income lies in the indicated range for that if-test, then the variables tax and bracket are calculated by the formula in that if-statement. Otherwise, nothing is done in that if-statement. Note that, in every execution of the program, each of the if-tests is performed, but that the conditions describing the ranges for income have been written carefully to guarantee that only one range and one tax computation formula applies for each possible value of income less than or equal to $10,000.

To be more specific, let us look at a few sample executions of income-tax1, in which the computer is supplied with different values as input for the variable income.

```
run incometax1

The tax on $ 100.00 is $ 14.00
This income is in the 14% tax bracket.
run incometax1

The tax on $ 1200.00 is $ 177.00
This income is in the 16% tax bracket.
```

```
run incometax1
```

```
The tax on $ 7500.00 is $ 1470.00
This income is in the 24% tax bracket.
```

```
run incometax1
```

```
Input data   income: 75000.00
Taxable income too high for this program
```

Consider the second run with a taxable income of $1200. The only condition in the tax computation section which this taxable income satisfies is

```
(income > 1000) and (income <= 1500)
```

The tax is computed by the formula in that fourth statement:

```
tax := 145 + 0.16 * (income - 1000)
     = 145 + 0.16 * 200
     = 145 + 32
     = 177
```

The second assignment statement of the fourth if-statement assigns a tax bracket of 16 (percent) to the variable bracket. All of the other if-tests in the tax computation section are made, but none of the other conditions is satisfied and so no other action is taken for a taxable income of $1200.

The final if-test of the program controls the printout. Since the value of income is $1200, which is less than $10,000, the two sentences giving the tax and the tax bracket are printed.

In the last of the sample executions using a taxable income of $75,000, none of the conditions in the tax computation section is satisfied, so tax and bracket are not assigned values at all. In this execution, the final if-test causes the computer to print a warning that the taxable income is too large for the program. It is good programming practice to warn the user when a situation occurs that the program is not designed to handle.

The Boolean Operators And, Or, and Not

The keywords "and", "or", and "not" may be used to specify conditions that cannot be described using only one comparison. In the program incometax1, most of the ranges for income are described by two comparisons. For example,

```
if (income > 1000) and (income <= 1500) then
if (income > 1500) and (income <= 2000) then
if (income > 2000) and (income <= 4000) then
```

Both comparisons must be true before the then-clause is executed. On the other hand, the program explainor below helps explain under what circumstances an if-test consisting of two conditions connected by the operator "or" is satisfied.

```
program explainor (input, output);

  var
    x, y : integer;

  begin
  read (x, y);
  writeln ('Input data  x: ', x :1);
  writeln ('             y: ', y :1);
```

```
if (x = 0) or (y = 0) then
  writeln ('At least one of the variables x or y is zero.')
else
  writeln ('Neither x nor y is zero.');
end.
```

```
run explainor

Input data  x: 0
            y: 0
At least one of the variables x or y is zero.

run explainor

Input data  x: 0
            y: 1
At least one of the variables x or y is zero.

run explainor

Input data  x: 1
            y: 0
At least one of the variables x or y is zero.

run explainor

Input data  x: 1
            y: 1
Neither x nor y is zero.
```

As can be seen from the sample executions, whenever x is zero or y is zero the if-test is satisfied. Consequently, the writeln statement in the then-clause causes the computer to print "At least one of the variables x or y is zero." If both x and y are zero, there are two reasons for printing the message. Only if x and y are both nonzero is the writeln statement in the else-clause executed to print the sentence "Neither x nor y is zero."

In Pascal, a comparison that is one of the operands of an "and" or "or" operation must be enclosed in parentheses to achieve the desired effect. This is because boolean operators are evaluated before comparison operators in the absence of parentheses.

The boolean operator "not" applied to a logical value changes it. If it is true, it becomes false; if it is false, it becomes true.

In expressions without parentheses, the "not" operator is applied first, then the "and" operator, and finally the "or" operator. If a, b, and c are type boolean, the expression

```
a and not b or c
```

would be evaluated as if it were the expression

```
(a and (not b)) or c
```

Case-Statements

Pascal has another construct for handling situations where there are multiple alternatives, the **case-statement**. The case-statement is well suited to the situation where the alternatives may be distinguished simply on the basis of the value of a single variable or expression.

At one time, telephone exchanges were alphabetic and most telephones still have letters of the alphabet on the dial. The letters shared dialing positions or buttons with digits. When telephone companies decided to switch to all-digit dialing, it was a simple matter to replace each letter in an exchange by the digit on the same button. The telephone number WAlnut 6-8024 became the all-digit telephone number 926-8024 by replacing the letter "W" with the digit "9" and the letter "A" with the digit "2". The program digitdialing shows how to use a case-statement to do the conversion.

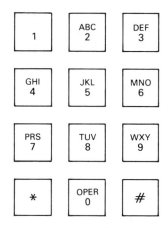

Figure 4.6 Telephone buttons, showing correspondence of letters to digits.

```
program digitdialing (input, output);
   { Converts a letter in a telephone exchange
      to its digit equivalent. }

var
   letter : char;
   digit : integer;

begin
read (letter);
write ('The letter ', letter, ' becomes the digit ');

case letter of
   'A', 'B', 'C':  digit := 2;
   'D', 'E', 'F':  digit := 3;
   'G', 'H', 'I':  digit := 4;
   'J', 'K', 'L':  digit := 5;
   'M', 'N', 'O':  digit := 6;
   'P', 'R', 'S':  digit := 7;
   'T', 'U', 'V':  digit := 8;
   'W', 'X', 'Y':  digit := 9;
   end; { of the case statement }

writeln (digit :1);
end.
```

```
run digitdialing

The letter W becomes the digit 9
run digitdialing

The letter A becomes the digit 2
```

In the case-statement of the program digitdialing, the variable letter is the **selector variable**, which is used to distinguish between cases. Each case is described by a list of the values of the selector variable which fall in that case. In this example, only one statement is executed in each case. However it is always permissible to use a compound statement, as the executable instructions in a case of a case-statement.

The general form of a case-statement is as follows:

```
case expression of
  constant, constant, ..., constant :
    statement ;
  constant, constant, ..., constant :
      .
      .
      .
    statement ;
  constant, constant, ..., constant :
    statement ;
  end
```

Two points should be noted. First, the selection of the proper case can be on the basis of the value of an expression rather than the value of a single variable. This is a minor convenience, because if it were not permitted, you could always calculate the value of the expression and assign it to a variable before the case-statement. Second, the case-statement ends with the keyword "end". When case-statements are present in a program, the number of times the keyword "begin" appears will not be the same as the number of times that the keyword "end" appears. The syntax chart for the case-statement appears in Figure 4.7.

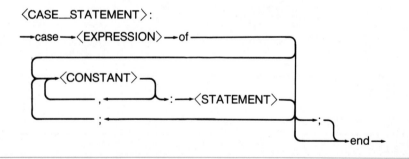

Figure 4.7 Case-statement syntax chart.

The next program, lettergrade, shows how a selector expression may be used to reduce the size of the lists of values specifying the cases. In this example, a test score from 0 to 100 is read. The program prints out an appropriate letter grade. Although you might expect a total of 101 items in the case lists, the use of a selector expression reduces the number greatly.

```
program lettergrade (input, output);
  { Prints a letter grade for each number grade
    from 0 to 100 }
```

```
var
   numbergrade : 0..100;  { a subrange of type integer }

begin
read (numbergrade);
write ('A grade of ', numbergrade :1);

case numbergrade div 10 of
   9, 10:  writeln (' is an A.');
   8    :  writeln (' is a B.');
   7    :  writeln (' is a C.');
   6    :  writeln (' is a D.');
   0, 1, 2, 3, 4, 5:
           begin
           writeln (' is an F.');
           writeln ('Please see me after class.');
           end;
   end; { case statement }
end.
```

```
run lettergrade

A grade of 85 is a B.

run lettergrade

A grade of 55 is an F.
Please see me after class.
```

Subrange Type

The integer quotient (div) of the number grade divided by 10 produces an answer between 0 an 10. Thus there are only 11 possible cases instead of 101. The declaration of the variable numbergrade illustrates a new feature of Pascal, **subrange type**. We know that a number grade will be in the range 0 to 100. Also we know that a number grade outside of that range, like 136, will cause severe problems in the program. Therefore, we declare the type of the variable numbergrade to the **subrange** of integers consisting of only the numbers 0 to 100.

```
var
   numbergrade : 0..100;
```

Many Pascal compilers will check the values assigned to a variable of subrange type and print an error message if the value is outside the declared range.

The program lettergrade also illustrates the use of a compound statement in the last case. There is no "else" clause in a case-statement in standard Pascal, so it would be a programming error if the value of the selector expression were not in one of the lists of values describing the cases.

Comparison of Case- and If-Statements

Many program decisions can be handled either by a case-statement or by a sequence of if-statements with mutually exclusive conditions. Compare the flow of control in Figures 4.8 and 4.9. To give an idea of when a case-statement is preferable and when if-statements are preferable, the case-statement from the program digitdialing can be rewritten as a sequence of if-statements:

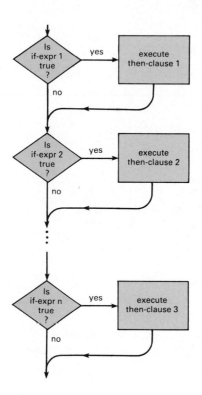

Figure 4.8 Flow of control for a sequence of if-statements.

```
if (letter = 'A') or (letter = 'B') or (letter = 'C') then
   digit := 2;
if (letter = 'D') or (letter = 'E') or (letter = 'F') then
   digit := 3;
if (letter = 'G') or (letter = 'H') or (letter = 'I') then
   digit := 4;
if (letter = 'J') or (letter = 'K') or (letter = 'L') then
   digit := 5;
if (letter = 'M') or (letter = 'N') or (letter = 'O') then
   digit := 6;
if (letter = 'P') or (letter = 'R') or (letter = 'S') then
   digit := 7;
if (letter = 'T') or (letter = 'U') or (letter = 'V') then
   digit := 8;
if (letter = 'W') or (letter = 'X') or (letter = 'Y') then
   digit := 9;
```

Although the sequence of if-statements certainly is readable, this method of programming the decisions is more cumbersome than the single case-statement used in the program digitdialing, and probably it is less clear.

Case-statements work very well when a single selector variable distinguishes between the cases and when the selector variable does not take on too many different values.

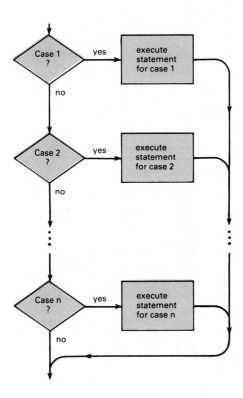

Figure 4.9   Flow of control for a case-statement.

In the program lettergrade, the obvious selector variable, numbergrade, takes on 101 different values, so a case-statement based on this variable would have to contain very long lists of constants to specify the case. Using some ingenuity, a selector-expression

    numbergrade div 10

can be found which distinguishes between the cases, but takes on only 11 possible values. In some sense, we were lucky that the grading system was so regular and predictable; the lowest number grade for each letter grade was a multiple of 10. If that were not the case, still greater ingenuity would be required to find a suitable selector expression. Suppose the As started at 92, the Bs at 84, the Cs at 71, and the Ds at 57. The following sequence of if-statements would do the job. It is likely that any case-statement for this situation would be long, obscure, and confusing.

```
if numbergrade >= 2 then
  writeln (' is an A.')
if (numbergrade >= 84) and (numbergrade < 92) then
  writeln (' is a B.')
if (numbergrade >= 71) and (numbergrade < 84) then
  writeln (' is a C.')
if (numbergrade >= 57) and (numbergrade < 71) then
  writeln (' is a D.')
```

```
if numbergrade < 57 then
  begin
  writeln (' is an F.');
  writeln ('Please see me after class.');
  end;
```

As these examples show, a sequence of if-statements is much more general and capable of handling a greater variety of situations. However, when it is applicable, a case-statement is generally shorter and clearer.

Self-Test Questions

1. Find and correct all syntax errors in the following case-statements.

a.
```
case code of
  1:  x := 1;
  2, 3, 4:
    begin
    x := 1;
    y := 1;
    end
  5, 6:  y := 1;
  7:  z := 1;
```

b.
```
case digit of
  1, 3, 7:  writeln ('Case 1');
  2, 4, 6:  writeln ('Case 2');
  5, 8:     writeln ('Case 3');
  else:     writeln ('Bad data');
```

c.
```
case compasspoint of
  'N', 'S':  writeln ('vertical');
  'E', 'W':  writeln ('horizontal');
  end
```

2. Write a case-statement that prints the word "vowel" if the value of the variable letter is a vowel (i.e., a, e, i, o, or u) and the word "consonant" if the value of letter is any other letter of the alphabet. Only lowercase letters can appear.

3. Write an if-statement or a sequence of if-statements to do the same thing as the case-statement written for Question 2.

Exercises

1. For nonresident married persons earning income in New York State who elect to file a joint federal income tax return but separate New York State returns, Table 4.2 shows the progressive tax rate schedule on taxable income. Write a program that calculates for any taxable income supplied as input the New York State income tax according to this schedule.

2. The Enlightened Corporation is pleased when its employees enroll in college classes. It offers them an 80 percent rebate on the first $500 of tuition, a 60 percent rebate on the second $400, and a 40 percent rebate on the next $300. Write a program that computes the rebate for an amount of tuition supplied as input.

3. The ranges of taxable income for each tax bracket all start and end on multiples of $500. Use this fact to write the sequence of if-statements in the program incometax in this section as a case-statement. Compare the result with the if-statements in the program incometax for clarity.

Table 4.2 New York State Tax Rate Schedule for Certain Persons

IF TAXABLE INCOME IS

OVER	BUT NOT OVER	THEN INCOME TAX IS		
$0	$1,000		2% of taxable income	
$1,000	$3,000	$20 plus	3% of excess over	$1,000
$3,000	$5,000	$80 plus	4% of excess over	$3,000
$5,000	$7,000	$160 plus	5% of excess over	$5,000
$7,000	$9,000	$260 plus	6% of excess over	$7,000
$9,000	$11,000	$380 plus	7% of excess over	$9,000
$11,000	$13,000	$520 plus	8% of excess over	$11,000
$13,000	$15,000	$680 plus	9% of excess over	$13,000
$15,000	$17,000	$860 plus	10% of excess over	$15,000
$17,000	$19,000	$1,060 plus	11% of excess over	$17,000
$19,000	$21,000	$1,280 plus	12% of excess over	$19,000
$21,000	$23,000	$1,520 plus	13% of excess over	$21,000
$23,000	$25,000	$1,780 plus	14% of excess over	$23,000
$25,000		$2,060 plus	15% of excess over	$25,000

4.3   Nested If-Statements

Section Preview

Nested if-statements:

In an if-statement, the then-clause and the else-clause may be any Pascal statement, including other if-statements. The inner if-statements are **nested** within the outer if-statement.

Most general form of if-statements nested to depth 2:

```
if condition then
  if condition 1 then
    statement 1a
  else
    statement 1b
else
  if condition 2 then
    statement 2a
  else
    statement 2b
```

Else Ambiguity:

In nested if-statements, an else-clause always belongs to the closest if-statement that is not yet completed by a semicolon or a closer else-clause.

Else-If Construction:

When only the else-clause has another if-statement nexted within it, a construction like a case-statement, only more powerful, is obtained. Note that the indentation conventions are supressed in this case.

General form of the else-if construction:

>if *condition 1* then
>   *statement 1*
>else if *condition 2* then
>   *statement 2*
>else if *condition 3* then
>   *statement 3*
>   .
>   .
>   .
>else if *condition n* then
>   *statement n*
>else
>   *statement n + 1*

Three Related Decision Procedures

We open this section with three related examples of programs using if-statements. In each of the three applications, a test has been given. The test contains not only the regular questions, which are marked normally, but also three bonus questions. The input data for all the programs consists of four items. The first item is a numerical test score for the regular questions. Each of the remaining three items is either the character R, for "right", or W, for "wrong", depending on which of the bonus questions are answered correctly. There is no partial credit for the bonus questions. The comparison operator equals (=) may be used to compare two characters.

```
program extra1 (input, output);
{ five extra points for each bonus question answered correctly }

   const
     right = 'R';

   var
     score : integer;
     bonus1, bonus2, bonus3 : char;

   begin
   writeln;
   read (score, bonus1, bonus2, bonus3);
   writeln ('Input data  score: ', score :1);
   writeln ('             bonus1: ', bonus1 :1);
   writeln ('             bonus2: ', bonus2 :1);
   writeln ('             bonus3: ', bonus3 :1);
   if bonus1 = right then
     score := score + 5;
   if bonus2 = right then
     score := score + 5;
   if bonus3 = right then
     score := score + 5;
   writeln ('Adjusted test score = ', score :1);
   end.
```

```
run extra1

Input data   score: 83
             bonus1: R
             bonus2: W
             bonus3: R
Adjusted test score = 93
```

In the program extra1, the variable score is increased by 5 every time a bonus question is answered correctly. Thus an adjusted test score can be as much as 15 points higher than the score on the regular questions if all three bonus questions were answered correctly.

In the next example, the instructor has decided to adjust the regular test score only if all three bonus questions are answered correctly. No adjustment is to be made if only one or two bonus questions are answered correctly.

```
program extra2 (input, output);
{ five extra points if all three bonus questions answered correctly }

  const
    right = 'R';

  var
    score : integer;
    bonus1, bonus2, bonus3 : char;

  begin
  writeln;
  read (score, bonus1, bonus2, bonus3);
  writeln ('Input data   score: ', score :1);
  writeln ('             bonus1: ', bonus1 :1);
  writeln ('             bonus2: ', bonus2 :1);
  writeln ('             bonus3: ', bonus3 :1);
  if (bonus1 = right) and (bonus2 = right)
     and (bonus3 = right) then
    score := score + 5;
  writeln ('Adjusted test score = ', score :1);
  end.
```

```
run extra2

Input data   score: 83
             bonus1: R
             bonus2: W
             bonus3: R
Adjusted test score = 83
```

The if-test has three comparisons separated by the keyword "and". Commas or other punctuation that might be used if this were an English sentence are not used in Pascal. The parentheses must not be omitted.

In the next example, test scores are to be adjusted by five points if any bonus question is answered correctly. There is no additional credit for a second or third bonus question that is also answered correctly.

```
program extra3 (input, output);
{ five extra points if at least one bonus question answered correctly }

   const
     right = 'R';

   var
     score : integer;
     bonus1, bonus2, bonus3 : char;

   begin
   writeln;
   read (score, bonus1, bonus2, bonus3);
   writeln ('Input data  score: ', score :1);
   writeln ('               bonus1: ', bonus1 :1);
   writeln ('               bonus2: ', bonus2 :1);
   writeln ('               bonus3: ', bonus3 :1);
   if (bonus1 = right) or (bonus2 = right) or
      (bonus3 = right) then
     score := score + 5;
   writeln ('Adjusted test score = ', score :1);
   end.
run extra3

Input data   score: 83
             bonus1: R
             bonus2: W
             bonus3: R
Adjusted test score = 88
```

This program is identical to the previous program, except that "and" has been changed to "or". The regular test score thus is increased by five points if one, two, or three of the bonus questions are answered correctly and is unchanged only if none of the bonus questions is answered correctly. The parentheses must not be omitted.

Nesting

We now show how to program the last two applications without using either "and" or "or". The programs become somewhat longer and probably less clear.

```
program extra2b (input, output);
{ five extra points if all three bonus questions answered correctly }

   const
     right = 'R';

   var
     score : integer;
     bonus1, bonus2, bonus3 : char;

   begin
   writeln;
   read (score, bonus1, bonus2, bonus3);
```

```
writeln ('Input data   score: ', score :1);
writeln ('              bonus1: ', bonus1 :1);
writeln ('              bonus2: ', bonus2 :1);
writeln ('              bonus3: ', bonus3 :1);
if bonus1 = right then
  if bonus2 = right then
    if bonus3 = right then
      score := score + 5;
writeln ('Adjusted test score = ', score :1);
end.

run extra2b

Input data   score: 83
             bonus1: R
             bonus2: W
             bonus3: R
Adjusted test score = 83
```

In this program, there are three if-statements, one nested within the next. They start on different lines, but each one ends after the assignment statement. None of these if-statements has an else-clause, so if any one of the three tests is not satisfied, the computer procedes to the writeln statement (see Figure 4.10). The program extra2b is grammatically correct and executes properly, but it is more confusing than extra2, which is therefore preferred.

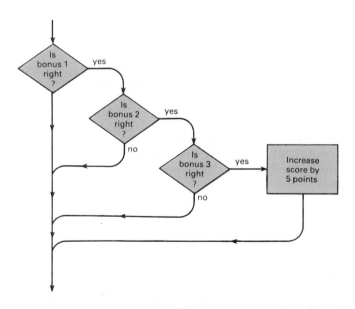

Figure 4.10   Nested if-statement structure of the program extra2b. All three if-conditions must be satisfied to earn the 5-point bonus.

In order to eliminate the keyword "or" from the program extra3, a similar nesting of if-statements is necessary. This time the nesting occurs in the else-clause.

```
program extra3b (input, output);
{ five extra points if at least one bonus question answered correctly }

  const
    right = 'R';

  var
    score : integer;
    bonus1, bonus2, bonus3 : char;

  begin
  writeln;
  read (score, bonus1, bonus2, bonus3);
  writeln ('Input data  score: ', score :1);
  writeln ('              bonus1: ', bonus1 :1);
  writeln ('              bonus2: ', bonus2 :1);
  writeln ('              bonus3: ', bonus3 :1);
  if bonus1 = right then
    score := score + 5
  else
    if bonus2 = right then
      score := score + 5
    else
      if bonus3 = right then
        score := score + 5;
  writeln ('Adjusted test score = ', score :1);
  end.
run extra3b

Input data  score: 83
              bonus1: R
              bonus2: W
              bonus3: R
Adjusted test score = 88
```

With effort, it can be verified that this program is correct (see Figure 4.11). However, the program using the keyword "or" is clearly preferable. The program can be made a little clearer by writing the keyword "else" and the if-test following it on one line, as shown below.

```
if bonus1 = right then
  score := score + 5
else if bonus2 = right then
  score := score + 5
else if bonus3 = right then
  score := score + 5
```

This form is much more readable than the nested if-statements in the program extra3b, which are syntactically *identical* to the nested if-statements here. The indentation of the nested if-statements in the program extra3b is done following the usual rules of indentation to show the exact nature of the nesting. Although this else-if form of indentation makes the nested if-statements more readable, they are still less readable than the single if-statement using the boolean operator "or" in the program extra3.

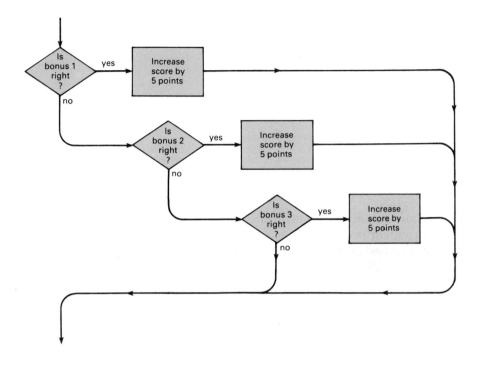

Figure 4.11   Nested if-statement structure of the program extra3b. The 5-point bonus is awarded if any of the three bonus questions is answered correctly.

The Else Ambiguity

The following if-statement, deliberately presented without indentation, illustrates a point of possible confusion in the Pascal language.

```
if x > 0 then
if y > 0 then
n := 1
else
n := 2
```

It is not clear to which condition the "else" belongs. To prevent ambiguity, Pascal associates an else-clause with the most recent incomplete if-statement. Thus the proper indentation is:

```
if x > 0 then
  if y > 0 then
    n := 1
  else
    n := 2
```

Suppose x = y = −1. The first if-test is false and the remainder of the statement is skipped, so that the value of n is not changed. Suppose x = 1 and y = −1. The first if-test is true, so the next if-statement is executed. Since y > 0 is false, the else-clause is executed, setting n equal to 2.

It is possible to force the else to go with the first if-statement in at least two ways. One is to use a begin-end pair of keywords to enclose the inner if-statement in a single compound statement, giving it a definite end. The other way is to add another "else" with an empty else-clause to complete the inner if-statement. The two resulting statements follow.

```
if x > 0 then
  begin
  if y > 0 then
    n := 1
  end
else
  n := 2
if x > 0 then
  if y > 0 then
    n := 1
  else
else
  n := 2
```

Each of the two statements above has been indented correctly to show its structure, but it is the text of the program that determines what is to be computed and the indentation has no effect whatsoever. With or without proper indentation, the begin-end version is probably clearer.

Self-Test Questions

To test your understanding of the syntax of if-statements and the placement of semicolons in a Pascal program, hand simulate the programs example1 to example6 using the values 45, 75, and 95 as input data (18 simulations in all). Check your answers with a computer, if possible, as well as against the answers in the book. *Caution:* These simulations are tricky and, to add to the challenge, some of these programs are syntactically incorrect and cannot be executed at all. Try to determine which are incorrect before the computer gives you an error message.

1.
```
program example1 (input, output);
  var
    x : integer;
  begin
  read (x);
  if x > 50 then
    if x > 90 then
      begin
      write ('Input data x = ', x :1);
      writeln (' is very high.')
      end
    else
      begin
      write ('Input data x = ', x :1);
      writeln (' is high.')
      end
  end.
```

2.
```
program example2 (input, output);
  var
    x : integer;
  begin
  read (x);
```

```
    if x > 50 then
      if x > 90 then
        begin
        write ('Input data x = ', x :1);
        writeln (' is very high.');
        end
      else
        begin
        write ('Input data x = ', x :1);
        writeln (' is high.');
        end;
      end.
```

3.
```
program example3 (input, output);
  var
    x : integer;
  begin;
  read (x);
  if x > 50 then
    if x > 90 then
      begin;
      write ('Input data x = ', x :1);
      writeln (' is very high.');
      end
    else
      begin;
      write ('Input data x = ', x :1);
      writeln (' is high.');
      end;
    end.
```

4.
```
program example4 (input, output);
  var
    x : integer;
  begin
  read (x);
  if x > 50 then
    if x > 90 then
      begin
      write ('Input data x = ', x :1);
      writeln (' is very high.');
      end
    else;
      begin
      write ('Input data x = ', x :1);
      writeln (' is high.');
      end
    end.
```

5.
```
program example5 (input, output);
  var
    x : integer;
  begin
  read (x);
```

```
        if x > 50 then
          if x > 90 then
            begin
            write ('Input data x = ', x :1);
            writeln (' is very high.');
            end;
          else
            begin
            write ('Input data x = ', x :1);
            writeln (' is high.');
            end;
          end.
```

6.
```
    program example6 (input, output);
      var
        x : integer;
      begin
      read (x);
      if x > 50 then;
        if x > 90 then
          begin
          write ('Input data x = ', x :1);
          writeln (' is very high.');
          end
        else
          begin
          write ('Input data x = ', x :1);
          writeln (' is high.');
          end
        end.
```

Exercises

1. Social security benefits are available to men starting at age 65 and women
    starting at age 62. Write a program that accepts as input the code M or F
    designating the sex of the applicant and an integer designating the age of
    the applicant. The program should print "eligible" if the applicant is eli-
    gible for social security benefits and "ineligible" if not. Write the pro-
    gram two ways: once using compound if-conditions and once using nested
    if-statements. Compare the two versions from the point of view of pro-
    gram clarity.

2. The price of an issue of a popular computing magazine is given in the fol-
    lowing table:

	Subscription	Newstand
U. S.	$1.75	$3.50
Canada	$1.95	$3.95

    Write a program that accepts a country code U or C and a location code S
    or N and prints out the price of the magazine.

3. A toll bridge charges $1.50 for passenger cars, $2.00 for busses, $3.00 for
    trucks under 10,000 pounds, and $5.00 for trucks over 10,000 pounds.
    Write a program that first accepts as input the letters c, b, and t,
    representing the vehicle class. If the vehicle class code is t (for truck),
    the program should ask for one of the characters "<" or ">". The pro-
    gram should then print out the toll charge.

4.4   Character String Comparisons

Both character and character string values may be compared in if-tests. This section reviews character and character string data types and explains how comparisons work for these types.

Section Preview

Character Data:

Pascal has an intrinsic data type char permitting any one machine-representable character as value.

Example:

```
const
    lastletter = 'z';
var
    alphabetic : char;
```

Character Strings:

A character string is a packed array of characters.

Examples (both character strings of length 3):

```
const
    zooword = 'zoo';
var
    word : packed array [1..3] of char;
```

Collating Sequence:

The built-in function ord gives the ordinal position of a character in the collating sequence. The built-in function chr gives the character with a given ordinal position.

Comparison of Characters and Character Strings:

For single characters, the character with lower ordinal position in the collating sequence is considered "lower". For character strings, the relative ordinal positions of the first characters that differ determine which will be considered the "smaller" character string. This ordering extends ordinary lexicographic order.

Character strings to be compared or assigned must be of exactly the same lenth.

The following example illustrates declaration, assignment, and comparison of character strings in standard Pascal.

```
program example (output);

    const
      first = 'lisa ';

    var
      name, name2 : packed array [1..5] of char;

    begin
    name : = 'pam ';
    if name < first then
      name2 := name
```

```
         else
            name2 := 'julie'
         writeln (name2);
         end.
```

Character Data Type

In addition to the data types integer and real, there is a character data type denoted by **char**. A variable may be declared to be type character as illustrated in the following declaration.

```
      var
         q23, c1, initial : char;
```

The value of such a variable may be any single computer-representable character. Most computers use either the 128-character **ASCII character set** or the 256-character **EBCDIC character set**. The acronym ASCII stands for "American Standard Code for Information Interchange", and the acronym EBCDIC stands for "Extended Binary Coded Decimal Interchange Code". Both character sets include uppercase and lowercase letters, numerals, standard punctuation signs, and all the characters on the keyboard of you computer terminal or keypunch. Tables 4.3 and 4.4 list most of the printable characters in the ASCII and EBCDIC character codes.

Constants also may be of type character. The values of such constants are given by a single character enclosed by apostrophes. The following are declarations of typical character constants.

```
      const
         eggs = 'x';
         signal = '*';
```

The Built-In Functions Ord and Chr

The 128 possible characters of the ASCII character set or the 256 possible characters of the EBCDIC character set have an intrinsic ordering derived from the most usual ways of storing or representing character data in a computer. This ordering is the **collating sequence** for the character set. As Tables 4.3 and 4.4 show, the collating sequences for the ASCII and EBCDIC character sets do not agree on important particulars. However, they do agree that both uppercse and lowercase letters are in alphabetic order and that the digits are in numeric order.

In Pascal, the six comparison operators

```
      <    >    =    <=    >=    <>
```

may be used to compare character values according to the intrinsic ordering of the character set used. Thus

```
      'A' < 'B' < 'C' < 'D'
      'a' < 'b' < 'c' < 'd'
      '1' < '2' < '3' < '4'
```

in either the ASCII or the EBCDIC collating sequences. However, the question of whether 'A' is less than 'a' or vice versa will have a different answer on two different computers if one uses the ASCII collating sequence and the other uses the EBCDIC collating sequence. All examples in this book will run on computers with either collating sequence.

The built-in function **ord** assigns to each possible character value its **ordinal position** in the character set. On a computer using the ASCII character set, the values of the built-in function ord range from 0 to 127. When EBCDIC is used, they range from 0 to 255. It is possible to determine the character code used on your computer by executing the program chars below.

Table 4.3 The collating sequence for a selection of printable ASCII characters.

```
blank ! " # $ % & ' ( ) * + , - . /
0 1 2 3 4 5 6 7 8 9 : ; < = > ? @
A B C D E F G H I J K L M N O P Q R S T U V W X Y Z [ ] ^ _ `
a b c d e f g h i j k l m n o p q r s t u v w x y z { | } ~
```

Table 4.4 The collating sequence for a selection of printable EBCDIC characters.

```
blank ] . < ( + ! & [ $ * ) ; ^ - / , % _ > ? : # @ ' = "
a b c d e f g h i j k l m n o p q r s t u v w x y z
A B C D E F G H I J K L M N O P Q R S T U V W X Y Z
0 1 2 3 4 5 6 7 8 9
```

```pascal
program chars (output);
  var
    code : 0..127;
  begin
  for code := 0 to 127 do
    begin
    write (code :6, chr (code) :2);
    if code mod 8 = 7 then
      writeln;
    end; { for loop }
  end.

run chars
```

0	1	2	3	4	5	6	7
8	9	10					
11	12	13	14	15			
16	17	18	19	20	21	22	23
24	25	26	27	28	29	30	31
32	33 !	34 "	35 #	36 $	37 %	38 &	39 '
40 (	41)	42 *	43 +	44 ,	45 –	46 .	47 /
48 0	49 1	50 2	51 3	52 4	53 5	54 6	55 7
56 8	57 9	58 :	59 ;	60 <	61 =	62 >	63 ?
64 @	65 A	66 B	67 C	68 D	69 E	70 F	71 G
72 H	73 I	74 J	75 K	76 L	77 M	78 N	79 O
80 P	81 Q	82 R	83 S	84 T	85 U	86 V	87 W
88 X	89 Y	90 Z	91 [	92	93]	94 ^	95 _
96 `	97 a	98 b	99 c	100 d	101 e	102 f	103 g
104 h	105 i	106 j	107 k	108 l	109 m	110 n	111 o
112 p	113 q	114 r	115 s	116 t	117 u	118 v	119 w
120 x	121 y	122 z	123 {	124		125 }	126 ~	127

The value of the built-in function chr is the character whose code or position in the collating sequence is the integer that is the argument of chr. For example, on a computer that uses the ASCII code, chr (65) = 'A', and chr (66) = 'B'.

The program chars will take some experimentation to run. You must determine if the computer uses the 128-character ASCII character set (as shown) or the 256-character EBCDIC character set, or some other character set of another size. Also, the output is bound to look peculiar in places. Most of the characters from 0 to 31 do not print. Some, like the line, feed, chr (10), direct the printer to perform some action rather than print a character. The sample output shown is typical; it was produced on the VAX 11/750 computer using the ASCII character code. The output device used for computer-controlled typesetting also modified the spacing.

The built-in function ord may be applied to an expression of type char. It produces an integer that represents the position of that character in the collating sequence. Ord and chr are inverse functions

chr (ord (c)) = c

as long as c is a character and

ord (chr (n)) = n

provided that n is a valid ASCII or EBCDIC character code.

Character Strings

Character string constants have been used since Section 2.1 to identify the output of a program. For example, the statement

```
writeln ('The sum of 6 and 5 is ', 6 + 5)
```
not only prints the sum, 11, but it also prints the identifying character string constant 'The sum of 6 and 5 is ' preceding the answer:

```
The sum of 6 and 5 is 11
```

Character string constants also may be declared in the constant declaration (const) part of a program. For example, the declarations

```
const
  su = 'State University';
  password = 'rumplesnort';
  signal = 'zzz';
```
assign character string values of lengths greater than one to these three constants.

A variable of type char must have as its value one single character. **Character string variables** are also possible. In a program, a character string variable is declared to be either an **array** or a **packed array** of characters. Although we do not explain arrays at this point, the declaration of the character string variables below can be used as models for declaring character string variables of different lengths.

```
var
  tenlettername : packed array [1..10] of char;
  threeletterword : packed array [1..3] of char;
  fiveletterword : packed array [1..5] of char;
```

The length of a character string variable or constant is important because two character strings may be compared (in standard Pascal) only if they have *exactly the same length*.

For example, the test

```
if tenlettername = 'David' then
```
is invalid, but the tests

```
if tenlettername = 'David    ' then
if tenlettername = 'Michael J.' then
```

are both valid. Blanks within a character string are perfectly legal characters. In the ASCII code, a blank is chr (32).

If the first character of one character string precedes the first character of the second character string in the collating sequence, then we say the first character string is less than the second. If the first characters are equal, the second characters are used to decide which character string is "smaller". If the second characters match also, the third characters are used to decide, and so on. Since the two character strings have the same length, either every character in the first string matches the corresponding character in the second string, in which case the two character strings are equal, or there is a first character position in which they differ. The character string with the "smaller" character, i.e, the one earlier in the collating sequence, in the first position where they disagree is considered the "smaller" character string.

For example,

```
'apple     ' < 'bug       ' < 'cacophony' < 'doldrums '
'earache ' < 'elephant' < 'empathy ' < 'equine    '
'phlegmatic    ' < 'phonograph    ' < 'photosynthetic'
'dipole    ' < 'duplicate' = 'duplicate' < 'dynamic   '
```

In the first line of comparisons, decisions are made on the basis of the first letter of the strings. In the second line, since each string has first letter "e", decisions are made on the basis of the relative collating position of the second letters. In the third set of comparisons, third or fourth letters differ.

From these examples, it is clear that the natural order of character strings corresponds exactly to ordinary alphabetic order when the character strings are words written either entirely in uppercase or entirely in lowercase letters. String ordering is an extension of ordinary **lexicographic order** because it orders nonsense "words" as well as those that have English meaning and because it orders character strings that include characters such as "#", "%", and "?" that do not appear in words.

String ordering does not take meaning into account. For example, although

```
'1' < '2'< '3' < '4'
```

as expected, it is also true that

```
'four ' < 'one  ' < 'three' < 'two
```

and, worse yet,

```
'12' < '2 '
```

Self-Test Questions

1. Which of the following constant declarations are correct?
    ```
    const
      signal = 'stop';
      bee = 'b';
    ```

2. Which of the following variable declarations are correct?
    ```
    var
      firstname : packed array of char;
      signal : packed array [1..4] of char;
    ```

3.   Which of the following assignment statements are correct?

```
a.   see := 'c'
b.   word := 'certainly'
c.   'yes' := 'no '
```

4.   Which of the following comparisons are valid and, if valid, which are true?

```
a.   if 'one' < 'two' then ...
b.   if 'two' < 'three' then ...
c.   if 'five' < 6 then ...
d.   if 'five' < '6' then ...
e.   if 'a' < 'A' then ...
f.   if 'albatross' < 'albumen  ' then ...
```

Exercises

1.   What is the value of each of the following expressions?

```
chr (ord ('*'))
chr (ord ('a') + 1)
ord ('7') - ord ('0')
```

2.   Compare the two character strings 'ABC' and '123' using the ASCII and the EBCDIC collating sequences given in Tables 4.3 and 4.4. Which string comes first (i.e., collates low) in ASCII? Which in EBCDIC?

3.   Write a program to read three characters as input and to check them against a 3-character password declared as three character constants in the program. Print the message "okay" if they match or "try again" if they don't.

4.   Modify the program chars in this section (if necessary) and run it on your computer. Determine whether your computer uses the ASCII collating sequence, the EBCDIC collating sequence, or some other collating sequence. What effect do the following characters have on the printed or displayed output on your computer?

chr	name
7	bell
8	backspace
10	line feed
12	form feed
13	carriage return
27	escape
32	blank
92	backslash
127	delete

4.5   What You Should Know

1.   The if-statement is built using other statements.
2.   The condition in the if-test is a boolean expression.
3.   The only values a boolean expression can have are true and false.
4.   The then-clause of an if-statement is executed if the boolean condition is true.
5.   The else-clause of an if-statement is executed if the condition is false.

6. The else-clause may be omitted if no action is required when the condition is false.

7. The then-clause of an if-statement may be any single Pascal statement. The same is true for the else-clause.

8. A compound statement is a group of Pascal statements headed by "begin" and ending with "end". It may be used any place a simple statement may be used, including then- or else-clauses in an if-statement.

9. When one of the clauses of an if-statement is itself an if-statement, the if-statements are said to be nested.

10. In nested if-statements, an else-clause always belongs to the closest if-statement that is not yet completed by a semicolon or a closer else-clause.

11. A sequence of if-tests with mutually exclusive conditions can handle a decision with more than two alternatives.

12. Case-statements handle multiple alternatives very well when a single selector variable distinguishes between the cases and when the selector variable does not take on too many different values.

13. Nesting each one of a sequence of if-statements in the else-clause of the previous if-statement eliminates the need to make the conditions mutually exclusive. This nesting is called "the else-if construction".

14. The six arithmetic comparison operators may be used to construct boolean conditions. They are $>$, $<$, $=$, $>=$, $<=$, and $<>$.

15. A flowchart is a way of depicting the sequence in which instructions are executed. It is particularaly useful for analyzing the effect of if-statements and nested if-statements.

16. The first version of a program should use terms from the original problem statement. The steps in this version need not be executable Pascal statements.

17. Unrefined statements are refined by placing them by instructions in Pascal that direct a computer to do what the English statements say to do.

18. Since the refined program is really the same program with more of the details spelled out, the same program name is used before and after refinement.

19. When a program is tested, there should be at least one set of test data to test each alternative in the program.

20. A syntax chart is a way of depicting correct Pascal syntax. Any complete path from the beginning to the end of a syntax chart represents a syntactically correct Pascal construct. Complete syntax charts for Pascal appear in Appendix B.

21. It is good programming practice to warn the user when a situation occurs that the program is not designed to handle.

22. The boolean operators "and", "or", and "not" may be used to build more comlplex boolean expressions.

23. The value of type char may be any single compter-representable character. The two most common character sets are the 128-character ASCII set and the 256-character EBCDIC set.

24. The built-in function ord converts a character to a number, its ordinal position in the character set. The function chr reverses the process: it yields the character represented by the ASCII or EBCDIC code.

25. Character comparisons are based on the collating sequence for the character set. Characters with lower ordinal positions are considered less than characters with higher ordinal positions. The six character comparison operations are denoted by the same symbols as the arithmetic comparison operators.

26. A character string constant is a sequence of characters enclosed in apostrophes.

27. A character string variable is a packed array of characters.
28. In standard Pascal, character strings may be compared only if they have exactly the same length.
29. String ordering is an extension of alphabetic ordering. One character string is less than a second character string if it precedes the second character string in alphabetic order.

LOOP STRUCTURES 5

The value of a variable may change not only from one run to the next as a result of different values of the input data, but also during the course of a single run. The reassignment of new values to a variable during execution is a crucial feature of many programs, particularly of those containing a **loop**, which is a sequence of instruction to be executed repeatedly.

All of the programs so far suffer from the defect that each instruction is executed exactly once. At the enormous speed at which computers execute instructions, it would be difficult to keep a computer busy for very long using this type of program. By the simple expedient of having the computer execute some instructions more than once, perhaps a large number of times, it is possible to produce a computer program that takes longer to execute than to write. Such programs can also do useful data processing and calculation.

The simplest loop in Pascal, the **for-loop**, is introduced in Section 5.1. The more general flexible loop structures, the **while-loop** and the **repeat-until-loop**, are introduced in Section 5.2. Since some variables repeatedly have their values changed during execution of a loop, this chapter provides an opportunity to take a closer look at the underlying nature of a variable in a computer program.

Section 5.3 explores the relationship between for-loops and character strings and other arrays. The remainder of the chapter treats the use of a loop to calculate a sum and average, and the special problems involved in debugging a program that contains a loop.

5.1   For-Loops

Quite frequently, the successive values taken on by a variable follow a simple pattern, like 1, 2, 3, 4, 5, 6, 7, 8, 9, 10, or 7, 6, 5, 4. Because these sequences occur so often in programming, there is a simple means of assigning successive values to a variable in Pascal, the for-statement.

Section Preview

For-Loop:

General Form:

> for *variable* := *expression* to *expression* do
> statement

> for *variable* := *expression* downto *expression* do
> statement

Examples:

```
for n := 1 to 20 do
  writeln (n)
```

```
for value := 20 downto 1 do
  sum := sum + value
```

```
for letter := 1 to 10 do
  begin
  read (singlecharacter);
  write (singlecharacter);
  end
```

Syntax Chart for a For-Statement:

⟨FOR_STATEMENT⟩:

→for→⟨IDENTIFIER⟩→:=→⟨EXPRESSION⟩

        ┌─to─┐
        └─downto─┘→⟨EXPRESSION⟩→do→⟨STATEMENT⟩→

Step Size:

In Pascal, successive values of a for-variable either increase by 1 or decrease by 1. No other other step size is permitted.

Semicolons:

Semicolons *separate* statements. If a semicolon immediately precedes the keyword "end" in a compound statement, a harmless empty statement is assumed to follow the semicolon. If a semicolon follows the keyword "do" in a for-statement, the body of the for-loop is empty.

Counting Forward

The program tennumbers tells a computer to print the numbers from 1 to 10. It uses a **for-statement** to print the numbers.

```
program tennumbers (output);
  var
    number : integer;
  begin
  for number := 1 to 10 do
    write (number :3);
  writeln;
  end.
run tennumbers

  1   2   3   4   5   6   7   8   9  10
```

The for-statement in the program tennumbers, also called a **for-loop** consists of two parts, a statement

```
write (number :3)
```

that prints the current value of the variable number using three columns, and a **for-loop heading**

```
for number := 1 to 10 do
```

that tells the computer how many times to execute the write statement and what the values of the **for-variable** number should be each time. The first time the write statement is executed, the for-variable number has the value 1, and this number is printed at the beginning of the output line. Then the for-variable number takes on the value 2, which is printed three columns to the right. Then the for-variable takes on the values 3, 4, 5, 6, 7, 8, 9, and 10 for successive repetitions of the write statement. At this point, the possible values for the for-variable number specified in the for-loop heading are exhausted and the program execution proceeds to the next statement,

```
writeln
```

which writes carriage return and line feed characters to bring the printer to the beginning of a new line. On some computer systems, a partial output line may be lost if the program execution ends before a writeln statement is executed. See if this is true on your computer system by omitting the writeln statement.

The For-Statement

The values of a for-variable may either increase, as in the program tennumbers, or decrease, as in later examples. The general form of an ascending for-statement is

```
for variable := expression to expression do
    statement
```

As we shall see in later examples, it is permissible to use expressions to specify the starting and stopping values of a for-variable. The for-statement in the program tennumbers used constants 1 and 10. The statement to be executed repeatedly in the for-loop is the **body** of the for-loop. It also is permissible to write a compound statement for the body of the for-loop if you want to repeat more than one statement.

A Table of Squares and Square Roots

A structurally minor modification of the program tennumbers can produce a program sqrandsqrt to print a table of squares and square roots of numbers from 1 to 10.

```
program sqrandsqrt (output);
  var
    number : integer;
  begin
  writeln ('Number' :10, 'Square' :10, 'Square root' :15);
  for number := 1 to 10 do
    writeln (number :10, sqr (number) :10, sqrt (number) :15:3);
  end.
```

```
run sqrandsqrt
```

Number	Square	Square root
1	1	1.000
2	4	1.414
3	9	1.732
4	16	2.000
5	25	2.236
6	36	2.449
7	49	2.646
8	64	2.828
9	81	3.000
10	100	3.162

Eleven lines of output are printed by the program sqrandsqrt. The first writeln command that prints the heading of the columns is executed only once, because it is not within the for-loop. Indenting the body of a for-loop makes it easier to see which instructions are to be repeated. After the headings are printed, the writeln command within the for-loop prints a number, its square, and its square root, for each value of the variable number from 1 to 10. Using columns indicators on all output expressions forces proper placement on the print line, so the headings are positioned directly above the columns of numbers they identify.

Counting Backward

In Pascal, it is possible to have a for-variable count backwards. It is possible to print the complete words to the popular camp song "Ninety-Nine Bottles of Beer on the Wall" using a for-loop with the keyword **downto**. Note that "downto" is a single keyword; no space is permitted within the keyword. The program beer, which tells the computer to print the verses, is given below, and the music is given in Figure 5.1.

```
program beer (output);
for n := 99 downto 1 do
   begin
```

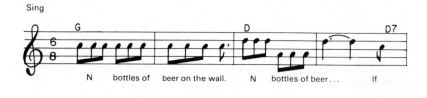

Figure 5.1 A musical for-loop for a 5-mile hike.

```
program beer (output);
   var
      n : integer;
```

```
    begin
    for n := 99 downto 1 do
      begin
      writeln;
      writeln (n :1, ' bottles of beer on the wall.');
      writeln (n :1, ' bottles of beer.');
      writeln ('If one of those bottles should happen to fall,');
      writeln ('There''d be ', n — 1 :1, ' bottles of beer on the wall.');
      end; { verse loop }
    end.
  run beer
```

```
  99 bottles of beer on the wall.
  99 bottles of beer.
  If one of those bottles should happen to fall,
  There'd be 98 bottles of beer on the wall.

  98 bottles of beer on the wall.
  98 bottles of beer.
  If one of those bottles should happen to fall,
  There'd be 97 bottles of beer on the wall.

  97 bottles of beer on the wall.
  97 bottles of beer.
  If one of those bottles should happen to fall,
  There'd be 96 bottles of beer on the wall.
            .
            .
            .
  1 bottles of beer on the wall.
  1 bottles of beer.
  If one of those bottles should happen to fall,
  There'd be 0 bottles of beer on the wall.
```

A short name n is chosen for the for-variable to make it easier to sing the program listing. The execution printout shown is abbreviated after three full verses, with the last verse also given to show how the loop ends.

Note that the last line of each verse of the song contains an apostrophe. Because apostrophes are used to delimit the character string within the program in Pascal, the apostrophe in "there'd" would normally be taken as the end of the character string. To avoid this difficulty two consecutive apostrophes in a program listing stand for a single apostrophe in a character string.

In the last verse of the song, shown in the abbreviated sample execution, and in the next to last verse, not shown, the computer printout continues to use "bottles", even though there is only one bottle of beer left on the wall. The users of computers see so much violation of the rules of English grammar in their printouts that it has come to be recognized as a trademark or characteristic of a computerized operation. This need not happen.

The grammar shown is incorrect not because a computer is incapable of producing correct grammar, but because it is easier to write a program that allows the computer to err in these two cases than it is to write a program that treats all cases properly. What happens in the program beer is that the convenience of the programmer has taken inappropriate precedence over the convenience of the user of the program. For this application, it is not too difficult to correct the grammar of the last verses.

Variable Limits for a For-Loop

For users who do not need or want all the lyrics of the popular camp song printed, the modified program anybeer allows a choice of which verses to print. The starting value and the stopping value need not be constants, but may also be given as the values of variables or other expressions. Of course, if a variable is used in specifying the starting value or stopping value for a for-variable, then it must be assigned a value before the for-loop is reached.

```
program anybeer (input, output);
  var
    first, last, n : integer;
  begin
  read (first, last);
  writeln ('Input data  first: ', first :1);
  writeln ('            last: ', last :1);
  for n := first downto last do
    begin
    writeln;
    writeln (n :1, ' bottles of beer on the wall.');
    writeln (n :1, ' bottles of beer.');
    writeln ('If one of these bottles should happen to fall,');
    writeln ('There''d be ', n — 1 :1, ' bottles of beer on the wall.');
    end;
  end.

run anybeer

Input data  first: 83
            last: 81

83 bottles of beer on the wall.
    .
    .
    .
```

Descending For-Statements

When the values of the for-variable descend (by one each time), the keyword "to" in the for-statement is replaced by the keyword "downto". The general form of a **descending** for-statement is

    for *variable* := *expression* downto *expression* do
        statement

In Pascal, increasing by one and decreasing by one are the only possible changes in a for-variable between successive iterations of a for-loop.

For-Loops That Are Executed No Times

Sometimes, the body of a for-loop is executed no times at all. For instance, the loop

```
for n := 1 to numberofentries do
    print the nth entry;
```

could be used to print all the entries in some collection. When numberofentries is 0, this loop reduces to

```
for n := 1 to 0 do
  print the nth entry
```

In Pascal, this for-loop executes no times at all, which is exactly what you want—since the collection has no entries. It is a tremendous convenience to programmers to be able to use this same for-loop even when the number of entries happens to be zero.

Counting By Twos

In Pascal, the differences between successive values of a for-variable must always be 1 or −1, as they have been in the previous examples. However, it is possible to achieve the effect of differences that are not 1 or −1, as is illustrated by the program countbytwos.

```
program countbytwos1 (output);
  var
    m : integer;
  begin
  for m := 1 to 5 do
    write (2 * m :3);
  writeln;
  end.
run countbytwos1

  2  4  6  8 10
```

Although the for-variable m does not increase by 2 each time, the value of the expression 2 * m does increase by 2. With a little practice, it is possible to write an expression that increases (or decreases) by any step size and has any starting value. For example, to print the sequence,

1, 11, 21, 31, 41, 51, 61, 71, 81, 91

the expression 1 + 10 * m starts at 1 when m is zero and increases by 10 each time m increases by 1. The program skipbytens uses this expression to print the sequence.

```
program skipbytens (output);
  var
    m : integer;
  begin
  for m := 0 to 9 do
    write (1 + 10 * m :3);
  writeln;
  end.
run skipbytens

  1 11 21 31 41 51 61 71 81 91
```

Nesting an If-Statement in a For-Loop

The **body**, of a for-loop may be any Pascal statement, and if it is a compound statement, it may contain any Pascal statements. The program tenbyten uses an if-statement **nested** within a for-loop to print the numbers from 1 to 100 on ten lines. Each time a multiple of ten is reached (recognized because n mod 10 is zero), a new output line is started. Otherwise, the program tenbyten closely resembles the program tennumbers.

```
program tenbyten (output);
  var
    n : integer;
  begin
  for n := 1 to 100 do
    begin
    write (n :4);
    { if-statement nested in a for-loop }
    if n mod 10 = 0 then
      writeln;
    end;  { for-loop }
  end.

run tenbyten
```

```
 1   2   3   4   5   6   7   8   9  10
11  12  13  14  15  16  17  18  19  20
21  22  23  24  25  26  27  28  29  30
31  32  33  34  35  36  37  38  39  40
41  42  43  44  45  46  47  48  49  50
51  52  53  54  55  56  57  58  59  60
61  62  63  64  65  66  67  68  69  70
71  72  73  74  75  76  77  78  79  80
81  82  83  84  85  86  87  88  89  90
91  92  93  94  95  96  97  98  99 100
```

Self-Test Questions

1.   Which of the following for-loops are syntactically correct?

a.
```
for n = 1 to 10 do
  writeln (n * n)
```

b.
```
for x := 10 downto 3
  writeln (x)
```

c.
```
for year := 1960 to 1984 do
  read (profit)
```

d.
```
for n := 1 to 9 do sum := sum + n
```

e.
```
for n := 1 to 9 do
  sum := sum + n
```

f.
```
for count := 1 to n do
  begin
  read (score);
  sum := sum + score;
  end
```

g.
```
for time := 1 to 3 do
  begin
  total := total + 1
  end
```

2.   Correct those for-loops in Question 1 that have syntax errors.

3.   Hand simulate the execution of the following compound statement, keeping track of the value of n and product after the execution of each statement.

```
begin
product := 1;
for n := 2 to 4 do
  product := product * n;
end
```

4. What output is produced by the following program?

```
program example4 (output);
  var
    m : integer;
  begin
  for m := 1 to 20 do
    if odd (m) then
      write (m :3);
  writeln;
  end.
```

Exercises

1. Write a program to print a table of the numbers from 1 to 10 and their cubes.
2. Write a program to print the numbers from 1 to 100 on 10 lines, with the numbers from 1 to 10 going down the first column, the numbers from 11 to 20 going down the second column, and so on.
3. Modify the program tennumbers to print the numbers from 1 to 25.
4. Modify the program tennumbers to read a number n as input and to print the numbers from 1 to n.
5. Write a program to print all integers less than 100 that are perfect squares, i. e., that are squares of other integers. *Hint:* a number is a perfect square if trunc (sqrt (n)) = sqrt (n).
6. Write a program tensandunits to produce the same output as the program tenbyten. The program tensandunits should contain a for-loop running through all the possible units digits nested in a for-loop running through all the possible tens digits.

5.2   While-Loops and Repeat-Until-Loops

Although a for-loop is very convenient Pascal when it applies, the for-loop is often too specialized for many applications. The number of times a for-loop is to execute must be known, if not when the program is written, at least before the for-loop is entered during program execution. The while- and repeat-until-loops, introduced in this section, have no such restrictions. They can be used when termination of a loop depends on testing a calculated value or on recognizing a signal value in the input data.

Section Preview

While-Statement:

General Form:

while *condition* do
  statement

A **while-loop** usually requires **initialization** of at least one variable used in the test condition and some means of changing that variable in the body of the while-loop.

Examples of While-Loops:

```
n := 1;
while n <= 1000 do
   begin
   writeln (n);
   n := n * 2;
   end { body of the while-loop }
singlecharacter := ' ';
while singlecharacter <> '.' do
   begin
   read (singlecharacter);
   write (singlecharacter);
   end
```

Syntax Chart for a While-Statement:

```
⟨WHILE_STATEMENT⟩:

→ while → ⟨EXPRESSION⟩ → do → ⟨STATEMENT⟩ ——→
```

Repeat-Until-Statement:

A loop construct closely resembling the while-loop in power, except the **exit test** is performed *after* each iteration of the body of the loop, rather than before each iteration as in a while-loop. The body of a repeat-until-loop is always performed at least once.

General form:

```
   repeat
      statement;
      statement;
      .

      .

      .
      statement
      until condition
```

Examples:

```
repeat
   read (singlecharacter);
   write (singlecharacter);
   until singlecharacter = '.'
n := 1;
repeat
   writeln (n);
   n := n * 2;
   until n > 1000
```

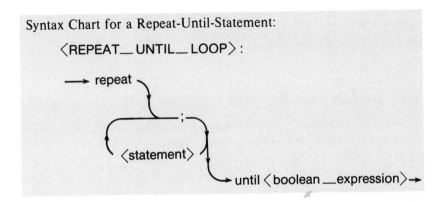

Syntax Chart for a Repeat-Until-Statement:

⟨REPEAT__UNTIL__LOOP⟩:

repeat

;

⟨statement⟩

until ⟨boolean __expression⟩→

A Recipe

A recipe is a program a person follows to prepare a kind of food. Recipes resemble computer programs closely enough that the preparation of a soup will provide the first examples of while- and repeat-until-loops. In both examples, the loop inplements the final step in the preparation of a soup,

```
salt to taste
```

First, the while-loop version, souppreparation1 is given.

```
recipe souppreparation1; { while-loop version }
  begin
  prepare soup;
  toobland := true;   { initial condition }
  while toobland do   { while-loop to salt to taste }
    begin
    stir;
    taste;
    if taste is just right then
      toobland := false
    else
      add a pinch of salt;
    end;   { while-loop }
  serve;
  end.
```

Having completed all the other preparations for the soup, the chef wishes to add just the right amount of salt. On each iteration of the while-loop, the soup is stirred and tasted. If the taste is "just right", the chef notes that the soup is no longer "toobland", a boolean condition tested in the while-statement. As a result, the while-loop is terminated before the next iteration and the soup is served. If the taste is not "just right", the chef adds a pinch of salt and the sequence of operations is repeated.

A for-loop could not be used to salt a soup to taste. The best a recipe could do using a for-loop is

```
{ add 17 pinches of salt }
for n := 1 to 17 do
  begin
  add a pinch of salt;
  stir;
  end;   { for-loop }
serve
```

The more sophisticated rule adds two pinches of salt for each quart; it compensates for different quantites of soup, but is still doesn't salt to taste.

```
for n := 1 to 2 * volumeinquarts do
  { add 2 pinches of salt per quart }
  begin
  add a pinch of salt;
  stir;
  end;  { for-loop }
serve
```

The **repeat-until** loop resembles the while-loop in power, but differs from it in several major syntactic and semantic ways. As we can see in the recipe souppreparation2 the exit test is performed at the bottom of the loop body and not at the top. Also, the repeat-until construction does not require a compound statement if the body of the loop consists of more than one statement.

```
recipe souppreparation2;  { repeat-until-loop version }
  begin
  prepare soup;
  repeat
    add a pinch of salt;
    stir;
    taste;
    until taste is just right;
  serve;
  end.
```

The major "defect" in a repeat-until-loop is that the body of the loop *must* be executed at least once before an exit test is made. Thus, if it were likely that the soup would be "just right" before even the first pinch of salt is added, the repeat-until-loop in the recipe souppreparation2 should not be used. A minor defect is that the exit condition is written at the bottom of the loop in the until-clause instead of up front at the top of the loop where it is easier to find.

Notice that the keywords "repeat" and "until" enclose a sequence of statements, the **body** of the repeat-until-loop, without making the sequence of statements into a compound statement by enclosing them with the keywords "begin" and "end". This is unusual for a Pascal construct.

Loops With Calculated Exit Conditions

Suppose we wish to write a program to find the first (smallest) power of 2 that exceeds 1000. Pascal does not have a raising-to-the-power operation, but successive powers of 2 may be calculated by starting with a small power of 2, say $2^0 = 1$, and repeatedly doubling that number. Doubling is repeated until a power of 2 is found that exceeds 1000. That power of 2 is printed and the program bigpower1 ends.

```
program bigpower1 (output);
  var
    n : integer;
  begin
  n := 1;  { initialization }
  repeat
    { double n to get the next power of 2 }
    n := n * 2;
    until n > 1000;
  writeln (n :1, ' is the first power of 2 that exceeds 1000.')
  end.
```

```
run bigpower1
```

```
1024 is the first power of 2 that exceeds 1000.
```

It is natural to think of a loop as intended to be executed many times. In this way of thinking, a loop is repeated until something happens to indicate that repetition should stop. The repeat-until-statement captures this conception of a loop pretty well. The keyword "while", on the other hand, seems to be making the opposite assumption about repetition of the loop. The loop must constantly prove (by passing a test) that it qualifies for the next repetition. Even the first iteration of the loop body must pass the test.

Since "until" and "while" have opposite meanings, the repetition test

```
until n > 1000
```

may by translated into the while-test

```
while not (n > 1000) do
```

or more simply

```
while n <= 1000 do
```

It is now easy to write a while-loop version of the program bigpower1.

```
program bigpower2 (output);
  var
    n : integer;
  begin
    n := 1;  { initialization }
    while n <= 1000 do
      { double n to get the next power of 2 }
      n := n * 2;
    writeln (n :1, ' is the first power of 2 that exceeds 1000.')
  end.
run bigpower2
```

```
1024 is the first power of 2 that exceeds 1000.
```

Loops Terminated By Special Data

Many kinds of input data ordinarily come in groups whose exact size or length cannot be predicted in advance at the time the program is written. Although the amount of data actually present can be counted by the user at the time the input file is prepared, people are not particularly good at counting more than a few items. The computer, on the other hand, is very good at repetitive tasks like counting.

The next set of programs shows how to make a computer count the number of items in the input data. In these examples, the input data consists of an English sentence. Since sentences come in varying lengths, we make the simplifying assumption that every sentence ends with one of the standard punctuation marks ".", "!", or "?". The programs will count the number of characters in the input sentence, including all blank characters between words and all punctuation marks. Also the sentence is echoed to the standard output device, which makes good sense if the program is not run interactively. If execution is interactive, the echo of input data should be replaced with a prompt requesting the user to type a sentence.

```
program countcharacters (input, output);
  var
    inputcharacter : char;
    count : integer;
  begin
  count : = 0; { initialization }
  write ('Input data: ');
  repeat
    read (inputcharacter);
    write (inputcharacter);
    count := count + 1;
    until (inputcharacter = '.') or
          (inputcharacter = '!') or
          (inputcharacter = '?');
  writeln;
  writeln ('There are ', count :1, ' characters in the sentence,');
  writeln ('including blanks and punctuation marks.');
  end.
run countcharacters

Input data: Never mind the why's and wherefore's.
There are 37 characters in the sentence,
including blanks and punctuation marks.
```

After the variable count is initialized to zero and the identifying message (or prompt) "Input data: " is printed, the computer repeats the three steps of the body of the repeat-until-loop until the period, exclamation point, or question mark at the end of the sentence is reached. The steps are to read a character, echo it to the printer or screen, and increase the count by one. The assignment statement

```
count := count + 1
```

directs the computer to take the previous value of the variable count, add one to it, and to store the result as the new value of the variable count.

The first while-loop version of the program differs little from the repeat-until-loop version.

```
program countcharacters2 (input, output);
  var
    inputcharacter : char;
    count : integer;
  begin
  count : = 0; { genuine initialization }
  write ('Input data: ');
  inputcharacter := ' '; { "fake" initialization for while-loop}
  while (inputcharacter <> '.') and
        (inputcharacter <> '!') and
        (inputcharacter <> '?') do
    begin
    read (inputcharacter);
    write (inputcharacter);
    count := count + 1;
    end;   { while-loop }
```

```
    writeln;
    writeln ('There are ', count :1, ' characters in the sentence,');
    writeln ('including blanks and punctuation marks.');
    end.
```

    run countcharacters2

    Input data: To be, or not to be?
    There are 20 characters in the sentence,
    including blanks and punctuation marks.

Most of the program countcharacters2 is the same as the program countcharacters. The while-condition that must be successfully passed before each iteration of the loop

```
    while (inputcharacter <> '.') and
          (inputcharacter <> '!') and
          (inputcharacter <> '?') do
```

is probably less clear than the until-condition in the program countcharacters. Moreover, there is an additional problem caused by the fact that the while-condition must be tested before even the first iteration of the loop. Without the "fake" initialization of the variable inputcharacter, that variable would not have been assigned a value going into the first while-test, and the attempt to use an undefined variable would stop the execution with an error or warning message on most Pascal systems. We call this initialization a "fake" initialization because it is there only to trick the while-test into allowing a first iteration in which the variable inputcharacter gets its "true" first value, namely the first character of the input sentence.

The while-loop and repeat-until-loop are essentially similar constructs. The differences between them must not be overemphasized. The repeat-until-loop is useful because it exits at the beginning. An expert programmer can benefit from knowing both constructs. A beginner is better advised to master one of them and use it consistently, even at the expense of slight awkwardness in some programs.

Self-Test Questions

1. Which of the following loops are syntactically correct? Which have problems with uninitialized variables? Which have other problems? What is the final value of the variable when the program segment ends?

a.
```
    n := 1;
    while n < 10 do
       n := n + 1;
```

b.
```
    n := 1;
    while n > 1 do;
       n := n - 1;
```

c.
```
    repeat
       n := n + 1
    until n > 10
```

d.
```
    while datavalue <> 0 do
       read (datavalue)
```

e.
```
    inchar := 'x';
    while inchar = 'x' do
       read (inchar);
       write (inchar);
```

f.
```
until inchar = '.' do
  read (inchar);
repeat
```

2. Correct the mistakes in the loops of Question 1.
3. Rewrite the following repeat-until-loop as a while-loop.
```
count := 0;
repeat
  count := count + 1;
  n := count * 13;
until n > 1000;
writeln (n :1, ' is the first multiple of 13');
writeln ('that exceeds 100');
```

4. The body of a repeat-until-loop is always executed at least once. How would you modify the following program fragment to print nothing in case the value read for the variable times is 0? Do not switch to a while-loop.
```
read (times);
count := 0;
repeat
  writeln ('Hello');
  count := count + 1;
until count = times
```

Exercises

1. Write a program to read integers and to count how many nonzero integers there are in the input before the first zero.
2. Write a program to read integers and to find the average of all the nonzero values in the input that precede the first zero.
3. Write a program to read integers and to print out the nonzero value from the input data that immediately precedes the first zero value. *Hint:* Before you read a new value that might be zero, save the old value in a second variable.
4. Write a program to calculate and print the first power of 3 that exceeds 1000.
5. A number q is the square root of a number n if the quotient $n/q = q$. Write a program to read an integer n and attempt to find the square root of n by trying $= 1, 2, 3, ...,$ until either $n/q = q$, in which case the square root q has been found, or until $n/q < q$, in which case the square root of n is not an integer, but it lies between $q - 1$ and q. Your program should distinguish between the two cases and print appropriate messages and answers.
6. Write a program that reads a sentence properly terminated by a period, exclamation point, or question mark and prints only the letters in the input data, excluding all spaces, punctuation marks, special characters, etc.
7. The population of New Jersey was 7,168,162 in 1970 and it was increasing at the rate of 18% per decade. The area of New Jersey is 7521 square miles. Write a program that estimates the population of New Jersey every 10 years by multiplying the previous decade's population by 1.18. Stop the program when the number of square feet per person in New Jersey is less than 10 feet × 10 feet. Print out all estimates.

5.3   Character Strings and Arrays

In Pascal, single-character data is handled by the intrinsic data type char. **Character strings**, on the other hand, are derived, programmer-defined data types. Although Pascal provides some features for assigning, comparing, and writing character strings as wholes, it is sometimes necessary to process the characters in a character string one by one. This section discusses the use of loops to process the characters in a character string one by one.

Section Preview

Character Strings:

A character string is an **array** or **packed array** of characters. The following example illustrates declaration, input, and output of character strings in standard Pascal.

Example:

```
program example (input, output);
   var
      name : packed array [1..20] of char;
      letter : integer;
   begin
   for letter := 1 to 20 do
      read (name [letter]);
   writeln (name);
   end.
```

Arrays:

Arrays of type other than **char** are permitted. Subscript bounds need not start at one.

Examples:

```
var
   profit : array [1970..1984] of real;
   squares : array [0..100] of integer;
```

Packed Arrays of Characters

A character string is declared to be an **array** or **packed array** of type char. As shown in the following example, a character string variable of length 7 is declared to be an array of 7 characters.

```
var
   sevenletterword : packed array [1..7] of char;
```

The only effect of the optional keyword "packed" is to indicate that as many characters as possible should be stored together in the computer's memory. However, in some Pascal systems, operations can be performed on packed arrays of characters that cannot be done with ordinary arrays of characters. Therefore, all strings in this book will be declared as packed arrays of characters. Figure 5.3 indicates the difference between a packed array and an ordinary array.

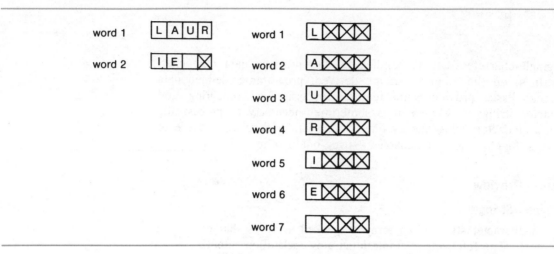

Figure 5.2 Packed and unpacked storage of the character string 'Laurie '.

Input and Output of Character Strings

The somewhat facetious program named "who" illustrates the declaration, input, and output of character strings.

```
program who (input, output);
  var
    whatsisname : packed array [1..14] of char;
    letter : integer;
  begin
  writeln ('Do I remember whatsisname?');
  write ('Of course, I remember ');
  for letter := 1 to 14 do
    read (whatsisname [letter]);
  writeln (whatsisname);
  end.
run who

Do I remember whatsisname?
Of course, I remember Roger Kaputnik
```

The variable name whatsisname refers to the whole character string or array. The individual characters that comprise the string are denoted

```
whatsisname [1]
whatsisname [2]
whatsisname [3]
    .
    .
    .
whatsisname [14]
```

An entire character string may be written by putting its name in a write or writeln command, as shown in the program who. However, the value of a character string (in standard Pascal) must be read one character at a time, usually by using a for-loop.

```
for letter := 1 to 14 do
  read (whatsisname [letter])
```

This for-loop serves as a convenient abbreviation for the 14 read statements

```
read  (whatsisname  [1]);
read  (whatsisname  [2]);
read  (whatsisname  [3]);
        .
        .
        .
read  (whatsisname  [14]);
```

each reading one character of the input string. Reading of character strings takes this form because what must appear within the parentheses of a read or readln command is a simple variable or array element, not a whole array of characters. This for-loop closely resembles the for-loop in the program ten-numbers. Each time the read statement is executed, the for-variable letter takes on its next value, producing the combined effect of the 14 read statements shown above.

If you like, you also can write a for-loop to print a character string.

```
for  letter  := 1  to  14  do
    write  (whatsisname  [letter]);
writeln
```

Many Pascal systems have extensions to read whole strings. Details vary considerably, however, so get descriptions of the local extensions from the instructor or system manuals.

Arrays of Integers or Reals

Just as a collection of individual characters can be organized into a character string using an array, so collections of other types of data, like integer data or real data, can be organized into arrays. For instance, suppose that the author of a popular textbook wants to write a program concerned with the number of copies her book sold in the years 1972 to 1983 and her royalties in those years. The declarations

```
sales  :  array  [1972..1983]  of  integer;
royalty  :  array  [1972..1983]  of  real;
```

would enable her to use the integer-valued quantities sales [1972], sales [1973], ..., sales [1983] and real-valued quantities royalty [1972], royalty [1973], ..., royalty [1983] in her program.

In the same way that a for-loop can tell the computer to read the letters of a character string one letter at a time, a for-loop can tell the computer to read the sales figures or royalties one year at a time, as follows:

```
for  year  := 1972  to  1983  do
    read  (sales  [year]);
for  year  := 1972  to  1983  do
    read  (royalty  [year]);
```

or better still

```
for  year  := 1972  to  1983  do
    read  (sales  [year],  royalty  [year]);
```

These fragmentary examples barely hint at the possible uses of for-loops in conjunction with arrays. An array allows a number of related values of the same kind to be stored in memory locations with the same array name, but with different relative locations. The relative location of an individual element in an array is indicated by its **subscript**, the integer written between square brackets.

A for-loop allows all of the data items to be processed simply. The for-variable—instead of the relative address number of an individual array element—is written in the square brackets. Thus, when such a statement is executed repeatedly under control of a for-statement, the subscript changes each time, until it runs through all the values indicated in the for-statement.

Self-Test Questions

1. Which of the following constant declarations are correct?

    ```
    const
      signal = 'stop';
      bee = 'b';
    ```

2. Which of the following variable declarations are correct?

    ```
    var
      firstname : packed array of char;
      signal : packed array [1..4] of char;
      vector : packed array [1..3 of real;
    ```

3. Which of the following assignment statements are correct?

    ```
    bee := 'b'
    word := 'certainly'
    ```

4. How many characters are read by the for statement

    ```
    for letter := 1 to 20 do
      read (alphabetic [letter]);
    ```

5. How many reals can be stored in the array profit declared below?

    ```
    var
      profit : array [10..20] of real;
    ```

Exercises

1. Write a program that reads an 8-letter word as input and tests to see if it is equal to a password given in a character string constant declaration in the program. The program should print out "okay" if the password is correct and "sorry, wrong password" if the password is wrong.
2. Write a program to read a 5-letter word and to print it out backward.
3. A word like "radar" that reads the same forward or backward is a palindrome. Write a program that reads a 5-letter word and tests whether the word is a palindrome.
4. Write a program to read a list of 12 integers and print them out.
5. Write a program to read a list of 12 integers and print them out in two columns in the following order:

    ```
              list [1]      list [7]
              list [2]      list [8]

                   .             .
                   .             .
                   .             .

              list [6]      list [12]
    ```

    Hint: Use the writeln statement

    ```
    writeln (list [n] :15, list [n + 6] :15)
    ```

6. Write a program to read a list of 12 integers and to print them in three columns in the following order.

    ```
          list [1]      list [2]      list [3]
          list [4]      list [5]      list [6]
          list [7]      list [8]      list [9]
          list [10]     list [11]     list [12]
    ```

Hint: The last subscript in each line is a multiple of 3. Start by modifying the program countbytwos in Section 5.1 to count by 3s. Then use the writeln statement

```
writeln (list [3*m-2] :15, list [3*m-1] :15, list [3*m] :15)
```

5.4 For-Loops To Calculate Averages

Calculating the total of a column of numbers is basically a repetitive task: each new number is added to the running total. In this section, a loop is used to calculate a total and to examine how the values of the varibles change during the execution of a loop.

Section Preview

Accumulating Totals:

The statement

```
sum := sum + nextscore
```

increases the value of the variable sum by the value of the variable nextscore. Used repeatedly in a loop, this kind of statement forms the key step in programs to calculate the sum (and subsequently, the average) of many quantities.

Example:

```
sum := 0;
for i := 1 to 10 do
  begin
  read (nextscore);
  sum := sum + nextscore;
  end
```

Hand Simulation:

This is a technique in which you put yourself in the role of the computer and perform by hand the steps which the computer is directed to perform by its program. It is important for understanding and debugging programs.

Arrays:

An array can hold a list of values. The sum of these values may be found using a for-loop.

Example:

```
sum := 0;
for subscript := 1 to 20 do
  sum := sum + value [subscript]
```

Calculating an Average of Many Numbers

Suppose an instructor wishes to find the average of the test scores that the 27 students in a class earned on their first examination. The instructor could write a program averageof27 using 27 constants.

However, if the instructor knows that there will be several more examinations during the semester, it might be desirable to write a program that can be used for subsequent examinations as well. The program averageof27 uses variables instead of specific numbers written in the program, so that it can find the average of any 27 numbers. Recall that Pascal statements that do not fit on one line may be continued on subsequent lines.

```
program averageof27 (input, output);

    var
      a,b,c,d,e,f,g,h,i,j,k,l,m,n,o,p,q,r,s,t,
        u,v,w,x,y,z,aa : real;

    begin
    read (a,b,c,d,e,f,g,h,i,j,k,l,m,n,o,p,q,
        r,s,t,u,v,w,x,y,z,aa);
    writeln ((a + b + c + d + e + f + g + h + i + j
        + k + l + m + n + o + p + q + r + s + t
        + u + v + w + x + y + z + aa) / 27 :1:2);
    end.
    run averageof27

    82.30
```

The fact that more than 26 variables are needed is no hardship since the name of a variable can be more than one letter long. The absence of input echoes makes it impossible to tell whether 82.30 is indeed the correct answer, because it is impossible to tell what input data was used. Despite the extra trouble, input echoes would have been added if this program were not going to be replaced immediately with a better one.

Using a Loop to Calculate an Average

Averageof27 does not exploit the basic repetitiveness of the process of adding the 27 test scores. The program avgof27version2, however, uses a Pascal for-statement of the simplest kind to reflect in the program the repetitiveness of the task. A side benefit is reducing the number of variables needed to two, namely sum and nextscore. Now it is reasonable to print the input data for the program.

```
program avgof27version2 (input, output);

    const
      numberofscores = 27;

    var
      count : integer;
      sum, nextscore : real;

    begin
    sum := 0;
    for count := 1 to numberofscores do
      begin
      read (nextscore);
      writeln ('Input data  nextscore: ', nextscore :7:2);
```

```
    sum := sum + nextscore;
    end; { for-loop }
  writeln ('Average test score = ', sum / numberofscores :1:2);
  end.
```

The first assignment statement of the program avgof27version2 gives the variable sum its initial value of zero. The next six lines, which comprise a for-statement, tell the computer to read and to add up the test scores, and the final writeln statement tells the computer to print the answer.

Execution of a For-Loop

The for-loop of the program avgof27version2 is executed as if the 81 statements

```
    read (nextscore);
    writeln ('Input data  nextscore:', nextscore :7:2);
    sum := sum + nextscore;
    read (nextscore);
    writeln ('Input data  nextscore:', nextscore :7:2);
    sum := sum + nextscore;
    read (nextscore);
    writeln ('Input data  nextscore:', nextscore :7:2);
    sum := sum + nextscore;

        .
        .
        .

    read (nextscore);
    writeln ('Input data  nextscore:', nextscore :7:2);
    sum := sum + nextscore;
```

were written instead of the 6-line for-statement. Since the read and writeln commands are executed 27 times, the execution printout is much longer than the actual program.

```
    run avgof27version2

    Input data   nextscore:     85.00
    Input data   nextscore:     97.00
    Input data   nextscore:     68.00
    Input data   nextscore:     86.00
    Input data   nextscore:     75.00
    Input data   nextscore:     90.00
    Input data   nextscore:     82.00
    Input data   nextscore:    100.00
    Input data   nextscore:     87.00
    Input data   nextscore:     63.00
    Input data   nextscore:     79.00
    Input data   nextscore:     85.00
    Input data   nextscore:     93.00
    Input data   nextscore:     62.00
    Input data   nextscore:     88.00
    Input data   nextscore:     76.00
    Input data   nextscore:     38.00
    Input data   nextscore:     70.00
    Input data   nextscore:     87.00
    Input data   nextscore:     93.00
    Input data   nextscore:     98.00
```

```
Input data   nextscore:    81.00
Input data   nextscore:    95.00
Input data   nextscore:    72.00
Input data   nextscore:    89.00
Input data   nextscore:    99.00
Input data   nextscore:    84.00
Average test score =   82.30
```

The echo of input data is extremely useful in checking that all the test scores were entered correctly.

Increasing the Value of a Variable

The meaning of the assignment statement

```
sum := sum + nextscore
```

is: "Add the values of the variables sum and nextscore and assign their sum as the new value of the variable sum". The value of the variable nextscore is not changed by this statement.

The assignment statement is *not* a mathematical equation in which the variable sum can be cancelled on both sides of the assignment operator to "solve" the assignment statement for the variable nextscore := 0. This distinction is emphasized by using := as the assignment operator instead of the equal sign by itself (=) as is done in some other programming languages. Each variable on the right of the assignment operator has its value determined before execution of the assignment statement begins, while the variable on the left is assigned a new value as a result of the statement.

Hand Simulation

To show in more detail how a for-loop works, we follow the steps, one at a time, that a computer performs during the execution of the program avgof27version2. Since the statements inside the loop are executed 27 times and the statements outside the loop are executed only once, almost all the steps of the execution correspond to instructions in the loop. Of particular interest are the changing values of the variables nextscore and sum. Following the steps in this manner is **hand simulation** because the computer's computations are simulated by hand. It is perfectly ethical to use a hand calculator to do the arithmetic when hand simulating a program.

The first statement of the program avgof27version2 assigns the variable sum its initial value of 0. The other variable nextscore does not yet have a value. The for-loop is then started. In each of the 27 repetitions of the loop, the computer reads a number and assigns that number to the variable nextscore. Then it prints an echo of the value that it read. Finally, it adds the value of nextscore to the current value of the variable sum to obtain a new value for the variable sum.

During the first pass through the repeated statements, the number 85.0 is read and assigned to the variable nextscore. The first echo of input data line

```
Input data   nextscore:    85.00
```

of the printout confirms that the first number supplied as input data is indeed 85.0. Then the value 85.0 of nextscore is added to the current value, 0.0, of the variable sum to obtain a new sum 0.0 + 85.0 = 85.0, which is assigned as the new value for sum. Thus the values of the variables nextscore and sum after the first pass through the repeated instructions are 85.0 and 85.0. Table 5.1 shows the values of these variables after each of the 27 passes.

Table 5.1 Values of the variables nextscore and sum during execution of the program avgof27version2 using data from the sample run.

NEXTSCORE	SUM	PASS THROUGH THE FOR LOOP
undefined	0.0	before the 1st pass
85.0	85.0	after the 1st pass
97.0	182.0	after the 2nd pass
68.0	250.0	after the 3rd pass
86.0	336.0	after the 4th pass
75.0	411.0	after the 5th pass
90.0	501.0	after the 6th pass
82.0	583.0	after the 7th pass
100.0	683.0	after the 8th pass
87.0	770.0	after the 9th pass
63.0	833.0	after the 10th pass
79.0	912.0	after the 11th pass
85.0	997.0	after the 12th pass
93.0	1090.0	after the 13th pass
62.0	1152.0	after the 14th pass
88.0	1240.0	after the 15th pass
76.0	1316.0	after the 16th pass
38.0	1354.0	after the 17th pass
70.0	1424.0	after the 18th pass
87.0	1511.0	after the 19th pass
93.0	1604.0	after the 20th pass
98.0	1702.0	after the 21st pass
81.0	1783.0	after the 22nd pass
95.0	1878.0	after the 23rd pass
72.0	1950.0	after the 24th pass
89.0	2039.0	after the 25th pass
99.0	2138.0	after the 26th pass
84.0	2222.0	after the 27th pass

After 27 complete passes, the loop is not repeated and the computer execution proceeds to the final writeln statement. By then all of the test scores which were the successive values for the variable nextscore already have been added to accumulate their sum 2222.0, which is the final value of the variable sum. When the final writeln statement specifies printing the expression sum / 27, the average 82.30 of all 27 test scores is printed.

Top-Down Program Design

Next, we attempt to redesign the averaging program in a top-down fashion. The result is an equivalent, but slightly different program avgof27version3.

The top-down analysis of the problem of averaging 27 test scores proceeds as follows: to calculate an average, you first have to calculate the sum of the scores. Of course, the computer can't calculate the sum of the scores until after it has read the scores, so that must come first. Finally, the computer should print the answer, not just keep it to itself. As a result of this analysis, a first version of the program avgof27version3 might look like this:

```
program avgof27version3 (input, output); { top-down design }
  begin
  read all the scores;
  calculate their sum;
  average := sum / 27;
  writeln ('Average test score = ', average :1 :2);
  end.
```

Notice that the step

```
read all the scores
```

is now a separate step from calculating the average. It is easy to program this
step using an array of test scores and a for-loop.

```
var
  score : array [1..27] of real;

for student := 1 to 27 do
  read (score [student];
```

A simple variable, nextscore, would not serve the purpose in this version of the
program because all 27 test scores must be stored in the computer *simultaneously* at the end of this step, and a simple variable can hold only one value at a
time. An array of length 27 can hold 27 different test scores in its 27 components, score [1], score [2], score [3], ..., score [27].

The for-loop to calculate the sum of the test scores differs only slightly
from avgof27version2. The most important change is that the scores already
have been read in the previous step, so the loop is simpler.

```
sum := 0;
for student := 1 to 27 do
  sum := sum + score [student]
```

Putting the details together, and adding echoes of input data in the read
step, we get the following program avgof27version3.

```
program avgof27version3 (input, output);

  var
    score : array [1..27] of real;
    student : integer;
    sum, average : real;

  begin
  { read all the scores }
  writeln ('Student' :10, 'Score' :10); { print headings }
  for student := 1 to 27 do
    begin
    read (score [student]);
    writeln (student :10, score [student] :10 :2);
    end; { for-loop to read all the scores }

  { calculate the sum of the test scores }
  sum := 0;
  for student := 1 to 27 do
    sum := sum + score [student];
  average := sum / 27;
  writeln ('Average test score = ', average :7 :2);
  end.
```

```
run avg27version3
```

```
Student        Score
        1      85.00
        2      97.00
        3      68.00
        .        .
        .        .
        .        .
       26      99.00
       27      84.00
Average test score =    82.30
```

Self-Test Questions

1. What is the meaning of the statement

    ```
    sum := sum + 1
    ```

2. What is the value of the variable sum at the conclusion of the following loops?

a.
```
sum := 0;
for n := 1 to 10 do
  sum := sum + 1
```

b.
```
sum := 0;
for n := 1 to 5 do
  sum := sum + n * n
```

c.
```
sum := 0;
for n := 1 to 4 do
  sum := sum + n * n
```

d.
```
sum := 0;
for n := 5 downto 1 do
  sum := sum + n
```

3. Hand simulate the execution of the following compound statement recording the values of n and product after the execution of each statement.

    ```
    begin
    product := 1;
    for n := 2 to 4 do
      product := product * n;
    end
    ```

4. Which of the following loops are syntactically correct? Which require initialization not shown? Give a plausible initialization statement. If a sum is accumulated, what is its final value?

a.
```
for n := 1 to 9 do sum := sum + n
```

b.
```
sum := 1;
for n := 2 to 9 do;
  sum := sum + n;
```

c.
```
sum := 0;
for count := 1 to n do
  begin
  read (score);
  sum := sum + score;
  end
```

d.
```
for coord := 1 to 3 do
  begin
  read (vector [coord]);
  end
```

Exercises

1. Write a program to find the sum of the numbers from 10 to 100.
2. Write a program to add the numbers 0, 0.1, 0.2, 0.3, ..., 10.0. *Hint:* Use 10 times the number to be added as the values of the for-variable.
3. Write a program that asks the user how many numbers will follow and then finds the average of those numbers.
4. A 3-dimensional vector v is a quantity described by means of 3 components, v_1, v_2, and v_3. The magnitude of a vector is the square root of the sum of the squares of the 3 components. Write a program to read the three components of a 3-dimensional vector as input and to calculate its magnitude.

5.5   Debugging a Loop

The projects for this section are to improve the averaging programs of Section 5.4 to allow a variable amount of data for averaging. Also shown are case studies of typical bugs that might occur in programs like these and how they are located.

> **Section Preview**
>
> **Debugging:**
>
> > Removing bugs, that is, errors, from a program. Two case studies show the use of *echoes of input data* in debugging.

A More General Program for Averaging

A slight modification of avgof27version2 produces a program avgofscores that can compute the average of any number of test scores.

```
program avgofscores (input, output);

var
  enrollment, count : integer;
  sum, nextscore : real;
```

```
begin
read (enrollment);
writeln ('Input data  enrollment: ', enrollment :1);
sum := 0;
for count := 1 to enrollment do
   begin
   read (nextscore);
   writeln ('Input data  nextscore: ', nextscore :7:2);
   sum := sum + nextscore;
   end; { for-loop }
writeln; { write a blank line }
writeln ('Average test score = ', sum / enrollment :1:2);
end.
```

The new feature in this program is that the number of times the for-loop is repeated is a variable. Of course, a value for this variable enrollment must be assigned before the for-loop can be started. The statement

```
read (enrollment)
```

obtains this value from an input device before any of the test scores are read. Thus the data for the more general program avgofscores must consist of a first number giving the number of test scores to be averaged, and then an appropriate number of test scores.

The sample run of avgofscores uses only 6 scores to be averaged, although the program would work just as well with 60 or 600. It is a great convenience to be able to test a program on a small number of data items, because the results can be checked more easily by hand.

```
run avgofscores

Input data  enrollment: 6
Input data  nextscore:   82.00
Input data  nextscore:   78.00
Input data  nextscore:   93.00
Input data  nextscore:   91.00
Input data  nextscore:   52.00
Input data  nextscore:   72.00

Average test score =  78.00
```

The program avgofscores can be used by any instructor for a class of any size. Even an instructor who does not know how to program can be told how to prepare input data for avgofscores.

Debugging

The practice of detecting and removing errors from a program is **debugging**. Carefully rereading the program, or rereading selected parts of it, is an obvious first step. Hand simulation, described in the previous section, is a highly valuable technique. Another debugging method, to be elaborated upon later, is the insertion of write commands at carefully selected places in a program, to monitor the execution. In a large program, periodic monitoring can help localize the possible source of an error to a small enough region in the program that critical rereading of that section is likely to turn up the error.

Discovering Mistakes in a Program

The usual cause of a disappointing program execution is a mistake in the program. When a programmer means to write one thing but accidentally writes another, the computer executes the program it actually sees, not the one that would have made sense. The program attemptavg contains a mistake of this kind.

```
program attemptavg (input, output);
{ This program contains a bug! }

  var
    enrollment, count : integer;
    sum, nextscore : real;

  begin
  read (enrollment);
  writeln ('Input data  enrollment: ', enrollment :1);
  sum := 0;
  for count := 1 to enrollment do
    begin
    read (nextscore);
    writeln ('Input data  nextscore: ', nextscore :7:2);
    sum := nextscore;
    end; { for }
  writeln;
  writeln ('Average test score = ', sum / enrollment :1:2);
  end.
run attemptavg

Input data  enrollment: 5
Input data  nextscore:   72.00
Input data  nextscore:   46.00
Input data  nextscore:   93.00
Input data  nextscore:   86.00
Input data  nextscore:   75.00

Average test score =  15.00
```

A programmer usually can determine whether or not there is an error in a program by carefully choosing test data and independently calculating what results to expect. The actual average of the five test scores in the illustrative test run is 74.4. The value 15 for the average test score shown in the execution printout is obviously wrong, because it is smaller than any of the supplied test scores.

In a program this short, there is not much room for an error to hide. Once one is known to exist, the programmer usually can find it by critically rereading the program. Examination of the echoes of input data in the execution output indicates that the value for enrollment was read correctly, as were each of the five test scores. This means that the loop was executed the correct number of times. Very little of the program is left to check for possible errors. In this case, the statement

```
sum := nextscore
```

should be changed to

```
sum := sum + nextscore
```

After making this change, which seems to explain the erroneous execution, the program should be rerun, first with the same test data and then with a representative range of reasonable test scores, including extreme values such as 100 and 0, if these are the limits of valid input data.

Mistakes in the Input Data

Even after exercising considerable care in writing a program, a programmer may sometimes still find the execution printout disappointing. Even a correct program cannot be expected to give correct results if there is a mistake in the input data. This is illustrated using the program avgofscores. Suppose the data for this program consists of the seven test scores 45, 98, 77, 64, 38, 86, and 53, but the first required data item, the enrollment, is inadvertently omitted, a common mistake.

```
run avgofscores

Input data   enrollment:  45
Input data   nextscore:   98.00
Input data   nextscore:   77.00
Input data   nextscore:   64.00
Input data   nextscore:   38.00
Input data   nextscore:   86.00
Input data   nextscore:   53.00
INPUT ERROR:  end of file reached
```

Because the sample execution printout contains clearly identified echoes of all input data, the cause of the erroneous program execution is not hard to find. The program avgofscores tells the computer that the first number it reads is the value for the variable enrollment. Accordingly, when the first number in the input data is 45, the computer anticipates 45 test scores in the data. When it finds only 6 more numbers, it is unable to continue with the program execution and prints an error message saying that it has run out of data, that is, that it has come to the end of the input file without having found all the numbers that it needs. The cure is simply to rerun the program with the enrollment data included.

Self-Test Questions

1. Find the bug in the following program to sum the numbers from 1 to 5. If you have a computer available, type the program in as given below and debug from the output. If no computer is available, hand simulate the execution of the program, especially the writeln statements, and debug from the simulated output.

```
program bug1 (output);
  var
    n, sum : integer;
  begin
  sum := 0;
```

```
   for n := 1 to 5 do
     begin
     sum := sum + 1;
     writeln ('n = ', n :1, '   sum = ', sum :1);
     end; { for-loop }
   writeln ('Final sum = ', sum :1);
   end.
```

Exercises

1.   Discuss the following programs from the point of view of clarity, self-
     documentation, and ease of debugging. They all were intended to have
     the same execution, except for input echoes and identification of output.
     Which one or ones of these contain bugs? Can you be certain? Which
     one is the hardest to verify that it is correct or to debug in case it is not?
     You may use a computer if you have one. What conclusions can you
     draw from this?

a.   program avgofscores (input, output);

```
     var
        enrollment, count : integer;
        sum, nextscore : real;

     begin
     read (enrollment);
     writeln ('Input data  enrollment: ', enrollment :1);
     sum := 0;
     for count := 1 to enrollment do
       begin
       read (nextscore);
       writeln ('Input data  nextscore: ', nextscore :7:2);
       sum := sum + nextscore;
       end; { for-loop }
     writeln;  { write a blank line }
     writeln ('Average test score = ', sum / enrollment :1:2);
     end.
```

b.   program t (input, output);
```
     var
        c, n : integer;
        s, x : real;
     begin
     read (n);
     s := 0;
     for c := 1 to n do
       begin
       read (x);
       s := s + x;
       end;
     writeln ('Average test score = ', s / n);
     end.
```

c.
```
program avg (input, output);
var c, n : integer; s, x : real;
begin
read (n); s := 0;
for c := 1 to n do begin
read (x); s := s + x; end;
writeln (s / n); end.
```

d.
```
program confusing (input, output);

    var
      dinner, plate : integer;
      wine, abook : real;

    begin
    read (dinner);
    writeln ('Input data  dinner: ', dinner);
    wine := 0;
    for plate := 1 to dinner do
      begin
      read (abook);
      writeln ('Input data  abook: ', abook :7:2);
      wine := wine + abook;
      end;
    writeln ('A delightful meal = ', wine / dinner :1:2);
    end.
```

5.6 What You Should Know

1. The for-statement consists of a heading and a body.
2. The body of a for-loop may be any other Pascal statement, and if it is a compound statement, it may contain any Pascal statement.
3. The heading specifies how many times the loop will be executed and what the values of the for-variable will be in each repetition.
4. The values of the for-variable can only increase or decrease by 1 between iterations.
5. Sometimes the body of a for-loop is executed no times at all.
6. While-loops test a boolean condition before each iteration of the loop body.
7. Repeat-until loops test a boolean condition after each iteration of the loop body.
8. The loop body of a repeat-until statement is a sequence of Pascal statements. This is unusual; most constructs use a compound statement.
9. Variable length input data is handled by loops that terminate either when a programmer-defined signal value is recognized or when the built-in function eoln (end of line) or eof (end of file) are true.
10. A character string is a packed array of characters.
11. In standard Pascal, the characters of a character string must be read one at a time.
12. Character strings may be written either by referencing the array name or by a loop writing one character at a time.
13. Pascal permits arrays of integers and reals.

14. An array is used when a number of different values of the same kind must be stored in the computer simultaneously.

15. The relative location of an individual element in an array is indicated by its subscript. The subscript is written in square brackets after the array name.

16. Hand simulation means putting yourself in the place of the computer and simulating the steps the computer would take in executing the program.

17. Echoes of input data are extremely useful in debugging. They tell whether the input has been prepared and read correctly.

18. You should know how to write a loop to accumulate a sum and calculate an average.

19. You should know how to read variable length input data and count how many values were read.

PROCEDURES MODULARITY AND STEP-WISE REFINEMENT 6

Every program in this book uses the built-in procedures read, write, and writeln. They are by now familiar and easy to use. In fact, you may be wondering why they are called procedures instead of just garden-variety Pascal statements. A partial answer is that beneath their apparent simplicity lies a complex sequence of steps. The built-in procedure read must scan the sequence of input characters looking for digits, signs, decimal points, e's, and blanks; it must decide if the input number is in integer form, positional real form, or exponential real form; it must evaluate the number and convert it to an appropriate internal form; and it must store the value just computed in the proper place in memory. The procedures write and writeln perform essentially the same steps, but in reverse, adding rounding and field spacing as well.

Using a built-in procedure in a Pascal program is a simple way to call for a possibly complex sequence of steps. Writers of Pascal programs never need to know about the details, some of which depend not only on Pascal but also on the specific computer being used to run the programs. The designers of the Pascal compiler and the operating system have taken care of these details.

Programmer-defined procedures work the same way: they provide a simple way to specify a possibly complex sequence of steps in a program. The only difference is that, in this case, the programmer must supply the details. The heart of this chapter is the complete top-down analysis, in Sections 6.2 to 6.4, of a large problem, from the initial statement of the problem to the final executable Pascal program of over 100 lines.

6.1 Declaring and Calling a Procedure

When a program is planned from the top down, the steps that appear in a high-level analysis of the problem often will take many Pascal statements to refine. One good way to prevent the high-level organization of the problem from becoming submerged in a sea of details is to refine these steps as procedure calls to programmer-defined procedures. The procedure call preserves the organization, and the procedure declaration supplies the details.

In this section, we discuss how to write programmer-defined procedures and where to place them in a program.

Section Preview

General forms of a procedure and its placement in a program:

```
program program name (list of files);
  const
    ...;
  var
    ...;

  procedure procedure name;
    begin
    ...;
    Pascal statements;
    ...;
    end; { of procedure declaration }

  begin { main program }
  ...;
  Pascal statements;
  ...;
  procedure name; { This line calls the procedure }
  ...;
  Pascal statements;
  ...;
  end. { of the main program }
```

Example:

```
program afewsums (input, output);
  var
    j, n, sum, time : integer;

  procedure summer;
    begin
    sum := 0;
    for j := 1 to n do
      sum := sum + j;
    end;   { of the procedure summer }

  begin  { main program }
  for time := 1 to 3 do
    begin
    read (n);
    { Call the procedure summer }
    summer;
    writeln ('The sum to ', n :1, ' is ', sum);
    end; { of the for-loop }
  end.  { of the main program }
```

Global Variables:

A global variable is known by the same name throughout the program. In the form given above, all constant and variable declarations made are outside of the procedure declaration and are, therefore, global variables.

Note: Procedures really have a much more powerful general form than the one given here, but this form using global variables to exchange information will do for the present.

One way to find class averages for several classes is to repeat several times the process of finding the class average for one class. The program avgof-several implements this strategy, refining the step of finding the class average for one class by a **procedure call**

```
avgoneclass
```

to a **programmer-defined** procedure named avgoneclass. Like a built-in procedure, a programmer-defined procedure is **called** by writing its name as a statement in the Pascal program. Programmer-defined procedures enable a programmer to write a program in larger conceptual units, making it easier to keep from getting lost in the mass of details:

```
program avgofseveral (input, output);
{ missing variable and procedure declarations }

   begin { main program to find the average test scores
           for several classes }
   read (numberofclasses);
   writeln ('Input data  numberofclasses: ', numberofclasses :1);
   for classcount := 1 to numberofclasses do
     begin
     writeln; writeln;
     avgoneclass;   { find average for one class }
     end; { for-loop }
   end. { avgofseveral }
```

Refining a step in the program by a procedure call does not relieve the programmer of responsibility for supplying the details for that step. It just moves the details from the main program to a separate **procedure declaration** that precedes the main program, as shown below.

```
program avgofseveral (input, output);

   var
      enrollment, count : integer;
      numberofclasses, classcount : integer;
      sum, nextscore : real;

   procedure avgoneclass;   { procedure declaration }
     begin
     read (enrollment);
     writeln ('Input data  enrollment: ', enrollment :1);
     sum := 0;
     for count := 1 to enrollment do
       begin
       read (nextscore);
       writeln ('Input data  nextscore: ', nextscore :7:2);
       sum := sum + nextscore;
       end; { for-loop }
     writeln;
     writeln ('Average test score = ', sum / enrollment :1:2);
     end; { avgoneclass }

   begin { main program to find the average test scores
           for several classes }
   read (numberofclasses);
   writeln ('Input data  numberofclasses: ', numberofclasses :1);
```

```
    for classcount := 1 to numberofclasses do
      begin
      writeln; writeln;
      avgoneclass;   { procedure call }
      end; { for-loop }
    end. { avgofseveral }
  run avgofseveral

  Input data  numberofclasses: 3


  Input data  enrollment: 6
  Input data  nextscore:   73.00
  Input data  nextscore:   68.00
  Input data  nextscore:   94.00
  Input data  nextscore:   88.00
  Input data  nextscore:   75.00
  Input data  nextscore:   79.00

  Average test score =  79.50


  Input data  enrollment: 2
  Input data  nextscore:   76.00
  Input data  nextscore:   83.00

  Average test score =  79.50


  Input data  enrollment: 4
  Input data  nextscore:   99.00
  Input data  nextscore:   77.00
  Input data  nextscore:   64.00
  Input data  nextscore:   73.00

  Average test score =  78.25
```

The details of the programmer-defined procedure avgoneclass appear above the main begin-end block of the program avgofseveralclasses for the following reason. Pascal regards specifying the details of a programmer-defined procedure as a definition of the meaning of the procedure name. Consistent with the Pascal policy that definitions and other declarations must precede their use in a program, the procedure declaration for the programmer-defined procedure avgoneclass is placed before the main program that calls for its execution. This placement makes good theoretical sense and simplifies the design of Pascal compilers, especially for smaller computers.

Not all programming languages subscribe to this theory. Top-down design is based on planning the main program first and looking at the details later. From this point of view it is clearer and more natural to put the highest level executive or main program first and the details later. However, Pascal programmers simply learn to seek the main program near the end of the program listing.

Self-Test Questions

1. How do you call a programmer-defined procedure?
2. Where does the declaration of a programmer-defined procedure go in a program?
3. True/false:

    a. A procedure may be called only once in a given program execution.

    b. The main program must not use the same variable names as the procedure.

    c. A programmer-defined procedure is used the same way as a built-in procedure.

    d. Programmer-defined procedures enable a programmer to think and write a program in terms of larger, more natural conceptual units.

    e. Programmer-defined procedures augment the vocabulary of Pascal.

Exercises

1. A test consists of three parts, each worth a maximum of 50 points. A student's grade on this test is the sum of the two highest point scores. Write a program avg3parts that reads the part scores for each student and finds the class average for this test. Use a programmer-defined procedure getonescore to read the three part scores and to determine the test score for one student, so that these details do not appear in the main program.
2. An input file contains a list of one month's transaction for a checking account, represented as follows. First comes an integer, giving the number of transactions for the month. Next come pairs of entries, each consisting of a one-character transaction code and the amount of the transaction. Valid transaction codes are "I" for initial balance brought forward from the previous month, "C" for check, "D" for deposit, and "S" for service charge. Handle the processing for each transaction type in a separate programmer-defined procedure, and let the main program decide which procedure to call. The program should print the final balance.
3. Modify the program in Exercise 2 so that it calculates the service charges. Service charges are $3 per month to maintain the account, 10 cents per check, and a $15 overdraft charge whenever a check brings the balance below $0.00.
4. The quadratic equation $ax^2 + bx + c = 0$ has two real roots, two complex roots, or one real root, depending on whether the quantity $b^2 - 4ac$ is positive, negative, or zero, respectively. Write a program to find and print the roots of any quadratic equation. Use a separate programmer-defined procedure for each of the three cases.

6.2   Top-Down Analysis of a Problem

The time has come to put all the pieces together for a full-scale test. It is time to try out our tools on a large, real problem. We have at our disposal all the major programming features of Pascal: input, output, arithmetic calculations, assignment, character strings and arrays, if-statements, case-statements, loops, and procedures. We have a methodology for attacking complex problems described in Chapter 3: **top-down design** with **successive refinements** We are now in a position to trace the entire course of a problem solution from the initial statement of the problem to the final executable Pascal program to solve the problem.

Section Preview

Top-Down Analysis:

A problem is attacked first at a high conceptual level that is natural to the human program planner and close to the statement of the problem.

Successive Refinement:

Each level of solution of the problem is refined by replacing relatively higher-level descriptions of steps by more detailed, lower-level descriptions of the same steps. Ultimately, an executable program is produced.

Modularity:

Readability of the final program is maintained by breaking it into modules called **programmer-defined procedures**. This method also retains a record of the top-down analysis of the problem.

The Problem: Preparation of Grade Reports

South Mountain College is a liberal arts school with 1037 students presently enrolled. Although some administrative tasks are done by the computer, until recently each student's grade report was prepared by hand and typed. Gradepoint averages were computed on hand calculators and typed into the report as well. In the fall of last year as a senior project, newly declared computer science major Rena Little prepared an analysis of the system then in effect and the extent to which it might be automated. We follow her analysis.

She observed that the registrar maintains a file of index cards prepared during registration, one for each student, with the student's roster of courses written on the card. This roster includes the name of each course and the number of credits that each course is worth. In most courses, the number of credits equals the number of hours per week that a course meets.

At the end of a semester, the instructors send copies of the grades to the registrar, and the registrar's assistants transfer the grades to these index cards. The grade reports are prepared from these index cards. For instance, Figure 6.1 shows a report for a student named Gordon Grimswell.

Name: Gordon Grimswell   Class: 1986
Semester: Fall, 1983   GPA: 3.06

Course	*Credits*	*Grade*
Applications Programming for Turing Machines 105	3	B
Survey of Inca Music 321	2	A
Phrenology 294	4	A
Conversational Aztec 308	5	C
Precambrian Art & Architecture 220	4	B

Figure 6.1 A grade report for a student at South Mountain College.

To calculate a gradepoint average (abbreviated GPA) at South Mountain College, the first step is to convert letter grades A, B, C, D, and F to the respective numerical values 4, 3, 2, 1, and 0, which are called number grades. The product of the number grade for a course and the number of credits is the student's gradepoint score in the course. For example, Gordon Grimswell has a gradepoint score of $3 \times 3 = 9$ in Applications Programming for Turing Machines 105 and a score of $2 \times 4 = 8$ in Survey of Inca Music 321. Overall, he earned a total gradepoint score of

$$3 \times 3 \; + \; 2 \times 4 \; + \; 4 \times 4 \; + \; 5 \times 2 \; + \; 4 \times 3 \; = \; 55$$

in the fall semester of 1983.

The gradepoint average is calculated by dividing the total gradepoint score by the total number of credits taken. Since Grimswell took

$$3 + 2 + 4 + 5 + 4 \; = \; 18$$

credits and earned 55 gradepoints, his GPA is

$$55 \, / \, 18 \; = \; 3.055555...$$

The gradepoint average is rounded to two decimal places and recorded on the grade report. As a first step toward automation, Rena Little suggested that the GPA calculation be done on a computer. We follow her suggestion and describe how a program to calculate gradepoint averages might be written.

How to Begin Writing a Program

We are faced with the task of constructing a program complex enough that it might not be obvious where to begin programming. Top-down programming means to begin to write a program in a form understandable to humans, almost as though you were writing for a much smarter computer than you actually have available, a mythical computer that understands and can execute many more operations and processes than can reasonably be expected of a computer. Then you go back over the program and refine it.

If some of the steps happen to be in a computer-executable language, so much the better. If not, the refinement process continues until they are. Even in parts of the program description that are not yet computer-executable, choose constructions that resemble keywords and phrases of the **target language**, Pascal. This makes the task of converting preliminary descriptions into executable statements a little easier.

The following version of the program gradeptavg might be a suitable beginning for the refinement process.

```
program gradepointaverages (input, output);  { initial version }
{ calculates gradepoint average for entire college }
   begin
   Read the input data that is common to all students;
   For every student.in the college do
     Process the grade report for that student;
   end.
```

Although this initial version of the program might appear vague or even ambiguous because of its lack of detail, it is a small but definite step in the right direction. It expresses quite clearly the obvious, but undeniable, fact that the way to do grade reports for the entire college is to do them one student at a time until they are all done.

The structure of this initial version makes some token gestures in the direction of Pascal syntax, but the statements are really designed to be read by people, and then only by people who understand the procedure of the registrar's office.

The top-down analysis has been partially successful; we now have three simpler problems to solve (see also Figure 6.2). They are:

1.   How do we read the input data common to all students?
2.   Which Pascal loop structure should be used to implement the English phrase "for every student in the college"?
3.   How do we process a grade report for one student?

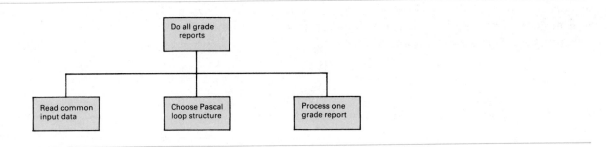

Figure 6.2 A breakdown of the gradepoint problem into three parts.

Knowing that initialization statements are best refined last, and assuming that there will be little difficulty in choosing an appropriate loop structure once the rest of the details are settled, we pass over Steps 1 and 2 and refine Step 3:

    Process one grade report

Modularity

Processing the grade report for one student has all the hallmarks of a **modular subprocess:**

1.   It is reasonably self-contained.
2.   It is described easily. (We just did it in seven words.)
3.   It is a meaningful conceptual unit to the designer and reader of the program.

    Therefore we refine this subprocess into a procedure call.

    processonegradereport

and supply the details in the programmer-defined procedure processonegradereport (process one grade report). Drawing on our analysis of how gradepoint averages and hence grade reports are prepared, we may write the following refinement of the procedure processonegradereport.

```
procedure processonegradereport;
    { for one student only }
    begin
    Read all the input data for this student;
    Convert letter grades to number grades;
    Calculate the gradepoint average (GPA);
    Print the finished grade report;
    end;  { of the procedure processonegradereport }
```

Even though more details have been supplied, we are still asking too much of a computer. It would have to be able to read and understand the preceding pages of this section. It would have to know that the input data consists of the information found on the registrar's index cards. It would have to know how to convert letter grades to number grades and how to calculate a gradepoint average. And it would have to know what information belongs in the finished grade report and how to print it.

Although it is easy to find humans who understand these instructions (for example, the clerical staff in the registrar's office), we do not expect to find a computer that will understand them without further elaboration of the details. Therefore, we continue with the process of refining the program, which means the process of making the program's meaning more explicit by spelling out some of the steps in greater detail. We may measure our progress, as shown in Figure 6.3, by the fact that we have broken up the subproblem of processing one grade report into four still smaller problems:

1. Reading all the input data for one student.
2. Converting letter grades to number grades.
3. Calculating the gradepoint average.
4. Printing the final report for the one student.

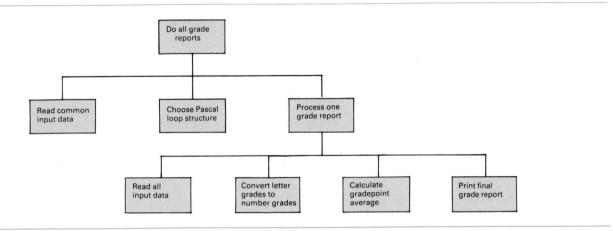

Figure 6.3 A further breakdown: one part of the gradepoint problem is decomposed into four subparts.

Refining the Output Statement

Since we do not have a super-smart computer that can execute this version of the procedure processonegradereport, we must refine the program by replacing one or more of its statements by other statements describing the same part of the program in greater detail. Each refinement of a program is a little bit further along the way toward converting the program into the target computer programming language.

Often, a good place to start refining a program is either with the input or output statement. Such a refinement will make explicit exactly what answers we want the program to print and what input data must be supplied to the computer so that it has enough information to calculate these answers. In the process, we also will make explicit the names of some of the variables that appear in the input and output sections of the program.

In this program as in most programs, the output section is easier to refine first because the form of the output is specified in the problem description. Stated simply, the registrar would like the output to look like the grade report shown earlier in Figure 6.1. With a copy of Figure 6.1 in front of us, it is not hard to write a procedure that produces output resembling it. Don't worry too much now about the exact spacing of the fields in the grade report. All we want to do is to get close to the specified appearance of the grade report, and then we will hash out the final details with the registrar later. A sample grade report, done on graph paper, was used to get the columns indicators used below.

```
procedure printgradereport;
  begin
  writeln;
  write ('Name:   ', name :35, ' ' :5);
  writeln ('Class:  ', class :1);
  write ('Semester:  ', semester :15, ' ' :21);
  writeln ('GPA:  ', gpa :1 :2);
  writeln;
  writeln (' ' :10, 'Course', 'Credit' :28, 'Grade' :15);
```

```
  for course := 1 to numberofcourses do
    writeln (title [course] :25, credit [course] :16,
        lettergrade [course] :16);
  writeln;
  end;  { procedure printgradereport }
```

First, notice that the procedure printgradereport is written entirely in Pascal. This branch of the top-down design process has produced a refinement that is an executable procedure in the target language.

Second, notice that in order to write executable Pascal code, it was necessary to choose names for the variables whose values will be printed on the final grade report. We discuss these choices now.

The student's name will be in a character string of length 35 called name. Few names are longer than 35 characters, so this should be enough room.

```
  var
    name : packed array [1..35] of char;
```

The student's graduating class will be kept in an integer type variable called class, the semester will be in a character string of length 15 called semester, and the student's gradepoint average will be the value of a real type variable called gpa. All of these variable names are **self-documenting**, that is, each variable name, in large measure, explains what its values will represent.

```
  var
    class : integer;
    semester : packed array [1..15] of char;
    gpa : real;
```

Arrays

Some of the variables had to be arrays because there was more than one piece of data of that type. For example, there is ordinarily one letter grade for each course, and a student usually takes more than one course per semester. Assuming that no student takes more than 12 courses in a semester, we make the following declaration for the variable lettergrade.

```
  var
    lettergrade : array [1..12] of char;
```

The array element lettergrade [1] will hold the letter grade for the first course the student took, the array element lettergrade [2] will hold the letter grade for the second course the student took, and so forth. If the value of the integer type variable numberofcourses is the number of courses the student took in the semester of the grade report, the array element lettergrade [numberofcourses] will hold the letter grade for the last course the student took. All array elements with higher subscripts will either have undefined values or values left over from the grade report of some previous student. In any event, they will not be used in the current grade report because the for-loop variable runs only from 1 to numberofcourses.

The variable lettergrade is not declared to be a packed array of characters because it is not a character string. It is a collection of up to 12 isolated characters.

Since the number of credits for each course is always an integer, (at least at South Mountain College), the following declaration for the array credit is suitable.

```
  var
    credit : array [1..12] of integer;
```

If South Mountain College ever introduces fractional credit for courses, we simply change "integer" to "real".

Programmer-Defined Data Types

There is also one course title for each course taken, and each course title is a character string. This suggests declaring the variable title as an array of character strings, and indeed this is permissible in Pascal. The following declarations show one clear way to do this.

```
type
   titletype = packed array [1..25] of char;
var
   title : array [1..12] of titletype;
```

One of the nicest features of Pascal is illustrated here, **programmer-defined data types**. Standard Pascal does not have character string of length 25 as an intrinsic data type; it has only the intrinsic type "char" for single characters. The **type declaration** declares a new, programmer-defined data type named "titletype" consisting of character strings (i. e., packed arrays) of length 25. Once defined in a type declaration, the new data type titletype may be used in additional type declarations, or, as shown, in variable declarations.

Two additional variables, whose values do not appear in the printed output, were necessary to write the procedure printgradereport. They are the for-variable course and its upper limit numberofcourses, both of type integer. Since neither the variable numberofcourses nor any of the printed variables is assigned a value in the procedure printgradereport, using and printing these values in the procedure imposes an obligation on the rest of the program to assign values to them before the procedure printgradereport is executed.

Converting Letter Grades to Number Grades

For those who are keeping track of our progress, we are working on the subproblem "Process one grade report", which was refined to four subproblems. The score is one down ("Print final grade report"), three to go. We even have some executable Pascal code to show for our efforts, although the planning that went into the preliminary version actually represents more progress than the executable code.

We shift to high gear and look for another subproblem to conquer. If success with the output problem suggests attempting the input subproblem, we suppress the idea because reading input is a kind of initialization, and we still do not know for sure exactly what values must be read until we have explored the details of the calculations that will be done on them.

So, we write a procedure to convert letter grades to number grades. The task is straightforward and there are no difficulties. We need another array variable numbergrade to hold the number grades. The best news is that a case-statement is perfectly suited for doing the actual conversion of individual letter grades to the equivalent number grades.

```
var
   numbergrade : array [1..12] of integer;

procedure convertlettergradestonumbergrades;
   begin
   for course := 1 to numberofcourses do
      case lettergrade [course] of
         'A' : numbergrade [course] := 4;
         'B' : numbergrade [course] := 3;
```

```
        'C' : numbergrade [course] := 2;
        'D' : numbergrade [course] := 1;
        'F' : numbergrade [course] := 0;
        end;  { case-statement }
    end;  { procedure convertlettergradestonumbergrades }
```

Experienced Pascal programmers might notice that we placed the additional variable declaration above the procedure declaration. As will be explained in Chapter 8, it is permissible to declare variables within a procedure, but this makes them local variables, known only within the procedure in which they are declared. Here, we wish every variable to be known by name throughout the entire program, so all variable declarations will appear at the top of the main program gradepointaverages.

Calculating the Gradepoint Average

Two down and two to go! We begin writing a procedure to calculate a gradepoint average. Each course contributes to the total gradepoint score a number of gradepoints equal to credit for the course times the numbergrade for the course. The gradepoint average is the quotient of the total gradepoint score and the total credits for courses taken in the semester. A first version of the procedure calculategpa follows immediately.

```
procedure calculategpa;  { gradepoint average }
    begin
    Calculate total gradepoint score;
    Calculate total credits;
    gpa := totalgradepoints / totalcredits;
    end;
```

As Figure 6.4 shows, calculategpa is refined to three subproblems, one of them already solved.

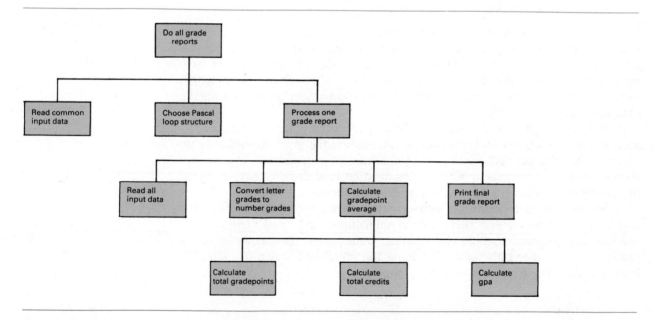

Figure 6.4 Refining the gradepoint average calculation to three subproblems.

The two subproblems are solved easily by for-loops modelled to accumulate the appropriate sums. Since the details are so short, we do not refine these subproblems into additional procedure calls. Instead, we place the initial version of the subproblem statement as a comment and place the for-loop that implements the accumulation of the sum below it.

```
var
   totalgradepoints, totalcredits : integer;

procedure calculategpa;  { final version }
   begin

   { Calculate total gradepoint score }
   totalgradepoints := 0;
   for course := 1 to numberofcourses do
      totalgradepoints := totalgradepoints +
          credit [course] * numbergrade [course];

   { Calculate total credits }
   totalcredits := 0;
   for course := 1 to numberofcourses do
      totalcredits := totalcredits + credit [course];

   { Calculate gpa }
   gpa := totalgradepoints / totalcredits;

   end;  { procedure calculategpa }
```

Three down, one to go! We refine the remaining level 3 subproblem, "read all input data for one student", in the next section. It consolidates some techniques used to handle the fact that the number of courses taken, and thus the amount of input data, will vary from one student to another.

1. Why did we refine the output procedure first?
2. What is a modular subprocess?
3. True/false:

    a. The first real progress was made when we wrote executable Pascal code for the output routine.

    b. A Pascal programmer can define new data types that are not intrinsic.

6.3   End-of-Data Signals

Refinement of the gradepoint average program continues in this section. The input procedures refined here use both programmer-defined and built-in signals to terminate reading of variable length data.

Section Preview

Eoln and **Eof:**

> The built-in functions eoln and eof detect, respectively, the end of an input line and the end of an entire input file of characters.

Programmer-Defined Termination Signals:

> A program can recognize certain input responses of the programmer's choosing as signals that no more data of the current kind will be forthcoming. Recognition of

termination signal data can be used to trigger termination
of a while- or repeat-until-loop by invalidating the test
condition controlling loop repetition.

Refining the Input Procedure

We have left the input procedure for last because it is the hardest. First of all,
until we had refined all the other subproblems, we couldn't be sure exactly
what information these procedures would need available, so we couldn't write
the input procedure to supply it. Second, the amount of input data in each
category is variable. The number of courses taken is not the same for all students. The number of students in the college varies from semester to semester. Finally, because of the way Pascal handles character strings, we have to
worry that the number of characters in a student's name varies from student to
student.

Since we now know what data is absolutely needed to calculate and print a
grade report for one student, we may write a first version of the procedure
readonestudentsdata (read one student's data). The characters string semester
is not read in this procedure because it is information common to all students.
Therefore it will be read in the main program outside the loop that runs
through all the students.

```
procedure readonestudentsdata;   { first version }
  { Read all input data for one student }
  begin
  Read the student's name;
  Read the student's graduating class;
  For every course this student took this semester do
    Read title [course];
    Read credit [course];
    Read lettergrade [course];
    end;   { of loop for courses }
  end;   { of procedure readonestudentsdata }
```

If the registrar's record-keeping operations had been computerized for
some time, it would be likely that the input information would already be available in some file that contains not only the relevant information read above,
but also lots of other information about the student and the courses. The only
way to skip information in an input file is to read it. The input procedure must
read all the available information for a student so that subsequent calls to the
procedure will be able to read information for the next student. The rest of the
program simply would ignore the extraneous information.

We have to decide whether reading input will be interactive, with input
entered during execution, or whether an input data file will be prepared for all
students in advance, and reading input will be done in a noninteractive mode.
Since the clerks in the registrar's office were used to typing the grade reports
anyway, Ms. Little suggested that execution be interactive. We agree. Fewer
mistakes will be made if someone can look at the output right away and catch
obvious errors.

Reading a Name

First, we analyze how to read a name conveniently. Since execution will be interactive, we prompt the person at the terminal that a student name is requested. Then, we face up to the problem that Pascal character strings are of fixed
length but student's names vary in length. We could ask the person at the terminal to pad each student's name with spaces at the end until it is exactly 35

exactly 35 characters long, the length we declared for the characters string name. This is a solution of absolutely last resort because it is so **user-unfriendly**.

The programs countcharacters (versions 1-3) in Section 5.2 suggest a better way. They read a sentence as input and stop when they see the punctuation mark (period, question mark, or exclamation point) at the end of the sentence. We could ask the typist to type a period after the last characters of each student's name and recognize the end of the name that way. However, Pascal has a built-in function, eoln (end-of-line), that recognizes when the carriage-return key is pressed. Using this built-in function is the standard way of treating variable-length character string input.

Notes

1. Some Pascal systems have nonstandard but very convenient built-in procedures for reading variable-length character string input. It would be foolish not to use these procedures if you have them. Simply ignore the gyrations we must go through in order to read such input in standard Pascal.
2. On some interactive Pascal systems, the authors have had problems with the eoln built-in function. If your system has such problems, adopt the period-at-the-end strategy.

End-of-Line and End-of-File Built-In Functions

The built-in function **eoln** (end of line) has boolean value true whenever the input file is positioned at the end of a line, and value false at all other times.

When a file is prepared for later use as an input file to a noninteractive execution, the carriage returns typed while preparing the file are stored in the file as end-of-line characters. If the file originates from cards or other fixed record length devices, the end of each card generates an end-of-line character in the file.

The end-of-line character sequence is not read by the eoln built-in function. When eoln is true, the very next read or readln statement will read the end-of-line character. The difference between the built-in procedures read and readln can now be explained. After the readln procedure finishes reading enough data to satisfy its input list, it continues reading until it reads an end-of-line character. Then it stops, positioned at the first character after the end of the line.

In interactive mode, the eoln function becomes true when the carriage return is pressed.

The built-in function **eof** (end of file) has boolean value true whenever the input file is positioned at its end. Otherwise, it has the value false. An attempt to read from the input file when eof is true will result in an "out-of-data" error in most Pascal systems. For interactive input, many systems have a special character that is typed to signal end-of-file. Because the user could always type more data, there is no other way for the computer to tell when the input file is at the end.

The built-in function eof provides a means of exiting from an input loop when all the data in an input file are exhausted. The program copytext illustrates how the built-in functions eoln and eof are used.

```
program copytext (input, output);

var
    onecharacter : char;
```

```
    begin
    while not eof do
      begin
      while not eoln do
        begin
        read (onecharacter);
        write (onecharacter);
        end;
      readln; { skip over end-of-line character }
      writeln;
      end;
    end.
  run copytext
```

The built-in function eoln has the value true
whenever the next character awaiting reading on
the file is an end-of-line character like
a carriage return. Otherwise, its value is false.
It may be used to terminate variable length
character strings in input data.

Buffered Input

There are three types of character strings that must be read in the gradepoint
average program: student names, course titles, and the semester (fall or
spring). All three character string types have different declared lengths, so we
will write a general-purpose procedure to read a whole input line of up to 80
characters into a holding area called a **buffer**, and then copy as many characters
as needed into one of the character strings. The procedure is called "readline".

```
  procedure readline;
    { Reads a line of up to 80 characters,
      adding blanks to fill the line }
    begin

    { Blank entire line }
    for position := 1 to 80 do
      line [position] := ' ';

    { Read input until end-of-line }
    position := 0;
    while (not eoln) and (position < 80) do
      begin
      position := position + 1;
      read (line [position]);
      end;   { of while-loop }
    readln;   { to pass over end-of-line character }
    end;
```

The procedure readname to read a name is easily written using the procedure readline. Since name is a character string of length 35, the first 35 characters of an input line are copied from line to name. Notice that once a procedure is defined, it becomes a part of the language and may be used to define
other procedures.

```
procedure readname;
  begin
  write ('Enter a student name: ');   { input prompt }
  readline;
  for position := 1 to 35 do
    name [position] := line [position];
  end;
```

The procedures readtitle and readsemester are written similarly.

```
procedure readtitle;
  begin
  write ('Enter next course title: ');   { input prompt }
  readline;
  for position := 1 to 25 do
    title [course] [position] := line [position];
  end;

procedure readsemester;
  begin
  write ('Enter semester and year: ');   { input prompt }
  readline;
  for position := 1 to 15 do
    semester [position] := line [position];
  end;
```

The only peculiarity is the array element

```
title [course] [position]
```

in the procedure readtitle. Remember that title is an array of character strings.
So each element of title, denoted by

```
title [course]
```

is itself an array of characters. The second subscript, position, refers to the location within this array of characters.

Counting the Number of Courses

The number of courses varies from one student to the next. We can't use the built-in function eof to tell when there are no more courses for a student because end-of-file means that there is no more data after it. This means that the data for the next student cannot be put after the end-of-file.

Therefore, programmer-defined end-of-data signal is used to terminate input for each student. The **termination signal** we choose is a course title of "No more courses". We now write a second version of the procedure readonestudentsdata that returns to the calling procedure as soon as it reads the signal course title "No more courses".

```
procedure readonestudentsdata;   { second version }
  { Read all input data for one student }
  begin
  readname;
  write ('Enter student's graduating class: ');
  read (class);
  morecourses := true;
  course := 0;
```

```
while morecourses do
  begin
  course := course + 1;
  readtitle;
  if title [course] = 'No more courses            ' then
    morecourses := false
  else
    begin
    read (credit [course]);
    write ('Enter letter grade for this course: ');
    read (lettergrade [course]);
    end;   { of else-clause and if-statement }
  end;   { of while-loop for courses }
{ don't count the signal as a course }
numberofcourses := course - 1;
{   This doesn't work if there are 12 courses;
It tries to put the signal into position 13, which doesn't exist. }
end;   { of procedure readonestudentsdata }
```

A Minor Bug

In an effort to write the while-loop that runs through all the courses as simply as possible, a bug has been introduced, one that would show up in rare but still in permitted circumstances. If the input data has 12 course titles *and* a termination signal, the computer would be asked to put the signal in the nonexistent array element title [13]. One obvious fix is to increase all relevant array upper bounds to 13 while keeping the upper limit for courses to 12.

We fix the bug in another way. We read course titles first into a buffer, titlebuffer, and transfer a title to the array only if it is not the termination signal.

```
var
  titlebuffer : titletype;
```

```
procedure readtitle;
  begin
  write ('Enter next course title: ');   { input prompt }
  readline;
  for position := 1 to 35 do
    titlebuffer [position] := line [position];
  end;
procedure readonestudentsdata;   { third version }
  { Read all input data for one student }
  begin
  readname;
  write ('Enter student's graduating class: ');
  read (class);
  morecourses := true;
  course := 0;
  while morecourses do
    begin
    course := course + 1;
    readtitle;
```

```
if titlebuffer = 'No more courses          ' then
  morecourses := false
else
  begin
  title [course] := titlebuffer;
  read (credit [course]);
  write ('Enter letter grade for this course: ');
  read (lettergrade [course]);
  end;  { of else-clause and if-statement }
end;  { of while-loop for courses }
{ don't count the signal as a course }
numberofcourses := course — 1;
end;  { of procedure readonestudentsdata }
```

Progress Report

Four down and none to go! Or at least, so it seems. In our elation at writing executable Pascal for all four subproblems of processing one grade report, we may have momentarily lost sight of the fact that this completely solves only one part of the main problem "Do all grade reports". There are still two of those to go, one easy and one slightly harder.

Stopping the Program Execution

Since we are ready to solve the remaining level 2 subproblems, we reproduce the initial version of the main program gradepointaverages for reference.

```
program gradepointaverages (input, output)  { initial version }
  { Prints grade reports for the entire college }
  begin
  Read input data common to all students;
  For every student in the college do
    Process the grade report for that student;
  end.
```

The input data common to all students turned out to consist only of the semester, so this step is refined by the single procedure call

```
readsemester
```

The procedure processonegradereport, with all its subordinate procedures, was the result of completely refining the subproblem of processing the grade report for one student. All that is left to do is to refine the loop structure that repeats the procedure processonegradereport for every student in the college.

One solution is to use the end-of-file character if it is available on your system. Another solution is to ask the user after each student's grade report is processed if there are any more students. If the answer is "no", or more simply "n", then execution is terminated. Otherwise, the step of processing the next students grade report is repeated. A graceful termination permits the printing of summary statistics, or at least a polite "goodbye" to the user.

```
program gradepointaverages (input, output); { Final version }
  { Prints grade reports for the entire college }
  begin
  readsemester;
```

```
repeat
  processonegradereport;
  write ('Are there any more students? (y/n) ');
  read (answer)
  until answer = 'n';
writeln;
writeln ('Goodbye.  Have a nice day.');
end.
```

The planning process is now complete. We leave the tasks of assembling the pieces and testing the program to the next section.

Self-Test Questions

1. What is the advantage of using the built-in function eoln to terminate variable-length character string input as compared to using a period, space, or a special character, such as "|"?
2. What is a buffer?
3. What do you think the user of the program should be instructed to do in case a mistake is made in typing the input data?

6.4 Refinement Using Procedures

In this section, we put together all the pieces of the solution of the gradepoint averaging program for the registrar's office at South Mountain College. These pieces have emerged from the top-down analysis of the problem in Sections 6.2 and 6.3. Then we test the program.

> **Section Preview**
>
> **Final Synthesis:**
>> The complete, executable Pascal program for the grade-point average problem is shown and tested.
>
> **Procedure Declarations:**
>> A procedure declaration must precede any call to the procedure.
>
> **Documentation:**
>> A program should be supplied with internal and external documentation and a manual for its use by nonprogrammers.

Procedure Declarations

It is a general rule in Pascal that declarations of any kind must precede the first use in the program of the thing being defined. This rule applies to procedure declarations as well as to constant, type, and variable declarations. As a result, (and contrary to the objective of having the top-down design of the program highly visible to a reader of a program), the highest level component of the problem solution, the main program, always comes last.

Following this reasoning down the line, all level 2 procedures must precede the main program and all level 3 procedures must precede the level 2 procedures that call them. Thus the procedures with the most specific details come first. Assuming all variables will be global, variable declarations must precede the procedure declarations, type declarations must precede the variable declarations (some of which use the programmer-declared types), and constant declarations must precede the type declarations (which are permitted to use programmer-declared constants).

The Complete Pascal Program Gradepointaverages

To get the complete, executable, final version of the program, we have to do the straightforward but time-consuming job of collecting all the final executable versions of the procedures written in Sections 6.2 and 6.3 as terminal stages in the top-down refinement process. They must be arranged in reverse order of the generality and declarations must be written for all the variable, types, and constants used in the program.

We can now see what we have accomplished. We have written a Pascal program of over a hundred lines to solve a complex problem.

```
program gradepointaverages (input, output); { Final version }
  { Prints grade reports for the entire college }

  type
    titletype = packed array [1..25] of char;

  var
    position : integer;
    line : packed array [1..80] of char;
    semester : packed array [1..15] of char;
    name : packed array [1..35] of char;
    class : integer;
    morecourses : boolean;
    course, numberofcourses : integer;
    titlebuffer : titletype;
    title : array [1..12] of titletype;
    credit : array [1..12] of integer;
    lettergrade : array [1..12] of char;
    numbergrade : array [1..12] of integer;
    totalgradepoints, totalcredits : integer;
    gpa : real;
    answer : char;

  procedure readline;
    { Reads a line of up to 80 characters,
      adding blanks to fill the line }
    begin

    { Blank entire line }
    for position := 1 to 80 do
      line [position] := ' ';

    { Read input until end-of-line }
    position := 0;
```

```
while (not eoln) and (position < 80) do
  begin
  position := position + 1;
  read (line [position]);
  end;  { of while-loop }

readln;  { to pass over end-of-line character }
end;  { of procedure readline }

procedure readsemester;
  begin
  write ('Enter semester and year:   ');  { input prompt }
  readline;

  for position := 1 to 15 do
    semester [position] := line [position];
  end;

procedure readname;
  begin
  write ('Enter a student name:   ');  { input prompt }
  readline;

  for position := 1 to 35 do
    name [position] := line [position];
  end;

procedure readtitle;
  begin
  write ('Enter next course title:   ');  { input prompt }
  readline;

  for position := 1 to 25 do
    titlebuffer [position] := line [position];
  end;

procedure readonestudentsdata;  { second version }
  { Read all input data for one student }
  begin
  writeln;
  readname;

  write ('Enter student''s graduating class:   ');
  readln (class);

  morecourses := true;
  course := 0;
  while (morecourses) and (course < 12) do
    begin
    course := course + 1;
    readtitle;

    if titlebuffer = 'No more courses             ' then
      morecourses := false
```

```
          else
            begin
            title [course] := titlebuffer;
            write ('Enter credit for this course:   ');
            readln (credit [course]);
            write ('Enter letter grade for this course:   ');
            readln (lettergrade [course]);
            end;   { of else-clause and if-statement }
          end;   { of while-loop for courses }

      { don't count the signal as a course }
      numberofcourses := course - 1;
      end;   { of procedure readonestudentsdata }

procedure convertlettergradestonumbergrades;
    begin
    for course := 1 to numberofcourses do
      case lettergrade [course] of
          'A' : numbergrade [course] := 4;
          'B' : numbergrade [course] := 3;
          'C' : numbergrade [course] := 2;
          'D' : numbergrade [course] := 1;
          'F' : numbergrade [course] := 0;
        end;   { case-statement }
      end;   { procedure convertlettergradestonumbergrades }

procedure calculategpa;   { final version }
    begin

    { Calculate total gradepoint score }
    totalgradepoints := 0;
    for course := 1 to numberofcourses do
      totalgradepoints := totalgradepoints +
          credit [course] * numbergrade [course];

    { Calculate total credits }
    totalcredits := 0;
    for course := 1 to numberofcourses do
      totalcredits := totalcredits + credit [course];

    { Calculate gpa }
    gpa := totalgradepoints / totalcredits;
    end;   { procedure calculategpa }

procedure printgradereport;
    begin
    writeln;
    write ('Name:   ', name :35, ' ' :5);
    writeln ('Class:   ', class :1);
    write ('Semester:   ', semester :15, ' ' :21);
    writeln ('GPA:   ', gpa :1 :2);
    writeln;
    writeln (' ' :10, 'Course', 'Credit' :28, 'Grade' :15);
```

```
    for course := 1 to numberofcourses do
      writeln (title [course] :25, credit [course] :16,
          lettergrade [course] :16);
    writeln;
    end;  { procedure printgradereport }

  procedure processonegradereport;  { final version }
    { for one student only }
    begin
    readonestudentsdata;
    convertlettergradestonumbergrades;
    calculategpa;  { gradepoint average }
    printgradereport;
    end;  { procedure processonegradereport }

  { Main program gradepointaverages, final version }
  begin
  readsemester;

  repeat
    processonegradereport;
    write ('Are there any more students? (y/n)  ');
    readln (answer);
    until answer = 'n';

  writeln;
  writeln ('Goodbye.  Have a nice day.');
  end.
run gradepointaverages

Enter semester and year:  Fall 1984

Enter a student name:  Gordon Grimswell
Enter student's graduating class:  1988
Enter next course title:  Prog. Turing Machines 105
Enter credit for this course:  3
Enter letter grade for this course:  B
Enter next course title:  Survey of Inca Music 321
Enter credit for this course:  2
Enter letter grade for this course:  A
Enter next course title:  Phrenology 294
Enter credit for this course:  4
Enter letter grade for this course:  A
Enter next course title:  Conversational Aztec 308
Enter credit for this course:  5
Enter letter grade for this course:  C
Enter next course title:  Precambrian Art Arch. 220
Enter credit for this course:  4
Enter letter grade for this course:  B
Enter next course title:  No more courses
```

```
Name:   Gordon Grimswell                          Class:   1988
Semester:  Fall 1984                              GPA:    3.06

            Course                    Credit            Grade
Prog. Turing Machines 105               3                 B
Survey of Inca Music 321                2                 A
Phrenology 294                          4                 A
Conversational Aztec 308                5                 C
Precambrian Art Arch. 220               4                 B

Are there any more students? (y/n)   y

Enter a student name:  Jeanne Adams
Enter student's graduating class:  1987
Enter next course title:  Physics 300
Enter credit for this course:  4
Enter letter grade for this course:  A
Enter next course title:  Calculus 320
Enter credit for this course:  3
Enter letter grade for this course:  B
Enter next course title:  Chemistry 210
Enter credit for this course:  5
Enter letter grade for this course:  A
Enter next course title:  No more courses

Name:   Jeanne Adams                              Class:   1987
Semester:  Fall 1984                              GPA:    3.75

            Course                    Credit            Grade
Physics 300                             4                 A
Calculus 320                            3                 B
Chemistry 210                           5                 A

Are there any more students? (y/n)   y

Enter a student name:  Tom Taylor
Enter student's graduating class:  1987
Enter next course title:  Arts and Leisure 101
Enter credit for this course:  5
Enter letter grade for this course:  C
Enter next course title:  Computer Science 105
Enter credit for this course:  3
Enter letter grade for this course:  F
Enter next course title:  No more courses

Name:   Tom Taylor                                Class:   1987
Semester:  Fall 1984                              GPA:    1.25

            Course                    Credit            Grade
Arts and Leisure 101                    5                 C
Computer Science 105                    3                 F

Are there any more students? (y/n)   n

Goodbye.  Have a nice day.
```

Documentation

This first test of the program looks correct. Other tests would then be conducted to satisfy the registrar that the program is reliable and correct. Perhaps, for a full semester's grade reports, this program would be used in parallel with the old, hand method of preparing grade reports and the results compared.

However, before the program is released for use by the clerks in the registrar's office, the program must be **documented**. Three types of documentation are usually required:

1. **Internal documentation:** this is documentation in the program listing for the benefit of programmers who will read the program later to modify it, to verify its correctness, or to fix a bug that shows up after the program has been released.

    Internal documentation includes the use of self-explanatory variable and procedure names, which this program has in abundance, and comments to explain its few potentially puzzling steps. The better the variable and procedure names, the fewer commments a program needs. Straightforward, top-down design minimizes the number of puzzling steps.

    Most beginners and experts alike need to be encouraged to include more comments, and to include them when the program is first written to aid in the debugging, not just after the fact to satisfy documentation standards. It is possible to overdo comments by explaining what is already clear in the porgram. Use your good judgment to decide what is necessary and useful.

2. **External documentaion:** a programmer should write down for the record what algorithms and methods were used in the solution. The statement of the problem and the method of calculating gradepoint averages at South Mountain College, as given in Section 6.2, should be included. Figures 6.2 to 6.4 showing the organization of the main modules would be helpful.

    Sometimes a condensed version of this information also is included in comments in the program listing.

    Important strategic decisions, like the choice to make the program execution interactive, should be chronicled, and the reasons for the ultimate decision documented. Options considered but not implemented in code should be described to make it easier to implement them later. For example, the programmer might discuss in the documentation how the program might be modified so that even though input remains interactive, the finished grade reports are written to a file for later printing.

3. A **manual** for use of the program: this manual should describe, *in terms understandable to nonprogrammers*, how to start the program, how to enter data at the appropriate times during the execution, and how to terminate the execution. It should describe all error halts (there are none in this program), what to do if data is entered incorrectly, limitations on permissible data (like the maximum number of courses, or the maximum length of a student name or course title), and a description of any quirks in the use of the program.

    A transcript of a typical program execution, like the one shown in the section, is an important adjunct to the verbal description of the program use and should be included in the documentation. The execution transcript, perhaps annotated with comments at pivotal points in the execution, is ofter clearer and easier for the user to follow than verbal instructions, but including both in the documentation is still better.

Self-Test Questions

1.   In what order do the procedure declarations for subtasks appear in the final program listing?
2.   What are the three major kinds of documentation that should accompany a program? Give examples of what is included under each heading.
3.   How many times should you test a program?

Exercises

1.   Modify the program gradepointaverages so that it tests each letter grade in the input to see whether it is one of the allowable grades A, B, C, D, or F for which numeric equivalents are given. If one or more letter grades in the input file are in error, print an error message instead of a gradepoint average. *Hint:* Introduce a variable named errorcount.
2.   Some schools use a grading scheme different from that of South Mountain College. For example, there may be grades of A+ and A−, B+ and B−, etc, in addition to the grades A, B, C, D, and F. Modify the program gradepointaverages so that it computes gradepoint averages according to the system used at your school, if it differs from that of South Mountain College.
3.   Modify the program gradepointaverages to handle grades of W (withdrawn), P (passing), and I (incomplete). Although their effects on the total number of credits accumulated toward a degree differ, all three grades W, P, and I have the same effect on the current semester's gradepoint average, that is, the courses for which they are given are to be excluded from the gradepoint average calculation. *Hint:* Use an array excludefromgpa [1..maxcourses] of type character or boolean to keep track of which courses are excluded.
4.   Modify the program gradepointaverages so that it runs in batch mode with input data in a prepared file. Document the format of the prepared input file.
5.   What happens in the program gradepointaverages in this section if a student takes no courses this semester? Will the program crash (a) always, or (b) only if the user handles this case the wrong way? What should the user be told to do to handle this case?
6.   Modify the program gradepointaverages in this section so that no problems develop if the user enters "No more courses" before any course titles are entered.

Major project: A library allows books to be borrowed for a period of 2 weeks and charges a fine of 5 cents a day for the first week a book is overdue, 10 cents a day for the second week, and 25 cents a day thereafter. The following program is for computing the amount of the fine, if any, on a borrowed book:

```
program libraryfine (input, output);   { preliminary version }
   begin
   Read withdrawal and return dates;
   Calculate number of days overdue;
   Determine fine, if any;
   Print fine or message saying that none is due;
   end.
```

Refine the program libraryfine to an executable Pascal program. Some hints are given below concerning calendar computations, and important steps in the complete problem solution are described separately below as Exercises 7 to 14.

7.   Refine the program libraryfine to an executable Pascal program, using procedures and procedure calls for program steps that involve too much

detail. An answer to this exercise is acceptable if the main program is entirely in Pascal, but some of the procedures still require further refinement.

8. The amount of the fine on an overdue book depends only on the number of days the book is overdue. One way to calculate the number of days the book is overdue is based on numbering the days of a year from 1 for January 1 to 365 (or 366 in leap years) for December 31. For days in the same year, simple subtraction suffices to determine the number of days for which a book is borrowed. For borrowing periods that start in one year and end in another year, the formula is only slightly more complex.

   Refine the procedure or program steps that determine this fine on an overdue book to an executable program. For this exercise, it is not necessary to refine the step that converts a month and day of the month to a day-of-the-year number from 1 to 365 (or 366), if it is done in a procedure. This is saved for Exercise 9.

9. January 1 is the first day of the year, and December 31 is the 365th day of an ordinary year or the 366th day of a leap year. It is easy to convert a month and day of the month to a day of the year for ordinary years using the information contained in Table 6.1.

Table 6.1 Converting a month and day of the month to a day of the year for ordinary (nonleap) years.

	MONTH	DAY OF THE YEAR
1	January	0 + day of the month
2	February	31 + day of the month
3	March	59 + day of the month
4	April	90 + day of the month
5	May	120 + day of the month
6	June	151 + day of the month
7	July	181 + day of the month
8	August	212 + day of the month
9	September	243 + day of the month
10	October	273 + day of the month
11	November	304 + day of the month
12	December	334 + day of the month

For example, October 26 is the 273 + 26 = 299th day of an ordinary year. Write a program to convert a given month and day of the month to a day of the year and refine it to an executable procedure. For this exercise, you may make the simplifying assumption that all years are ordinary years; that is, ignore leap years.

10. For the years from 1901 to 2099, any year that is exactly divisible by 4 (with remainder 0) is a leap year and has a twenty-ninth day in February. Improve the procedure written in Exercise 9 to work correctly for leap years also. To refine this program to an executable Pascal procedure, use the integer operator mod. The value of the operator mod is the integer remainder when two integers are divided. Thus a year from 1901 to 2099 is a leap year if and only if

   year mod 4 = 0

11.   Include a leap year correction in the procedure for Exercise 8.

12.   Refine the procedure or program steps written for Exercise 7 that read the withdrawal date and the return date. You must make sure that all the information required to calculate the number of days overdue is obtained or calculated. Otherwise the program libraryfine will not work when all the procedures are included in the program. This is why the refinement of this step is saved for last. The answer to this exercise depends on whether the procedure written for Exercise 9 to calculate the day of the year uses the full names January, February, and so on, or abbreviations such as Jan, Feb, and so on, for the months, or requires the month to be specified as a number from 1 to 12.

13.   What effect would it have on the program libraryfine if the withdrawal and return dates were entered as numbers from 1 to 365 (or 366)? Are there any problems with this from the standpoint of a user of the program libraryfine?

14.   What is the effect on the program libraryfine of entering the withdrawal and return dates as days of the century, from 1 to 36525? Is this desirable?

Program testing hints: Self-contained modules often may be tested independently, apart from the larger program that uses them. Exercises 15 to 17 contain suggestions for independent testing of modules written to help solve the library fine problem.

15.   The procedure described in Exercise 9 for ordinary years, and in Exercise 10 for leap years, for converting a month and day of the month into a day of the year from 1 to 365 (or 366) is a useful calculation in other applications besides library fines. Write a driving program whose sole purpose is to call and test thoroughly the procedure written in Exercise 9 or 10. What date should be used in conjunction with this testing program to establish with reasonable certainty that the procedure is written correctly?

16.   The procedure described in Exercise 8 to calculate the number of days elapsed between two given calendar dates is also useful in other applications, like interest calculations on deposits and loans. Write a driving program to test thoroughly the procedure written for Exercise 8. What data should be used to be reasonably sure the procedure will always do what it is supposed to do?

17.   Write a program to test the procedure that calculates the fines on overdue books. Design data to test it.

6.5   What You Should Know

1.   Procedure declarations follow the variable declarations in a program.
2.   A procedure is called by writing its name as a statement in a program.
3.   A procedure declaration must precede any call to that procedure.
4.   Since the main program calls all of the other procedures directly or indirectly, the body of the main program always comes last in the program listing.
5.   A global variable is a variable known by the same name throughout the program.
6.   Global variables are declared in the variables section at the head of the main program.
7.   The high-level analysis of a problem is preserved in the final program by making subprocesses procedures.

8. Programmer-defined procedures enable a programmer to write a program in larger conceptual units.

9. Top-down programming means to first write a program in a form understandable to humans, almost as though you had a much smarter computer than you actually have available. Then you go back over the program, describing in more detail those processes that the available computer cannot understand.

10. Even in parts of the program description that are not yet computer-executable, choose constructions that resemble keywords and phrases for the target language, Pascal.

11. The hallmarks of a modular process are:

    a. It is reasonably self-contained.
    b. It is described easily.
    c. It is a meaningful conceptual unit to the designer and reader of the program.

12. A self-documenting variable name explains, in large measure, what its values will represent.

13. Arrays are used to store a list of similar values. The value of the subscript indicates which item in the list is being referenced.

14. Pascal allows the programmer to define new data types and use them in place of intrinsic types.

15. The built-in function eoln (end-of-line) is true whenever the input file is positioned at the end of a line.

16. The built-in function eof (end-of-file) is true whenever the input file is positioned at the end of the input data.

17. A programmer also can define a termination signal, which the program tests for, to end reading of data.

18. Internal documentation appears in the program listing for the benefit of programmers who will read the program later to modify it, to verify its correctness, or to fix a bug.

19. External documentation includes a record of the analysis of the problem, the strategic choices made, the algorithms chosen, and charts showing the organization of the main modules.

20. A manual for using the program should be written in terms a nonprogrammer can understand.

MORE ABOUT LOOP STRUCTURES 7

Loops are so important in computer programming that no single chapter can cover them completely. There will be no additional loop constructs introduced in this chapter; the for-, while-, and repeat-until-loop structures introduced in Chapter 5 are sufficient for any problem. This chapter covers new ways to use these three loop structures.

Sections 7.1 and 7.2 deal with while-loops whose exit is controlled by two or more independent conditions. Section 7.3 compares the three loop constructs in Pascal and discusses the circumstances under which each loop construct is preferable. Section 7.4 treats while-loops that might have been for-loops if the the Pascal for-statement allowed step sizes other than one or minus one.

Sections 7.5 and 7.6 deal with special debugging problems that arise in programs with loops. Finally, Section 7.7 treats programmer-defined **enumerated data types** and their use in loops.

7.1 Multiple Exit Conditions

Industrial processes have the potential to cause major environmental changes. Simulations are a safe and rapid way to study the effects of these changes, which may take decades to appear and may be irreversible. Such simulations can predict the effects of current policies and alternative courses of action, so that intelligent choices can be made among them.

The while-loops used in the simulation of this section have two termination criteria: a maximum time limit for the simulation model and a simulation parameter exceeding some target conditions.

Section Preview

Independent Exit Criteria:

The while-loop

while *condition1* and *condition2* do
statement

---

is terminated when either *condition1* or *condition2* becomes false.

Deterministic Simulation:

A mathematical model is built incorporating the major measurable quantities of a real situation and equations or algorithms describing how these quantities change. The computer calculates predictions of future values of these quantities based on the mathematical model and supplied starting values.

Compound Conditions

Sometimes there is more than one criterion for terminating a loop. In the programs in this section, there are two criteria: (1) the value of a variable achieving a desired objective, and (2) a "time-out" condition to prevent the program from running forever without achieving the objective. The situation is handled by making the condition in a while-statement

    while *condition* do
        statement

a compound condition formed using the boolean operators "and" or "or". Combining two conditions with the operator *and* in a while-statement

    while *condition1* and *condition2* do
        statement

means that both conditions must be satisfied in order for the loop to continue to the next iteration. Failure of either condition terminates the loop.

The same effect may be achieved in a repeat-until-loop by using the boolean operator *or*.

    repeat
        statement;
        ... ;
        statement
    until (not *condition1*) or (not *condition2*)

Mathematical Modeling and Simulation

In order to understand a phenomenon and to perform experiments that are either too time-consuming, too expensive, or too dangerous to be done using the real situation and materials, a scientist constructs a **model** of the situation and performs the experiments on the model. Sometimes the model is a physical model exhibiting the same phenomena on a much smaller and more tractable scale. More often these days, with computers available to do the huge amounts of computation involved, the model is a mathematical one.

All model building, of necessity, involves a compromise between a desire to retain as many characteristics of the original as possible and a desire to simplify the model so it can be solved or examined more conveniently. In mathematical model building, the values of the important physically meaningful quantities are included in the model along with mathematical rules describing how these values change. These rules model the physical laws that determine the behavior of the original physical system.

In a **deterministic simulation** of a situation, the mathematical rules describing how the values of the important quantities change are used to predict future values of these quantities. The word "deterministic" means that there is no element of chance in the rules for predicting future values.

Garbage In, Garbage Out

Neatly printed computer output has the ring of authority and truth. Especially in the area of simulation, the user needs to be reminded of the standard computer science warning: "Garbage in, garbage out!" If the mathematical model does not capture the important features of the original or if the starting data is in error, the predictions generated by the simulation program are worthless, even though they may be printed to seven decimal places. However, if the model is correct in essential detail and the data used are accurate, the results of the simulation are likely to be accurate predictions of what will happen in the real situation.

A Water Quality Problem

The residents of Mudville, located on the shore of Lake Sludge, notice that the quality of the water in their beautiful lake has deteriorated in recent years, and they make a special study of the situation illustrated in Figure 7.1.

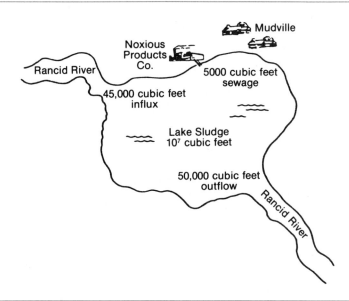

Figure 7.1   The environs of Mudville.

First, they observe that the volume of Lake Sludge is 10 million cubic feet, and that the lake is 0.5 percent polluted. That is, the quantity of polluting materials is

$0.005 \times 10,000,000 = 50,000$ cubic feet

Second, the influx from the Rancid River, which is 0.2 percent polluted, is 45,000 cubic feet per day. Third, the town of Mudville puts 5000 cubic feet of sewage into the lake daily. 10 percent of this sewage is concentrated polluting materials.

A Simulation of the Water Flow

A deterministic simulation which can calculate when the pollution level in the lake reaches 1 percent needs to record only one item of information, the amount of pollutants in Lake Sludge. The variable lakegunk will hold this value in the program pollute. The initial value of lakegunk is the current quantity of pollutants in the lake, which is $0.005 \times 1,000,000$ cubic feet. Each day, counted by the variable day, the value of lakegunk is increased by the quantity of pollutants coming from sewage and the influx of the Rancid River. The value of lakegunk is then decreased by the amount of pollutants that flow out of the lake. This calculation is repeated until the proportion of pollutants in the lake, lakegunk / lakevolume, is more than 1 percent.

In the program pollute, some simplifying assumptions have been made.

1.   There is no loss of water by evaporation, so the amount of liquid flowing out of Lake Sludge is equal to the amount flowing in.
2.   The pollutants in the lake are completely mixed, so that the proportion of pollutants leaving Lake Sludge via the river is the same as the proportion for the whole lake.

The first simplification can be removed easily and is left for an exercise at the end of this section. The second would result in a very much more complex model. The program pollute calulates how long Mudville has before the pollution level reaches 1%.

```
program pollute (output);

const
   lakevolume = 1.0e7;        { cubic feet }
   riverinflux = 45000.0;     { cubic feet / day }
   sewageinflux = 5000.0;     { cubic feet / day }
   riverpollution = 0.002;
   sewagepollution = 0.10;
   initialpollution = 0.005;
   maxpollution = 0.01;
   maxdays = 10000;

var
   lakegunk, rivergunk, sewagegunk : real;
   riveroutflow : real;
   day : 0..maxdays;
   toopolluted : boolean;

begin
rivergunk := riverpollution * riverinflux;
sewagegunk := sewagepollution * sewageinflux;
riveroutflow := sewageinflux + riverinflux;
lakegunk := initialpollution * lakevolume;
toopolluted := false;
day := 0;
while (day < maxdays) and (not toopolluted) do
   begin
   day := day + 1;
   lakegunk := lakegunk + rivergunk + sewagegunk;
   lakegunk := lakegunk - (lakegunk / lakevolume) * riveroutflow;
   if lakegunk / lakevolume > maxpollution then
      toopolluted := true;
   end; { while-loop }
```

```
    if`toopolluted then
      writeln ('Mudville is doomed in ', day :1, ' days.')
    else
      writeln ('There is no danger to Mudville for at least ',
          maxdays :1, ' days.');
    end.
  run pollute

  Mudville is doomed in 271 days.
```

Testing Corrective Actions

If the Noxious Products plant were closed and sewage treatment facilities built, the town could reduce the pollutant level of the sewage going into the lake to 0.1 percent. If the septic tanks along the Rancid River were replaced by a sewer system, the pollutant level of the river would drop to 0.03 percent. If these actions could be implemented immediately, how long would it be before the pollution level of the lake dropped to 0.1 percent?

The program cleanup is similar to the program pollute. The pollutant levels of the water sources have been changed, and the simulation is stopped when lakegunk $< 0.001 \times$ lakevolume. Simply by changing the numbers in the program cleanup, it is possible to predict the effect on the lake of any other changes in the pollutant levels of the river or of the town's sewage.

```
  program cleanup (output);

    const
      lakevolume = 1.0e7;
      riverinflux = 45000.0;
      sewageinflux = 5000.0;
      riverpollution = 0.0003;
      sewagepollution = 0.001;
      initialpollution = 0.005;
      minpollution = 0.001;
      maxdays = 1000;

    var
      lakegunk, rivergunk, sewagegunk : real;
      riveroutflow : real;
      day : 0..maxdays;
      cleanedup : boolean;

    begin
    rivergunk := riverpollution * riverinflux;
    sewagegunk := sewagepollution * sewageinflux;
    riveroutflow := sewageinflux + riverinflux;
    lakegunk := initialpollution * lakevolume;
    cleanedup := false;
    day := 0;
```

```
while (day < maxdays) and (not cleanedup) do
  begin
  day := day + 1;
  lakegunk := lakegunk + rivergunk + sewagegunk;
  lakegunk := lakegunk - (lakegunk / lakevolume) * riveroutflow;
  if lakegunk / lakevolume < minpollution then
    cleanedup := true;
  end; { while-loop }

if cleanedup then
  writeln ('Pollutant level down to ', minpollution * 100 :1:1,
          '% after ', day :1, ' days.')
else
  writeln ('Pollutant level still not below ', minpollution * 100 :1:1,
          '% after ', maxdays :1, ' days.');
end.
run cleanup

Pollutant level down to  0.1% after 398 days.
```

The simulation technique illustrated in the program cleanup is being used to solve some very complex problems. In *American Scientist*, Walter Orr Roberts discusses a simulation program to model the weather system of the entire world:

> Not only will the model, when built and tested, permit experiments to refine weather and climate forecasting research, but also we anticipate, ... that such a model will permit experiments in global weather modification—safely in the model, and not in nature. We should be able, for example, to level the Rockies or rotate the earth backwards and see what the impact is on weather. Or more usefully and realistically, we hope to be able to simulate, for a few thousand dollars, cleaning up world air pollution, so that we may be able to evaluate the meteorological consequences of such a clean-up—giving us a handle to the value of so doing in the real world. This would be a very powerful decision-making aid.*

Self-Test Questions

1. What is the maximum number of input integers the program example will examine looking for the integer value zero? What is the final value of the variable count?

    ```
    program example (input, output);
      var
        x, count : integer;
        zerofound : boolean;
      begin
      count := 0;
      zerofound := false;
      while (count < 10) and (not zerofound) do
        begin
        read (x);
    ```

---

*"Man on a Changing Earth", *American Scientist*, 59 (1971): 16-19.

```
        if x = 0 then
          zerofound := true
        else
          count := count + 1;
      end;   { while-loop }
    writeln ('Count = ', count :1);
    end.
```

2.   What does "garbage in, garbage out" mean?
3.   Why is it necessary to simplify in building a model? What is the danger of oversimplification?

Exercises

1.   The population of the United States in 1970 was 203.2 million. By 1980 it had increased 11.5 percent to 226.5 million. If it increases by 11.5 percent each decade, what will the population of the United States be in 2000? In 2050?

2.   The town of Bettysburg had 10,324 residents in the year 2073. Every year there is a new baby born for each 173 residents and one death for every 211 residents. Every year exactly 47 new residents move to town, and 76 move away. Write a deterministic simulation that will determine the population in the year 2084.

3.   Suppose the pollutant level of the Rancid River is reduced to 0.03 percent, but the residents of Mudville are not willing to close the Noxious Products plant because most of them would lose their jobs. Therefore the pollutant level in the town's sewage will be 1 percent, even after installation of a treatment facility. What will happen to the pollution level of the lake? Put a writeln statement in the simulation program that will display the pollution level of the lake only every 30 days.

4.   Modify the Lake Sludge program pollute to reflect the assumption that 500 cubic feet of pure, unpolluted water evaporate each day and the flow of water out of the lake into the Rancid River is 49,500 cubic feet.

5.   The individuals of certain species of birds may be any one of three genetic types: BB, Bb, or bb. Individuals of types BB and Bb have brown eyes, and those of type bb have blue eyes. Each year during mating season, mating between the members of each pair of genetic types produces a number of offspring, which is equal to 10 percent of the number of individuals in the smaller of the two groups. In other words, if there are 16.3 million BB adults and 75.6 million bb adults, they will produce 0.1×16.3 million = 1.63 million offspring. The genotype of each offspring is determined by selecting at random one of the genes (B or b) from each parent. Each of the four not necessarily distinct genotypes comprises one-fourth of the offspring generation. Each year, after the offspring are produced, 15 percent of the brown-eyed adults and 5 percent of the blue-eyed adults die. The new offspring become reproducing adults in 1 year.

     If the current population distribution, which is atypical, is given by the following table

TYPE	POPULATION (MILLIONS)
BB	16.3
Bb	41.2
bb	75.6

what will be the population of each type in 30 years?

6.   A husband and wife plan to save money from their paychecks to make a
      down payment on a home. They intend to make monthly deposits of
      $800 in a savings account on which the bank pays monthly interest at the
      rate of 7/12 of 1 percent. (The bank advertises a nominal annual rate of
      7 percent, but it actually pays somewhat more, because the interest is
      compounded monthly.) How many months will they need to accumulate
      $30,000?

7.   A house is purchased for $75,000 with a down payment of $15,000. The
      $60,000 balance is borrowed at an interest rate of 12 percent per annum.
      Payments are to be made monthly, and from each payment is deducted
      the interest due for 1 month. The remainder of the payment is applied to
      reducing the principal. To the nearest dollar, how much should the pay-
      ments be in order that the loan will be repaid in 25 years? The payments
      are to be level, that is, the same amount each month. Try simulating
      with payments varying in size until the number of payments comes out
      right. *Note:* The formula for computing the correct monthly payment,
      given in Section 7.4, can be used to check the answer, but the point of
      this exercise is to simulate the steady decrease of the outstanding princi-
      pal.

7.2   End-Of-Line and Variable-Length Input

In this section, compound exit conditions are used to provide both unusual and
early exits from loops involving interactive input. The concept of **interactive
dialogue** is introduced and used to write a simple program for computer-assisted
instruction.

> **Section Preview**
>
> **Compound Conditions:**
>   The while-statement
>
>   while (not eoln) and (letter < maxnamesize) do
>   . . .
>
>   terminates on either end-of-line or end of the array name
>   [1..maxnamesize]. The while-statement
>
>   while (not answerok) and (chance <= 3) do
>   . . .
>
>   terminates on either a correct answer or after the third
>   chance to give the correct answer.

Early Exits

In Pascal, a character string variable is declared as a packed array of fixed
length. However, the data to be stored in that character string variable, perhaps
a name, may be variable length. A loop to read a variable-length value for a
character string variable may end on either of two exit conditions: 1) end of
input line, or 2) reaching the declared end of the character string array.

   A loop to give the user up to three tries to give the correct answer to a
problem also has two exit conditions. It ends either after the three tries are up
or after the user supplies the correct answer.

Computer-Assisted Instruction

Educational theorists emphasize the value of immediate reinforcement of correct responses in improving rates of learning. Yet the average classroom teacher has too many students to give each one an immediate pat on the back for a right answer or to correct a wrong answer, except on an occasional basis. For some types of learning, a computer terminal can be programmed to provide greater individual attention to the student than a classroom teacher, while still retaining far greater flexibility in instruction than a textbook or workbook. This section discusses how to write an interactive program to conduct a drill on the addition of numbers and how to modify that program to conduct drills on the other arithmetic operations. Such drills are one aspect of **computer-assisted instruction**.

In order to present the student with a more varied selection of problems during the computer-assisted arithmetic drills, a random number generating function is used so that the problems are never the same twice.

Teaching Addition: A Dramatization

The interactive addition drill described here is intended for a young school child. The child sits at a computer terminal, and someone starts the program running. The first few times it might be an older person, perhaps a teacher, who explains what to do, but thereafter the child might well be able to do it alone. The session opens with a mutual introduction.

Computer:	Hello. I'm a computer.
	What's your name?
Child types name:	Jessica
Computer:	Nice to meet you, Jessica.
	Today we are going to do
	twenty addition problems.

Then, as it promises, the computer poses 20 problems, each requiring the addition of two one-digit numbers. For each problem, the child has three chances to give a correct answer before the computer provides the correct answer and goes on to the next problem. When the child replies correctly on the first try, the dialogue for that problem might look something like this:

Computer:	Please tell me, Jessica,
	How much is 5 and 2?
Child types answer:	7
Computer:	Correct, Jessica. Very good.

When the child makes one or two mistakes before giving the right answer, the problem printout might look like this:

Computer:	Please tell me, Jessica,
	How much is 7 and 8?
Child types answer:	19
Computer:	That's not right, Jessica.
	Please try again.
Child types another answer:	15
Computer:	Correct, Jessica. Very good.
Computer:	Please tell me, Jessica,
	How much is 8 and 8?
Child types answer:	18
Computer:	That's not right, Jessica.
	Please try again.
Child types another answer:	15

Computer:	That's not right, Jessica. Please try again.
Child types a third answer:	16
Computer:	Correct, Jessica. Very good.

An example of printout when the child does not give the right answer in the three allowed tries might be the following:

Computer:	Please tell me, Jessica, How much is 9 and 6?
Child types answer:	13
Computer:	That's not right, Jessica. Please try again.
Child types another answer:	16
Computer:	That's not right, Jessica Please try again.
Child types a third answer:	19
Computer:	Still wrong, Jessica. The right answer is 15.

At the conclusion of the drill, the computer tells the child how many of the 20 problems were answered correctly before the three chances ran out. For example, the computer might print

| Computer: | You answered 18 out of 20 correctly.
That is very good.
This was fun. Goodbye, Jessica. |

Interactive Dialogue

Computer-assisted instruction is the first application in this book that absolutely requires interactive execution. It simply makes no sense to execute a computer-assisted instruction program when the student is not present. Interactive execution calls for **interactive dialogue**, a different sequence of input and output operations than used in previous noninteractive programs. While a noninteractive program reads data from a previously prepared input file and echoes it in the output file, an interactive program prints an **input prompt** before each read statement, telling the user what information is expected by the next read statement.

An interactive program has the ability to check input data for correctness or feasibility and to allow the user to make immediate corrections. In the addition drill dramatization, the student has three chances to get the problem right before the computer supplies the correct answer. The use of the student's name in the computer's responses and input prompts adds a nice personal touch to the dialogue.

A Simpler Teaching Program: One Problem, One Chance

Before working out a nested loop structure to conduct the intended addition drill with 20 problems, it may be helpful to consider a less ambitious program simpledrill that poses only one problem and allows only one chance. This program illustrates the essential features of problem posing and interactive dialogue. The first version leaves two steps unrefined: reading the student's name and posing the problem.

```
program simpledrill (input, output);
{ one problem, one chance }
{ unrefined version }

  var
    studentname : packed array [1..20] of char;
    x, y, answer : integer;

  begin
  writeln ('Hello, I''m a computer. What''s your name?');
  write ('Please type your name: ');
  read the student's name into the array studentname;
  writeln ('Nice to meet you, ', studentname);
  writeln ('Today we are going to do an addition problem.');
  pose a problem, that is, choose two integers x and y;
  writeln ('Please tell me, ', studentname);
  writeln ('How much is ', x :1, ' and ', y :1, '?');
  write ('Type the answer: ');
  read (answer);
  if answer = x + y then
    begin
    writeln ('Correct, ', studentname);
    writeln ('Very good.');
    end
  else
    begin
    writeln ('That''s not right, ', studentname);
    writeln ('The answer is ', x + y :1);
    end;
  end.
```

Variable-Length Character String Input

In Section 6.3, the problem of reading variable-length character strings is solved by reading first into a very long buffer and then copying as many characters as will fit into the character string variable. In this section, we solve the problem with a compound exit condition for the input loop. The loop ends either on end-of-line or when the character string array is full, whichever comes first.

```
const
  maxnamesize = 20;
var
  studentname : packed array [1..maxnamesize] of char;
  letter : 0..maxnamesize;

procedure readname;
  begin
  for letter := 1 to maxnamesize do
    studentname [letter] := ' ';
  letter := 0;
```

```
while (not eoln) and (letter < maxnamesize) do
  begin
  letter := letter + 1;
  read (studentname [letter]);
  end; { loop }
readln;
end; { readname }
```

After filling the entire studentname with blanks using a for-loop, the program enters a while-loop which can terminate only if an end-of-line character is encountered or the value of letter is at least as great as maxnamesize. Since letter increases by one each time, this second termination condition is equivalent to termination when letter equals maxnamesize.

A Debugging Trick

It is a standard debugging practice to replace an unwritten step by an oversimplified but functional refinement that allows the rest of the program execution to proceed after a fashion. The refinement

```
x := 3;  { temporary refinement to  }
y := 4;  { pose one fixed problem    }
```

is adequate for present purposes, because it poses the problem, but not in a realistic way. This new version of the program simpledrill and a sample execution are given below.

```
program simpledrill (input, output);
{ one problem, one chance }
{ temporarily poses only the problem 3 + 4 = ? }

  const
    maxnamesize = 20;

  var
    studentname : packed array [1..maxnamesize] of char;
    x, y, answer : integer;
    letter : integer;

  procedure readname;
    ... end; { readname }

  begin
  writeln ('Hello, I''m a computer. What''s your name?');
  write ('Please type your name: ');
  readname;
  writeln ('Nice to meet you, ', studentname);
  writeln ('Today we are going to do an addition problem.');
  x := 3; { temporary refinement to  }
  y := 4; { pose one fixed problem }
  writeln ('Please tell me, ', studentname);
  writeln ('How much is ', x :1, ' and ', y :1, '?');
  write ('Type the answer: ');
  read (answer);
```

```
    if answer = x + y then
      begin
      writeln ('Correct, ', studentname);
      writeln ('Very good.');
      end
    else
      begin
      writeln ('That''s not right, ', studentname);
      writeln ('The answer is ', x + y :1);
      end;
    end.
  run simpledrill

  Hello, I'm a computer. What's your name?
  Please type your name: David
  Nice to meet you, David
  Today we are going to do an addition problem.
  Please tell me, David
  How much is 3 and 4?
  Type the answer: 7
  Correct, David
  Very good.
```

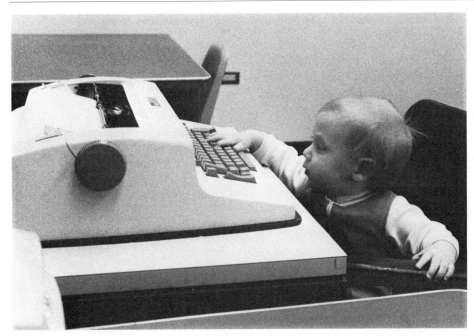

Figure 7.2 Even a small child can operate a computer terminal.

Varying the Problems By Using the Function Randominteger

The method of generating a problem used in simpledrill can only generate one problem, 3 + 4. The program teachadd must not only present 20 problems, but the problems must be different in every drill. Some Pascal systems have a built-in function that can be used to generate random problems. Even on Pascal systems that do not have such a function built in, however, the function randominteger may be used as though it were built in when the function definition presented here is copied into a program.

For any two integers r and s, the value of the expression

```
randominteger (r, s)
```

is one of the integers from r to s, although exactly which one it will be cannot be predicted in advance. For instance, the value of the expression

```
randominteger (0, 9)
```

could be any one of the integers 0 through 9. The likelihood that any one of these possibilities will be the computed value is the same as the likelihood that any other one will be. The user does not know in advance which of these 10 possible values will occur when the computer evaluates the expression

```
randominteger (0, 9)
```

The user only knows that each possible value has a 1/10 chance of occurring. Moreover, each time the expression is evaluated, a completely new and independent choice is made for the random integer from the complete set of possibilities.

The step of simpledrill which poses the problem may now be refined as

```
x := randominteger (0, 9);
y := randominteger (0, 9);
```

Properties of Random Integers

In two consecutive evaluations of a function generating random integers the second random integer is neither necessarily the same as nor necessarily different from the first. In fact, about 1/10 of the time they are the same, and about 9/10 of the time they are different. This property is illustrated by the program randomdigits that chooses a random integer from zero to nine, 50 consecutive times.

```
program randomdigits (output);

   var
     i, j, seed : integer;

   function randominteger (r, s : integer) : integer;
   { generates an integer in the interval [r..s] }
   { uses and changes the global variable seed }
     const
       maxseed = 10000;
       multiplier = 201;
       adder = 3437;
     begin
     seed := (multiplier * seed + adder) mod maxseed;
     randominteger := r + seed * (s - r + 1) div maxseed;
     end; { randominteger }

   begin
   seed := 1;
   for i := 1 to 10 do
     begin
     for j := 1 to 5 do
       write (randominteger (0, 9) :5);
     writeln;
     end; { for-loop }
   end.
```

```
run randomdigits
```

3	4	3	8	2
2	0	6	9	9
7	2	4	4	1
6	8	7	4	8
0	9	5	9	0
9	5	9	9	8
3	6	7	5	0
2	2	0	5	7
7	4	8	0	9
6	0	1	0	6

Evaluation of the same expression randominteger (0, 9) in the write statement of the program randomdigits results in all 50 random digits. Not every one of the 10 digits occurs exactly the same number of times, but surprising as it may be at first, this is to be expected. Suppose, to make an analogy, that an experiment consisted of tossing a coin 8 times. The probability of obtaining exactly 4 heads and 4 tails is not a virtual certainty, but actually is less than 1/3. This may be verified either analytically by those who know how to compute combinatorial probabilities, or empirically by performing the experiment of tossing 8 coins a large number of times. To further illustrate why an exactly equal number of heads and tails in the coin tossing experiment, or exactly 5 repetitions of each digit in the random number table, is not the most reasonable or the most probable occurrence, imagine what a scrupulously fair coin would do in an experiment consisting of 5 coin tosses. Would it have to show up heads 2½ times?

Programmer-Defined Functions: A Look Ahead

To use the function randominteger, copy the following lines into your program below the variable declarations:

```
function randominteger (r, s : integer) : integer;
{ generates an integer in the interval [r..s] }
{ uses and changes the global variable seed }
  const
    maxseed = 10000;
    multiplier = 201;
    adder = 3437;
  begin
  seed := (multiplier * seed + adder) mod maxseed;
  randominteger := r + seed * (s - r + 1) div maxseed;
  end; { randominteger }
```

What you are actually doing when you insert these lines is declaring a programmer-defined function.

There are two important rules for using the function randominteger. Both of its arguments, the two numbers in the parentheses, should be integers, and the second integer should be at least as large as the first.

A program using the function randominteger must contain a declaration of the integer variable seed and a statement initializing the variable seed to some value between 1 and maxseed. For different initial values of the variable seed, different sequences of random numbers will be generated.

Pseudorandom Numbers

Computers don't really generate random numbers: What they generate has all of the important properties of a truly random collection of numbers, but it cannot actually be random because it is calculated by an algorithm.

Suppose, for example, that randominteger (1, 73) is computed 7,300 times. The numbers produced would appear to be random, for our simple purposes, if each of the integers 1 to 73 is generated approximately 100 times, that is, approximately 1/73 of the time, and if there is no discernible pattern in the numbers generated. Of course, each will not occur exactly 100 times, but perhaps one number will occur 84 times, another will occur 107 times, and so on.

The function randominteger generates its random numbers in two stages. First, an unpredictable value between 0 and maxseed $-$ 1 is calculated for the variable seed. Then, the value of seed is scaled to produce integers in the correct range, from r to s. In the first step, the current value of seed is multiplied by the constant multiplier and adder is added to the result. Then the result is reduced to the range 0 to maxseed $-$ 1 using the integer operator mod. When maxseed is 10,000 as it is in this case, all but the last four digits of the new value of seed are discarded.

Seed takes on more possible values than the s $-$ r $+$ 1 allowed values for the function randominteger (r, s). Multiplying by s $-$ r $+$ 1 and dividing by maxseed produces the correct number values, and adding r makes the values start at r.

With the variable seed initialized to the value 1, the first ten values produced by randominteger (1, 100) are

37 47 32 90 22 29   9 63 92 94

It is no easy matter to decide whether the function randominteger does a good job of behaving like a true random generator, but it is entirely adequate for the present purpose of getting different problems for a small child.

Twenty Problems, Three Chances Each

Now that the use of the function randominteger to pose varied addition problems in a sequence the child cannot guess has been explained, and now that the simple drill program has shown how the playscript can be converted into computer terminal dialogue, it is time to write the intended program teachadd. Its initial form is the following.

```
program teachadd (input, output);
  begin
  initialize;
  make mutual introduction of computer and child;
  for problem := 1 to 20 do
    begin
    pose an addition problem;
    while (not answerok) and (chance <= 3) do
      evaluate and process the answer, possibly terminating
                  the loop before three chances in case the answer
                  is correct by setting answerok to true;
```

```
   if answerok then
     give the child a pat on the back
   else
     give the child the correct answer;
   end;  { for-loop }
 evaluate the child's total performance and say goodbye;
 end.
```

The basic loop structure of the program teachadd is a while-loop nested within a for-loop. The outer for-loop poses and evaluates 20 problems, including for each problem an execution of the inner while-loop that permits up to three chances. Outside the for-loop, and only executed once, are the mutual introduction, the initialization, and the evaluation of the total drill performance.

As is often the case when programs are written for two similar applications, some of the program steps in an early version of the second program already have been refined while writing the first program. For example, the refinement of the mutual introduction is adapted easily from the mutual introduction in the program simpledrill:

```
{ make mutual introduction of computer and child }
writeln ('Hello, I''m a computer. What''s your name?');
writeln ('Please type your name: ');
readname;
writeln ('Nice to meet you, ', studentname);
writeln ('Today we are going to do twenty addition problems.');
```

The posing of a random addition problem can use the same refinement in the program teachadd as in the program simpledrill.

```
{ pose an addition problem }
x := randominteger (0, 9);
y := randominteger (0, 9);
writeln;
writeln ('Please tell me, ', studentname);
writeln ('How much is ', x :1, ' and ', y :1, '?');
```

Nested If-Statements

The while-loop that gives the child up to three chances to give the correct answer is refined next. The printed output produced by this loop must conform to the playscript at the beginning of the section in case the child gives one or more incorrect answers.

```
{ allow the pupil three chances to answer correctly }
chance := 1;
answerok := false;
while (not answerok) and (chance <= 3) do
  begin
  writeln ('Type the answer: ');
  read (answer);
  if answer = x + y then
    answerok := true
  else
```

```
     if chance < 3 then
       begin
       writeln ('That''s not right, ', studentname);
       writeln ('Please try again.');
       end;
     chance := chance + 1;
   end; { while-loop }
```

The most notable programming technique in this refinement is the nesting of one if-statement within another if-statement. The else-clause of the outer if-statement is itself an if-statement, this time with no else-clause. The writeln statement terminates both of the if-statements. Notice that if the problem is not answered correctly on the third try, then nothing is printed and the while-loop is completed because three is the largest value for the variable chance that passes the while-statement.

Another if-statement that adapts readily from the program simpledrill is the statement that either congratulates the child who has given a correct answer or corrects the child who has missed it three times.

```
{ either acknowledge answer correct or tell correct answer }
if answerok then
  begin
  numberright := numberright + 1;
  writeln ('Correct, ', studentname);
  writeln ('Very good.');
  end
else
  begin
  writeln ('Still wrong, ', studentname);
  writeln ('The correct answer is ', x + y :1);
  end;
```

Evaluating the Drill Performance

In the playscript, the drill session ends with an evaluation of the child's performance. Teachadd implements a very simple evaluation, which consists of a summary of how many questions the child got right and an opinion of how good or bad a performance this represents. Ideally, the opinion should be expressed in a positive manner and should take into account the pupil's age and past experience with arithmetic, among other factors, and the programmer might well consult a specialist in elementary education for guidance.

The evaluation of the child's performance given in the program teachadd is only a sample of what can be done.

```
{ evaluate child's performance and say goodbye }
case numberright of
  20 :
    opinion := 'excellent.          ';
  18, 19 :
    opinion := 'very good.          ';
  16, 17 :
    opinion := 'good.               ';
  14, 15 :
    opinion := 'fair.               ';
  0, 1, 2, 3, 4, 5, 6, 7, 8, 9, 10, 11, 12, 13 :
    opinion := 'not as good as I hoped.  ';
  end; { case }
```

   This sample evaluation procedure is based only on the number of problems the child answered correctly within the three allotted chances. The 21
possible values of the variable numberright are grouped into five different
cases. In each ease a different value is assigned to the character string variable
opinion. The character string constants assigned to opinion are all padded with
blanks so that they have exactly the same length, 25, the declared length of the
character string opinion. The effect of the student evaluation is shown in the
sample execution of the program teachadd, now fully refined.

```
program teachadd (input, output);

   const
     maxnamesize = 20;

   var
     studentname : packed array [1..maxnamesize] of char;
     opinion : packed array [1..25] of char;
     x, y, answer : integer;
     seed, letter : integer;
     numberright, problem, chance : integer;
     answerok : boolean;

   function randominteger (r, s : integer) : integer;
       ... end; { randominteger }

   procedure readname;
       ... end; { readname }

   begin
   seed := 1;

   { make mutual introduction of computer and child }
   writeln ('Hello, I''m a computer. What''s your name?');
   writeln ('Please type your name: ');
   readname;
   writeln ('Nice to meet you, ', studentname);
   writeln ('Today we are going to do twenty addition problems.');

   { computer poses 20 problems, allowing the child up to
     three chances on each before telling the numberright answer }
   numberright := 0;
   for problem := 1 to 20 do
     begin
     { pose an addition problem }
     x := randominteger (0, 9);
     y := randominteger (0, 9);
     writeln;
     writeln ('Please tell me, ', studentname);
     writeln ('How much is ', x :1, ' and ', y :1, '?');

       { allow the pupil three chances to answer correctly }
       chance := 1;
       answerok := false;
```

```pascal
    while (not answerok) and (chance <= 3) do
      begin
      writeln ('Type the answer: ');
      read (answer);
      if answer = x + y then
        answerok := true
      else
        if chance < 3 then
          begin
          writeln ('That''s not right ', studentname);
          writeln ('Please try again.');
          end;
      chance := chance + 1;
      end; { while-loop }

    { either acknowledge answer correct or tell correct answer }
    if answerok then
      begin
      numberright := numberright + 1;
      writeln ('Correct, ', studentname);
      writeln ('Very good.');
      end
    else
      begin
      writeln ('Still wrong, ', studentname);
      writeln ('The correct answer is ', x + y :1);
      end;
    end; { for-loop }

{ evaluate child's performance and say goodbye }
case numberright of
  20 :
    opinion := 'excellent.             ';
  18, 19 :
    opinion := 'very good.             ';
  16, 17 :
    opinion := 'good.                  ';
  14, 15 :
    opinion := 'fair.                  ';
  0, 1, 2, 3, 4, 5, 6, 7, 8, 9, 10, 11, 12, 13 :
    opinion := 'not as good as I hoped. ';
end; { case }

writeln ('You answered ', numberright :1, ' out of 20 correctly.');
writeln ('That is ', opinion);
if numberright < 16 then
  writeln ('You need more practice.');
writeln ('This was fun.  Goodbye, ', studentname);
end.
```

```
run teachadd

Hello, I'm a computer. What's your name?
Please type your name: Jessica
Nice to meet you, Jessica
Today we are going to do twenty addition problems.

Please tell me, Jessica
How much is 3 and 4?
Type the answer: 7
Correct, Jessica
Very good.
        .
        .   (18 more problems)
        .
Please tell me, Jessica
How much is 5 and 7?
Type answer: 12
Correct, Jessica
Very good.

You answered 19 out of 20 correctly.
That is very good.
This was fun.  Goodbye, Jessica
```

Teaching Other Arithmetic Operations

It isn't hard to modify the program teachadd into other programs that teach multiplication, subtraction, and division. Once the details of the problem posing step for these other arithmetic operations are straightened out, the minor changes needed follow naturally, both in the while-loop that allows up to three chances and in the final if-statement that either acknowledges or reveals the correct answer.

   Although modifying the program teachadd to teach the multiplication of small integers is sufficiently easy to leave as an exercise, there is a slight difficulty in making the modification needed to obtain a program that conducts a drill on subtraction, namely, that there are good reasons to begin with proper subtraction, avoiding problems in which the difference is negative. If the variables x and y are randomly selected integers from 0 to 9, then y might be larger than x. The following while-loop is not an efficient way to obtain a proper subtraction problem.

```
{ pose a proper subtraction problem, inefficiently }
proper := false;
while not proper do
  begin
  x := randominteger (0,9);
  y := randominteger (0,9);
  if x - y >= 0 then
    proper := true;
  end; { while-loop }
writeln ('Please tell me, ', studentname);
writeln ('How much is ', x :1, ' minus ', y :1, '?');
```

   The inefficient part is waiting for the computer to generate values for the variables x and y so that their difference is not negative. Since there is a better than even chance that a random value for y will be less than or equal to a random value for x, the waiting time ordinarily will be imperceptibly short to the child sitting at a terminal. Thus it is not a terrible way to generate a proper subtraction problem. Nonetheless, choosing the value for y as a random integer from 0 to x instead of from 0 to 9 always guarantees a nonnegative difference the first time. This method is used in the second way of generating a subtraction problem.

```
{ pose a proper subtraction problem, second way }
x := randominteger (0, 9);
y := randominteger (0, x);
writeln ('Please tell me, ', studentname);
writeln ('How much is ', x :1, ' minus ', y :1, '?');
```

Persons acquainted with elementary probability theory may recognize that, while precisely the same 55 proper subtraction problems can be posed by either of the two methods described so far, the frequency of occurrence of a given problem is not the same for both methods. When the first method is used, each of the 55 possible proper subtraction problems is equally likely to occur, so each occurs about 1/55 of the time. When the second method is used, however, the problem of finding the difference zero minus zero is the most likely to occur, because whenever the variable x is assigned the value zero, the variable y necessarily will be assigned the value zero also. Since x is assigned the value zero about 1/10 of the time, zero minus zero will occur as the subtraction problem about 1/10 of the time. Another method of generating the same 55 proper subtraction problems by swapping unsuitable values for x and y is discussed in Exercise 4.

Uniformly Distributed Proper Subtraction Problems

A slightly different approach to generating proper subtraction problems ensures that each occurs with the same frequency. With this new approach, instead of assigning random values to x and y, we assign random values to y and z = x − y. x is obtained as the sum of y and z, the standard way of checking a subtraction problem.

```
{ pose a proper subtraction problem, third way }
y := randominteger (0, 9);
z := randominteger (0, 9);
x := y + z;
writeln ('Please tell me, ', studentname);
writeln ('how much is ', x :1, ' minus ', y :1, '?');
```

This third way permits x to be as large as 18, while y may be only as large as 9. The notion is reinforced that subtraction is the inverse operation of addition, because there is now a subtraction problem corresponding to every one-digit addition problem.

It is easy to modify this method to provide a highly satisfactory method for posing drill problems involving division of integers without remainder. Modifying the rest of the program teachadd so that it might be used in a subtraction drill based on this third way of obtaining a proper subtraction problem is left as an exercise.

Self-Test Questions

1. Under what conditions is the built-in function eoln true?
2. True/false:

a. The while-loop
> while *condition1* and *condition2* do
> > *statement*

terminates when both *condition1* and *condition2* are true.

b. The while-loop
> while *condition1* or *condition2* do
> > *statement*

terminates when both *condition1* and *condition2* are false.

Exercises

1. Write an arithmetic teaching program that poses five problems, each giving three chances to add a one-digit number to a two-digit number.

2. Write a program that teaches multiplication.

3. Modify the program teachadd in this section to conduct a drill on proper subtraction problems. (Some of the modifications are described in detail in the section.)

4. One cannot obtain a proper subtraction problem (i.e., with a difference greater than or equal to 0) by choosing two random integers from 0 to 9 for x and y and then asking for the difference x − y because almost half of the time the random integer chosen for y will be greater than the random integer chosen for x. However, it is possible to modify this procedure to pose proper subtraction problems by swapping the values of x and y in case the value of y is the larger of the two. Incorporate this method of generating proper subtraction problems into a program that teaches proper subtraction of one-digit numbers.

5. Revise the evaluation procedure of the program teachadd so that it tells the pupil how many problems were answered correctly on the first try, how many correctly on the second try, how many correctly on the third try, and how many were not answered correctly.

6. Modify the assigning of an opinion to describe the child's performance in the program teachadd to take into account the more detailed record keeping described in Exercise 5. One way is to assign three points for each problem answered correctly on the first try, two points for each problem answered correctly on the second try, one point for each problem answered correctly on the third try, and no points for problems still not answered correctly. Then the expression of opinion may be based on this weighted total of correct answers.

7. Revise the program teachadd so that, after an incorrect answer, it gives the pupil a hint by saying whether the correct answer is higher or lower.

8. A neighboring entry of a product in the multiplication table is an entry one vertical position above or below the correct product, or an entry one horizontal position to the right or left of the correct product. Thus the neighboring entries of $7 \times 8 = 56$ are $6 \times 8 = 48$, $8 \times 8 = 64$, $7 \times 7 = 49$, and $7 \times 9 = 63$. A common error in remembering multiplication facts is giving a neighboring entry as the answer instead of the correct product. Write a multiplication teaching program that recognizes when a neighboring entry has been given mistakenly as the answer and informs the student of this fact. For example, if the pupil gives 48 as the answer to 7×8, then the computer might print

```
No, Josh.  48 is 6 times 8.
Please try again.
```

9. A good way of generating integer division problems with remainder is to select the divisor, the quotient, and the remainder randomly and then to calculate the dividend by the formula

```
dividend := divisor * quotient + remainder
```

Write a program that teaches integer division with remainder using this method to generate problems. Both the divisor and the quotient should be less than 10, and the divisor must not be 0. Recall also that, in division with remainder, the remainder is always less than the divisor and may be 0 if the divisor divides the dividend exactly. Be careful in your program to use different variable names for the correct answers and the student's responses, which may or may not be correct.

10. Modify the program teachadd so that the computer's response changes with each wrong answer to a problem. The computer's response to correct answers should also change, depending on how many tries it takes for the child to get the problem right.

11. For each of the following three expressions, determine all possible values.

```
2 * randominteger (0, 5)
randominteger (0, 10)
randominteger (0, 5) + randominteger (0, 5)
```

12. Which two of the three expressions in Exercise 11 are the most nearly alike? How does the other expression differ from these two?

13. Which of the following relationships is always true?

$$\text{sqrt (sqr (x))} = x \text{ for all } x$$
$$\text{sqr (sqrt (x))} = x \text{ for all } x >= 0$$

14. Rewrite the following two expressions using the integer operator mod. Assume n is type integer.

```
n - (n div 100) * 100
not odd (n)
```

15. An integer larger than one is called *prime* if there is no way to express it as a product of two positive integer factors unless the number itself is one of the factors. Write a program that divides a positive integer n, supplied as input, by as many of the numbers 2, 3, 4, ..., n − 1 as you think necessary to decide whether or not n is prime.

16. Prove that, if a positive integer is not prime (see Exercise 15), then the smaller of the two integers that factor the given number must lie between 2 and the square root of the given number. Use this fact in a program to test whether a number n supplied as input is prime.

17. Prove that, in deciding as in Exercises 15 and 16 whether an integer is prime, there is no need to divide by any even number except 2. Use this fact in a program to test whether a number is prime.

18. A proper divisor of a positive integer n is any exact divisor of n except n itself. (1 is considered a proper divisor of any positive integer.) Write a program that lists all the proper divisors of a number n supplied as input.

19. A positive integer is called *perfect* if it equals the sum of its proper divisors (see Exercise 18). For example, the numbers 6 and 28 are perfect because

$$6 = 1 + 2 + 3$$
$$28 = 1 + 2 + 4 + 7 + 14$$

Write a procedure to decide whether a positive integer is perfect. Write a program to find the smallest perfect number greater than 28.

20. Write a program whose purpose is to find the smallest perfect odd number (see Exercise 19). Do you know whether the execution of your program is certain to terminate?

21. Evaluate the expression

```
x + abs (x)
```

for the following values of x: -2, -1.5, -1, -0.5, 0, 0.5, 1, 1.5, and 2.

22.   Do the following two expressions always have the same value for any value of the variable x?

```
abs (x)
sqrt (sqr (x))
```

23.   Write a program to conduct a vocabulary drill in the form of multiple-answer questions. For example, a question might be

Please tell me, Pam, what is the meaning of apathy?
(a) boredom (b) laziness (c) sloth (d) disinterest (e) I don't care what the meaning is

Give 10 questions and allow the student to answer with either the letter (a to e) of the correct answer or the correct answer itself. Evaluation of the drill should be similar to that of teachadd.

24.   Modify the vocabulary drill program in Exercise 24 so that, whenever the student gives an incorrect answer, the computer gives the definition of the student's answer and an explanation of why it is not the correct answer.

7.3   A Comparison of Loop Structures

There are three major loop constructs in Pascal: the for-loop, the while-loop, and the repeat-until-loop. This section shows how closely the while- and repeat-until-loops resemble each other. The structure of these loops is studied in detail.

This section also compares the while- and repeat-until-loops with the for-loop, a more natural construct for an entirely different class of programs.

Section Preview

A loop contains four major parts:

1.   Initialization
2.   Repetition vs. Exit Test
3.   Loop Body
4.   Modification of Loop Control Variable(s) in the Loop Body

For-loops are a natural loop construct to use if a sequence of consecutive integers is involved and if the number of iterations of the loop body is known before the loop is entered.

While-loops and repeat-until-loops are used in all other situations.

Unknown Number of Iterations

In the first group of programs, we want to find the first positive integer whose square exceeds 1000. A while-loop provides a clear program. The number of iterations of the loop is not known in advance.

```
program testsquares1 (output);
   var
      n : integer;
   begin
```

```
n := 0;
while n * n <= 1000 do
  n := n + 1;
writeln (n :1, ' is the smallest number ',
    'whose square exceeds 1000.');
end.
```

```
run testsquares1
```

```
32 is the smallest number whose square exceeds 1000.
```

For this example, a repeat-until-loop is equally clear.

```
program testsquares2 (output);
  var
    n : integer;
  begin
n := 0;
repeat
  n := n + 1;
  until n * n > 1000;
  writeln (n :1, ' is the smallest number ',
      'whose square exceeds 1000.');
  end.
```

```
run testsquares2
```

```
32 is the smallest number whose square exceeds 1000.
```

Notice that the boolean condition in both a while-test and a repeat-until-test
may be any boolean expression involving comparison operators as well as the
boolean operations and, or, and not. There is no completely satisfactory way to
write this program using a for-loop.

Number of Iterations Known in Advance

On the other hand, when the loop limits are known in advance, the for-
loop provides a natural program and both the while-loop and the repeat-until-
loop are slightly awkward. For comparison, all three programs below print a
table of squares from 1 to 10.

```
program squares1 (output);
  var
    n : integer;
  begin
  writeln ('number  square');
for n := 1 to 10 do
  writeln (n :4, n * n :8);
  end.
```

```
run squares1
```

```
number   square
   1        1
   2        4
   3        9
   4       16
   5       25
   6       36
```

```
    7        49
    8        64
    9        81
   10       100
program squares2 (output);
  var
    n : integer;
  begin
  writeln ('number  square');
  n := 1;
  while n <= 10 do
    begin
    writeln (n :4, n * n :8);
    n := n + 1;
    end; { while-loop }
  end.
program squares3 (output);
  var
    n : integer;
  begin
  writeln ('number  square');
  n := 1;
  repeat
    writeln (n :4, n * n :8);
    n := n + 1;
    until n > 10;
  end.
```

Execution printouts are not shown for squares2 and squares3 because they duplicate that of squares1. Notice that both the while-loop and the repeat-until-loop require explicit **initialization**

```
    n := 1
```

and **incrementation**

```
    n := n + 1
```

statements as well as their termination test expressions

```
    while n <= 10
```

and

```
    until n > 10
```

A for-loop is preferable for this application because it condenses these details into the loop heading. For-loops also are ideally suited for any kind of processing that runs through a complete character string or other array, or through a fixed portion of the array known in advance.

Parts of While- and Repeat-Until-Loops

A while-loop or repeat-until-loop always consists of four parts:

1. Initialization
2. Repetition vs. exit test
3. Loop body
4. Loop control variable modification step

The while-test at the top of a while-loop and the until-test at the bottom of a repeat-until-loop test the truth of a relationship involving one or more variables or constants. In general, the while- or until-condition must contain at

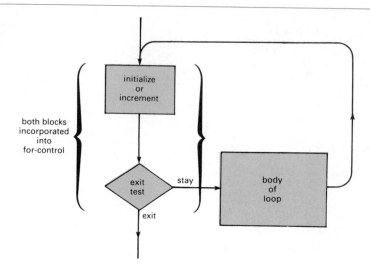

Figure 7.3 Control of flow maintained by a for-loop.

least one variable, because, if it contained only constants, the test always would give the same result. The loop body either would never be executed or it would be executed forever.

Since the first action of a computer executing a while-statement is to perform the while-test, the while-statement must be preceded by initialization statements assigning starting values to each of the variables in the while-test. These variables are **control variables** for the loop. In the programs testsquares1 and squares2, there is only one control variable, n, for the while-loop. It is initialized immediately before the while-statement.

The mere fact that a while-test contains variables is not sufficient to guarantee that the truth of the while-condition can change. There must be at least one statement in the body of the loop to change the value of a variable used in the while-test. This statement is a **loop control variable modification step**. If the change in a loop control variable is accomplished by adding something to it, the step is incrementation and the amount added is the **increment**. The programs testsquares1 and squares2 contain the increment step

```
n := n + 1
```

A loop control variable can change when its value is calculated or a new value is read from input data. While-loops frequently are used to read input data, terminating when the input value read is a signal value.

Repeat-until-loops usually have the same four parts as while-loops. However, since the until-test comes at the bottom of the loop following the loop body, it is sometimes unnecessary to have an initialization step. For example, if all the variables in the until-test are read from input data in the body of the repeat-until-loop, an initialization step is unnecessary. Thus, the loop

```
repeat
   read (a, b, c);
until a > b
```

requires no initialization for the loop control variables a or b. It terminates the first time the input value of a exceeds the input value for b. The body of this loop consists only of the control variable modification statement.

Similarly, no explicit initialization step may be necessary in a repeat-until-loop when all of the loop control variables are assigned values in the body of the loop. If the new values of the loop control variables depend on the old

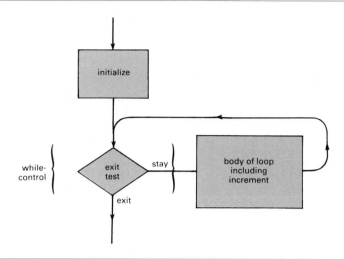

Figure 7.4 Control of flow maintained by a while-loop.

values, as they do in the programs testsquares2 and squares3, an initialization step is necessary.

A loop also may contain an initialization step not directly concerned with the loop control variables. The programs testsquares3 and sumofinputdata below have such initialization steps.

```
program testsquares3 (output);
  var
    n, square : integer;
    begin
    n := 0;  { initialization step }
    repeat
      n := n + 1;
      square := n * n;
      until square > 1000;
    writeln (n :1, ' is the smallest number ',
        'whose square exceeds 1000.');
    end.
```

The difference between the programs testsquares2 and testsquares3 is that instead of testing the expression n * n against the upper limit 1000, the program testsquares3 uses a new variable, square, and tests square against 1000 in the until-condition. The loop control variable square is not directly initialized above the repeat-until-loop. Since the value of square is calculated from the value of n, square is initialized *indirectly* when n is initialized.

The repeat-until-loop in the program sumofinputdata terminates when a signal value of zero is read, so no initialization is necessary for value, the loop control variable. However, there is an initialization step for the variable sum used in the loop.

```
program sumofinputdata (input, output);
  const
    signal = 0;
  var
    value, sum : integer;
    begin
    sum := 0;  { initialization step }
```

```
    repeat
      read (value);
      writeln ('Input data  value: ', value :1);
      sum := sum + value;
      until (value = signal);
    writeln ('Sum = ', sum :1);
    end.
  run sumofinputdata

  Input data   value: 35
  Input data   value: 45
  Input data   value: 16
  Input data   value: 0
  Sum = 96
```

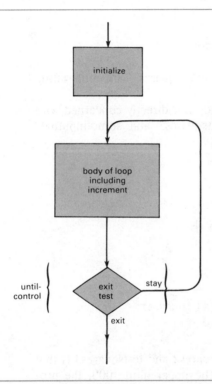

Figure 7.5 Control of flow maintained by a repeat-until-loop.

Many programmers prefer to use the built-in function eof to recognize the end of the input data. The while-loop in sumofinputdata2 also handles the possibility that there is no input data at all.

```
  program sumofinputdata2 (input, output);
    var
      value, sum : integer;
    begin
    sum := 0;  { initialization step }
    while (not eof) do
      begin
      readln (value);
      writeln ('Input data  value: ', value :1);
      sum := sum + value;
      end;
    writeln ('Sum = ', sum :1);
    end.
```

```
    writeln ('Sum = ', sum :1);
    end.
run sumofinputdata2

Input data   value: 35
Input data   value: 45
Input data   value: 16
Sum = 96
```

Self-Test Questions

1.   What are the four parts of a loop?
2.   Under what circumstances does a repeat-until-loop have no initialization step?
3.   When is a for-loop preferable to a while-loop or a repeat-until-loop?
4.   When is a while-loop or a repeat-until-loop preferable to a for-loop?
5.   The text doesn't say, but where do you think the four parts of a loop are in a for-loop?

Exercises

1.   Rewrite the program sumofinput data in this section to use a while-loop.
2.   Write a program to print the numbers 10, 20, 30, 40, 50, 60, 70, 80, 90 using a while-loop.
3.   Write a program to print the numbers 10, 20, 30, 40, 50, 60, 70, 80, 90 using a repeat-until-loop.
4.   Write a program to print the numbers 10, 20, 30, 40, 50, 60, 70, 80, 90 using a for-loop. (*Hint:* this sequence of numbers is closely related to a sequence of numbers that can be taken on by a for-variable.)
5.   Write three programs to print the first 10 powers of two, one program using each of the loop constructs. Compare the three programs.
6.   Explain why the simulation program pollute in Section 7.1 could not have been written using a for-loop. Rewrite it using a repeat-until-loop.

7.4   While-Loops That Stand In for For-Loops

Other computer languages allow greater flexibility in their equivalent of the for-loop. Some allow arbitrary real starting values, stopping values, and step sizes. This section discusses while-loops that stand in for such generalized for-loops.

Section Preview

The for-loop construct in Pascal is extremely restricted compared to related loop constructs in other programming languages, which allow arbitrary increments. In some languages, the for-variable and step size may be type real.

Using top-down program design, when a problem naturally calls for a **generalized for-loop**, the generalized for-loop should be used in the early versions of the program, then refined to a while-loop (or repeat-until-loop) in the final version of the program.

The "generalized for-loop"

> for *variable* := *expression1* to *expression2*
>   in steps of *expression3* do
>   *statement*

is refined to the while-loop

> *variable* := *expression1*;
> while *variable* <= *expression2* do
>   begin
>   *statement*;
>   *variable* := *variable* + *expression3*;
>   end

Counting By Twos

In Pascal, the differences between successive values of a for-variable must always be 1 or −1, as they have been in the previous examples. However, it is possible to achieve the effect of differences that are not 1 or −1, as is illustrated by the following two programs. The output from only one of these programs is shown, because both programs produce the same output.

```
program countbytwos1 (output);
  var
    m : integer;
  begin
  for m := 1 to 5 do
    write (2 * m :3);
  writeln;
  end.
program countbytwos2 (output);
  var
    n : integer;
  begin
  n := 2;
  while n <= 10 do
    begin
    write (n :3);
    n := n + 2;
    end; { loop }
  writeln;
  end.
run countbytwos1

  2  4  6  8 10
```

The first of these programs preserves the flavor of a for-loop headed by the non-Pascal statement

```
for n := 2 to 10 in steps of 2 do { not Pascal }
```

which is convenient to use for planning programs, but, of course, must be refined to valid Pascal statements for execution. In the program countbytwos1, the role of the variable n (which does not appear) is played by 2 * m.

The second of these programs converts the for-loop to a while-loop. To do the three jobs done by a for-statement, the programmer must supply a separate initialization statement

```
n := 2
```

before the loop and a separate incrementing statement

    n := n + 2

within the loop, since the while-statement heading

    while n <= 10 do

merely tests for completion of the for-loop.

Calculating a Mortgage Table

Nearly everyone who buys a house needs a mortgage in order to borrow some of the money for its purchase. A bank provides the needed money when the house is purchased, and the homeowner repays the bank in equal monthly installments over a relatively long period of time. What a prospective homeowner needs to know before buying a house and taking out a mortgage on it is how much the equal monthly payments are going to be. Neither the homeowner nor the bank wants to enter into a mortgage agreement where the monthly payments are more than the homeowner can afford to pay. Table 7.1 shows the basic form of a useful table of monthly payment amounts, keyed to the interest rate. For a $20,000 mortgage, the monthly payment is doubled, for a $30,000 mortgage, it is tripled. A different table is needed if the duration of the mortgage is other than 25 years.

Table 7.1 Monthly Payments on a 25-Year Mortgage of $10,000 for a Few Possible Interest Rates.

Annual Interest Rate (%)	Monthly Payments ($)
11	98.01131
11.25	99.82395
11.5	101.6469
11.75	103.4798
12	105.3224

A Formula for Mortgage Installments

The formula for the amount a of the equal monthly installment on a mortgage of p dollars is

$$a = \frac{p \times i \times c}{c - 1}$$

where

> p = principal = amount borrowed
> i = monthly interest rate = annual interest rate / 12
> n = number of monthly payments = number of years $\times$ 12
> $c = (1 + i)^n$

The derivation of this formula is of no immediate interest from a programming point of view, although persons who can derive the formula can check that no errors have been made in copying it.

Incrementing Variables By a Value Other Than One

The program mortgage1, given below in preliminary form, again illustrates a situation in which a variable is to be incremented by a value different from one each time the loop is executed. The intended values of the interest rate are every quarter of a percent from the lowest interest rate specified by the user to the highest rate. Because Pascal does not permit a for-variable to be incremented by any values other than plus or minus one, some other means must be used to set and increment the value of the interest rate. The program mortgage1 uses a while-loop patterned on the program countbytwos2.

```
program mortgage1 (input, output);
{ unrefined version }
  begin
  read values for the following:
      principal = the amount borrowed,
      years = the number of years mortgage runs,
      lowest = the lowest percentage rate,
      highest = the highest percentage rate;
  print table headings;
  rate := lowest;
  while rate <= highest do
    calculate the monthly payment;
    write rate and payment;
    increase rate by 0.25;
  end.
```

In the refined version of this program, the formula for calculating the monthly payments is as recognizable as typography allows, because most of the original variable names in the formula are retained in the program. Longer variable names could be made more self-documenting, but they would make the formula longer and less readable. Often a programmer must choose between giving a long variable name that completely describes what values are assigned to a variable and a shorter name that is more convenient to use. In this case, we have chosen the short variable names of the original formula, except for the variable principal that appears in an input echo or prompt. The original formula given earlier might be appended as documentation to a copy of the program. Note that a loop is used to raise $1 + i$ to the nth power.

```
program mortgage1 (input, output);

  const
    increment = 0.25;

  var
    years, n, power : integer;
    principal, lowrate, highrate,
        rate, annualrate, i, c, payment : real;

  procedure readvalues;
    begin
    read (principal);
    writeln ('Input data  principal: ', principal :1:2);
    read (years);
    writeln ('Input data  years: ', years :1);
    n := 12 * years;
```

```
      read (lowrate);
      writeln ('Input data  lowrate: ', lowrate :1:2);
      read (highrate);
      writeln ('Input data  highrate: ', highrate :1:2);
      end; { readvalues }

   procedure printheadings;
     begin
     writeln;
     writeln ('Table of monthly payments on a ', years :1,
         '-year mortgage of $', principal :1:2);
     writeln;
     writeln ('Annual interest rate (%)' :30, 'Monthly payments' :20);
     writeln;
     end; { printheadings }

   begin
   readvalues;
   printheadings;
   rate := lowrate;
   while rate <= highrate do
     begin

     { calculate the monthly payment }
     annualrate := rate / 100;
     i := annualrate / 12;

     { calculate c := 1 + i to the nth power }
     c := 1;
     for power := 1 to n do
       c := c * (1 + i);

     payment := principal * i * c / (c - 1);
     writeln (rate :30:2, payment :20:2);
     rate := rate + increment;
     end; { while-loop }
   end.
run mortgage1
```

```
Input data  principal:  25000.00
Input data  years: 20
Input data  lowrate:  11.00
Input data  highrate:  13.00
```

```
Table of monthly payments on a 20-year mortgage of $ 25000.00
```

Annual interest rate (%)	Monthly payments
11.00	258.05
11.25	262.31
11.50	266.61
11.75	270.93

12.00	275.27
12.25	279.64
12.50	284.04
12.75	288.45
13.00	292.89

A Second Method For Stopping the Mortgage Calculations

If the loop that calculates one mortgage payment is to be terminated when the monthly payment exceeds some upper limit specified by the borrower, the while-condition may be changed to the one in the program mortgage2. In this program, the loop terminates when the monthly payment exceeds some maximum specified by the user as part of the input data. A boolean variable paymentok is used to terminate the loop when the payment gets too large. As with the program mortgage1, the loop will also terminate when the mortgage payment for the highest interest rate has been calculated, if the maximum payment has not been exceeded.

```
program mortgage2 (input, output);
{ unrefined version }
  begin
  read the values for:
      principal = the amount borrowed,
      years = the number of years mortgage runs,
      lowest = the lowest percentage rate,
      highest = the highest percentage rate,
      limit = the borrower's limit on monthly payments;
  print table headings;
  rate := lowest;
  paymentok := true;
  while (rate <= highest) and (paymentok) do
    calculate the monthly payment;
    if payment > limit then
      paymentok := false
    else
      write rate and payment;
      increase rate by 0.25;
  end.
```

Since the details of refining the mortgage2 are nearly identical to those of refining the program mortgage1, they are left as an exercise. The sample execution shows input data for which the loop is terminated because the monthly payment exceeds the maximum. The monthly payment on a 25-year mortgage of $30,000.00 at 9 percent is $251.76, which exceeds the borrower's upper limit on monthly payments of $250.00. If the borrower's limit on monthly payments were raised to $275.00, the resulting program execution (not shown) would terminate when the variable rate reached the upper limit of 10 percent because, even at 10 percent, the monthly payment on a 25-year mortgage of $30,000.00 is $272.61, which does not exceed the borrower's increased limit on monthly payments.

```
run mortgage2

Input data  principal:  30000.00
Input data  years: 25
Input data  lowrate:  8.00
Input data  highrate:  10.00
Input data  maxpayment:  250.00

Table of monthly payments on a 25-year mortgage of $ 30000.00
```

Annual interest rate (%)	Monthly payments
8.00	231.54
8.25	236.54
8.50	241.57
8.75	246.64

Self-Test Questions

1. Convert the non-Pascal generalized for-loop

    ```
    for x := 10 to 20 in steps of 0.1 do
      writeln (x)
    ```

    to a while-loop.

2. What output is printed by the following while-loop? Summarize the effect of this loop by a generalized for-loop.

    ```
    top := 100;
    bottom := 1;
    x := top;
    while x >= bottom do
      begin
      writeln (x);
      x := x - 1/3;
      end;  { while-loop }
    ```

Exercises

1. If the price of an imported cheese is $3.85 per pound, write a program to print the cost of any number of ounces of the cheese from 1 ounce to 2 pounds. There are 16 ounces in a pound.
2. If pickled herring sells for $4.17 per pound, write a program using a while-loop that prints out the price for each whole number of pounds of pickled herring that can be purchased for less than $17.00. How many people will this feed if each person eats 2 ounces of pickled herring?
3. Use the built-in function trunc, introduced in Section 2.4, to write a more efficient program for the application in Exercise 2.
4. The polynomial $x^2 - 2$ has the value 0 for some value of x between 1 and 2. Write a program to print out the values of the polynomial $x^2 - 2$ for values of x between 1 and 2 at intervals of 1/100.
5. Write a program that computes the value of the polynomial $x^2 - 2$ for values of x between 1 and 2 at intervals of 0.0001 and prints the largest of these for which the polynomial has a negative value. (This is not the most efficient way to approximate the square root of 2.)
6. Rewrite the program mortgage1 in this section using a for-loop in which the for-variable k takes on the values 1, 2, 3, ..., 25, 26 and the annual interest rate is computed as (k + 19) / 400.

7. Compare the program mortgage1 with the modifications made in it for Exercise 6 on the basis of program readability. If written properly, the printed output produced by each program is the same.

8. Actual banking practice for treating the fractions of a cent in the monthly payment is to increase any fraction of a cent, no matter how small, to the next larger penny, so that the final payment will be a few cents less than the other payments rather than a few cents more. Use the built-in function round, introduced in Section 2.4, to modify any one of the mortgage programs in this section to calculate the monthly payments in this way.

9. Write a program to list all the odd numbers starting with 3 that do not exceed the square root of 271. You may use the built-in function sqrt.

10. Write a program to test whether the number 271 is divisible by either the number 2, or by any odd number starting with 3 but less than the square root of 271. *Hint:* One integer a divides another integer b if and only if

$$b \bmod a = 0$$

where mod is the integer operator described in Section 2.4 that finds the remainder when b is divided by a. If an integer divisor of 271 is found, print it and the quotient. Otherwise, print a statement saying that no divisors have been found.

7.5 Debugging an Endless Loop

For-loops always terminate after the specified number of iterations. If they seem to run forever, it is either because the specified number of iterations is larger than expected or the computer is slower than expected.

While-loops actually can run forever, or at least until the operator pulls the plug. They can fail to terminate for a variety or reasons. This section treats the problem of debugging an endless loop.

Section Preview

An endless while-loop has a test condition that is never false.

There are two major reasons why a while-condition might never become false:

1. The loop control variables used in the while-test are never changed in the body of the loop (or all the loop control variables are constants).
2. The loop control variables change in such a way that the while-condition is never satisfied.

The cause of a nonterminating loop usually can be discovered (if rereading the program doesn't give the answer immediately) by inserting a write statement in the body of the loop to print out the loop control and other relevant variables for each iteration.

If too much output is generated before the critical iteration is reached, the debugging printout can be made selective by enclosing the write statement in an if-statement.

Some Endless Loops

Consider the following while-loop.

```
n := 2;
while n <= 10 do
    compute
```

Unless the procedure compute changes the value of the variable n, its value will always be 2 and the loop will never terminate.

A mistake is harder to see when variables are used for the starting value, stopping value, or step size in a while-loop that implements a generalized for-loop construction. The program endlessloop2 tries to find the sum of the even numbers from 0 to 10, inclusive, but it does not succeed because a programming error turns its loop into one like the preceding example. The nondescriptive variable names used in endlessloop2 help to conceal the error, showing what poor choices they are.

```
program endlessloop2 (output);
{ contains a programming error that
  creates an endless while-loop }
  const
    x = 0;
    y = 10;
    z = 2;
  var
    sum, n : integer;
  begin
  sum := 0;
  n := z;
  while n <= y do
    begin
    sum := sum + n;
    n := n + x;
    end; { while-loop }
  writeln ('The sum is ', sum :1);
  end.
run endlessloop2
```

Execution terminated-- 50000 statements executed

The exact nature of the error message varies from installation to installation, and some computer systems may even allow the program to run forever. It is essential for users of such systems to learn how to interrupt a program execution and to do so as soon as reasonable hope for normal program termination is lost.

In any event, the writeln statement in the program endlessloop2 is never executed, because the step size x by which the variable n is incremented has a value of zero and the condition in the while statement is always true. The intended correct program is obtained by exchanging the values assigned to the variables x and z. It is doubtful that this particular error could have passed unnoticed if the variable names had been the more self-explanatory names smallest, largest, and stepsize.

The Use Of Input Echoes In Debugging

Suppose one wants to find the sum of the numbers 0, 2, 4, 6, ..., 100. Since the difference between successive numbers in this sequence is constant, it is natural to use a loop to compute the sum and increment a variable by 2 each time through the loop. However, a slightly more general program can find the sum of any arithmetic progresssion, a sequence of values whose successive terms differ by a constant. The plan is simple enough—to read values for the smallest number in the sequence, the largest number in the sequence, and the constant difference, and then to compute the sum using a loop. The completed program and sample execution are given now without further ado. Remember that the columns indicator :1 causes each quantity to be printed using only as many columns as the number requires.

```
program sumofanyprog (input, output);
  var
    smallest, largest, difference,
        sum, n : integer;
  begin
  read (smallest, largest, difference);
  writeln ('Input data. smallest: ', smallest :1);
  writeln ('            largest: ', largest :1);
  writeln ('            difference: ', difference :1);
  sum := 0;
  n := smallest;
  while n <= largest do
    begin
    sum := sum + n;
    n := n + difference;
    end; { while-loop }
  writeln ('The sum of the terms of the arithmetic progression is ',
      sum :1);
  end.
run sumofanyprog


Input data   smallest: 2
             largest: 100
             difference: 0
Execution terminated.. 50000 statements executed
```

Fortunately, the computer system being used does not allow this program execution to go on forever, chewing up valuable and expensive minutes of computer time. However, no answer at all is printed, so something is amiss. The sample execution is not a complete waste for two reasons. First, meaningful names have been used for the variables of the program and, second, the echo of input data provided allows us to look at what the values of some of these variables are when they are read in from the input file. When the echoes of input data are compared to the program listing, it is not difficult to see that a value of zero for the variable difference spells trouble.

Since the input file contains only values, and not the names of the variables to which these values are to be assigned, one might guess that what has probably happened is that the three data values have been entered into the file in the wrong order. The intended values are smallest: 0, largest: 100, and difference: 2. With less descriptive variable names such as x, y, and z, as in the program endlessloop2, the error might have been harder to spot and, without an echo of the input data, the error would have been impossible to spot from the execution printout. This is one reason that inserting a programmer-supplied echo of input data is always recommended. Similarly, if this program is run interactively from a computer terminal with appropriate input prompting messages, it is less likely that the user will muddle the input data in this way.

Selective Printing For Program Verification

Since the reversal of the order of the input data fully explains the endless loop that occurred in the sample execution of the program sumofanyprog, one would hope that placing the data in the correct order is all that is necessary to ensure correct computer execution. However, the programmer, having grown somewhat more cautious, might ask this question: "Suppose the program execution now prints an answer, as there is good reason to believe it will. What reason is there to believe that the answer is correct?"

Certainly, the apparent correctness of the program listing is one bit of evidence, but more convincing proof can be obtained by selectively printing the value of some of the variables during the execution of the program. This selective printing could show, if the execution is correct, that the calculation is progressing exactly as anticipated. On the other hand, if for some reason the program execution still contains an error, the selective printing might help pinpoint the error. The program sumwithdebug is designed to provide evidence of the correctness of the program execution, or to provide information helpful in locating an error, should there be one, without printing an excessive number of lines of output.

```
program sumwithdebug (input, output);
  var
    smallest, largest, difference,
         sum, n : integer;
  begin
  read (smallest, largest, difference);
  writeln ('Input data   smallest: ', smallest :1);
  writeln ('              largest: ', largest :1);
  writeln ('              difference: ', difference :1);
  sum := 0;
  writeln ('Initial sum is ', sum :1);
  n := smallest;
  while n <= largest do
    begin
    sum := sum + n;
    { the if-statement is for debugging purposes }
    if n <= 10 then
      writeln ('n = ', n :1, ' sum = ', sum :1);
    n := n + difference;
    end; { while-loop }
  writeln ('The sum of the terms of the arithmetic progression is
      sum :1);
  end.
run sumwithdebug

Input data   smallest: 0
              largest: 100
              difference: 2
```

```
Initial sum is 0
n = 0 sum = 0
n = 2 sum = 2
n = 4 sum = 6
n = 6 sum = 12
n = 8 sum = 20
n = 10 sum = 30
```
The sum of the terms of the arithmetic progression is 2550

Not only is the answer printed, but the progress of the computation is monitored as far as n = 10. Since everything seems correct up to that point, and since the echo of input data for the stopping value seems correct, there is reason to believe that the answer is correct. Exercise 2 discusses what would happen if the reversal of the input data had not been corrected, and why the selective printing would provide ample indication of the exact nature of the original error. For the programmer who is still skeptical about whether the loop terminates correctly, another write command, selectively executed for values of n greater than 96, would provide additional confirmation of a correct execution.

Self-Test Questions

1. Which of the following debugging aids is particularly useful in debugging an endless loop?
    a. Self-explanatory variable names
    b. Clear program structure
    c. Careful rereading of the program listing
    d. A write statement in the loop printing the loop control variable(s)
    e. Hand simulation

2. If a loop is expected to repeat a large number of times before terminating, how can you still get a representative tracing of its progress? It is especially important to trace the iterations which are expected to produce the correct exit condition for the loop.

Exercises

1. Insert write commands into the program endlessloop2 that would help a programmer to determine the reason the loop does not terminate. As the program endlessloop2 now stands, the only printed output is the error message saying that the execution time limit has been exceeded.
2. Hand simulate the execution of the program sumwithdebug using the original data that caused an endless loop in the sample execution of the program sumofanyprog. Would the selective printing of values for the variables sum and n help pinpoint the exact nature of the error?
3. The following program, sumattempt, is supposed to find out when the sum of the consecutive integers 1 + 2 + 3 + · · ·, reaches 100. Debug it using the techniques in this section.

```
program sumattempt (output);
  var
    n, sum : integer;
  begin
  sum := 0;
  n : = 0;
```

```
      while not (sum = 100) do
        begin
        sum := sum + n;
        end;
      writeln ('The sum has reached 100 when n = ', n :1);
      end.

  run sumattempt

  Execution terminated-- 50000 statements executed
```

7.6   Upper Limits That Are Not Attained Exactly

When a while-loop implements a generalized for-loop with step size different
from one, there is always a chance that the values of the loop control variable
will never exactly match the upper limit in the while-test. This section
discusses how this can happen intentionally and how it can happen accidentally.

> **Section Preview**
>
> Often a loop control variable takes on a sequence of values
> intended to terminate when the variable reaches an upper limit.
> There are two major reasons why a test for equality with the
> upper limit sometimes fails.
>
> 1.   The exact upper limit might not be a value in the
>   sequence of values taken on by the loop control variable.
>   The phrase "terminated at the upper limit" should be
>   "terminated at the first value that exceeds the upper
>   limit".
> 2.   Although the sequence of values for the loop control vari-
>   able should reach the upper limit exactly using ordinary
>   noncomputer arithmetic, roundoff error, might make a
>   reasonable-looking equality test fail. An inequality test
>   for exceeding the upper limit would not fail.

Treated as a collection of English phrases, the unrefined loop control
heading

```
      for n := start to finish  in steps of stepsize { not Pascal }
```

carries with it an implication that, after a sufficient number of steps, the variable n will finally take on the value finish for the last iteration of the loop.
However, there are two important reasons why this does not always happen for
the standard while-loop refinement of this construct.

```
      n := start;
      while n <= finish do
        begin ...; n := n + stepsize end;
```

1.   Because of minor differences between computer arithmetic and ordinary
     arithmetic, the values actually computed for the variable n can sometimes
     differ from the intended values by just enough to prevent equality
     between the final value of n and the value of finish. For example, since
     $1/3 + 1/3 + 1/3 = 1$, but $0.3333333 + 0.3333333 + 0.3333333 = 0.9999999$, a loop controlled by the statements

```
{ while-loop refinement of
  for n := 1/3 to 1 in steps of 1/3 }
n := 1/3;
while n <= 1 do
  begin ...; n := n + 1/3; end;
```

is unlikely to produce a final value for n of exactly one in actual computer execution.

2.   In some programs, the programmer never intends the upper limit to be reached exactly. Consider trying to print all multiples of 13 that are less than or equal to 500. The criterion for stopping is simple: when the loop control variable exceeds 500. It might not be obvious what the last multiple of 13 should be. However, as shown in the program multiples, it is not necessary to know the final value in advance.

```
program multiples (output);
  const
    limit = 500;
    factor = 13;
  var
    multiple : integer;
  begin
  multiple := factor;
  while multiple <= limit do
    begin
    writeln (multiple :4);
    multiple := multiple + factor;
    end; { loop }
  end.
```

run multiples

```
    13
    26
    39

     .
     .
     .

   481
   494
```

For debugging purposes, the abbreviated execution printout shown above could be generated by changing the unconditional writeln statement to the following if-statement:

```
if (multiple <= 40) or (multiple >= 480) then
  writeln (multiple :4);
```

Self-Test Questions

1.   Why should while-tests sometimes not use the equality comparison?
2.   When is it safe to use an equality test at the upper limit?

Exercises

1.   Write a program to find the closest multiple of 17 to 100,000.
2.   Write a program to print the multiples of 1/6 from 1/6 to 20. Print as many decimal places as your computer will permit. Are any of the values that should be integers miscalculated?

7.7 Enumerated Data Types in Loops

Pascal is rich in data types. In Pascal, you don't have to encode the days of the week with integers from 1 to 7 nor the positions in a baseball team with integers from 1 to 9. Pascal allows the programmer to define new data types by enumerating the possible values a variable of that type can have. These new enumerated data types may be used in most ways that ordered intrinsic data types can.

Section Preview

Enumerated Data Types:

General form:
```
type
    typename = (elementname, elementname, ..., elementname);
var
    variablename : typename;
```

Example:
```
type
  primarycolor = (red, green, blue);
var
  flash, color : primarycolor;
  tvsignal : array [red..blue] of real;
```

Subscripts and For-Loops may use enumerated data types.

Example:
```
for color := red to blue do
  write (tvsignal [color]);
```

Enumerated Data Types

It is possible for the programmer to define a completely new data type by enumerating all the names of constants for the type. In Pascal, these new types are called **enumerated data types**.

The type declaration
```
type
    day = (sun, mon, tue, wed, thu, fri, sat);
```
declares a new, programmer-defined enumerated data type whose possible values are the constants sun, mon, tue, wed, thu, fri, and sat. Any variable declared to be type day, for example,
```
var
    today : day;
```
can be assigned a value consisting of one of these constants. However, a variable that has an enumerated data type cannot be read or written.

The values of an enumerated data type are considered to be ordered by their appearance in the type declaration. Thus, for our enumerated type called day,

sun < sat

thu > = tue

are both true expressions.

It doesn't make any sense to apply arithmetic operators such as + and mod to enumerated data type values, but there are three built-in functions whose **argument** may be an enumerated data type. The built-in function **ord** (ordinal position) applies to values in an enumerated data type. Its value is the ordinal position in the enumeration, beginning with zero. In our example,

    ord (sun) = 0
    ord (mon) = 1
                .
                .
                .
    ord (sat) = 6

The function ord may also be used with an argument of type char or boolean. For a boolean argument,

    ord (false) = 0
    ord (true) = 1

For an enumerated data type, the built-in function **succ** (successor) gives the next value in the enumeration of values in the type declaration. This function is not defined for the last value. In our example,

    succ (sun) = mon
    succ (mon) = tue
                .
                .
                .
    succ (fri) = sat

and succ (sat) is not defined.

The built-in function **pred** (predecessor) gives the value preceding its argument. It is not defined for the first value of an enumerated data type. Thus pred (sun) is not defined, but

    pred (mon) = sun
    pred (tue) = mon
                .
                .
                .
    pred (sat) = fri

Some relationships that hold between the functions ord, pred, and succ are

    pred (succ (x)) = x, unless x is largest
    succ (pred (x)) = x, unless x is smallest
    ord (x) + 1 = ord (succ (x)), unless x is largest
    ord (x) − 1 = ord (pred (x)), unless x is smallest
    x < y if and only if ord (x) < ord (y)

It is possible to have a subrange of an enumerated data type. For example,

```
type
   workday = mon..fri;
```

declares workday to be an enumerated data type that is a subrange of the type day. Variables declared to be type workday could then assume only the values mon, tue, wed, thu, and fri.

Subscripts and For-Loops

Enumerated data types and subranges of enumerated data types may be used as subscripts. For example,

```
var
   temperature : array [day] of real;
   dowjones : array [workday] of real;
```

could be used to declare an array temperature to record a temperature for each day of the week and to declare an array dowjones to record the Dow Jones stock market indicator for each work day of the week. With this declaration, dowjones [fri] would be the week's closing average.

A for-variable may be an enumerated data type. For example, if d is a variable declared to be type day or workday, then

```
for d := mon to fri do
   write (dowjones [d]);
```

writes the Dow Jones average for each day of the work week.

Self-Test Questions

1.   How do you declare a programmer-defined enumerated data type with possible values tic, tac, and toe?
2.   For the enumerated data type day declared in this section, what is

     a.   ord (wed)
     b.   pred (thu)
     c.   succ (sat)

3.   Using the declarations in this section what does the for-loop

```
for d := wed to sat do
   write (temperature [d])
```

     direct the computer to do?

Exercises

1.   Write a program using the enumerated data type day in this section to read daily high and low temperatures for a week and to print the high and low temperatures only for the workdays mon..fri.

7.8   What You Should Know

1.   Sometimes there is more than one criterion for determining when to terminate a loop.
2.   The boolean operators "and", "or", and "not" are used to write compound exit conditions.
3.   A model of a situation is something that exhibits the same characteristics as the original on a much smaller and more manageable scale. Sometimes the model is physical; sometimes it is mathematical.
4.   The popular board games, including chess, Monopoly, and psychological role-playing games, like Dungeons and Dragons, are simulations of modelled situations.
5.   In a mathematical model, the values of the important quantities in the situation are measured and the laws determining how they change are modelled by equations or algorithms.

6. All model building involves a compromise between a desire to retain as many characteristics as possible and a desire to simplify the model so it can be solved or examined more conveniently.

7. Garbage in, garbage out: if the input data to a model is in error or the model does not accurately capture the essential features, the answers will be worthless.

8. In a deterministic simulation, the mathematical rules describing how the values of important quantities change are used to predict future values for these quantities.

9. Experiments can be performed on a model that could not easily be performed in the real situation.

10. In interactive dialogue, the computer responds to what the user types and the user responds to what the computer writes.

11. A computer is very good at posing routine drill questions and evaluating the answers. This is one small aspect of computer-assisted instruction.

12. Giving a child three chances to answer a problem correctly is an example of a loop with compound exit conditions. The two exits occur when the child gives a correct answer or when the allotted number of tries is used up.

13. In case the student cannot guess the right answer, the loop exit after a maximum number of tries prevents an infinite loop.

14. Although a computer algorithm cannot generate truly random numbers, it can generate apparently unpredictable numbers, good enough for most purposes.

15. A loop contains four major parts: initialization, repetition vs. exit test, loop body, and modification of loop control in the loop body.

16. Initialization precedes the loop and may be absent in special circumstances.

17. In a while-loop, the exit test is at the top of the loop.

18. In a repeat-until-loop, the exit test is at the bottom of the loop.

19. In a for-loop, the initialization, the exit test, and the modification of the loop control variable are combined in the loop heading.

20. A while- or a repeat-until-loop must be used if the number of iterations is not known in advance.

21. A for-loop is the natural loop construct to use if a sequence of consecutive integers is involved and if the number of iterations is known before the loop is entered.

22. To prevent an infinite while- or repeat-until-loop, there must be a way to change one or more of the loop control variables in the body of the loop.

23. Adding a fixed quantity to a loop control variable is called incrementation and the amount added is the increment.

24. The built-in function eof may be used to recognize the end of the input data.

25. The built-in function eoln may be used to recognize the end of lines of input data.

26. Other languages have generalizations of the for-loop that are more powerful than Pascal's. When such a generalized for-loop comes up naturally in the program solution, it should be used in the early refinements of the program and changed to a while- or repeat-until-loop later.

27. For-loops always terminate after the specified number of iterations. If they seem to run forever, it is either because the specified number of iterations is larger than expected or the computer is slower than expected.

28. While- and repeat-until loops have greater potential for infinite looping. Writing values of the control variables in the body of the loop is useful for debugging infinite loops.

29. Echoes of input data verify that the input file has been prepared and read properly.
30. A programmer can define a new data type by enumerating its elements.
31. Enumerated data types can be used as subscripts and for-loop variables.
32. For the purposes of the six comparison operators, one element of an enumerated data type is "less than" another if it precedes it in the enumeration.
33. The values of the built-in functions ord, pred, and succ are determined by the enumerated order.

PROCEDURES AND FUNCTIONS WITH PARAMETERS 8

In previous chapters, calling programs have communicated with a procedure by means of global variables known by the same name in both the calling program and the procedure. This method is easy to learn and permits the modularization of programs at an early stage. However, it has enough drawbacks that experienced programmers rarely pass information to their procedures through global variables except in special circumstances.

The twin themes of this chapter are

1. Parameters provide a flexible and reliable channel for passing information to and from a procedure.
2. Localization of variables provides increased independence of procedures and calling programs from each other.

When a large program is written using a common global environment for all procedures, close coordination is required between the programmers writing each procedure. Each procedure has a specific and well-defined task to perform. However, in a global environment, each procedure has access to all of the variables in every other procedure. It is easy to make unintentional changes in the values of these other variables. Such programs are more fragile than modularized programs.

For example, a common, self-explanatory variable name like "count" might be used to retain a count of how many data items were read in one procedure. If another procedure accidentally used "count" as a loop control variable, the original value of count would probably be be lost. **Side effects** are peripheral effects of one on another procedure, effects unrelated to the well-defined task of the offending procedure. They are usually unintentional and make debugging very difficult, When a variable shows an unexpected change, the cause can be *anywhere* in the program.

Experienced programmers make almost all variables used in a procedure **local** to that procedure. Then, even if a variable in another procedure or in a calling program happens to have the same name as a local variable, Pascal considers the two to be different. Changes in a local variable cannot *ever* cause side effects in another procedure.

Pascal has two **argument passing** conventions. In one convention, information is passed from the supplied argument to the corresponding dummy argument, but no information may be returned from that dummy argument. In the other argument-passing convention, information may flow in both directions.

A function is a construction closely resembling a procedure. When the purpose of a programming process is to obtain a single value, that process may be written as a function rather than as a procedure. Generating a random number is an example of such a process. Arguments may be passed to functions as well as to procedures.

8.1   Argument Passing

There are two aspects of modularization: isolation and communication. The modularization isolates the procedures from each other. The programmer can then control how much information is to be exchanged between modules. Communication channels are established with **parameter lists**. A one-to-one correspondence is set up between **actual parameters** in the calling procedure and **dummy parameters** in the subordinate procedure. The corresponding parameters need not have the same name, and the correspondence is temporary, lasting only for the duration of the procedure call. Parameters also are called arguments and actual parameters are called **supplied arguments**.

   This section describes how to write and use procedures with explicit arguments. It introduces extremely useful procedures named swap and readlist that reappear several times in this book. The section also contains a discussion of localization of procedure variables, which is a technique for guaranteeing that a procedure does not create undesirable side effects by accidentally reusing a variable name already used in the calling program.

Section Preview

Dummy Argument List:

   In a procedure declaration, the procedure name may be followed by a list of dummy parameters, also called dummy arguments.

Supplied Argument List:

   In a procedure call, the procedure name is followed by a list of supplied arguments, also called actual parameters. Each supplied argument is associated with the corresponding dummy argument for the duration of the procedure call.

Value Arguments:

   A dummy argument not preceded by the keyword "var" can only receive an initial value from the corresponding supplied argument. A change in the value of such a dummy argument during execution of the procedure does not cause a change in the corresponding supplied argument (actual parameter), even if the corresponding supplied argument is a variable.

Reference Arguments:

   A dummy argument preceded by the keyword "var" is a parameter called by reference. Any reference to the dummy argument in the procedure causes the computer to behave as if the reference were to the corresponding supplied argument, which must be a variable. Statements in the procedure causing changes to such a dummy argument cause the same changes to the corresponding supplied argument.

Local Variables:

Constants, types, variables, and even other procedures may be declared in a procedure. These constants, types, variables, and "internal procedures" are *local* to the procedure in which they are declared; that is, they are known within the procedure in which they are declared and all its subprocedures, but they are distinct from any constant, type, variable, or procedure of the same name declared in an enclosing main program or in a procedure external to the one in which they are declared.

Compatibility of Supplied Arguments and Dummy Arguments:

Dummy arguments must have simple (i.e, one-word) types. Supplied arguments must have types which can be assigned to the corresponding dummy argument types. If a supplied argument is a call-by-reference argument (i.e., "var"), its corresponding supplied argument must be a variable of exactly the same simple type.

Example:

```
program powers (output);

   var
      s, c, fourth, sixth, ninth : integer;
      inverse : real;  { main program variable }

   procedure squarecube (n : integer;
                            var square, cube : integer);
      var
         inverse : real;  { local variable }

      begin
      square := n * n;
      inverse := 1 / n;  { assigns to local variable }
      cube := round (square * square * inverse);
      end;  { procedure squarecube }

   begin  { main program }
   squarecube (2, s, c);
   squarecube (c, sixth, ninth);
   inverse := 1 / sixth;  { assigns to main progr variable }
   squarecube (s, fourth, sixth);
   writeln (sixth * inverse, ' should be 1');
   end.  { program squarecube }
```

Swapping the Values of Two Variables

The purpose of the procedure swapintegers presented here is to exchange two integer values, a fairly common programming operation. Although the program swapintegers contains only three executable statements, there is a good deal of merit in keeping these three lines from continually cluttering up the many programs that need this common operation.

```
procedure swapintegers (var a, b : integer);
  begin
  temporary := a;
  a := b;
  b := temporary;
  end;  { swapintegers }
```

Dummy Arguments

The listing for the procedure swapintegers looks like the listings of procedures
in previous chapters, except for one thing. In the title line, the procedure
name swapintegers is followed by a list

```
(var   a, b :  integer)
```

of variable declarations enclosed in parentheses. The variables a and b in that
list are the **dummy arguments** of the procedure swapintegers.

Three ways to pose a proper subtraction problem to a child were presented
in Section 7.2. The procedure swapintegers facilitates the design of a fourth
method: if the second random number generated for the subtraction problem is
larger than the first, then they are swapped.

```
program propersubtraction (input, output);

  var
    x, y, answer : integer;
    seed : integer;
    temporary : integer;

  function randominteger (r, s : integer) : integer;
  { generates an integer in the interval [r..s] }
  { uses and changes the global variable seed }
    const
      maxseed = 10000;
      multiplier = 201;
      adder = 3437;

    begin
    seed := (multiplier * seed + adder) mod maxseed;
    randominteger := r + seed * (s − r + 1) div maxseed;
    end; { randominteger }

  procedure swapintegers (var a, b : integer);
    begin
    temporary := a;
    a := b;
    b := temporary;
    end; { swapintegers }

  begin
  seed := 1;
  x := randominteger (0, 9);
  y := randominteger (0, 9);
  if y > x then
    swapintegers (x, y);
  writeln ('Please tell me, how much is ',
      x :1, ' minus ', y :1);
  writeln ('Input data  answer: ');
```

```
      readln (answer);
      if answer = x − y then
        writeln ('Correct.   Very good.')
      else
        writeln ('Incorrect.   The answer is ', x − y :1);
      end.
   run propersubtraction

   Please tell me, how much is 4 minus 3
   Input data  answer: 1
   Correct.   Very good.
```

```
program propersubtraction (input, output);
   .
   .
   .
   begin

   seed := 1;

   x := randominteger (0, 9);
   y := randominteger (0, 9);
   if y > x then
     swapintegers (x, y);
   writeln ('Please tell me, how much is ',
     x :1, 'minus ', y :1);
   writeln ('Input data answer: ');
   readln (answer);
   if answer = x − y then
     writeln ('Correct. Very good.')
   else
     writeln ('Incorrect. The answer is ', x − y :1);
   end.
```

```
procedure swapintegers
           x  y
   (var a, b : integer);
   begin
                       x
   temporary := a;

           x  y
   a := b;

           y
   b := temporary;
   end; {swapintegers}
```

Figure 8.1 Supplying arguments to a procedure.

Suppose that in executing the first two statements of the program proper-subtraction, the computer assigns to the variable x the randomly generated integer 3 and assigns to the variable y the randomly generated integer 4.

Since 4, the value of y, is greater than 3, the value of x, the computer executes the then-clause

```
swapintegers (x, y)
```

During execution of the procedure swapintegers, it is as if every occurrence of the dummy argument a in swapintegers were replaced by the variable x, and every occurrence of the dummy argument b in swapintegers were replaced by the variable y. Figure 8.1 shows this replacement. In executing the statement

```
temporary := a
```

of the procedure swapintegers, the computer assigns to the variable temporary the value 3 of the variable x in the program propersubtraction, just as if the statement were written

```
temporary := x
```

In executing the statement

```
a := b
```

of the procedure swapintegers, the computer assigns to the variable x the value 4 of the variable y, as though the statement were written

```
x := y
```

Finally, the value 3 that is saved as the value of the variable temporary is assigned to the variable y by the statement

```
b := temporary
```

as though it were written

```
y := temporary
```

Supplied Arguments

The variables x and y in the statement

```
swapintegers (x, y)
```

are the **supplied arguments** of the procedure call. There is no need for the supplied arguments to have the same names as the dummy arguments. Whatever the names of the dummy arguments, during the execution of the procedure, it is always as if the names of the supplied arguments were copied in place of the dummy arguments. This is why the supplied arguments are declared in the calling program to have the *same types* as declared for the dummy arguments in the procedure heading.

Local Variables

It would not matter if a calling program happened to use variables whose names coincided with those of the dummy arguments a and b of swapintegers. When swapintegers is called, it is executed as if the supplied arguments were written in place of the dummy arguments. This leaves leave no opportunity for the execution of swapintegers to affect calling program variables named a or b, unless those variables are supplied arguments.

On the other hand, execution of swapintegers could change the value of a variable named temporary in the calling program, because the procedure swapintegers also has a variable named temporary. If a programmer desires to have a procedure affect nothing in the calling program except the supplied arguments, the variables of the procedure are **localized**. The following version of the procedure swapintegers, which is used in place of the previous version in all future applications, localizes the variable temporary.

```
procedure swapintegers (var a, b : integer);
  var
    temporary : integer;
  begin
  temporary := a;
  a := b;
  b := temporary;
  end; { swapintegers }
```

The declaration in this version of the procedure swapintegers

```
var
  temporary : integer;
```

tells the computer that whenever the variable temporary appears in the procedure, it is to be regarded as a private variable for that procedure, and not as a variable in the calling program that happens to have the same name. In general, it is a good programming practice to declare procedure variables locally within the procedure, unless there is a compelling reason to do otherwise.

The declaration section of a procedure may contain all of the kinds of declarations that can occur in a program. Thus a procedure may contain declarations of constants and types as well as declarations of variables. Indeed, since a procedure is a declaration, procedures may contain declarations of other procedures. All constants, types, variables, and procedures that are declared within a procedure are local to that procedure.

The program local illustrates how some of these concepts work. Note that two variable or constant names in different procedures may not only have different values, but may have different data types as well. In the program local, the variable temporary is a character, but it is type integer in the procedure swapintegers. A name could represent a simple variable in the main program and an array in a procedure called by the program. Note also that although the dummy arguments a and b of the procedure swapintegers have the same names as constants in the calling program local, the values of the constants a and b in the main program are unaffected by execution of the procedure swapintegers.

```
program local (output);

    const
      a = 1; b = 2;

    var
      c, d : integer;
      temporary : char;

    procedure swapintegers (var a, b : integer);
      var
        temporary : integer;
      begin
      temporary := a;
      a := b;
      b := temporary;
      end; { swapintegers }

    begin
    temporary := 'x';
    c := 3; d := 4;
    swapintegers (c, d);
    writeln (temporary :2, a :2, b :2, c :2, d :2);
    end.
run local

    x 1 2 4 3
```

Compatibility of Supplied Arguments With Dummy Arguments

For a procedure call to be correct, the calling program must supply the same number of arguments specified in the procedure heading. Because the supplied argument must be assignable to the dummy argument, the data type of each supplied argument and its corresponding dummy argument must agree. For example, if the dummy argument is type char, then the supplied argument could be type char or a subrange of type char. One consequence of this rule is that a different procedure must be written to swap two real values, since swapintegers swaps two integer values. The procedure swapreals is the same as swapintegers except that all variables in swapreals are declared to be type real.

```
procedure swapreals (var a, b : real);
  var
    temporary : real;
  begin
  temporary := a;
  a := b;
  b := temporary;
  end; { swapreals }
```

To avoid writing a different procedure to swap two characters, and additional procedures to swap two strings of length 7 or two 4 × 5 arrays of real values, it is possible to use a programmer-defined data type to write a procedure that will swap two quantities of any type. The procedure swap illustrates how this is done.

```
procedure swap (var a, b : datatype);
  var
    temporary : datatype;
  begin
  temporary := a;
  a := b;
  b := temporary;
  end; { swap }
```

A program that uses the procedure swap must contain a declaration of the type datatype, and the values to be swapped must be declared to be of that type. For example, if the procedure swap is to be used to swap integer values, then the program calling swap must contain the type declaration

```
type
  datatype = integer;
```

Scope of a Declaration

Every constant, type, variable, or procedure used in a Pascal program must be declared in at least one procedure or program that encloses the references to it.

The **scope** of a declaration is the set of lines in the program listing to which that declaration applies. Any declaration made at the head of a procedure or program, including constant, type, variable, and procedure declarations, applies to all parts of the procedure or program in which it is declared. In particular, a variable declaration applies in the procedure in which it is declared and in all procedures declared within that enclosing procedure. If a name is used within the scope of two declaratives, the innermost declaration applies. The variable temporary in the program local, earlier in this section, is declared both in the main program and in the procedure swapintegers. Its use within the procedure swapintegers refers to the local integer variable temporary, and its use in the main program refers to a character variable.

Scope rules for declarations allow selective sharing of constants, variables, types, and procedures between associated procedures. However, not all consequences of the scope rules are beneficial. If it is necessary to swap quantities of two different data types within the same program, then two different swapping procedures must be used. At any line of the program listing, only one declaration for the type datatype will be in force.

An Array as an Argument

There is no restriction that an argument of a procedure must be a simple variable. Lists and tables are permitted. The purpose of the procedure readlist is to partially fill an array from data given as input. The procedure readlist reads data, adding each item to the array until stopped by a termination signal. The procedure is similar to the procedure readline to read a character string of varying length in Section 7.2. Dummy arguments and general type names (declared in the calling program) are used to make this procedure as general as possible, and local variables are used to prevent any possible side effects on the calling program or any other procedure.

```
procedure readlist (var list : listtype;
                    maxlistsize : listsizetype;
                    signal : listdatatype;
                    var numberofelements : listsizetype);

var
  datum : listdatatype;
  i : listsizetype;
  moredata : boolean;

begin
moredata := true;
i := 0;
while (i < maxlistsize) and (moredata) do
  begin
  read (datum);
  writeln ('Input data  datum: ', datum);
  if datum = signal then
    moredata := false
  else
    begin
    i := i + 1;
    list [i] := datum;
    end; { else }
  end; { while-loop }
if moredata then
  numberofelements := maxlistsize
else
  numberofelements := i;
end; { readlist }
```

Declaring the variable i to be local is important. If the localization of the variable i were omitted, and if the calling program also contained a variable named i, then executing the procedure readlist would affect the value of the variable i in the calling program. The programmer-defined data types listtype, listsizetype, and listdatatype are used in the procedure readlist to allow the calling program to decide what type of data is to be stored in the list and what subscript bounds will apply to the array list.

Testing a Procedure

In order to test the procedure readlist, it is necessary to have a calling program supply arguments for list, maxlistsize, signal, and numberofelements. The program testreadlist is written expressly to test the procedure readlist.

```
program testreadlist (input, output);

const
  maxlistsize = 9;
  signal = -1;

type
  listdatatype = integer;
  listtype = array [1..maxlistsize] of listdatatype;
  listsizetype = 0..maxlistsize;

var
  i : 1..maxlistsize;
  actuallistsize : listsizetype;
  evennumbers : listtype;

procedure readlist (var list : listtype;
                        maxlistsize : listsizetype;
                        signal : listdatatype;
                        var numberofelements : listsizetype);
  ... end; { readlist }

begin
readlist (evennumbers, maxlistsize, signal, actuallistsize);
for i := 1 to actuallistsize do
  write (evennumbers [i]);
writeln;
end.
run testreadlist

Input data  datum:         2
Input data  datum:         4
Input data  datum:         6
Input data  datum:        -1
            2          4          6
```

Since the execution printout shows that the complete list has been
accepted without the termination signal, it is reasonable to suppose that the
procedure readlist works correctly. A cautious programmer might design a few
additional tests.

Declaration of Dummy Arguments

In declaring a dummy argument of a procedure in the procedure heading, it is
necessary to make two choices. One is the type of the dummy argument, and
the other is whether to precede the declaration with the keyword var.

In a procedure heading, the declared type of a dummy argument must be
a *one-word* type name. This means that arrays, subrange types, and other composite types must be replaced by programmer-defined types. So far in this
book, declaring programmer-defined types has been recommended from a
stylistic point of view. In a procedure heading, these types are not only stylisti-
cally desirable, they are unavoidable.

If a variable is not declared var, a one-way communication channel is
established. The value of the supplied argument becomes the inital value of
the dummy argument, but any changes in the value of the dummy argument do
not affect the value of the supplied argument.

When a dummy argument is declared var, a two-way communication channel is established. All changes in the value of the dummy variable are reflected in the value of the supplied argument.

The types of the supplied and dummy arguments must be identical or closely related. Specifically, the values of the supplied argument must be assignable to variables of the dummy argument type.

Dummy arguments whose values are not changed during the execution of the procedure should be declared as constant by omitting the keyword var in the procedure heading. Constants and expressions of all kinds (including a single variable) may be supplied arguments for constant dummy arguments. The types of the supplied arguments must be such that their values can be assigned to the corresponding dummy arguments. A dummy argument is declared as var (variable) if the procedure contains a means of changing its value by reading, assignment, or another procedure call. The supplied argument also must be a variable or array element and must be declared to be the same type. Neither constants nor expressions more complicated than a single variable name may be supplied arguments for dummy arguments declared as var.

Var arguments are also called reference parameters and non-var arguments are called value parameters. Value parameters are local to the procedure in which they are declared, but reference parameters merely point back to their supplied arguments (the actual parameters). A procedure is permitted a value parameter, but corresponding actual parameters are not affected by the change. This practice, while permitted, is confusing and is not recommended. Sometimes array arguments that are not going to be changed are declared as var to avoid copying them to the dummy parameters.

Constants as Supplied Arguments

Constants may be supplied to a procedure as arguments if the program that results from simultaneously replacing every occurrence of each dummy argument in the procedure by its corresponding supplied argument must be executable. For example, the single statement

    readlist (numbers, arraysize, -1, numberofnumbers)

could do the same job for the program readlist as the two statements

    signal := -1;
    readlist (numbers, arraysize, signal, numberofnumbers);

In addition, signal could be the name of a constant, as in testreadlist, as well as a variable.

On the other hand, the procedure call

    swapintegers (2, 3)

is a mistake, because replacement of the dummy arguments a and b of the procedure swapintegers by the supplied arguments 2 and 3 changes the perfectly reasonable statements

    temporary := a;
    a := b;
    b := temporary

into the statements

    temporary := 2;
    2 := 3;
    3 := temporary

The first of these three resulting statements makes sense, but the other two are nonsense. Constants should not be supplied arguments for var dummy arguments for this reason. Similarly, expressions should not be supplied for var arguments.

Self-Test Questions

1.   True/false:

a. A dummy argument must have the same name as its supplied argument.

b. A supplied argument must have the same type as its dummy argument.

c. A constant may be used as a supplied argument.

d. When you write a Pascal procedure, you do not have to declare a variable that has the same name as one in the main program.

2.   Why are local variables used?

3.   When are dummy arguments called by reference, and when are they called by value?

Exercises

1.   Modify the procedures written for the gradepoint average program in Sections 6.2−6.4 to use parameter lists and local variables.

2.   Inserting an item at location k of list of length n means increasing the list length to n + 1, moving the values in locations k, k + 1, k + 2, ..., n to locations k + 1, k + 2, k + 3, ..., n + 1, respectively, and storing the value of the new item at location k. Write a program that accepts as input a list of integers, a location in the list where a value is to be inserted, and a value to be inserted at that location; it then should insert the value at the prescribed location and print out the new list. Does it help to use the procedure swap?

3.   Write a procedure

```
insert (var list : listtype;
        location : listindextype;
        newitem : listdatatype;
        var numberofelements : listsizetype);
```

that inserts a new item in a list at a specified location as described in Exercise 2.

4.   The purpose of the program largestof4 is to determine the maximum of four numbers supplied as input. Hand simulate its executions for the following cases:

a. The variable temporary of the procedure swap is local.

b. The variable temporary is global.

Enter as input the numbers 23, 7, 3, and 14.

```
program largestof4 (input, output);
{ designed to illustrate the need for local variables }
{ not the best way to find the largest of four numbers }

   type
     datatype = integer;

   var
     n1, n2, n3, n4, temporary, largest : datatype;

   procedure swap (var a, b : datatype);
      ... end; { swap }
```

```
begin
read (n1, n2, n3, n4);
writeln ('Input data  n1: ', n1);
writeln ('              n2: ', n2);
writeln ('              n3: ', n3);
writeln ('              n4: ', n4);
{ set temporary = larger of n1 and n2 }
if n1 >= n2 then
  temporary := n1
else
  temporary := n2;
{ make sure that n3 is not less than n4 }
if n3 < n4 then
  swap (n3, n4);
{ now pick the larger of temporary and n3 }
if n3 > temporary then
  largest := n3
else
  largest := temporary;
writeln (largest :1, ' is the largest.');
end.
```

5. A simple rotation of a list of length n is obtained by transferring the values at locations 1, 2, ..., n − 1 into locations 2, 3, ..., n, respectively, and transferring the value at location n into location 1. This is something like a kindergarten snack line operated so that the child who is at the end of the line on one day moves to the front of the line the next day, causing everyone else to move back by one position. Write a procedure that performs the simple rotation of a list supplied as argument.

6. A *random transposition* in a list of length n is obtained by generating two random integers i and j from 1 to n and exchanging the value of the list item at location i with the value of the list item at location j. Write a procedure that shuffles a list of n numbers by performing n random transpositions.

7. A permutation of a list of distinct values is called a *derangement* if no value ends up in the same location it started in. A list of 10 distinct items is to be shuffled by the method in Exercise 6. Write a program that shuffles the list

    1 2 3 4 5 6 7 8 9 10

100 times and counts the number of such shufflings that result in derangements.

8. Write a program that performs random transpositions (Exercise 6) on a list of numbers until it is deranged (Exercise 7) and counts the number of random transpositions required.

9. Suppose that the value of the integer variable i is 1, that the value of a [1] is 2, and that the value of a [2] is 3. The array a is also type integer. What are the values of these variables after execution of the following statement? Test your answer on a computer, if possible.

    swapintegers (i, a [i])

10. Write a procedure

```
drop (var list : listtype;
      n, maxlistsize : listsizetype;
      var numberofelements : listsizetype);
```

that drops the first n elements from a list of the specified size containing the designated number of elements.

8.2   A Debugging Trace

In this section, we show a program with a bug of a slightly more subtle kind than previously encountered. The echoes of input data show that the input was read successfully, but the printout of the answer shows the program failed to work properly. The error lies somewhere in between. We find the bug by inserting debugging printouts, **snapshots**, making the computer trace the progress of the execution.

> **Section Preview**
>
> **Snapshot:**
>
> > A snapshot is a printout (or other record) of the values of one or more variables at one instant during the execution of a program.
>
> **Execution Trace:**
>
> > Tracing a program execution means having the computer keep a record of the progress of the execution by printing snapshots of the values of important variables whenever selected steps of the program are reached.
>
> **Snapshot procedure:**
>
> > When a sufficient number of variables are sampled in a snapshot or greater care is taken to ensure readability of the output of a snapshot, the statements to produce the snapshot often are written as a separate procedure.

Swapping Items in a List

Either or both of the arguments supplied to any of the swapping procedures may be individual array elements, because replacing occurrences of the dummy arguments by such subscripted entries makes perfectly good sense. That is, the replacement results in program steps the computer can execute. For instance, the program tryreversal supplies two arguments with subscripts to the procedure swapintegers. The purpose of the program tryreversal is to read a list of numbers and then to reverse the list and print the result. The printout shows that tryreversal does not succeed. Try to diagnose the error yourself before reading the explanation.

```
program tryreversal (input, output);
{ Read a list, reverse it, and print the result. }
{ Why does this program seem to accomplish nothing? }
{ Try to determine the programming error. }

  const
    maxlistsize = 9;
    maxdata = 9999;
    signal = -maxdata;

  type
    listdatatype = -maxdata..maxdata;
    listtype = array [1..maxlistsize] of listdatatype;
    listsizetype = 0..maxlistsize;
    datatype = listdatatype; { for swap }
```

```
    var
      i : 1.. maxlistsize;
      numberofv : listsizetype;
      v : listtype;

procedure readlist (var list : listtype;
                        maxlistsize : listsizetype;
                        signal : listdatatype;
                        var numberofelements : listsizetype);

    var
      datum : listdatatype;
      i : listsizetype;
      moredata : boolean;

  begin
  moredata := true;
  i := 0;
  while (i < maxlistsize) and (moredata) do
    begin
    read (datum);
    writeln ('Input data  datum: ', datum);
    if datum = signal then
      moredata := false
    else
      begin
      i := i + 1;
      list [i] := datum;
      end; { else }
    end; { while-loop }
  if moredata then
    numberofelements := maxlistsize
  else
    numberofelements := i;
  end; { readlist }

  procedure swap (var a, b : datatype);
    var
      temporary : datatype;
    begin
    temporary := a;
    a := b;
    b := temporary;
    end; { swap }

  begin
  readlist (v, maxlistsize, signal, numberofv);
  writeln ('Original list: ');
  for i := 1 to numberofv do
    write (v [i] :5);
  writeln;
  for i := 1 to numberofv do
    swap (v [i], v [numberofv - i + 1]);
```

```
writeln ('Reversed list: ');
for i := 1 to numberofv do
  write (v [i] :5);
writeln;
end.
```

run tryreversal

```
Input data   datum:              2
Input data   datum:              3
Input data   datum:              5
Input data   datum:              7
Input data   datum:             11
Input data   datum:             13
Input data   datum:          −9999
Original list:
   2    3    5    7   11   13
Reversed list:
   2    3    5    7   11   13
```

It is evident from the execution printout of tryreversal that something is the matter, because the list has not been reversed. In proofreading the program for possible errors, what might stand out as most suspicious is the subscript numberofv − i + 1 in the statement that calls the procedure swap.

Since the procedure readlist discards the termination signal, the number of elements in the list v in the sample execution is 6. (Like any other list read by the procedure readlist, the list v has the number 1 for its lower bound.) It follows that when the for-variable i has the value 1, the expression numberofv − i + 1 has the value 6. Thus the first time the procedure swap is called, it is asked to exchange the arguments v [1] and v [6], exactly what is supposed to happen. When the number 2 is the value of the for-variable i, the value of the expression numberofv − i + 1 is 5. Hence, the second time swap is called, it is asked to exchange the values of v [2] and v [5], again the exchange wanted.

Careful scrutiny of the suspicious looking expression has produced nothing but evidence of its correctness. The supposedly reversed list is still in the original order. Is it possible that the for-loop is never executed? To investigate, we resort to **tracing**, another standard tool in a programmer's debugging repertoire, generally employed when hand simulation does not locate the mistake easily.

A Debugging Trace

Inserting a **debugging trace** into a program makes the computer print the successive values of critical variables as those values occur during a program execution. To monitor the execution of the for-loop, we insert a writeln statement immediately after the procedure call, obtaining the following modified loop.

```
for i := 1 to numberofv do
  begin
  swap (v [i], v [numberofv − i + 1]);
  writeln (v [1] :5, v [2] :5, v [3] :5,
      v [4] :5, v [5] :5, v [6] :5, '   i = ', i :1);
  end; { for i }
```

After changing the program name to trywithdebug, it is rerun, using the same test data.

```
run trywithdebug

Input data  datum:            2
Input data  datum:            3
Input data  datum:            5
Input data  datum:            7
Input data  datum:           11
Input data  datum:           13
Input data  datum:         -9999
Original list:
    2     3     5     7    11    13
   13     3     5     7    11     2   i = 1
   13    11     5     7     3     2   i = 2
   13    11     7     5     3     2   i = 3
   13    11     5     7     3     2   i = 4
   13     3     5     7    11     2   i = 5
    2     3     5     7    11    13   i = 6
Reversed list:
    2     3     5     7    11    13
```

The six trace lines in the execution printout of the program trywithdebug reveal the source of the problem. The first of these six lines

```
   13     3     5     7    11     2   i = 1
```

shows that, after one iteration of the for-loop, the first and last numbers are exchanged. The second of the six trace lines

```
   13    11     5     7     3     2   i = 2
```

indicates that, after two iterations of the for-loop, the second and the next to last numbers have been exchanged.

The third trace line

```
   13    11     7     5     3     2   i = 3
```

demonstrates that, after the third iteration of the for-loop, the list is in reverse order. The fourth, fifth, and sixth trace lines, however, indicate that the fourth, fifth, and sixth iterations of the for-loop undo the achievements of the first three iterations by exchanging elements of the list back into their original locations.

Choice of Test Data

The choice of test data is often quite important in successful debugging. The test data used so far in sample executions of the reversing program possess several simple but important virtues. First, the input list is in increasing order. This makes it easy to see whether all or part of the list is reversed. Second, the number of items in the list is small enough that the entire execution may be hand simulated or traced, if necessary, but not so small that the program execution is trivial.

In this instance, virtue is rewarded. The test data uncover the existence of a programming error, and the debugging trace gives enough additional information to attribute the source of the error to swapping each pair of values twice. The correction that suggests itself is to limit the for-loop to half as many iterations as before.

An alert programmer might immediately notice potential trouble in trying to halve the number of iterations of the for-loop. If the number of elements in the input list were odd, then the proposed number of exchanges would not be an integer. The corrected program reversealist resolves this problem by truncating, if necessary, to obtain an integer, using the integer operator div. The execution printouts for the two sample runs indicate that the corrected program works, both for an input list of even length and for an input list of odd length.

```
program reversealist (input, output);
{ Read a list, reverse it, and print the result. }

  const
    maxlistsize = 9;
    maxdata = 9999;
    signal = -maxdata;

  type
    listdatatype = -maxdata..maxdata;
    listtype = array [1..maxlistsize] of listdatatype;
    listsizetype = 0..maxlistsize;
    datatype = listdatatype; { for swap }

  var
    i : 1..maxlistsize;
    numberofv : listsizetype;
    v : listtype;

  procedure readlist (var list : listtype;
                          maxlistsize : listsizetype;
                          signal : listdatatype;
                          var numberofelements : listsizetype);
    ... end; { readlist }

  procedure swap (var a, b : datatype);
    ... end; { swap }

  begin
  readlist (v, maxlistsize, signal, numberofv);
  writeln ('Original list: ');
  for i := 1 to numberofv do
    write (v [i] :5);
  writeln;
  for i := 1 to numberofv div 2 do
    swap (v [i], v [numberofv - i + 1]);
  writeln ('Reversed list: ');
  for i := 1 to numberofv do
    write (v [i] :5);
  writeln;
  end.

run reversealist

Input data  datum:          2
Input data  datum:          3
Input data  datum:          5
Input data  datum:          7
Input data  datum:         11
Input data  datum:         13
Input data  datum:      -9999
```

```
Original list:
    2    3    5    7   11   13
Reversed list:
   13   11    7    5    3    2

run reversealist

Input data  datum:          17
Input data  datum:          19
Input data  datum:          23
Input data  datum:          29
Input data  datum:          31
Input data  datum:       -9999
Original list:
   17   19   23   29   31
Reversed list:
   31   29   23   19   17
```

To prove that a program works, all the essentially different possible executions should be tested. In addition, if any test reveals an error, a correction should be made in the program and the resulting program retested with the same test data that were improperly processed by the previous program version. It seems sufficient to test the program reversealist for one input list of even length and one input list of odd length, as representatives of the only two essentially different cases.

Tests using randomly generated data are sometimes a valuable extra precaution because they can disclose possibilities not anticipated by the programmer. However, test cases carefully constructed by the programmer to tax all capabilities of the program usually are more productive in detecting errors.

Why Write Procedures

Removing integral portions of a computational process from the main program and encoding them as procedures often makes it easier to understand the flow of the main program. If such a portion might be reused in other computational processes, then encoding it as a procedure with explicit arguments makes it possible for the variable names to make sense both in the procedure and in all the programs that call it. Once a procedure has been tested thoroughly, it may be used in many applications without the extensive debugging frequently needed for new programs.

Using A Procedure to Assist In Tracing

In debugging a complicated program, sometimes the trace takes the form of a procedure. If it seems advisable to record the values of variables at several different locations in the program, and if more than one program statement is needed to take such a snapshot, a programmer might design a tracing procedure, giving it a name like **snapshot**. Then procedure calls to snapshot could be inserted at the critical program locations. For example, the debugging writeln statement of trywithdebug could be replaced by this procedure call and the following procedure snapshot.

```
procedure snapshot;
  var
    j : 1..maxlistsize;
```

```
begin
for j := 1 to numberofv do
   write (v [j] :5);
writeln ('   i = ', i :1);
end; {snapshot }
```

Sometimes it is helpful if the tracing procedure is coded with explicit arguments in order to make it more flexible.

Some Pascal systems have built-in tracing features. A programmer using such a system should learn both how to use the built-in feature and how to design a trace.

Self-Test Questions

1.   True/false:

     a. Random test data is the safest way to verify the correctness of a program, because it avoids the possibility of testing only with values guaranteed to work.

     b. Inserting a debugging trace into a program is also called "hand simulation".

     c. Snapshots are never placed in the middle of a loop because too much output will be printed.

     d. One of the main reasons for modularizing a program into procedures is to enable you to test each procedure independently of the rest of the program.

2.   What are the advantages of computer tracing over hand simulation?

3.   What are the advantages of hand simulation over computer tracing?

Exercises

1.   Debug the following program by inserting one or more snapshots. The program is supposed to find the average of a list of input numbers, terminated by a signal value of −1.

```
program averageattempt (input, output);
   const
      signal = -1;
   var
      value, count, sum : integer;
      average : real;
   begin
   sum := 0;
   count := 0;
   value := 0;  { initialization for while-test }
   while value <> signal do
      begin
      count := count + 1;
      read (value);
      writeln ('Input data  value: ', value);
      sum := sum + value;
      end;  { while-loop }
   average := sum / count;
   writeln ('Average = ', average :1 :2);
   end.  { program averageattempt }
```

8.3   Functions and Function Values

A **function** is a construction that looks a lot like a procedure but is used like a built-in function to compute a single value. It is a programmer's way of augmenting a language to include functions that are not built in.

Section Preview

Function Declaration:

General Form:

function *functionname* (<optional var> *dummyvariable* : *type*;
                        <optional var> *dummyvariable* : *type*;
                        ...
                        <optional var> *dummyvariable* : *type*) : *type*;

        const
          constant declarations;
        type
          type declarations;
        var
          local variable declarations;
        local procedure and function declarations;
        begin
        statement;
        ...
        functionname := *expression*; { at least one such assignment }
        ...
        statement;
        end; { of function declaration }

Example:

```
function smallest (first, second, third : integer) : integer;
  var
    smaller : integer;  { local variable }
  begin
  if first < second then
    smaller := first
  else
    smaller := second;
  if smaller < third then
    smallest := smaller  { function value assignment }
  else
    smallest := third;  { function value assignment }
  end;  { of function smallest }
```

Function Call:

A function is called by using it in an expression.

Example:

```
sum := smallest (a, b, c) + smallest (x, y, z)
```

Side Effects:

A function ordinarily is designed to compute one single value, the function value, on the basis of the values of the supplied arguments. Any other effect on the calling program is usually considered a side effect and is usually avoided by using local variables and call-by-value parameters. *Note:* There are exceptions to these rules and not all experienced programmers agree 100% with these conventions.

Functions and Procedures

Like a procedure, a function has a title line that might list some dummy arguments, followed by a body of statements. The title line contains a declaration of the type of value returned by the function as well as declarations of any dummy arguments. Like a procedure, a function is executed as if supplied arguments were copied in place of the dummy arguments. One difference, however, is that a procedure is called *explicitly* by a procedure call statement, while a function is called *implicitly* whenever the computer executes a program statement that uses the function's name.

Exponentiation

Our first example of a function is concerned with raising an integer to a power that is a nonnegative integer. The function intpower computes this value and returns it to the calling program. The driver program testintpower tests the function intpower.

```
program testintpower (output);

    function intpower (number, exponent : integer) : integer;

      var
        value, i : integer;

      begin
      value := 1;
      for i := 1 to exponent do
        value := value * number;
      intpower := value;
      end; { intpower }

    begin
    writeln (intpower (2, 10));
    end.
run testintpower

      1024
```

The function intpower has two dummy arguments, number and exponent, both declared to be type integer in the title line

```
    function intpower (number, exponent : integer) : integer;
```

By means of the type specifier integer following the argument list, the title line also declares that the value of the function intpower is type integer. In order to protect any possible calling program from unexpected side effects, the function intpower declares that its variables value and i are local and its arguments are not variable.

Assigning a Function Value

Most of the assignment statements in the function intpower are executed exactly as if they were in a procedure. The first assignment statement assigns the constant 1 to the local variable value. Each time the second assignment statement is executed, the value of the variable value is multiplied by the value of the number, which is 2. The last assignment statement

```
intpower := value
```

however, is a **function value assignment**, found only in functions. The difference is that the name on the left of the assignment is the function name, not a variable. This instruction is executed by evaluating the expression on the right of the assignment symbol and assigning it as the function value. The name of the function must not be used as a variable in the program; in particular, once assigned, its value must never be used in an expression within the function. However, the value of a function may be assigned more than once during execution of a function. The last value assigned is the one returned to the calling program.

```
                              2           10
    function intpower (~~number~~,  ~~exponent~~  : integer) : integer;

      var
        value, i : integer;

      begin
      value := 1;
                     10
      for i := 1 to ~~exponent~~  do
                          2
        value := value * ~~number~~;
      intpower := value;
      end; { intpower }
```

Figure 8.2 Supplying arguments to a function program.

Returning a Function Value to the Calling Program

When the execution of the function is completed, the function value is returned to the calling program, and the computer continues with the execution of the calling program.

Suppose, for example, that a program includes the calling statement

```
writeln (intpower (2, 10))
```

As illustrated in Figure 8.2, the value 2 is supplied to the function intpower to replace the dummy argument number, and the value 10 is supplied to replace the dummy argument exponent. The loop in the function intpower is executed 10 times, each time multiplying value by 2. When the loop is completed, the value is 2 to the 10th power (1024). The final assignment statement assigns 1024 as the value of the function.

Since execution of the function is now completed, the function value is returned to the calling program, and execution of the calling program resumes. In this case, the computer completes execution of the writeln statement that called intpower by printing the function value just calculated.

A function program is declared in exactly the same manner as a procedure. Function and procedure declarations may be mixed in any order.

Execution of any program that calls an available function program proceeds exactly as if the function were built in.

What Day of the Week is New Year's Day?

The program newyearsday calculates the day of the week on which the new year begins for every year in the twentieth century. As a precaution, the program checks the validity of the input data.

```
program newyearsday (input, output);
    read (year);
    if year is from 1901 to 2000 then
        Initialize jan1day to Tuesday { for the year 1901 }
        Calculate the day of Jan 1 for the input year
            by advancing jan1day by one for each year
            and one additional day for each leap year
        Convert the day to a character string and print it
    else
        Print an error message
```

Advancing of Calendar Dates and Days of the Week

Division of the number of days in an ordinary calendar year, 365, by the number of days in a week, 7, yields a quotient of 52 weeks and a remainder of 1 day. If New Year's Day of an ordinary year falls on a Thursday, for example, the remainder of 1 day will push New Year's Day of the following year to a Friday. After 52 weeks of an ordinary year beginning on a Monday, the day of the week will again be a Monday. The remainder of 1 day, the last day of the year, will cause the subsequent New Year's Day to be a Tuesday.

A leap year of 366 days has 52 whole weeks and two extra days. It follows that, if New Year's Day of a leap year falls on a Wednesday, the year after it will fall on a Friday. Leap year causes New Year's Day to advance 2 days of the week.

A similar progression occurs for other fixed dates in the calendar year. In successive years a fixed calendar date advances 1 day of the week unless a February 29 intervenes, in which case it advances 2 days.

Some Background Information For Calendar Computations

The twentieth century began on January 1, 1901, a Tuesday, and will end on December 31, 2000. It is a mistake to think that it began in 1900 and will end in 1999, because the first century began in the year 1 (there never was a year 0) and every century is 100 years long.

The only additional information needed to understand the calculations employed by the program newyearsday is which years of the twentieth century are leap years. Although most calendar years are 365 days long, the earth requires nearly 365 1/4 days to orbit the sun. In order to compensate for the extra fraction of a day beyond 365, nearly every fourth year is designated a leap year, during which the calendar is lengthened to 366 days by adding one day to February's normal 28.

It was arbitrarily decided long ago that, if the number 4 evenly divides the year number, or equivalently, if it evenly divides the last two digits of the year number, then the year is a leap year, except for one special case, the last year of a century. Although the year number of the last year of any century is always divisible by 4, such a year is not a leap year unless its year number is also divisible by 400. For example, the years 1800 and 1900 were not leap years, and the years 2100, 2200, and 2300 will not be leap years. On the other hand, 2000 and 2400 will be leap years.

The reason for this complication in the last year of a century is that the earth's orbiting time is about 365.24219879 days, a shade under 365 1/4 days, and the general goal of the rule for designating leap years is to keep the average length of the calendar year nearly equal to the earth's orbiting time.

Fortunately for the program newyearsday, it is not necessary to know the reasoning behind the assignment of leap years. It is enough to know that a year of the twentieth century is a leap year if and only if its year number is divisible by 4.

Testing the Program Newyearsday

The execution printouts for the executable refinement of the program newyearsday show that it is being tested with years whose starting dates are verified easily. An almanac is a convenient source of calendars for the past few years and the next few years.

```
program newyearsday (input, output);

   const
      daysinweek = 7;

   type
      day = (sun, mon, tue, wed, thu, fri, sat);
      string9 = packed array [1..9] of char;

   var
      dayname : array [day] of string9;
      year : integer;
      numberofleapyears : 0..24;
      advances : 0..6;
      i : 1..6;
      jan1day : day;

   function nextday (givenday : day) : day;
      begin
      if givenday = sat then
         nextday := sun
      else
         nextday := succ (givenday);
      end; { nextday }

   begin
   dayname [sun] := 'Sunday   ';
   dayname [mon] := 'Monday   ';
   dayname [tue] := 'Tuesday  ';
   dayname [wed] := 'Wednesday';
   dayname [thu] := 'Thursday ';
   dayname [fri] := 'Friday   ';
   dayname [sat] := 'Saturday ';
   read (year);
   writeln ('Input data  year: ', year);
```

```
  if (year >= 1901) and (year <= 2000) then
    begin
    numberofleapyears := (year - 1901) div 4;
    advances := (year - 1901 + numberofleapyears) mod daysinweek;
    janlday := tue; { 1901 Jan 1 was a Tuesday }
    for i := 1 to advances do
      janlday := nextday (janlday);
    writeln ('New Year''s Day, ', year :1,
        ', was or will be ', dayname [janlday]);
    end { if }
  else
    writeln ('The year must be an integer ',
        'from 1901 to 2000.');
  end.
```

run newyearsday

Input data year: 1981
New Year's Day, 1981, was or will be Thursday

run newyearsday

Input data year: 1984
New Year's Day, 1984, was or will be Sunday

The variable numberofleapyears is assigned a value equal to the number
of occurrences of February 29 between New Year's Day, 1901, and New Year's
Day of the given year. The variable advances is then assigned as its value the
total number of advances of New Year's Day from 1901 to the given year.
Since each 7 advances return the day of the week to the same day it was, the
variable advances is reduced mod 7 to shorten the for-loop that follows.

For example, the number of leap years from 1901 to 1981 is 20, the result
of dividing 80 by 4. The number of advances, therefore, is 100, one day's
advance for each of the 80 years from the base date January 1, 1901, to the
objective date January 1, 1981, plus one additional day's advance for each of
the 20 leap years between those two dates. If the day of the week is advanced
7 times, there is no change, so the number of advances made is the remainder
when the actual number of advances is divided by 7. For 1981, this is 100 mod
7 = 2, so the day of the week is advanced from Tuesday to Thursday. In the
second sample execution, the number of occurrences of February 29 between
New Year's Day, 1901, and New Year's Day, 1984, is also 20, the integer part
of (1984 - 1901) / 4. The number of advances therefore is 103, the sum of
83 and 20. Thus the day of the week is advanced 103 mod 7 = 5 times from
Tuesday to Sunday.

Enumerated Data Types

Since the program newyearsday deals primarily with days of the week, it is
natural to use the **enumerated data type**

```
type
    day = (sun, mon, tue, wed, thu, fri, sat);
```

whose seven possible values are abbreviations of the seven days of the week.
The function, nextday, accepts a supplied argument of type day and returns a
value of the same type. It uses the natural ordering of the data type day to
assign the successor of a givenday as the function value nextday in most cases.
The next day after Saturday is treated separately.

Expressions as Supplied Arguments

In general, a supplied argument to a function or procedure may be an expression. With a built-in function, the only restriction is that the function value be defined for the value of the supplied argument. However, in order for a procedure call or a call to a programmer-defined function to be executed when an expression is supplied as an argument, it is necessary that it makes sense to substitute the expression itself for each occurrence of the corresponding dummy argument. In particular, a dummy argument that receives an expression as a supplied argument should not be declared as a variable. For instance, the following calls to the function intpower are both executable, because the substitutions they specify all make sense if y is type integer.

```
write (intpower (y + 5, 4))
write (intpower (2 * y, y div 4))
```

Comparison of Functions and Procedures

A function listing looks so much like a procedure listing that one might wonder why both structures are included in a programming language. The reason is largely a matter of programming style.

The concept of a function is borrowed from mathematics, in which a function f assigns a value $f(x)$ or $f(x_1, x_2, ..., x_n)$ to each allowable value of its argument or list of arguments. To avoid confusion, Pascal functions should be reserved for precisely this usage. A procedure can be used for any other kind of subtask.

The guiding principle in deciding whether to isolate a part of the whole program as a function or as a procedure is that, if its purpose is to produce a single value, then usually a function is used. Otherwise a procedure is used. Beyond this guiding principle, however, there are some important conventions to be obeyed in writing functions.

Avoidance of Side Effects

The most important convention for writing functions is that a function should have no side effects. A statement like

```
jan1day := nextday (jan1day)
```

tells the computer to calculate the value of the function nextday and assign this value to the variable jan1day. If there is any other effect of executing this statement, a person reading the program in which the statement is contained would be totally unaware of it. Therefore, if execution of a function causes side effects, it is very difficult to determine the behavior of a program that calls that function.

Execution of a function should not change the values of its dummy arguments, nor should it change the value of any variables that are not local to the function. Accordingly, the dummy arguments of a function should never be declared variable, even though this is permitted in Pascal, and all variables used in a function should be declared local. If other effects on the calling program are necessary or desirable, the programmer should write a procedure instead of a function.*

Any effect of a procedure on a calling program not related to the procedure's stated computational purpose is a side effect and also should be

---

*These rules are violated once in this book in order to write the function randominteger, which is traditionally written as a function although it changes the value of the global variable named seed. It is written as a function so it can be used in arithmetic expressions. Explicit mention of the variable seed is suppressed, because it is not of primary concern to the user.

avoided. However, procedures commonly are used to achieve numerous effects on the calling program, including changing the values of some variables in the calling program. For example, the entire point of the procedure swap is to change the values of its arguments. Thus such a change in the arguments is not a side effect. On the other hand, changing the value of a calling program variable that happens to be named temporary is a side effect, easily avoided by localizing the procedure variable temporary.

Supplied Arguments Outside the Function Domain

It is a serious mistake to attempt to pass to a function or procedure a supplied argument that is incompatible with the corresponding dummy argument. For instance, supplying character strings to the function intpower won't work.

Even if a supplied argument is of the correct type, its value might still be outside the function domain. If, for example, the supplied argument to the built-in function log were −1, the function could not produce a value, because the logarithm of a negative number is not defined. Many computer systems would terminate execution of the program if this were attempted.

When a supplied argument is of the right type, it is still possible that the value might represent something of a nonstandard case. Under such circumstances, the function may return a special, recognizable signal instead of doing the usual calculations and returning their result.

For instance, a function to search a given list looking for the presence of a specific value might return as function value the location of that value in the list, if it is found. It might return a special signal function value in case the specific value is not in the list. Although the inability to find a particular entry in a list might be a disaster for one calling program, it might be merely a mild setback for another, and possibly a routine occurrence for a third calling program. Returning the special signal value enables the calling program to react according to its individual needs. The calling program is free either to test for the signal value or to continue computing without testing, at its own possible peril.

The burden of screening the values of supplied arguments does not always fall completely on the function or the procedure. Sometimes the calling program screens them itself in order to avoid meaningless computations or possible program termination.

Style Rule: Avoid Reassigning a Function Value

Although a function program may contain an unlimited number of function value assignment statements, only one of them should be executed during a single execution of the function program. It is essential, however, that at least one function value assignment be executed during a function call: otherwise, the function might return no value at all or a value unrelated to the current supplied arguments. For instance, it might return the function value computed for the supplied arguments in the previous call, or perhaps still worse, the garbage left by another program or programmer.

A function program is easier to read when not more than one function value assignment is made during a single function execution. When a function value assignment is encountered in the function program listing, it is then possible to conclude that at least one case of the computation is finally settled.

Nesting Procedure Calls and Function Calls

It is permissible for a function to call a procedure and for a procedure to call a function. Supplied arguments may pass through several levels of such mixed calls. Similarly, it is permissible to nest function declarations within procedure declarations and vice versa.

Self-Test Questions

1. How does a function differ from a procedure?
2. True/false:

   a. The parameters of a function do not all have to be of the same type.
   b. Procedure declarations and function declarations may be mixed in any order.
   c. The first value assigned to a function inside the function body is the value returned to the calling program.

Exercises

1. Write a function named average to find the average of a list of numbers supplied as the argument.
2. Write a function named even that returns the boolean value true if the supplied argument is an even integer or the value false if the supplied argument is an odd integer.
3. Write a program to test the function even for Exercise 2.
4. The quantity $n!$, called *n factorial*, is the number 1 if $n = 0$, and is the product

   $$n \times (n-1) \times (n-2) \times \cdots \times 3 \times 2 \times 1$$

   if n is a positive integer. When n is a positive integer, the quantity $n!$ is the number of ways of arranging n different items in a row. Write a function factorial that returns the function value n! if the argument n is a nonnegative integer, and the value -1 to signal an improper supplied argument otherwise.
5. Write a function listminimum to which a calling program supplies as argument a list of numbers and obtains in return the smallest number in that list.
6. Write a function locofmin that returns not the minimum number itself but the location of the minimum number in a list supplied as an argument.
7. Write a function remainder that works exactly the same as the operator mod.

The function oneyearinterest calculates the total interest accumulating in 1 year for a savings account that pays interest monthly. The initial amount and the annual rate are supplied as arguments. Exercises 8 to 11 are concerned with diagnosing and curing possible side-effects of the poorly written function.

```
function oneyearinterest
        (principal : real;
        var rate : real)
        : real;
{ causes possible undesirable side effects }
```

```
begin
balance := principal;
{ convert annual interest rate to a monthly rate }
rate := rate / 12;
for month := 1 to 12 do
   balance := balance + balance * rate;
oneyearinterest := balance - principal;
end; { oneyearinterest }
```

8. Hand simulate the execution of the driver program oneyeartest1 for the
    function oneyearinterest to find the undesirable side effect. What is it?

```
program oneyeartest1 (output);
{ one year's compound interest on $1000 at 5% and 6%
      annual rate, compounded monthly }

   const
     principal = 1000;

   var
      rate, balance : real;
      month : 1..12;

   function oneyearinterest ...end; { oneyearinterest }

   begin
   rate := 0.05;
   writeln ('One year''s compound interest on $1000');
   writeln ('    at 5%, compounded monthly = ',
       oneyearinterest (principal, rate) :1:2);
   rate := rate + 0.01;
   writeln ('One year''s compound interest on $1000');
   writeln ('    at 6%, compounded monthly = ',
       oneyearinterest (principal, rate) :1:2);
   end.
```

9. Hand simulate the execution of the driver program oneyeartest2 for the
    function oneyearinterest to find the undesirable side effect. What is it?

```
program oneyeartest2 (output);
{ interest accumulated for different starting amounts }

   var
      rate, balance : real;
      month : 1..12;

   function oneyearinterest ..end; { oneyearinterest }

   begin
   writeln ('Deposit' : 20, 'Interest at 10%' :20);
   balance := 100;
   while balance <= 500 do
      begin
      rate := 0.10;
      writeln (balance :20:2,
          oneyearinterest (balance, rate) :20:2);
```

```
        balance := balance + 100;
      end; { while-loop }
    end.
```

10. Write a calling program (to replace oneyeartest2) on which the function oneyearinterest has no side effects.

11. Rewrite the function oneyearinterest so that it has no side effect on any calling program.

12. The *median* of a list of numbers is the middle value, if the list has odd length, or the average of the two values closest to the middle, if the list has even length. Write a function median to calculate the median of a list of numbers. *Hint:* Write a procedure to count how many items of the list precede a given item in the list and how many items follow it.

13. Write a function that returns as its value the character string 'sorted   ' if a list of numbers supplied as argument is in ascending order, and the character string 'unsorted' otherwise.

14. Hand simulate the execution of the function illdefined for the supplied arguments −3.14, 8, and 6.4. Why is this function ill-defined? What kind of remedy is needed to make it well?

```
function illdefined (a, b, c : real) : boolean;
  begin
  if b <= a then
    illdefined := false;
  if (b > a) and (b <= c) then
    illdefined := true;
  end; { illdefined }
```

15. Write a function that accepts as arguments a month name, a number representing the day of the month, and a year number in the twentieth century and returns the number (from 1 to 366) of the day in the year on which the given date occurred. *Hint:* The function needs to include a list of the number of the days in the various months and a leap year test.

16. Write a program that calculates for any date in the twentieth century the day of the week on which it has occurred or will occur. *Hint:* Refer to Exercise 15 and to the program newyearsday.

17. Unfortunately, there is no built-in function that is the inverse of the function ord. For the enumerated type day in the program newyearsday, write a function called dayofweek that gives the nth day for any value of its argument n from 0 to 6. That is

    dayofweek (0) = sun
    dayofweek (1) = mon
        .
        .
        .
    dayofweek (6) = sat

18. Modify the function intpower so that its value is −1 if the exponent supplied is negative.

8.4 What You Should Know

1. Every procedure should have a specific and well-defined task to do.
2. Side effects, peripheral effects of one procedure on another, are effects unrelated to the task of the offending procedure.

3. In a global environment, each procedure has access to all of the variables in any other procedure. Unintentional side effects are hard to avoid when all variables are global.

4. All constants, types, variables, and procedures that are declared within a procedure are local to that procedure.

5. Changes in a local variable cannot *ever* cause side effects in another procedure.

6. A procedure may have a list of arguments through which it communicates with the calling program.

7. All references to a dummy argument which is declared as var are replaced with references to the corresponding supplied argument before the procedure executed. Supplied and dummy arguments must have exactly the same type.

8. Type names of dummy arguments can only be single words. Often, a programmer must declare a new type name to meet this requirement.

9. Dummy arguments which are not declared var are assigned the value of the corresponding supplied argument before procedure execution begins. Changes in the value of the dummy argument do not affect the supplied argument.

10. For non-var arguments, values of the type of the supplied argument must be assignable to the dummy argument. Therefore, constants and expressions are permitted as supplied arguments.

11. Arguments are also called parameters. In this terminology, dummy arguments are dummy parameters and supplied arguments are actual parameters.

12. A function is a construction like a procedure, with two major differences:

    a. A function returns a function value whose type is declared in the heading.

    b. A function is called implicitly by being written in an expression.

13. In general, a function should have no effect other than computing its function value.

14. In a function, the function values should be assigned exactly once in each execution.

15. The scope of a declaration is the set of lines in the program listing to which that declaration applies.

16. Any declaration made at the head of a program or procedure applies to all parts of that program or procedure.

17. If a name is used within the scope of two declarations, the innermost declaration applies.

18. Tracing is keeping track of the execution of a program by monitoring the values of selected variables.

19. A snapshot is a procedure designed to display the values of key variables in easy-to-read form. In debugging, calls to such procedures are strategically placed to give insight into how the execution is proceeding.

ARRAYS 9

When a programming application requires the processing of a number of different pieces of information of the same kind, it is natural to organize the data in an array. For example, in taking an average of test scores, each test score may be different, but they are all data of the same kind and each is to be treated in the same way by the program. The existence of a conceptual list of test scores, however, does not mean that the computer program must use an array.

In Section 5.4, an average of test scores was calculated without using an array by arranging the calculation so that only one test score is needed at a time in the computer. Each test score was read, echoed, added to the sum, and then discarded. It is fortunate that a discarded test score was not needed again later in the program execution, because it was no longer available. It was replaced by the next test score read into the same variable. In some sense, this program to average test scores is harder than one using arrays, because it distorts the natural organization of the data to make the computation possible.

In Section 6.2, the registrar's gradepoint average problem for an entire college was analyzed using a top-down approach. For each student, there was a list of courses taken, a list of letter grades in the courses, a list of credits for the courses, and so on. Mirroring the way the grade report was prepared by hand, it seemed natural to first read these lists of data, then to do the calculations, and finally to print the grade report.

For this plan of attack to work, the complete information for one student must be available *simultaneously* during the execution of the program. The use of arrays is now inevitable.

Although arrays have shown up at scattered places in this book—for example, in Pascal, character strings are formally arrays of characters—the fundamental syntax and interpretation of arrays in Pascal are collected and reviewed in this chapter. Then, the chapter discusses the extremely important applications of searching and sorting that fully exploit the systematic organization of an array.

9.1   Lists, Subscripts, and Index Variables

In ordinary usage, a **list** is a sequence of values, usually all representing data of the same kind, or otherwise related to one another. A list of students registered for a particular course and a list of all students enrolled at a college are examples. The roster of active players on an athletic team and the names of all the presidents of the United States are also lists. So are grocery lists and lists of entrants in a jousting tournament. Synonyms for the same concept are **one-dimensional array** and "vector". Sometimes the phrase "linear list" is used to distinguish it from the more general list structures that are beyond the scope of this discussion.

In Pascal, a collection of values of the same type is called an **array**, a keyword that must be used in the variable declaration for such a collection. Except in variable declarations, where no synonyms are permitted, we will refer to a one-dimensional array as a list. This section is concerned mainly with introducing the programming techniques associated with lists, including the concepts of **subscripts** and **index variables**.

Section Preview

Array:

An array is a list of values of the same type.

Array Declaration:

General Forms:

```
var
    arrayname : array [constant..constant] of type;
    arrayname : array [subrangetype] of type;
    arrayname : array [enumerateddatatype] of type;
    arrayname : arraytype;
```

Example:

```
type
  smallinteger = -10..10;
  string30 = packed array [1..30] of char;
  primarycolor = (red, green, blue);
var
  battingaverage : array [1..9] of real;
  frequency : array [smallinteger] of real;
  intensity : array [primarycolor] of real;
  name : string30;
```

Subscript:

The relative position within an array, written between the square brackets ([ ]), is the subscript of the array element.

Index Variables:

A subscript may be a variable! Indeed, there would hardly be any use for arrays if a subscript couldn't vary. A variable that appears as a subscript of an array is an index variable.

```
Example:
{ reads values for the 3 components of the array vector }
var
  vector : array [1..3] of real;
  i : 1..3;
  begin
  for i := 1 to 3 do
    read (vector [i]);
  end;
```

A Credit Card Checking Application

As an example of a problem concerned with a list, suppose that a company maintains a computerized list of credit cards either that have been reported lost or stolen or that are greatly in arrears in payments. The company needs a program to determine quickly whether a given credit card, presented by a customer wishing to charge a purchase, is on this list of credit cards that can no longer be honored.

Suppose that a company has a list of 8,262 credit cards reported lost or stolen, as illustrated in Table 9.1.

Table 9.1 List of the Account Numbers of Credit Cards Reported Lost or Stolen.

Account number of 1st lost credit card	2718281
Account number of 2nd lost credit card	7389056
Account number of 3rd lost credit card	1098612
Account number of 4th lost credit card	5459815
Account number of 5th lost credit card	1484131
.	.
.	.
.	.
Account number of 8262nd lost credit card	1383596

Since all of the 8,262 numbers in the list must be retained simultaneously in the computer's main memory for efficient searching, each number must be assigned as the value of a variable with a different name so that the computer can be instructed to compare each account number of a lost or stolen card against the account number of the card offered in payment for goods and services.

Subscripts

It is possible to use Pascal variable names

```
accountnumberof1stlostcreditcard
accountnumberof2ndlostcreditcard
accountnumberof3rdlostcreditcard

        .
        .

accountnumberof8262ndlostcreditcard
```

corresponding to the descriptive names in the left column of Table 9.1 with the blanks removed. Unfortunately, the Pascal language does not recognize the intended relationship between these variable names. (Some Pascal systems might even consider them all to be the same name, because the first 15 characters of all the names are the same.) Even the shorter variable names

```
numberof1stlostcard
numberof2ndlostcard
        .
        .
        .
numberof8262ndlostcard
```

whose relationship to each other is still perfectly clear to a person, do not bear any more relationship to one another in Pascal than do any 8,262 variable names chosen at random. The form used for designating the items in a Pascal list is the following:

```
numberoflostcard [1]
numberoflostcard [2]
numberoflostcard [3]
        .
        .
        .
numberoflostcard [8262]
```

This seemingly minor modification of otherwise perfectly acceptable variable names opens up a new dimension of programming capabilities. All the programs in this chapter, and a large number of the programs in succeeding chapters, cannot be written without this form. The numbers in square brackets that specify the location of an item within a list are **subscripts**, a name borrowed from mathematics. Although mathematical subscripts are usually written below the line (hence the name "subscript"), such a form of typography is impossible on most computer input devices. A substitute notation, enclosing the subscript in brackets or parentheses, is adopted in most computer languages. It is customary to read the expression x [3] as "x sub 3", just as if the number 3 were written below the line.

Why Use Subscripts?

The advantage of this method of naming the quantities over using the nearly identical variable names numberof1stlostcard, numberof2ndlostcard, ..., numberof8262ndlostcard springs from the following programming language capability: the subscript of an array variable may itself be a variable, or even a more complicated expression.

The consequences of this simple statement are much more profound than would appear at first sight. In fact, it is one of the most important principles in modern computer programming. This entire chapter, and much of the rest of this book, is devoted to exploring some of the uses of this facility.

For a start in describing the uses of a subscript that is itself a variable, the two statements

```
i := 1;
write (numberoflostcard [i])
```

produce exactly the same output as the single statement

```
write (numberoflostcard [1])
```

namely, 2718281, the account number of the first lost credit card on the list. Similarly, the account numbers of the first three lost credit cards may be written by the statements

```
i := 1;
write (numberoflostcard [i]);
i := 2;
write (numberoflostcard [i]);
i := 3;
write (numberoflostcard [i])
```

The effect is the same as executing the three statements

```
write (numberoflostcard [1]);
write (numberoflostcard [2]);
write (numberoflostcard [3])
```

Based on the data in Table 9.1, the sample output in both cases would be

```
2718281   7389056   1098612
```

In fact, the entire list of account numbers of lost credit cards can be written by the procedure printlostcards.

```
procedure printlostcards;
  var
    { i must be an integer from 1 to 8262 }
    i : 1..8262;
  begin
  for i := 1 to 8262 do
    writeln (numberoflostcard [i]);
  end; { printlostcards }
2718281
7389056
1098612

   .
   .
   .

1383596
```

The sample output resembles Table 9.1 without the names. The important thing to keep in mind when following the execution of the procedure printlostcards is that, each time the writeln command is executed, there is a different value for the subscript i, and consequently a different item in the list is printed. Figure 9.1 shows another example of how the value of the subscript distinguishes between elements of an array.

Index Variables

A variable used to indicate which item in a list is being referenced is an **index**. The variable subscript i in the procedure printlostcards is such an **index variable**. Traditionally, the name "i" is a very popular one for index variables, partly because it is the first letter in the word "index", and partly because the letter "i" is commonly used in mathematics for a variable subscript. The names "j" and "k" are popular also.

Local and Global Variables

The declaration of the variable i in the procedure printlostcards illustrates two features of Pascal. First, the variable i is declared as a subrange type, the subrange of integers from 1 to 8,262. There is no need for the other integers, because those values for the subscript i would be outside of the declared range of subscripts for the array numberoflostcard.

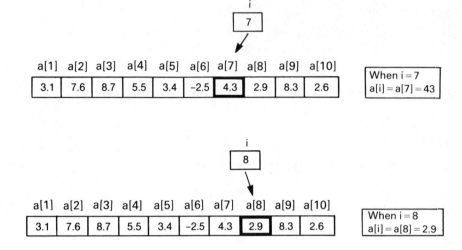

Figure 9.1 The effect of changing the value of the subscript i on the array element a [i].

Second, by declaring the variable in the procedure printlostcards, we make it a local variable. The variable i is used by the procedure printlostcards in a way that does not concern the calling program. The value of i before starting the procedure printlostcards has no effect on the execution of the procedure printlostcards, which initializes i to 1 in the for-loop, and the value of i upon completion of printlostcards is undefined. The variable i is declared in the procedure printlostcards because its meaning is local to that procedure.

Subrange Types

The variable i is declared to be a subrange type. In this case, the expression 1..8262 indicates that the permissible values for i are precisely those integers that lie in the range 1 to 8,262, inclusive. The values for i are a subrange of the integers because the lower bound 1 and the upper bound 8,262 are both integer constants.

Many debugging Pascal compilers provide execution-time error messages if a variable assumes a value outside its declared subrange.

It is possible to declare the values of a variable to be a subrange of characters or a subrange of a programmer-defined type. It is even permissible to declare a subrange of boolean values, although this usually isn't very useful. A variable must not be declared to be a subrange of real values.

For example, with the following declarations, the variable x may assume any two-digit positive, negative, or zero value, uppercaseletter may have a value that is any single upper case letter of the alphabet, and digit may be any single character that is a decimal digit. Although their declarations are similar, the values of the variable digit must be characters and the values of the variable number must be integers.

```
var
    x : -99..99;
    uppercaseletter : 'A'..'Z';
    digit : '0'..'9';
    number : 0..9;
```

In subrange declarations, it is good programming practice to use names of constants in place of the constants themselves in all but the simplest cases. Thus in the example above, the constant 99 probably should be given a name so that the declaration of x may appear as

```
const
    limit = 99;
var
    x : -limit..limit;
```

Naming a constant makes the program more readable and makes it easier to modify in case a different constant value becomes appropriate.

Array Declarations

The name of an array must obey the same rules as an ordinary variable name. Each array must be declared in the variable declaration section of the program. In a declaration of an array, the keyword "array" is followed by the range of subscripts of the array in brackets, followed by the keyword "of", and ending with the type of each element of the array. For example,

```
var
    x, y : array [1..9] of real;
    yesno : array ['a'..'z'] of boolean;
```

declares that x and y are lists of 9 real values that yesno is a list of 26 boolean values yesno ['a'], yesno ['b'], yesno ['c'], ..., yesno ['z']. This declaration implies that a subscript for x or y must be an integer expression with a value from 1 to 9 and that a subscript for yesno must be a character expression whose value is a lower case letter.

In Pascal, a character string is simply a list of characters. Often the keyword **packed** is attached to a character string declaration to indicate that the characters are to be packed in memory as densely as possible in order to save space. For example, the following declaration allows the variable name to store character strings of exactly 20 characters, including trailing blanks.

```
var
    name : packed array [1..20] of char;
```

A list of character strings may be declared in a form like the following.

```
var
    stringlist : array [1..17] of array [1..8] of char;
```

In this example, the variable stringlist is a list of 17 character strings, each of length 8. The equivalent form of declaration

```
var
    stringlist : array [1..17, 1..8] of char;
```

portrays the list of character strings as a table of characters, a conceptually different but equivalent structure.

Variable Length Lists

It is clearly absurd to assume that a company will always have exactly 8,262 credit cards reported lost or stolen. However, Pascal requires *fixed constant limits* for the range of subscripts in an array declaration. The way around this restriction is to declare a constant maxquantityofcards of, say, 10,000 to be used as the upper bound in array and subscript range declarations and a variable actualquantityofcards, whose current value would be 8,262 for the data of Figure 9.1.

In this light, we rewrite the procedure printlostcards and show the relevant declarations in the main program that uses the procedure

printlostcards, defining everything in terms of the single constant maxquantityofcards. In the main program, there would be declarations

```
const
  maxquantityofcards = 10000;
var
  actualquantityofcards : 0..maxquantityofcards;
  numberoflostcard : array [1..maxquantityofcards] of integer;
```

and the procedure itself would be rewritten as follows.

```
procedure printlostcards;
  var
    i : 1..maxquantityofcards;
  begin
  for i := 1 to actualquantityofcards do
    writeln (numberoflostcard [i]);
  end; { printlostcards }
```

With the availability of subrange declarations, very few variables need to
be declared to be type integer. It is a good programming practice to specify the
expected range of any integer quantity as a subrange type, whenever it is possible to do so.

Use of an Array When a Simple Variable Will Do

Some programs may be written either with or without arrays. The process is
illustrated again by comparing the program avgofscores2, which does not use an
array, with the program avgofscores, which does. Both programs accept varying
numbers of test scores in the input data and count the number of test scores.

```
program avgofscores2 (input, output);

  const
    signal = 9999;

  var
    enrollment : integer;
    outofdata : boolean;
    sum, nextscore : real;

  begin
  enrollment := 0;
  sum := 0;
  outofdata := false;
  while not outofdata do
    begin
    read (nextscore);
    if nextscore = signal then
      outofdata := true
    else
      begin
      writeln ('Input data  nextscore: ', nextscore :7:2);
      sum := sum + nextscore;
      enrollment := enrollment + 1;
      end; { else-clause }
    end; { while-loop }
```

```
writeln;
writeln ('There are ', enrollment :1, ' test scores.');
writeln ('Average test score = ', sum / enrollment :1:2);
end.
```

This program shows a typical use of the simple variables nextscore and sum in a loop. On each iteration, a new value of the variable nextscore is read, and except when the termination signal card is read, a new value of the running total sum is computed. Of course, the previous values of these variables are lost.

In contrast, the preliminary version of the program avgofscores3 cannot be refined without using an array, because all the test scores are stored simultaneously in the computer's memory after the reading step.

```
program avgoftestscores3 (input, output);
{ preliminary version }
   Read all the test scores
   Calculate the average
   Print the results
```

In refining the program avgofscores3, the programmer must recognize that the role filled by the simple variable nextscore in the program avgofscores and avgofscores2 now requires a list, score [1..maxenrollment]. The simple variable nextscore is retained as a buffer for holding the next score while the program tests whether this score value is the termination signal. The variable sum does not need to be a list, because only one value for sum is needed at a time.

```
program avgofscores3 (input, output);

   const
     maxenrollment = 100;
     signal = 9999;

   var
     enrollment : 0..maxenrollment;
     i : 1..maxenrollment;
     outofdata : boolean;
     sum, nextscore : real;
     score : array [1..maxenrollment] of real;

   begin
   enrollment := 0;

   { read all the test scores }
   outofdata := false;
   while (not outofdata) and (enrollment < maxenrollment) do
      begin
      read (nextscore);
      if nextscore = signal then
        outofdata := true
```

```
      else
        begin
        writeln ('Input data  nextscore: ', nextscore :7:2);
        enrollment := enrollment + 1;
        score [enrollment] := nextscore;
        end; { else }
    end; { while-loop }

  { check for more than 100 scores in data }
  if not outofdata then
    begin
    read (nextscore);
    if nextscore <> signal then
      begin
      writeln ('The input data consists of more than ',
          maxenrollment :1, ' scores.');
      writeln ('Only the first ', maxenrollment :1,
          ' have been used.');
      end;
    end;

  { calculate the average }
  sum := 0;
  for i := 1 to enrollment do
    sum := sum + score [i];

  { print the results }
  writeln;
  writeln ('There are ', enrollment :1, ' test scores.');
  writeln ('Average test score = ', sum / enrollment :1:2);
  end.
```

The difference between these two programs is twofold. First, the reading of the scores and the calculating of the sum can be separate loops when the test scores are stored in a list. The calculation of the sum is particularly clear when it is done separately from the reading. For this problem, the increase in computer time needed for separate loops is a cheap price to pay to obtain clarity. Second, the program using a list requires more memory locations for storing values. When a computer with thousands of memory locations is used, this may be of no consequence. However, when a programmable desk calculator is used, there may not be enough room to run the program using subscripts. This is probably why many programmable desk calculators do not have the instructions needed to implement arrays.

The program vectorsum further illustrates the reading and printing of lists.

```
program vectorsum (input, output);

const
  size = 3;

var
  i : 1..size;
  a, b, c : array [1..size] of integer;
```

```
begin
write ('Input data  a : ');
for i := 1 to size do
  begin
  read (a [i]); write (a [i] :1, ' ');
  end;
writeln;
write ('Input data  b : ');
for i := 1 to size do
  begin
  read (b [i]); write (b [i] :1, ' ');
  end;
for i := 1 to size do
  c [i] := a [i] + b [i];
writeln; writeln;
write ('The vector sum is ');
for i := 1 to size do
  write (c [i] :1, ' ');
writeln;
end.

run vectorsum

Input data  a : 1 4 9
Input data  b : 5 12 13

The vector sum is 6 16 22
```

Keeping Track of the Size of a List

Since the programmer must always declare one fixed size for each array, it is necessary to keep track of the actual number of values that have been put in the array at any time during execution of the program. This is usually done by using a variable declared to have values in the subrange of the integers from zero to the declared size of the list. The variable enrollment in the program avgofscores3 and the variable actualquantityofcards in the final version of the procedure printlostcards are used to keep track of the actual size of a variable length list.

Self-Test Questions

1. How do you declare the variable profit to be an array of 100 real values?
2. How do you declare a character string variable name to be length 30?
3. How do you handle lists of data that vary in length?
4. True/false:

    a. The smallest subscript in any array is always 1.
    b. Array subscripts must be integers.
    c. Subrange types are permitted as subscripts.
    d. If the problem has a list of values, then an array must be used.
    e. An array is always written or read using a for-loop.
    f. In an executable statement, the subscript written for an array element may be a variable.

Exercises

1. A sprinter wants to make a listing of her times in the 100-meter dash.
    Write a program that accepts as input the times to the nearest 1/10 second
    for 10 trials in this event and makes a listing of them with the trial
    numbers in the left column and the times in the right column. *Notes:* (a)
    This program does not require the use of an array, but use one anyway.
    (b) Programmers who like to experiment with fancy output might want to
    use the columns indicator and digits indicator described in Section 2.3.

2. The sprinter in Exercise 1 would like the listing of her times printed with
    the most recent one first. Modify the program written for Exercise 1 so
    that it prints the tenth trial and its time first, and the first trial and its time
    last. The input data are still in the same order as in Exercise 1.

3. The sprinter in Exercise 1 would like to know her average time for the
    sequence of 10 trials. Modify the program for Exercise 1 so that after
    printing the list of times it prints the average time.

4. Modify the program for Exercise 2 so that, after printing the list of trials
    and times with the most recent first, it also prints the average of the five
    more recent times, followed by the average of the five less recent times.

5. A chess player who specializes in endgame combinations likes to keep
    track of the number of moves it takes her to win. Write a program that
    first reads as input the number of games she played in a month, then
    reads as input the number of moves it took her to win each of these
    games, and then prints the average number of moves it took her to win a
    game during the month. *Note:* Again, this does not require an array, but
    the modification in the next exercise does.

6. The chess player in Exercise 5 also likes to play fast. Modify the program
    for Exercise 5 so that, after it reads the complete list of the number of
    moves in a game, it then reads as input a list of the time it took her to
    win each of these games and prints as output three columns of numbers:
    the number of moves, the time for the game, and the average time per
    move in that game.

7. An author enjoys dreaming about which of his overdue bills he will pay
    when his royalty check arrives. He receives 43 cents for each of the first
    1,500 copies that sell in a year and 57 cents for each copy thereafter.
    Write a program that accepts as input a list of the number of copies sold
    during each of the 12 months of the year and prints as output the author's
    royalties for the year. Use an array, even though it isn't absolutely neces-
    sary.

8. The first edition of the book written by the author in Exercise 7 has been
    in print for 5 years (60 months). Write a program that reads the numbers
    of copies sold for each of the 60 months and calculates the author's royal-
    ties two ways. First, compute the royalties based on a calendar year; that
    is, compute the royalties for the first 12 months as in Exercise 7, then for
    the next 12 months, and so on, and finally compute the total royalties for
    the 5 years. Second, compute the royalties on a July 1 to June 30 basis.
    That is, treat the first 6 months as a separate year for royalty purposes,
    then compute the royalties for the next 12 months, and so on. The final
    6 months are also treated as a separate year. Finally compute the total for
    the four whole years and two half years.

9. An amateur pianist, in training to play Chopin's "Minute Waltz" in less
    than 60 seconds, practices the piece between 25 and 40 times at a sitting.
    Write a program that reads as input a list of the times in seconds it takes
    the pianist to play the piece, followed by a termination signal, and prints
    as output the times for the last 10 performances of the waltz, followed by
    the average time for these 10 performances.

10.   Write a program that reads a list of data and prints out the odd-numbered items, list [1], list [3], and so on, followed by the even-numbered items. Place headings before each of these two output lists to identify them.

11.   Write a program that reads two lists and prints them side by side in two columns. Assume that both lists are the same length and that the length is read in as input before either list is read.

12.   Write a program that reads two lists of possibly different lengths and prints them side by side in two columns. The reading of each list should be terminated by the reading of a termination signal.

13.   Write a program that accepts as input a list and a number n and then extracts the first n items of the list as a new list, printing the result.

14.   Write a program that reads a list of real numbers and two integers, start and finish. Then it forms a new list consisting of those elements of the first list with subscripts from start to finish. The program should also print the new list.

15.   Write a program that reads as input a list and a number n and then deletes the first n items in the list. The program should also print the result.

16.   Write a program that reads as input a list and a number n and then rotates the list forward n locations. Thus, if the list is

     10 20 30 40 50 60 70 80

after rotating it forward three locations, the list will be

     40 50 60 70 80 10 20 30

Problems 17 and 18 are designed only for students with enough mathematical background.

17.   (Mathematical)   Write a procedure to compute the inner product of two vectors of dimension 3. Use it in a program to compute the length of a vector of dimension 3.

18.   (Mathematical)   Write a program to compute the angle between two vectors of dimension 3.

9.2   Sequential Searching

The previous section describes the appropriate terminology and some of the Pascal rules concerning lists and subscripts. This section makes a start toward illustrating the power of lists and subscripts as they are used in meaningful programs. The application throughout this section is that of checking a given credit card account number against a list of account numbers of lost or stolen cards. Increasingly more efficient programs are presented here and compared.

Section Preview

Sequential Search:

> In sequential search, the elements of an array are examined in sequence from the element with the lowest subscript to the element with the highest subscript (or vice versa).

Ordered Lists:

> When the array elements are in ascending or descending order, a sequential search for a value that is not in the list can "give up" when the correct position is reached, but the value is not found there.

> **Files:**
>
> Standard files input and output are available without being declared. Other files of characters must be declared. A file that is not sent to a terminal or other display device is saved permanently.

Credit Card Checking

When a customer presents a credit card in payment for goods or services, it is desirable to determine quickly whether it can be accepted or whether it previously has been reported lost or stolen or cancelled for any other reason. The programs in this section perform such an investigation. Companies that issue their own credit cards usually include such a card verification program in their combined charging, billing, and inventory control systems. Independent credit card companies offer a verification service, often by telephone, to the businesses that accept their credit cards.

Pascal Files

Between runs of a credit card checking program, the complete list of account numbers of cancelled cards is stored in computer-readable form on a magnetic disk. A read statement used to obtain information from a file other than the standard file named "input" is similar to a read statement used to read data from the file input except that it specifies which file to read from. For instance, if the variable cardfile is declared to be a file of characters, the statement

```
read (cardfile, actualnumberofcards)
```

tells the computer to read a value from the file named "cardfile" and to assign that value to the variable actualnumberofcards. Since many different files may be used by the same program, naming the particular file wanted is mandatory in any input or output statement that does not use the **default files** named input and output.

A **file** is a sequence of values, all of the same type. For the time being, we will consider only files of characters, which have the same format as the default files input and output. The name of such a file may be declared by a statement such as the following:

```
var
   cardfile : file of char;
```

The file names input and output are automatically declared to be files of characters in every Pascal program. That is, every program is treated as if it contained the declaration

```
var
   input, output : file of char;
```

These names are also special in that any input or output statement that does not contain a file name is assumed to specify either the file named input or the file named output.

All file names, including input and output, that are used by a Pascal program must appear within the parentheses of the program heading. The name of any file except input that is used for input in a Pascal program should appear as the argument of a **reset** procedure call before it is used. The procedure reset positions the file at its initial point in preparation for the first read command. For example, the statement

```
reset (cardfile)
```

appears in each of the credit card checking programs of this section prior to the first execution of a read statement for that file. Any Pascal file that is used for output, except the one named output, should appear as the argument of a rewrite command. The procedure **rewrite** removes all data from the file, if there is any, and prepares the file for writing. Pascal files will be discussed in much more detail in Chapter 11.

Sequential Search Through an Unordered List

The first and simplest strategy for checking a given credit card is simply to search from beginning to end through the list of cancelled credit cards, card by card, either until the given account number is found in the list, or until the end of the list is reached without finding that account number. In the program cardcheck, which implements this strategy, the **sequential search** is accomplished by a while-loop that scans the list until the given account number is found in the list or all of the numbers have been examined.

It is good programming practice to make the searching part of the program a separate module. Other versions of the credit card program in this section will be obtained by modifying this module and leaving the other modules essentially unchanged.

When writing programs that read data to be entered from a terminal, it is a good idea to precede the read statement with a message to the user describing what information is expected. Such a message eases the user's task of supplying exactly the right information at exactly the right time during the execution of the program. Printing such messages is more important when there is more than one kind of information to be entered.

There are two ways of exiting from the search loop. When the credit card being checked is not in the list, the search loop is executed until the list is exhausted. When the card being checked is found in the list, the boolean variable found is set to true, causing the loop to terminate. Then the boolean variable found is tested subsequently to decide which of two output messages is appropriate.

```
program cardcheck1 (input, output, cardfile);

  const
    maxquantityofcards = 10000;

  var
    actualquantityofcards : 0..maxquantityofcards;
    i : 1..maxquantityofcards;
    presentedcard : integer;
    cancelledcard : array [1..maxquantityofcards] of integer;
    cardfile : file of char;
    found : boolean;

  procedure readcards;
    begin
    reset (cardfile);
    read (cardfile, actualquantityofcards);
    for i := 1 to actualquantityofcards do
      read (cardfile, cancelledcard [i]);
    end; { readcards }
```

```
procedure seqsearch;
  begin
  i := 1;
  found := false;
  while (i <= actualquantityofcards) and (not found) do
    if presentedcard = cancelledcard [i] then
      found := true
    else
      i := i + 1;
  end; { seqsearch }
```

```
begin
readcards;
write ('Enter card number to be checked: ');
read (presentedcard);
seqsearch;
write ('Credit card #', presentedcard :1);
if found then
  writeln (' cannot be accepted.')
else
  writeln (' is acceptable.');
end.
run cardcheck1
```

```
Enter card number to be checked: 3572065
Credit card #3572065 is acceptable.
run cardcheck1
```

```
Enter card number to be checked: 2718281
Credit card #2718281 cannot be accepted.
```

The essential dilemma that previously had prevented the efficient programming of a sequential searching application is now solved by using a list. Each card number in the list can be referenced individually using cancelledcard [1], cancelledcard [2], cancelledcard [3], and so on, yet the single expression cancelledcard [i] may refer to any one card, because the value of the index variable i may be the location in the list of any particular card.

Improving the Efficiency

The basic strategy of the program cardcheck1 is to check a credit card account number, supplied as input, against each account number, in turn, in the list of cancelled cards, either until a match is found or until the list is exhausted. Most credit cards offered in payment for purchases or services represent the authorized use of active, valid accounts. In other words, by far the most usual execution of the program cardcheck1 terminates when the list is exhausted and the computer prints the message that the credit card presented is acceptable.

The number of comparisons a program must make before accepting a credit card is some measure of the efficiency of that program. For example, when searching for an acceptable credit card in a list of 10,000 cancelled credit cards, the program cardcheck1 always makes 10,000 comparisons. The actual elapsed computer time for the search section of the program depends on the time it takes the computer to make one comparison and to prepare to make the next comparison.

Sequential Search of an Ordered List

The disorder of the list of cancelled cards is the reason so many comparisons are needed before a presented card is accepted. If the list of cancelled credit cards is maintained in order of increasing card number, then some improvement is possible. The program cardcheck2 presumes that the list is in increasing order.

```
program cardcheck2 (input, output, cardfile);

  const
    maxquantityofcards = 10000;

  var
    actualquantityofcards : 0..maxquantityofcards;
    i : 1..maxactualquantityofcards;
    presentedcard : integer;
    cancelledcard : array [1..maxquantityofcards] of integer;
    cardfile : file of char;
    found, futile : boolean;

  procedure readcards;
      ... end; { readcards }

  procedure seqsearch2;
    begin
    i := 1;
    found := false;
    futile := false;
    while (i <= actualquantityofcards) and
          (not found) and (not futile) do
      if presentedcard <= cancelledcard [i] then
          if presentedcard = cancelledcard [i] then
            found := true
          else
            futile := true
        else
          i := i + 1;
    end; { seqsearch2 }

  begin
  readcards;
  write ('Enter card number to be checked: ');
  read (presentedcard);
  seqsearch2;
  write ('Credit card #', presentedcard :1);
  if found then
    writeln (' cannot be accepted.')
  else
    writeln (' is acceptable.');
  end.
run cardcheck2

Enter card number to be checked: 4629076
Credit card #4629076 is acceptable.
```

For the same input data, the output of the program cardcheck2 would be identical to that produced by the program cardcheck1, but the execution times are not identical. Before accepting a presented account number, cardcheck1 always must search the entire list, but cardcheck2 stops as soon as it reaches a number in the list of cancelled account numbers that is larger than the presented number.

Roughly speaking, the average number of comparisons needed for an acceptance by cardcheck2 is about half the list size, plus one additional comparison on the way out to determine whether the last entry examined was exactly the account number of the credit card being checked. For a list of 10,000 cancelled cards, it would take an average of 5,001 comparisons, significantly better than the 10,000 for cardcheck1.

To a limited extent, this increased efficiency in the checking program is counterbalanced by some additional computer time needed to maintain the list of cancelled credit cards in increasing order. Nevertheless, almost any increase in the efficiency of the checking program results, in practice, in an increase in the efficiency of the entire operation.

Self-Test Questions

1. True/false:

   a. In using a sequential search, the main advantage of scanning ordered data rather than unordered data is that ordered data is easier for humans to read.

   b. If you need to find something in a list, you should always sort the list first.

   c. Suppose you have a choice of searching an unordered list of objects or an ordered list containing the same objects. The search of the ordered list always will be faster.

2. What two purposes does the file cardfile serve in the credit card checking programs?

Exercises

1. Write a program to read as input a number and a list of four numbers and to determine whether the value of the single number is found in the list. The program should print its conclusion, either "yes" or "no".

2. Modify the program for Exercise 1 so that it also prints out the location in the list where the value of the single number is found.

3. Write a program to read a list of numbers and to produce a new list consisting of all the numbers found in the original list, but without duplicates. *Hint:* One way to do this is to copy a number into the new list if and only if no previous number in the original list is equal to it, and this can be determined by a search for equality.

4. Write a program that reads two lists and forms their union, a new list without duplicates consisting of all the numbers found in at least one of the two original lists. *Hint:* One way is to combine the lists without removing duplicates and then to use the program written for Exercise 4 to eliminate the duplicates.

5. Write a program that reads as input three lists of names of people who signed three circulating copies of a petition and produces a combined list, without duplicates, of all persons who signed the petition and a count of the number of such people.

6. Write a program that reads as input two lists and prints only those values that appear in both lists.

7. Write a program to read as input two lists and to print only those values that appear in exactly one of the two given lists.

8. Write a program that reads as input two lists and produces a third list whose values are the locations in the second list where the items of the first list are found. The length of the resulting list is the same as the length of the first list. If an item from the first list is not found in the second list, the corresponding entry in the resulting list should be zero. If an entry from the first list is found two or more times in the second list, the corresponding entry in the resulting list is the location of the first such occurrence.

9. Write a program to read two lists and to determine whether every element of the first list is also an element of the second list.

10. Write a program to read as input a list of numbers and to produce as output two lists, the first consisting of all the original numbers without duplication, and the second of the frequency of occurrence of these numbers. Print the two lists in side-by-side columns.

11. Write a program to read a list of test scores and to compute the mode, the test score that occurs most frequently in the list. *Hint:* Use the program written for Exercise 10. Note that the mode is more difficult for a computer to find than the average or mean. For people, it is often the other way around.

12. Write a program to read the first 10,000 digits of the number pi into a list and to determine whether the sequence of digits 1234567 ever occurs in those 10,000 digits. *Note:* Write a more general program to test whether the elements of any first list occur in order as elements of a second list, and test the program to find whether the digits 123 ever appear in order within the first 30 digits of pi.

13. Write a program to further test the more general program written for Exercise 12 by generating 10,000 random integers from 0 to 9, and testing to see whether the sequence of digits 1234567 ever occurs within the 10,000 random digits.

9.3 Better Algorithms For Searching

Sequential search is a brute force technique. It works well for short lists but succeeds only by sheer persistence for large ones. Significant improvements in efficiency are possible if the strategy is modified so that only small lists are searched sequentially. The correct page to search is located by skipping forward a whole page at a time until the correct one is found.

A somewhat different strategy, **divide and conquer**, is employed in a **binary search**. Half of the list can be eliminated at once by testing the middle element. Than half the remaining elements are eliminated by another test. Before long, there are hardly any candidates left and the search is completed quickly.

Section Preview

Multilevel Search:

If an ordered list is divided into "pages", it takes less time to search one entry per "page" and then to search that "page" for a given value than it takes to search the entire list sequentially.

If there are more levels, perhaps "volume", "chapter", "page", and "line", the search at each level is shorter and the total search time is shorter.

Binary Search:

Binary search uses a **divide and conquer** strategy to search an ordered list. At each step, the "middle" location still under consideration is tested, thereby eliminating half the remaining candidates for the location where the given value might be found. After very few steps, there is only one candidate left.

Multilevel Search

A better search strategy for a sequential search is to imitate the procedure of looking up a word in a dictionary. It makes no sense to search through every word in the dictionary, starting with "aardvark" in hopes of finding "zebra". Most dictionaries have the first and last words defined on a page printed at the top of that page, for easy visibility. There is no point in searching through all the words on a page if a glance at the top of the page confirms that the correct page has not yet been reached. For this purpose, 10,000 entries in a list of cancelled credit cards might be divided arbitrarily into 100 "pages" of 100 entries each.

The basic strategy of the program cardcheck3 is a **two-level search**, first for the correct page, and second for the correct entry (if there is one) on that page. Both the page search loop and the entry-by-entry search loop here are modelled on the search loop of cardcheck2, except that the page search loop does not have to check for exact agreement with the credit card number being presented.

```
program cardcheck3 (input, output, cardfile);

  const
    maxquantityofcards = 10000;
    pagesize = 100;

  var
    actualquantityofcards : 0..maxquantityofcards;
    i, firstonpage, lastonpage : 1..maxquantityofcards;
    presentedcard : integer;
    cancelledcard : array [1..maxquantityofcards] of integer;
    cardfile : file of char;
    entryfound, futile, pagefound : boolean;

  procedure readcards;
    ..: end; { readcards }

  procedure twolevelsearch;
    { the list of cancelled credit cards must be in
      increasing order by account number for this
      procedure to work }

    begin
    { search for the correct page }
    { each page has pagesize entries }
```

```
      pagefound := false;
     lastonpage := pagesize;
    while not pagefound do
       if lastonpage > actualquantityofcards then
         begin
         firstonpage := lastonpage - (pagesize - 1);
         lastonpage := actualquantityofcards;
         pagefound := true;
         end
       else
         if presentedcard <= cancelledcard [lastonpage] then
           begin
           firstonpage := lastonpage - (pagesize - 1);
           pagefound := true;
           end
         else
           lastonpage := lastonpage + pagesize;
      { end of while-loop }

     { search the page sequentially to see if
         the presented card is there }
    entryfound := false;
    futile := false;
    i := firstonpage;
    while (i <= lastonpage) and
           (not entryfound) and (not futile) do
       if presentedcard <= cancelledcard [i] then
         if presentedcard = cancelledcard [i] then
           entryfound := true
         else
           futile := true
       else
         i := i + 1; { end of while-loop }
    end; { twolevelsearch }

 begin
 readcards;
 write ('Enter card number to be checked: ');
 read (presentedcard);
 twolevelsearch;
 write ('Credit card #', presentedcard :1);
 if entryfound then
   writeln (' cannot be accepted.')
 else
   writeln (' is acceptable.');
 end.
```

Efficiency of a Multilevel Search

No sample execution output for the program cardcheck3 is given, because it would look identical to the output of cardcheck1 and to the output of card-check2. The speed of execution, however, is quite different. At the very worst, if the credit card presented is the last card in a list of 10,000 cancelled cards, the program cardcheck3 must scan through 100 pages and through 100 entries on the last page, and then make one final comparison for equality, a total of 201 comparisons. On the average, only half the pages must be checked, and only half the comparisons on the selected page are needed before a conclusion is reached. Thus the average number of comparisons of account numbers made by cardcheck3 is about 101, as compared to 5,001 for cardcheck2 and 10,000 for cardcheck1. The extra time spent writing the longer program cardcheck3 is quickly repaid in savings of computer time required for running the credit card checking program.

It is easy to see how a four-level search program could reduce the maximum number of comparisons to scan a list of 10,000 entries to $10 + 10 + 10 + 10 + 1 = 41$, with the average number of comparisons roughly half of that. The 10,000 entries are divided arbitrarily into blocks of 1,000, then the correct block of 1,000 is divided into subblocks of 100, then the correct block of 100 is divided into subblocks of 10, and finally the correct block of 10 is searched sequentially to see if the presented card is there. There are no new programming ideas in the writing of a program cardcheck4 to implement this four-level searching algorithm, so it is left as an exercise. A comparison of the efficiencies of cardcheck4 with the other programs of this section appears at the end of the section.

Binary Search

The number of comparisons required by the one-level, the two-level, and the four-level search procedures seems to indicate that, in spite of increasing the number of levels that must be checked, if the maximum number of comparisons on any one level is reduced, the total number of comparisons is reduced. Thus the ultimate in searching efficiency might be achieved by reducing the number of alternatives on each level to 2, even though the number of levels increases. This leads to an extremely efficient search procedure called a **binary search**. In fact, if the first alternative on any level is incorrect, then the second alternative must be correct. Thus only one test is needed on each level. With the use of such a binary search, it is possible to search a list of over 10,000 entries in only 15 comparisons, 14 comparisons to reduce the alternatives down to one entry, plus 1 more comparison to test that entry.

Surprisingly, the program cardcheck5 (listed later) to implement the binary search strategy has fewer statements than the program cardcheck3, which implements the much less efficient two-level search strategy. It is not necessary to write 14 successive loops for the binary search, because what is done at each level is sufficiently repetitive to form the only loop of the program. In order to clarify the details of a binary search, two examples are now provided.

Example 1.
Table 9.2 shows how a binary search is used to seek the number 2415495 in a list of 16 numbers. The numbers are given in increasing order in the first column. The presented number 2415495 is not in the list, but this fact plays no role in the search procedure until the very last step.

As a first step in binary searching, the list is divided in half. An asterisk follows the eighth number in column 1 because it is the last entry in the first half of the list. Since the given number 2415495 is less than (or equal to) the eighth entry 2980957, the second half of the list can be eliminated from further consideration. Column 2 shows only the first half of the original list, entries 1 through 8, retained as the segment still actively being searched.

The procedure is repeated. An asterisk follows the fourth entry in column 2 because it is the last entry in the first half of the segment of the list still actively being searched. Since the given number 2415495 is greater than the fourth number 1627547, this time it is the first half of the active segment that is eliminated and the second half (entries 5 through 8 of the original list) that is retained. This is shown in column 3 of Table 9.2.

Table 9.2 Binary search for the number 2415495 in a list of 16 numbers. An asterisk denotes the last entry of the first half of the segment still under active
consideration.

Before any comparisons	After one comparison	After two comparisons	After three comparisons	After four comparisons	Given number
1096633	1096633				
1202604	1202604				
1484131	1484131				
1627547	1627547*				
2008553	2008553	2008553			
2202646	2202646	2202646*			
2718281	2718281	2718281	2718281*	2718281 $\neq$	2415495
2980957*	2980957	2980957	2980957		
3269017					
4034287					
4424133					
5459815					
5987414					
7389056					
8103083					
8886110					

In the next stage, the second remaining number 2202646, which was the
sixth entry in the original list, is marked with an asterisk because it is the last
entry of the first half of the segment still being searched. Since this number is
exceeded by the given number 2415945, the second half of the segment in
column 3 (entries 7 and 8) is retained as the active segment in column 4. The
seventh entry of the original list, the number 2718281, is the last entry of the
first half of the remaining list of two entries and thus is marked with an asterisk
in column 4 to indicate its role as a comparison entry. Since the given number
2415495 is less than this, the other entry (the eighth original entry) is discarded, and column 5 shows that after four comparisons, only the seventh entry
2718281 remains.

Since only one entry remains, a test for equality is made between the
given number 2415495 and the one remaining entry 2718281. They are not
equal. Thus the given number is not in the list. Note that the previous comparisons of these two numbers was merely to determine whether the given
number was less than or equal to the seventh entry.

Example 2.

Table 9.3 shows how the binary search works for the number 7389056,
which is found in the list of 16 numbers.

As before, the first column lists the original numbers with an asterisk following the last number of the first half of the list, the eighth entry. The
number 7389056 is greater than the eighth entry, so the second half of the list
(entries 9 to 16) is retained in column 2. A comparison of the given number
7389056 with the last entry of the first half of the segment remaining in column
2, the twelfth original entry 5459815, eliminates entries 9 through 12.

A comparison with the fourteenth entry, followed by an asterisk in
column 3, eliminates the fifteenth and sixteenth entries. One more comparison
of the given number 7389056 against the thirteenth entry, followed by an asterisk in column 4, eliminates that entry and leaves only the fourteenth entry

Table 9.3 Binary search for the number 7389056 in a list of 16 numbers. An asterisk denotes the last entry of the first half of the segment still under active consideration.

Before any comparisons	After one comparison	After two comparisons	After three comparisons	After four comparisons	Given number
1096633					
1202604					
1484131					
1627547					
2008553					
2202646					
2718281					
2980957*					
3269017	3269017				
4034287	4034287				
4424133	4424133				
5459815	5459815*				
5987414	5987414	5987414	5987414*		
7389056	7389056	7389056*	7389056	7389056 =	7389056
8103083	8103083	8103083			
8886110	8886110	8886110			

7389056. The final test for equality of the given number and the only remaining candidate in the list yields success, and it can be reported that the given number is the fourteenth entry in the list.

It is most convenient when programming a binary search to use a list size that is an exact power of 2 (2, 4, 8, 16, 32,...). This avoids fractions when the size of the list segment still under consideration is halved repeatedly. Since the smallest power of 2 greater than 10,000 is 2 to the fourteenth power, which is 16,384, it takes the same number of comparisons to perform a binary search on a list of 16,384 entries as on a list of 10,000 entries. The program cardcheck5 does a binary search on a list of 16,384 entries. Actually, because the integer operator div is used to prevent fractional parts when locating the last element of the first half of the list segment still under active consideration, this binary search procedure applies to a list of arbitrary length.

```
program cardcheck5 (input, output, cardfile);

   const
     maxquantityofcards = 16384;

   var
     actualquantityofcards : 0..maxquantityofcards;
     i, onlyremaining : 1..maxquantityofcards;
     beginning, ending, endoffirsthalf : 1..maxquantityofcards;
     presentedcard : integer;
     cancelledcard : array [1..maxquantityofcards] of integer;
     cardfile : file of char;
     found : boolean;
```

```
procedure readcards;
    ... end;  { readcards }

procedure binarysearch;
    { The variables, beginning, ending, and endoffirsthalf
      refer to the part of the list still under consideration.
      Initially, this is the whole list. }
    begin
    beginning := 1;
    ending := actualquantityofcards;
    while beginning <> ending do
      begin
      endoffirsthalf := (beginning + ending - 1) div 2;
      if presentedcard <= cancelledcard [endoffirsthalf] then
        ending := endoffirsthalf
      else
        beginning := endoffirsthalf + 1;
      end;  { while-loop }

    { The only remaining location is beginning ( = ending ) }
    onlyremaining := beginning;
    found := presentedcard = cancelledcard [onlyremaining];
    end;  { binarysearch }

begin
readcards;
write ('Enter card number to be checked: ');
read (presentedcard);
binarysearch;
write ('Credit card #', presentedcard :1);
if found then
  writeln (' cannot be accepted.')
else
  writeln (' is acceptable.');
end.
```

The number of comparisons required in the binary search can be counted easily. With one comparison, the original list of 16,384 is cut down to 8,192. A second comparison leaves only 4,096 candidates. A third leaves 2,048; a fourth 1,024; a fifth 512; a sixth 256; a seventh 128; an eighth 64; a ninth 32; a tenth 16; an eleventh 8; a twelfth 4; a thirteenth 2; and finally a fourteenth comparison leaves only 1 candidate. The fifteenth and final comparison determines whether that candidate is the credit card being searched for or not. Thus, whether the presented credit card is in the list or not, the number of comparisons is always 15.

When the number of entries is less than 16,384, the number of candidates at each stage never exceeds the number of candidates for an original list size of 16,384. Thus 15 comparisons suffices for binary searching all lists of length up to 16,384 (= 2 to the 14th power), although sometimes even fewer are required.

Comparison of the Efficiency of the Search Procedures

Table 9.4 summarizes the number of comparisons required by each of the programs in this section to check a credit card against a list of 10,000 (or in the case of the binary search, 16,384) cancelled credit cards. For each program and search method, the minimum, maximum, and average number of comparisons is given for the most likely circumstance that the presented credit card is acceptable and is not to be found in the list.

Table 9.4 Comparison of Five Search Procedures Based on a 10,000-Entry List.

Search Method	Program Name	Comparisons		
		Minimum	Maximum	Average
Sequential search (unordered)	cardcheck1	10,000	10,000	10,000
Sequential search (ordered)	cardcheck2	2	10,001	5,001.5
Two-level sequential search	cardcheck3	3	201	102
Four-level sequential search	cardcheck4	5	41	23
Binary search	cardcheck5	15	15	15

The information in Table 9.4 shows the clear superiority of binary searching over all the other methods, even those whose programs are much more complicated. This superiority even increases as the list becomes longer, because it takes the binary search only one additional comparison to search a list with twice as many entries, 32,768, two additional comparisons to search 65,536 entries, and only three additional comparisons to extend the length of the list that can be searched to 131,072 entries.

The other searching methods cannot begin to match this feat, as shown in Table 9.5. Perhaps surprisingly, only the very slowest of the searching procedures is implemented by a program shorter than the binary search, and then not very much shorter. Binary search techniques are recommended, therefore, for searching all ordered lists, except possibly very short lists.

Table 9.5 Comparison of Five Search Procedures Based on a 100,000-Entry List.

Search Method	Program Name	Comparisons		
		Minimum	Maximum	Average
Sequential search (unordered)	cardcheck1	100,000	100,000	100,000
Sequential search (ordered)	cardcheck2	2	100,001	50,001.5
Two-level sequential search*	cardcheck3	3	634	318.5
Four-level sequential search**	cardcheck4	5	73	39
Binary search***	cardcheck5	18	18	18

*Based on $316 \times 317 = 100,172$ entries
**Based on $18 \times 18 \times 18 \times 18 = 104,976$ entries
***Based on $2^{17} = 131,072$ entries

Self-Test Questions

1.   True/false:

a. A sequential search is an efficient way to search an ordered list.

b. A sequential search is an efficient way to search an unordered list.

c. In general, the more levels a mulitlevel search has, the more efficient it is.

d. A binary search can be performed even if a list has gaps between adjacent values.

e. A binary search program is much more complicated than a multilevel search program.

f. Although binary search is more efficient than four-level search for lists of size 100,000, the four-level search catches up in efficiency for larger lists.

2.   Suppose a computer had memory space for a little more than 100 entries from a list. How could a list of 10,000 entries be searched efficiently on such a computer?

Exercises

1.   The information in Table 9.5 about the comparative speed of the two-level search program of 100,000 items is based on 316 pages of 317 entries each. How many comparisons would be necessary (minimum, maximum, and average) if the two-level searching procedure were based on 1,000 pages of 100 entries each? Can you formulate a general principle about minimizing the number of comparisons in a two-level search?

2.   Write a program cardcheck4 based on a four-level searching procedure.

9.4   Sorting

The credit card checking programs in the previous section search unordered and ordered lists of cancelled credit cards to determine whether a particular number is in the list. This section presents another kind of searching application, searching an unordered list to find the smallest element. (If the list is ordered, then finding the smallest element is very easy.) The program developed to search for the smallest element in an unordered list is employed subsequently as the basis for several programs to sort the entire unordered list into increasing order.

A second theme emphasized in this section is that programs need to be tested thoroughly. The programs written in this chapter are not completely obvious to most beginners, partly because understanding the concept of a subscript requires some practice and partly because the programs involve complex ways of processing data. It becomes increasingly important, therefore, for a programmer to know how to test a program to be sure that it does what it is supposed to do.

A third theme is while-loops. As illustrated by the credit card checking programs in the previous section, while-loops are essential for sequential scanning. Searching for the smallest element in an unordered list also requires sequential scanning.

Section Preview

Smallest Element In a List:

A sequential search loop is adapted to finding the smallest element in a list and its location by keeping, as running variables, the smallest value found so far and the location in the list of that smallest value.

Sorting:

The elements of alist may be located in increasing order by repeatedly finding the smallest element, copying it to the sorted list, and "crossing it out" by replacing it with a very large value. The second attempt to find the smallest element in the list will find the second smallest element of the original list, because the smallest element was "crossed out". The process continues for the remaining elements.

Interchange Sort:

Swapping the smallest element found in each pass with an appropriate element in the front (sorted) section of the list doubles the speed of sorting and halves the memory required.

Independent Testing of Procedures:

The input, output, and find-smallest-element procedures are sufficiently modular that they may be tested independently of the sorting procedure. With the correctness of the procedures independently verified in advance, there is little that could go wrong in the sorting program.

Parameters:

The procedures readlist, writelist, sort1, and sort2 in this section are of very general use in many applications, so they are written to operate on any list. Calling programs tell these procedures which list to operate on by putting the name of the list as an actual parameter (i.e., supplied argument) in the procedure call.

Earned Run Averages for Baseball Pitchers

In baseball, a pitcher's earned run average (ERA) is roughly the average number of runs per game scored against him and his team while he is pitching, not counting "unearned" runs scored because of fielding errors, which do not have a direct bearing on the pitcher's ability as a pitcher. While a low earned run average for a particular pitcher does not guarantee that his team will win the games he pitches, it certainly makes that outcome more likely. For this reason, newspapers and sports periodicals frequently publish lists of names of pitchers in ascending order of earned run average, so that the best pitcher in this regard appears first.

The program smallestera tells the computer to read data on pitchers and their earned run averages and to print out the name and earned run average for the pitcher with the smallest earned run average. Input data for the program consist of one line for each pitcher in the league, containing the pitcher's name and his earned run average, and a trailer line containing a termination signal. Data for the first sample execution are based on a memorable American League season.

Lists of Character Strings

The main part of the program smallestera resembles the program avgofscores3 in Section 9.1 in that both of them read all the data before the main processing is done. In choosing the names of the variables, the abbreviation "era" is used sometimes instead of the full phrase "earnedrunaverage", to keep the variable names from becoming too long. A new feature of this program is that the list pitcher has values that are character strings, that is, the names of the pitchers.

```
program smallestera (input, output);

  const
    maxnumberofpitchers = 1000;
    sizeofname = 20;
    signal = 'Aaron Gross           ';

  type
    listindex = 1..maxnumberofpitchers;
    nameindex = 1..sizeofname;
    nametype = packed array [nameindex] of char;

  var
    location, locsofar : listindex;
    letter : nameindex;
    i, numberofpitchers : 0..maxnumberofpitchers;
    name : nametype;
    pitcher : array [listindex] of nametype;
    era : array [listindex] of real;
    smallest, smallsofar : real;
    outofdata : boolean;

  procedure readeradata;
    begin
    i := 0;
    outofdata := false;
    while (i < maxnumberofpitchers) and (not outofdata) do
      begin
      for letter := 1 to sizeofname do
        read (name [letter]);
      writeln ('Input data  name: ', name);
      if name = signal then
        outofdata := true
```

```
        else
          begin
          i := i + 1;
          pitcher [i] := name;
          readln (era [i]);
          writeln ('Input data  era: ', era [i] :1:2);
          end; { else-clause }
      end; { while-loop }
    numberofpitchers := i;
  end; { readeradata }
```

```
procedure findsmallest;
  begin
  smallsofar := era [1];
  locsofar := 1;
  for i := 2 to numberofpitchers do
    if era [i] < smallsofar then
      begin
      smallsofar := era [i];
      locsofar := i;
      end; { if-statement and for-loop }
  smallest := smallsofar;
  location := locsofar;
  end; { findsmallest }
```

```
{ --------- main program ----------}
begin
readeradata;
findsmallest;
writeln ('Out of ', numberofpitchers :1, ' pitchers,');
writeln ('the best earned run average is ', smallest :1:2);
writeln ('pitched by ', pitcher [location]);
end.
```

The name "Aaron Gross" is used to terminate reading of the data. A termination signal of "***" is safer, but programmers need to have some fun. Actually, Aaron Gross converted from baseball to javelin at an early age and never pitched an inning of major league baseball, so his name cannot be confused with real data for this program. Baseball fans remember him best as a termination signal.

The basic strategy of the search is to examine each earned run average in turn and to remember it if it is the smallest encountered so far, or to forget it if it is not. The location of the smallest earned run average so far is also remembered, so that the pitcher's name may be printed out at the end.

Type Declarations

In Pascal, it is possible to declare a name to be a programmer-defined data type. These new data types can then be used in variable declarations in the same way that the ordinary Pascal types real, integer, char, boolean, and subranges may be used.

For example, the type declaration

```
type
  nameindex = 1..sizeofname;
```

indicates that nameindex is a type that is the same as the subrange 1..sizeof-name, which is the same as 1..20 in the program smallestera. The type declaration

```
nametype = packed array [nameindex] of char;
```

declares nametype to be a type that consists of character strings of length 20. Note that the type nameindex can be used in place of the subscript range 1..20 in the declaration.

Once a type has been declared, any variable can be declared to be that type. For example, in the program smallestera,

```
type
   listindex = 1..maxnumberofpitchers;
   nameindex = 1..sizeofname;
   nametype = packed array [nameindex] of char;

var
   name : nametype;
   pitcher : array [listindex] of nametype;
```

declares name to be a character string of length 20 and pitcher to be an array of 1,000 character strings, each of length 20.

Type declarations must be placed after constant declarations and before variable declarations. Note that the equals sign is used to separate the type name from its declaration.

Handling Ties

Before running this program, we make one improvement. In case of ties, the program smallestera locates and prints only the earliest of the equal entries. Since it makes little sense to ignore the other equally good pitchers, the following lines may be added to smallestera to print their names also.

```
for i := location + 1 to numberofpitchers do
  if era [i] = smallest then
    writeln ('and ', pitcher [i]);
```

This loop is another reason to find the location of the smallest earned run average in the list as well as its value. Incorporating these instructions to handle ties into the program smallestera results in the program smallestera2. The sample execution of the program smallestera2 has been reduced to reasonable size by using an alphabetical listing of only the best 10 pitchers in one season. The full execution, using all 122 pitchers who pitched in 12 or more games, is quite similar but much longer.

```
program smallestera2 (input, output);
   .
   .
   .
   { ·········· main program ··········}
   begin
   readeradata;
   findsmallest;
   writeln ('Out of ', numberofpitchers :1, ' pitchers,');
   writeln ('the best earned run average is ', smallest :1:2);
   writeln ('pitched by ', pitcher [location]);
   for i := location + 1 to numberofpitchers do
     if era [i] = smallest then
       writeln ('and ', pitcher [i]);
   end.
```

```
run smallestera2

Input data    name:  Vida Blue
Input data    era:   3.01
Input data    name:  Bert Blyleven
Input data    era:   3.00
Input data    name:  Steve Busby
Input data    era:   3.08
Input data    name:  Dennis Eckersley
Input data    era:   2.60
Input data    name:  Ed Figueroa
Input data    era:   2.90
Input data    name:  Catfish Hunter
Input data    era:   2.58
Input data    name:  Rudy May
Input data    era:   3.06
Input data    name:  Jim Palmer
Input data    era:   2.09
Input data    name:  Frank Tanana
Input data    era:   2.63
Input data    name:  Rusty Torrez
Input data    era:   3.06
Input data    name:  Aaron Gross
Out of 10 pitchers,
the best earned run average is   2.09
pitched by Jim Palmer
```

Program Testing

It is easy enough to check from the echoes of input data provided in the sample execution of smallestera2 that the correct smallest earned run average is found and printed. However, before adopting this program for regular use, additional checking should be done using different data to reduce or eliminate the likelihood that the program runs correctly only because of some special property of this first batch of data. Be especially suspicious of the testing data if the smallest earned run average turns out to be either the first one in the list or the last one in the list. Even an incorrect program might obtain the right answer in these very special circumstances.

Since the pitcher with the smallest earned run average in the sample execution is the eighth pitcher out of 10, the data used are suitable on this account. Of course, for a complete testing of the program, test data should also be used in which the smallest earned run average does come first or last, because programs also can fail when the data have special properties.

There is one eventuality allowed for in the program that is not tested by the data given, the possibility of ties. Since the actual historical data do not oblige us with a tie for the smallest earned run average, fictitious pitchers are manufactured to help test the tie feature. The career histories of two of them are of particular importance:

Carl Curveball was a reliable southpaw with a lot of stuff and good control. His career ended abruptly when he was traded to Mexico City and found that his curveball wouldn't curve in the thinner air.

Fireman Fink holds the major league record for appearances as a relief pitcher in a single season, at 162, not counting the playoffs and the World Series. His team did not make the playoffs or the World Series.

```
run smallestera2

Input data   name: Vida Blue
Input data   era:  3.01
Input data   name: Bert Blyleven
Input data   era:  3.00
Input data   name: Steve Busby
Input data   era:  3.08
Input data   name: Carl Curveball
Input data   era:  2.09
Input data   name: Dennis Eckersley
Input data   era:  2.60
Input data   name: Ed Figueroa
Input data   era:  2.90
Input data   name: Fireman Fink
Input data   era:  2.09
Input data   name: Catfish Hunter
Input data   era:  2.58
Input data   name: Rudy May
Input data   era:  3.06
Input data   name: Jim Palmer
Input data   era:  2.09
Input data   name: Frank Tanana
Input data   era:  2.63
Input data   name: Rusty Torrez
Input data   era:  3.06
Input data   name: Aaron Gross
Out of 12 pitchers,
the best earned run average is  2.09
pitched by Carl Curveball
and Fireman Fink
and Jim Palmer
```

After examining this somewhat fanciful execution, it is likely that the program smallestera2 could handle correctly the case of ties if that situation ever came up in real data.

A Uniform Main Program for Sorting

Sorting data is a very common and very important programming application. In the credit card checking application in Section 9.3, for instance, all the efficient programs require that the list of lost or stolen credit cards is already in increasing order.

In recognition of the need for sorting in many different applications, the sorting programs presented in this chapter use general variable names, like list and sortedlist, that fit many different circumstances. All the sorting programs in this chapter are refinements of the program dosort.

```
program dosort;
   Read all the data;
   Sort the data;
   Write the sorted list;
```

Although the input, output, and sorting procedures written in this section will use general, nonspecific names for their variables, the argument passing conventions introduced in Chapter 8 permit these subroutines to be used without change in any application.

Every sorting program in this chapter calls the same procedure readlist to read all the data. Readlist employs a loop whose execution is stopped when a termination signal is read. This procedure resembles the procedures readone-studentsdata and readline, written for the gradepoint application in Chapter 6. All these procedures place the data in an array, and all but readline also count the number of data items. An index variable is used to control where in the list the data are placed. When the signal data item is finally read, the value of this index variable gives the count of the items that were read.

```
const
  maxlistsize = 1000;
  signal = 9999;
type
  valuetype = -signal..signal;
  listindex = 1..maxlistsize;
  listsizetype = 0..maxlistsize;
  listtype = array [listindex] of valuetype;

procedure readlist (var list : listtype;
                    var listsize : listsizetype);
  var
    i : listsizetype;
    datum : valuetype;
    outofdata : boolean;

  begin
  i := 0;
  outofdata := false;
  while (i < maxlistsize) and (not outofdata) do
    begin
    read (datum);
    writeln ('Input data  datum: ', datum);
    if datum = signal then
      outofdata := true
    else
      begin
      i := i + 1;
      list [i] := datum;
      end; { else-clause }
    end; { while-loop }
  listsize := i;
  end; { readlist }
```

The procedure writelist is called to write the sorted list produced by the first sorting program to be considered. It employs a simple for-loop, and introduces no new features or methods.

```
procedure writelist (list : listtype;
                     listsize : listsizetype);
  var
    i : listindex;
  begin
  writeln;
  writeln ('The sorted list is as follows:');
  writeln;
```

```
      for i := 1 to listsize do
        writeln (sortedlist [i]);
      end; { writelist }
```

Testing the Input and Output Procedures

It is possible to test the input procedure readlist and the output procedure writelist without doing the sort in between. Since the sorting procedure is slightly more complicated than these procedures, it would be nice to know before checking the sorting procedure that the input and output procedures cannot contribute any errors that might be attributed falsely to the sorting procedure. A test program testio accomplishes this testing by copying the input list, without sorting, into the output list sortedlist. To avoid possible confusion, it writes a disclaimer that the output list remains unsorted.

```
program testio (input, output);

  const
    maxlistsize = 1000;
    signal = 9999;

  type
    valuetype = -signal..signal;
    listindex = 1..maxlistsize;
    listsizetype = 0..maxlistsize;
    listtype = array [listindex] of valuetype;

  var
    inputlist, sortedlist : listtype;
    listsize : listsizetype;

  procedure readlist (var list : listtype;
                      var listsize : listsizetype);
    ... end; { readlist }

  procedure writelist (list : listtype;
                       listsize : listsizetype);
    ... end; { writelist }

  { ----- test read and write procedures ----- }
  begin
  readlist (inputlist, listsize);
  sortedlist := list;
  writeln;
  writeln ('*** This is an I/O test program only. ***');
  writeln ('*** The data have not been sorted yet. ***');
  writelist (sortedlist, listsize);
  end.

  run testio

Input data datum:        256
Input data datum:        -37
Input data datum:          8
Input data datum:         45
Input data datum:       9999
```

```
*** This is an I/O test program only. ***
*** The data have not been sorted yet. ***

The sorted list is as follows:

        256
        -37
          8
         45
```

Assignment of Arrays

The statement that is used in the program testio to copy the values from the array inputlist to the array sortedlist is a single assignment statement. One array may be assigned to another provided they are both declared to be the same type. An array assignment was used in the program smallestera to set the values of character strings, which are actually arrays of characters.

Sorting by Finding the Smallest Element Remaining in a List

A procedure to find the smallest element in a list, can be used as a step in a procedure to sort a list. All that is required is to "cross out" the smallest element from the list after it has been placed in the new, sorted list. Then, the procedure finds the smallest remaining element, which was the second smallest original element. The second smallest is placed in the new list and "crossed out" in the original list. The next attempt to find the smallest remaining element will find the third smallest original element. Ultimately, the repetition of this process produces a sorted list consisting of all the original items in increasing order.

The sorting procedure sort1 repeatedly uses a procedure findsmallest to locate the smallest remaining element in the list. That smallest remaining element is then recorded in the sorted list. To trick the computer into thinking that the number has been "crossed out", it is replaced by a number too large to be plausible data. This number never will be found by the next application of the procedure findsmallest. The current procedure findsmallest is the procedure findsmallest in the earned run average example, with its variable names changed to conform to the greater generality of the current program.

```
procedure findsmallest (list : listtype;
                        listsize : listsizetype;
                        var smallest : valuetype;
                        var location : listindex);
    var
      smallsofar : valuetype;
      locsofar, i : listindex;

    begin
    smallsofar := list [1];
    locsofar := 1;
    for i := 2 to listsize do
      if list [i] < smallsofar then
        begin
        smallsofar := list [i];
        locsofar := i;
        end; { if and for-loop }
```

```
      smallest := smallsofar;
      location := locsofar;
   end;  { findsmallest }
procedure sort1 (list : listtype;
                 listsize : listsizetype;
                 var sortedlist : listtype);

   var
     locinsortedlist, location : listindex;
     smallest : valuetype;

   begin
   for locinsortedlist := 1 to listsize do
     begin
     findsmallest (list, listsize, smallest, location);
     sortedlist [locinsortedlist] := smallest;
     { cross out the smallest entry just found }
     list [location] := bignumber;  { a main prog constant }
     end;  { for-loop }
   end;  { sort1 }
```

If execution speed is important, a small amount of time could be saved by
using the same variables smallsofar and locsofar after the search as during the
search. However, the sorting procedure sort1 is by no means the most efficient
sorting procedure possible, only one of the simplest. Thus, improved clarity of
variable names is preferred in this case to increased execution speed. Accordingly, the last two instructions of the procedure findsmallest introduce two new
variables, smallest and location, to reflect the fact that the search has been
completed.

Testing Individual Procedures

It can be verified by hand that the procedure sort1 sorts a list into increasing
order, assuming that the procedure findsmallest supplies correct values for the
variables smallest and location. Verification that the procedure findsmallest
works properly might also be done by hand. Since findsmallest is a separate
procedure, it can be checked further using the small test program testfind, that
runs independently of the procedure sort1.

```
      program testfind (output);
      .
      .
      .
      { ----- test findsmallest procedure ----- }
      begin
      list [1] := 45; list [2] := 27; list [3] := 32;
      list [4] := 24; list [5] := 43;
      listsize := 5;
      findsmallest (list, listsize, smallest, location);
      writeln ('The smallest is ', smallest :1);
      writeln ('The location in the list is ', location :1);
      end.
```

```
run testfind

The smallest is 24
The location in the list is 4
```

More Program Testing

In the test program testfind, the values for the list are assigned by program steps to save the trouble of preparing input data. If more extensive testing is desired, the procedure readlist may be used to facilitate the reading of data to test findsmallest. The program morethorough illustrates this idea. Only one sample run is shown for this program, but it may be used as often as needed with different sets of test data, until the programmer is convinced that findsmallest works correctly for all possible data.

```
program morethorough (input, output);

    .
    .
    .

{ more thorough test of findsmallest procedure }
begin
readlist (list, listsize);
findsmallest (list, listsize, smallest, location);
writeln ('The smallest is ', smallest :1);
writeln ('The location in the list is ', location :1);
end.

run morethorough

Input data  datum:        81
Input data  datum:        35
Input data  datum:         0
Input data  datum:        14
Input data  datum:        -3
Input data  datum:        45
Input data  datum:       -27
Input data  datum:        36
Input data  datum:        12
Input data  datum:      9999
The smallest is -27
The location in the list is 7
```

The computer correctly recognizes that the number −27 is less than all positive numbers and less than the negative number −3. The echoes of input data that appear in the output are produced by the procedure readlist, which must be supplied along with the procedure findsmallest to create a complete executable program.

Fitting All The Procedures Together

The program dosort1 combines several procedures that have been checked more or less independently of each other, with favorable results in each case. The program dosort1 itself must now be tested to see if its way of combining the procedures actually provides a program for sorting data. The sample test run shown uses the same data used to test the procedure findsmallest, in order to guarantee that at least the first call to findsmallest will work correctly, permitting a test of what happens after the first time.

```
program dosort1 (input, output);

   const
     maxlistsize = 1000;
     signal = 9999;
     bignumber = signal;

   type
     valuetype = -signal..signal;
     listindex = 1..maxlistsize;
     listsizetype = 0..maxlistsize;
     listtype = array [listindex] of valuetype;

   var
     inputlist, sortedlist : listtype;
     listsize : listsizetype;

   procedure readlist (var list : listtype;
                       var listsize : listsizetype);
      ... end; { readlist };
   procedure writelist (list : listtype;
                        listsize : listsizetype);
      ... end; { writelist }
   procedure findsmallest (list : listtype;
                           listsize : listsizetype;
                           var smallest : valuetype;
                           var location : listindex);
      ... end; { findsmallest }
   procedure sort1 (list : listtype;
                    listsize : listsizetype;
                    var sortedlist : listtype);
      ... end; { sort1 }

   { ---------- main program ---------- }
   begin
   readlist (inputlist, listsize);
   sort1 (inputlist, listsize, sortedlist);
   writelist (sortedlist, listsize);
   end.
run dosort1
```

```
Input data  datum:          81
Input data  datum:          35
Input data  datum:           0
Input data  datum:          14
Input data  datum:          -3
Input data  datum:          45
Input data  datum:         -27
Input data  datum:          36
Input data  datum:          12
Input data  datum:        9999
```

The sorted list is as follows:

```
-27
-3
  0
 12
 14
 35
 36
 45
 81
```

Doubling the Sorting Speed While Saving Space As Well

The procedure sort1 is based on two key ideas. One is to use a search procedure to find the locations of the smallest remaining item. The other is to form a sorted list by transferring items there one at a time, in ascending order, from an unsorted list. Replacing numbers in the unsorted list with very large dummy numbers is more of an incidental trick than a key idea. In fact, the "crossing out" trick is unnecessarily expensive in both time and space.

Toward the end of the execution of sort1, when very few of the original numbers remain in the unsorted list, the search procedure spends most of its time examining and bypassing the dummy numbers, hardly productive labor. Moreover, the space occupied by the dummy numbers ultimately becomes as great as the space occupied by the whole original list.

Another sorting method, considered next, preserves both of the key ideas of sort1. However, by using an interchange, it saves both time and space. Consider starting with the list supplied as input in the sample execution of the program testio.

256 −37 8 45 (original list)

The first step in sorting by the interchange method is to locate the smallest by searching the original list in its entirety. It is the number −37 at location 2. The smallest item is then interchanged with the first item of the original list, as shown below. A vertical bar is drawn immediately after the sorted item in order to separate it from the remaining items. The sorted list is being formed to the left of the vertical bar.

−37 | 256 8 45

The second smallest item cannot be to the left of the vertical bar, because that is where the smallest item is. Thus the second smallest item of the original list is the smallest item to the right of the bar, and it can be found by searching the three locations to the right. This time the search locates the number 8 at location 3 of the list. This item, the second smallest item in the original list, is now interchanged with the item at location 2, yielding the following rearrangement of the list.

−37 8 | 256 45

This time the bar separates the two smallest items from the remaining items. To find the third smallest item of the original list, it is sufficient to search the items to the right of the bar, because the third smallest is the smallest of those two items.

The third smallest item of the original list is the number 45, at location 4 of the list. The interchange method of sorting now requires that it be exchanged with whatever number is at location 3 of the list as shown below.

−37 8 45 | 256

With each step, the sorted initial segment grows and the unsorted final segment shrinks. When the final segment disappears, the list is completely sorted. Indeed, when the unsorted final segment has length one, as it does here, the list is completely sorted because the last number must be the largest number of the original list.

Because the unsorted final segment is constantly shrinking, it takes the computer less and less time to find the smallest remaining item. By way of contrast, the search time for every item using the method of the procedure sort1 remains the same as the search time for the first item. Because of the reduced search time, this interchange method is about twice as fast as the "crossing out" method. The program dosort2 calls the procedure sort2 to apply this interchange method of sorting. The procedure writelist is changed slightly to make a procedure writelist2, because the sorted list is now formed in place of the original list instead of in a different list called sortedlist.

```
program dosort2 (input, output);

  const
    maxlistsize = 1000;
    signal = 9999;

  type
    valuetype = -signal..signal;
    listindex = 1..maxlistsize;
    listsizetype = 0..maxlistsize;
    listtype = array [listindex] of valuetype;

  var
    list : listtype;
    listsize : listsizetype;

  procedure readlist (var list : listtype;
                      var listsize : listsizetype);
      ... end; { readlist }
  procedure writelist (list : listtype;
                       listsize : listsizetype);
      ... end; { writelist }

  procedure findnextsmallest (list : listtype;
                              listsize : listsizetype;
                              var smallest : valuetype;
                              location : listindex;
                              numbersorted : listsizetype);
    var
      smallsofar : valuetype;
      locsofar, i : listindex;

    begin
      smallsofar := list [numbersorted + 1];
      locsofar := numbersorted + 1;
```

```
    for i := numbersorted + 2 to listsize do
      if list [i] < smallsofar then
        begin
        smallsofar := list [i];
        locsofar := i;
        end; { if-statement and for-loop }
    smallest := smallsofar;
    location := locsofar;
    end; { findnextsmallest }


  procedure sort2 (var list : listtype;
                    listsize : listsizetype);
    var
      numbersorted : listsizetype;
      location : listindex;
      smallest : valuetype;


    begin
    for numbersorted := 0 to listsize - 2 do
      begin
      findnextsmallest
          (list, listsize, smallest, location, numbersorted);
      { interchange smallest found with
        first item after sorted segment }
      list [location] := list [numbersorted + 1];
      list [numbersorted + 1] := smallest;
      end; { for-loop }
    end; { sort2 }


  { --------- main program --------- }
  begin
  readlist (list, listsize);
  sort2 (list, listsize);
  writelist (list, listsize);
  end.
run dosort2
```

```
Input data    datum:        81
Input data    datum:        35
Input data    datum:         0
Input data    datum:        14
Input data    datum:        -3
Input data    datum:        45
Input data    datum:       -27
Input data    datum:        36
Input data    datum:        12
Input data    datum:      9999
```

The sorted list is as follows:

```
      -27
       -3
        0
       12
       14
```

35
36
45
81

Readings

Donald E. Knuth, *The Art of Computer Programming,* Vol. 3, *Sorting and Searching,* Addison-Wesley, Reading, Mass., 1973.

William A. Martin, "Sorting", *Computing Surveys,* Vol. 3, pp. 147−174, 1971.

Robert P. Rich, *Internal Sorting Methods Illustrated with PL/I Programs,* Prentice-Hall, Englewood Cliffs, N.J., 1972.

Nicklaus Wirth, *Algorithms + Data Structures = Programs,* Prentice-Hall, Englewood Cliffs, N. J., 1976, Chapter 2.

Self-Test Questions

1. True/false:
    a. In executing procedure sort1, the computer examines every item in the unsorted list in order to determine which item is the smallest.
    b. If the input list to the "interchange sort" happens to be in sorted order, the execution time is less than for the usual case in which the input data are randomly ordered.
    c. The "interchange sort" works correctly even when there are duplicates in the input data.
2. What must be changed to make the sorting programs in this section sort into decreasing order, i.e., largest value first?

Exercises

1. Write a program to read a list of baseball players and their batting averages and to print the name and the batting average of the player with the highest batting average. Be sure your program can handle ties.
2. Modify the program for Exercise 1 so that, instead of a batting average for each player, the program reads the number of times the player officially came to bat in the season and the number of hits the player got. The batting average is the quotient of these numbers, that is, the number of hits divided by the number of times at bat.
3. Using the procedure sort1 as a model, write a program that starts to sort a list by finding the largest number in the list, putting it at the end of the sorted output list, and then "crossing out" the largest number by replacing it with a very small number. Then the process is repeated to find the largest remaining number in the list, and so on.
4. Test the program for Exercise 3 using the same data used in this section to run the program morethorough.
5. Modify the procedure sort2 so that it can sort the list of pitchers and earned run averages used in the programs smallestera and smallestera2. Be sure that whenever two earned run averages are swapped, the names of the pitchers corresponding to them are also swapped.
6. Using the program written for Exercise 5, write a program modelled on the program dosort2 that can read a list of pitchers and their earned run averages and print them out in increasing order.
7. Hand simulate the execution of the procedure sort1, starting with a list whose values are 45, 32, 16, 32, 45. This is an important type of data to

test, because the equality of two or more list items might upset the execution or the procedure findsmallest.

8. Write a program to test whether a list of names of persons is sorted into alphabetical order.

9. In Section 9.1, the list of lost credit cards was read from a file by the procedure readcards. All of the efficient searching methods require this list to be in ascending order. Write a program to read the file cardfile, sort it, and rewrite it in increasing order. You may use the procedure readcards to read the file and a similar procedure using the following statements to rewrite the file.

```
rewrite (cardfile);
write (cardfile, actualquantityofcards);
for i := 1 to actualquantityofcards do
  write (cardfile, cancelledcard [i]);
```

The sorted list should also be printed.

10. A different way to remove an item from a list is to move all the items with larger subscripts frontward one location. Write a program to sort a list by finding the smallest element, copying it into the sorted list, and then removing it from the unsorted data by this method, repeating these steps until the list of unsorted data is empty.

11. Modify the program readlist used in this section so that the termination signal is not set by the program but is read instead as the first item of data. Thus the valid data of the list are sandwiched between two termination signals, which act like a pair of parentheses.

12. What are the advantages of the program written for Exercise 11 over the original program readlist?

13. Write a program to decide what number occurs most frequently in a sorted list of numbers containing duplications.

14. Write a program that reads a list of numbers and prints out the following list derived from it:

> location of smallest
> location of second smallest
> location of third smallest
>
> .
>
> .
>
> .
>
> location of largest

15. Write a program that reads a list of numbers and prints out the following list derived from it:

> location of largest
> location of second largest
> location of third largest
>
> .
>
> .
>
> .
>
> location of smallest

16. The median of a list of numbers is defined to be that item in the list that has as many items greater than the item as less than it, if there is an odd number of items. If there is an even number of items in the list, the median is the average of the two middle items. Write a program to read a list of numbers and print the median. *Hint:* Sort the list first.

17. Prove that to sort a list of nine items the procedure sort1 requires 72 comparisons. How many comparisons does sort1 take for a list of length n?

18. Prove that to sort a list of nine items the procedure sort2 requires 36 comparisons. Now many comparisons does sort2 take for a list of length *n*? Contrast this answer to your answer for Exercise 17.
19. Use the test data in Exercise 7 to see how sort1 handles ties.

9.5 What You Should Know

1. A list is a sequence of values, all representing data of the same kind.
2. In Pascal, the most usual way of storing a list is in an array.
3. A subscript indicates which element of the list is referenced.
4. The subscript of a subscripted varaible may itself be a variable or an expression.
5. An index variable is a variable subscript.
6. In subrange declarations, it is good programming practice to use names of constants in place of the constants themselves.
7. Many Pascal compilers provide execution-time error messages if a subrange variable is out of bounds.
8. Pascal requires fixed constant limits for the range of subscripts in array declarations. Another variable is used to keep track of the number of elements actually in the list.
9. Standard files input and output are available without being declared. Other files of characters must be declared.
10. A file that is not sent to a terminal or other display device is saved permanently.
11. A sequential search algorithm examines each element of an array in increasing or decreasing order of subscript.
12. If the list is ordered, the sequential search does not have to stop on an exact match.
13. In a multilevel search, the list is scanned in large steps to determine quickly which smaller regions of the array should be searched in more detail.
14. A binary search quickly locates the position of a value in a list by halving the number of candidates with each step.
15. For large lists, multilevel search methods are much more efficient than sequential search methods and binary search methods are more efficient than muliltlevel search methods.
16. A list is sorted when its elements are in order.
17. Successful test runs with atypical data are not sufficient evidence that a program will run with more usual data. On the other hand, programs also must be tested with such unusual data, because they must work in all cases.
18. A list may be sorted by successively finding the smallest remaining element.
19. Modules may sometimes be tested independently. Thereafter, the debugging effort can be confined to testing whether the modules fit together.

MULTI-DIMENSIONAL ARRAYS 10

The array construct allows the name of a particular piece of information to be specified by a two-step process. First, the array name specifies a group of data items, and second, the subscript identifies a particular item within the group. The arrays in Chapter 9 were all one-dimensional arrays, also called **linear lists**, because position within the array or list is specified by one subscript.

Some data are naturally organized in such a way that it takes two independent indices to specify which item is meant. A **table** is an organization of data in which each entry is uniquely specified by its row number and its column number. In Pascal, such a structure would be called a **two-dimensional array**, a construct just like a one-dimensional array, except, of course, that two subscripts are used.

Digital images are pictures made by selectively coloring or shading a two-dimensional array of dots. Television images and newspaper or magazine pictures, called ''halftones'', are familiar examples. The individual dots are called **pixels**, short for ''picture elements''. The quality of the image depends on the size of the pixels. Large pixels create images that are obviously digital. Extremely small pixels, below the level of visual resolution at the usual viewing distances, create digital images indistinguishable from continuous images. The same principles of digital image processing apply to both coarse, low resolution digital images and to fine, high resolution computer graphics.

Sections 10.2 and 10.3 discuss how to write programs to produce **digital computer graphics** based on input data or equations, and to process digitally images acquired by photographic means. Depending on the hardware available for printing or displaying the image and the number of pixels that can be processed in the available computer time, the resulting image may vary from a ''cross stitch'' design with pixels the size of printed letters to a high resolution digital image with pixels the size of individual ink molecules.

10.1 Tables

An array variable with two subscripts is a **table**. The first subscript is often called the **row** number, and the second subscript the **column** number. After elementary examples involving a multiplication table and a telephone rate table, the next section concentrates on tables used in computer graphics, including visual image processing.

> **Section Preview**
>
> **Table:**
>
> A table is an array with two subscripts.
>
> General Forms:
>
> ```
> var
>     tablename : array [constant..constant, constant..constant] of type;
> type
>     rowtype = array [constant..constant] of type;
> var
>     tablename : array [constant..constant] of rowtype;
> ```
>
> Examples:
>
> ```
> type
>    rowtype = array [1..10] of real;
>    tabletype = array [1..5] of rowtype;
>
> var
>    table1 : array [1..5, 1..10] of real;
>    table2 : array [1..5] of rowtype
>    table3 : tabletype;
>    table4 : array [1..5] of array [1..10] of real;
> ```
>
> *Note:* All four variables, table1, table2, table3, and table4 are tables with 5 rows and 10 columns.

Multiplication Table

One of the most familiar tables is the multiplication table. Each entry is the product of its row number and its column number. The program printtable produces a copy of the multiplication table.

```
program printtable (output);
  var
    multtable : array [1..10, 1..10] of 1..100;
    row, column : 1..10;
  begin
  for row := 1 to 10 do
    for column := 1 to 10 do
      multtable [row, column] := row * column;
  { print table }
  for row := 1 to 10 do
    begin
    for column := 1 to 10 do
      write (multtable [row, column] :6);
    writeln;
    end;
  end.

run printtable
```

1	2	3	4	5	6	7	8	9	10
2	4	6	8	10	12	14	16	18	20
3	6	9	12	15	18	21	24	27	30
4	8	12	16	20	24	28	32	36	40

5	10	15	20	25	30	35	40	45	50
6	12	18	24	30	36	42	48	54	60
7	14	21	28	35	42	49	56	63	70
8	16	24	32	40	48	56	64	72	80
9	18	27	36	45	54	63	72	81	90
10	20	30	40	50	60	70	80	90	100

In Pascal, there are several different ways to declare a table. One is to declare the variable multtable to be an array of arrays, as in the following declaration.

```
var
   multtable : array [1..10] of array [1..10] of 1..100;
```

In a variation of this, a type called rowtype is declared and then multtable is defined to be an array [1..10] of rowtype. With this form of declaration, an assignment statement can assign the value of one row to another. In Pascal, a list of names is formally a two-dimensional array of characters. Each row in this two-dimensional array contains a single name. Assigning the type name nametype to the rows (as was done in the program smallestera in Section 9.4) allows the programmer to manipulate full names instead of individual characters.

In a third variation, a second type called table is defined to be an array of rows, then multtable is declared to be type table.

```
type
   rowtype = array [1..10] of 1..100;
   table = array [1..10] of rowtype;
var
   multtable : table;
```

If it is not necessary to name or manipulate any of the components of the table except the individual elements, then the declaration in the program printtable is suitable. It is simply an abbreviation of the first method, declaring multtable to be an array of arrays.

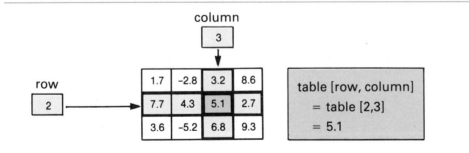

Figure 10.1 Referencing an entry in a table.

As shown in the assignment and write statements of the program printtable, two subscripts are written within brackets. The second subscript must be separated from the first by a comma. If the table multtable is considered an array of rows, then the ith row of multtable may be referenced as multtable [i]. The jth element in the ith row may be referenced by the form multtable [i] [j] as well as the form multtable [i, j]. As illustrated, it is quite common in programs that deal with tables to have a for-loop for the columns nested within a for-loop for the rows.

A Telephone Rate Table for Long-Distance Calls

Calculating the billing charges for a long-distance telephone call is another elementary example of the use of a table. The rates depend upon the time of the day the call is placed. To encourage use of the telephone company's facilities and equipment during under-utilized hours, the rates in effect during peak daytime hours are usually reduced somewhat in the evening, and further reduced at night. Table 10.1 is a simplified version of such a telephone rate table, giving the charge for the initial 3 minutes of direct-dialed long-distance calls from Fun City to selected garden spots on the eastern seaboard. Weekend and holiday rates are omitted to simplify the program phonecharges, which computes the long-distance telephone charges based on this table:

Table 10.1 Telephone Charges for the Initial 3 Minutes of Direct-Dialed Long-Distance Calls Placed from Fun City.

	Code for City	Day, Code 1	Evening, Code 2	Night, Code 3
Hoboken	1	.65	.45	.25
Paramus	2	.70	.50	.25
Peapack	3	.80	.55	.30
Piscataway	4	.70	.50	.25
Secaucus	5	.60	.40	.20
Tenafly	6	.60	.40	.20
Weehauken	7	.65	.45	.25

If a call lasts 3 minutes or less, then the customer pays the 3-minute basic rate. If the call runs over, there is an overtime charge proportional to the basic rate. The full charge before tax is the sum of the basic rate and the overtime charge. A tax of 10 percent is added, and the resulting amount is rounded to the nearest whole cent for printing.

```
program phonecharges (input, output, ratefile);

const
  nrofcities = 7;
  nrofrates = 3;
  basictime = 3.0;
  taxrate = 0.10;

var
  citycode : 1..nrofcities;
  ratecode : 1..nrofrates;
  rate : array [1..nrofcities, 1..nrofrates] of real;
  basiccharge, overtime, chargebeforetax, cost, duration : real;
  ratefile : file of char;

begin
{ read nrofrates from ratefile }
reset (ratefile);
for citycode := 1 to nrofcities do
  for ratecode := 1 to nrofrates do
    read (ratefile, rate [citycode, ratecode]);
```

```
{ read data pertinent to charges for this call }
read (citycode, ratecode, duration);
writeln ('Input data  citycode: ', citycode :1);
writeln ('              ratecode: ', ratecode :1);
writeln ('              duration: ', duration :1:2);

{ calculate the charge }
basiccharge := rate [citycode, ratecode];
if duration <= basictime then
  overtime := 0
else
  overtime := duration - basictime;
chargebeforetax := basiccharge + overtime * (basiccharge / basictime);
cost := chargebeforetax * (1 + taxrate);
{ print charge to customer }
writeln ('Charge for this call:  $', cost :1:2);
end.
run phonecharges

Input data  citycode: 3
            ratecode: 2
            duration:  19.00
Charge for this call:  $ 3.83
```

Self-Test Questions

1. How do you declare a 20 × 20 table of characters to use for storing a crossword puzzle?
2. The input data to the following program consists of the numbers 9, 7, 2, and 5. Hand simulate the execution of this program and tell what the output will look like. Describe what this program will do.

```
program example (input, output);
  var
    i, j : 1..2;
    a, b : array [1..2, 1..2] of 0..9;
  begin
  writeln ('Input data  a: ');
  for i := 1 to 2 do
    begin
    for j := 1 to 2 do
      begin
      read (a [i, j]);
      write (a [i, j] :2);
      end;  { j loop }
    writeln;
    end;  { i loop }
  b := a;
  writeln ('Table b: ');
  for i := 1 to 2 do
    begin
    for j := 1 to 2 do
      write (b [i, j] :2);
    writeln;
    end;  { i loop }
  end.
```

Exercises

1. Write a program that reads values for a 3 × 5 table and prints the table with a column of row totals on the right, a row of column totals along the bottom, and the total of all entries in the lower right-hand corner. Label the row of totals, the column of totals, and the grand total appropriately.

2. Write a program that prints a trigonometry table showing the sine, cosine, and tangent of each of the angles 0, 1, 2, ..., 45 degrees. *Hint:* Use the built-in functions described in Section 2.6. For the built-in functions sin and cos, the argument must be converted to radians by multiplying by $\pi/180$. Also $\tan(x) = \sin(x)/\cos(x)$.

3. Write a program that reads a table with the same number of rows as columns and prints the *transpose* of that table, that is, the table whose first row is the first column of the original table, whose second row is the original second column, and so on.

4. Write a program that performs a horizontal reflection on a table, that is, exchanges its leftmost column with its rightmost column, its next to leftmost column with its next to rightmost column, and so on.

5. Write a program that performs a vertical reflection of a table.

6. Write a program that converts a matrix (table) into a list, row by row.

7. Write a program that converts a matrix (table) into a list, column by column.

8. For each day of the month, a shot putter keeps a list of the distance he achieved in each of his shot puts that day. Write a program that reads each of these lists of distances into a row of a table and computes the average distance for the month for first puts, the average distance for second puts, and so on.

9. Modify the program for Exercise 8 so that it also prints out the number of the put in which the shot putter has the greatest average distance.

10. If the sum of the row number and column number is held constant, the resulting entries form a diagonal in a table. Write a program to extract all entries with a given sum in order of increasing column number.

11. Using the program written for Exercise 10, write a program that converts a table into a list by first taking all entries the sum of whose row and column is 2, then 3, then 4, and so on.

12. Ten student members of a committee would like to schedule a meeting when none of them has a class. Write a program that accepts as input the hours when each student has classes and which prints a table of the free hours when no one has class. *Hint:* Use an array

```
var
    free : array [9..17, mon..fri] of boolean;
```

in which each entry will represent whether no student has a class at that hour on that day. Hours greater than 12 represent afternoon classes.

13. The position of the pieces on a chess board may be described as an 8 × 8 table of integers. Negative numbers denote various kinds of white pieces and positive numbers denote black pieces. A zero denotes an empty position. Write a program to decide whether there is a white piece horizontally adjacent to a black piece.

14. Write a program that reads two tables of the same size and adds them together, entry for entry, to compute a third table. Print this last table.

10.2   Computer Graphics

Viewed from a sufficient distance, a closely spaced array of dots looks like a continuous image. The computer can produce digital images by controlling the intensity and location of the dots. The same techniques are used, regardless of the resolution of the image.

> **Section Preview**
>
> A **digital image** is made up of an array of pixels, or picture elements.
>
> In **printer graphics** each pixel is displayed as a printable character.
>
> **Superposition:**
>
> > A method of building a digital image by using an array to hold values for each pixel of the digital image. The values in the array may be modified, thereby "superimposing" several patterns, before the digital image is printed or displayed.

Digital Images

A **digital image** consists of a two-dimensional array of pixels. The digital image is produced by displaying or printing different shades of black, white, or gray, and different colors in some of the **pixels**.

In a newspaper photograph, each pixel is printed as a black dot whose size varies from pixel to pixel. Extremely dark regions have dots so large that they overlap and fill almost all the available space. Light regions have small dots with a great deal of white paper showing between them. A small magnifying glass will show the dots clearly. It is only when the digital image is viewed at a sufficient distance that the individual pixels are not the focus of attention and the effect of a continuous image is produced.

Television pictures are digital images produced using pixels of three different colors. If you look at a color television screen with a magnifying glass, you will see that its pixels come in groups of three, a red pixel, a green pixel, and a blue pixel. Each pixel is controlled individually to produce an intensity of its primary color from black (off) to the maximum intensity of that color the television screen is capable of producing.

Most computer display screens, including the ones usually used for displaying text, use digital images whose pixels are either on (bright) or off (dark). If you look at a display screen closely or with a magnifying glass, you will see how selected pixels are turned on and others turned off to form the letters and characters of the text. Many dot matrix printers use the same technique to form characters.

Although the size of the pixels and number of different possible colors or shades for an individual pixel certainly affect the resolution and quality of the digital image, the basic principles of digital image production are the same, no matter how many pixels are used. The standard language Pascal has no special features for controlling graphic output devices. However, in Pascal systems where graphic output is available, there are usually additional, nonstandard built-in procedures to control the graphic output devices.

In **printer graphics**, printable characters are used to display the pixels. The resolution is not good. Ten characters per inch horizontally and six characters per inch vertically is typical. However, the programming principles are the same, and a full page of printer graphics, viewed from a sufficient distance, appears somewhat continuous. The major problem is that no printable character is truly black, filling with ink 100% of the space allocated to a character.

The programs in Sections 10.2 and 10.3, as written, produce printer graphics. The higher resolution digital graphics shown in these two sections were produced using a microcomputer that supports Pascal and dot image graphics. The modifications to the programs were minor, consisting largely of increasing the size of the image arrays and using the nonstandard built-in procedures for graphic output.

Tables of Characters

There is no reason why the values in a table must be numeric. The program blockofasterisks "computes" and prints a 9×20 rectangle of asterisks, a simple graphic. Recall that when characters are printed, no extra blanks are inserted between them.

```
program blockofasterisks (output);

  const
    nrofrows = 9;
    nrofcolumns = 20;
    asterisk = '*';

  var
    block : array [1..nrofrows, 1..nrofcolumns] of char;
    row : 1..nrofrows;
    column : 1..nrofcolumns;

  begin
  { fill block with asterisks }
  for row := 1 to nrofrows do
    for column := 1 to nrofcolumns do
      block [row, column] := asterisk;

  { print block of asterisks }
  for row := 1 to nrofrows do
    begin
    for column := 1 to nrofcolumns do
      write (block [row, column]);
    writeln;
    end; { for row }
  end.
```

```
run blockofasterisks

* * * * * * * * * * * * * * * * * *
* * * * * * * * * * * * * * * * * *
* * * * * * * * * * * * * * * * * *
* * * * * * * * * * * * * * * * * *
* * * * * * * * * * * * * * * * * *
* * * * * * * * * * * * * * * * * *
* * * * * * * * * * * * * * * * * *
* * * * * * * * * * * * * * * * * *
* * * * * * * * * * * * * * * * * *
```

Superposition

The fundamental principle in printing more complicated graphics is to decompose them into simple shapes. In applying this principle, a programmer may make good use of **superposition**, superimposing new shapes over pre-existing parts of the graphic. The program printgraphic uses the superposition of shapes to produce a rectangular box with an X in it.

```
    program printgraphic (output);

      const
        nrofrows = 17;
        nrofcolumns = 48;
        star = '*';
        blank = ' ';

      var
        row : 1..nrofrows;
        column, startcol, stopcol : 1..nrofcolumns;
        graphic : array [1..nrofrows, 1..nrofcolumns] of char;

    begin
    { start with a block of stars }
    for row := 1 to nrofrows do
      for column := 1 to nrofcolumns do
        graphic [row, column] := star;

    { superimpose a block of blanks in the middle,
          leaving a border of stars }
    for row := 3 to nrofrows − 2 do
      for column := 4 to nrofcolumns − 3 do
        graphic [row, column] := blank;

    { diagonal bar from upper left to lower right }
    startcol := 4;
    for row := 3 to nrofrows − 2 do
      begin
      for column := startcol to startcol + 5 do
        graphic [row, column] := star;
      startcol := startcol + 3;
      end;
```

```
{ diagonal bar from upper right to lower left }
stopcol := nrofcolumns - 3;
for row := 3 to nrofrows - 2 do
  begin
  for column := stopcol - 5 to stopcol do
    graphic [row, column] := star;
  stopcol := stopcol - 3;
  end;

{ print the graphic }
for row := 1 to nrofrows do
  begin
  for column := 1 to nrofcolumns do
    write (graphic [row, column]);
  writeln;
  end; { for row }
end.
```

```
run printgraphic
```

```
* * * * * * * * * * * * * * * * * * * * * * * * * * * * * * * * * * * * * * * * * *
* * * * * * * * * * * * * * * * * * * * * * * * * * * * * * * * * * * * * * * * * *
* * * * * * * *                                               * * * * * * * *
* * *     * * * * * *                              * * * * * *      * * *
* * *       * * * * * *                          * * * * * *        * * *
* * *         * * * * * *                      * * * * * *          * * *
* * *           * * * * * *                  * * * * * *            * * *
* * *             * * * * * * * * * * * *                           * * *
* * *                 * * * * * *                                  * * *
* * *             * * * * * * * * * * * *                           * * *
* * *           * * * * * *          * * * * * *                    * * *
* * *         * * * * * *              * * * * * *                  * * *
* * *       * * * * * *                  * * * * * *                * * *
* * *     * * * * * *                      * * * * * *      * * *
* * * * * * * *                                               * * * * * * * *
* * * * * * * * * * * * * * * * * * * * * * * * * * * * * * * * * * * * * * * * * *
* * * * * * * * * * * * * * * * * * * * * * * * * * * * * * * * * * * * * * * * * *
```

Plotting a Histogram

Another type of computer graphic easily produced on a printer is a histogram, a frequency distribution bar graph. Suppose, for example, that at a liberal arts college the registrar reports that there were 5281 As, 6003 Bs, 6717 Cs, 3118 Ds, 2644 Fs, and 241 grades of "incomplete" given out in the fall semester. The program grades plots a vertical bar graph in which the height of each bar is proportional to the number of letter grades of that type given out. This makes it easier to see the general characteristics of the grade distribution pattern.

```
program grades (input, output);

   const
     letters = 6;
     nrofrows = 20;
     nrofcolumns = 36;
     star = '*';
     blank = ' ';
     line = '_____';

   type
     rowtype = packed array [1..nrofcolumns] of char;

   var
     histogram : array [1..nrofrows] of rowtype;
     allblank : rowtype;
     frequency : array [1..letters] of 0..10000;
     percent : array [1..letters] of real;
     letter : 1..letters;
     row : 1..nrofrows;
     column : 1..nrofcolumns;
     numberofgrades : 0..60000;
     barheight, topofbar : 0..21;

   begin
   { initialize allblank to all blanks }
   for column := 1 to nrofcolumns do
     allblank [column] := blank;

   { read grade frequencies and calculate total number of grades }
   { 1, 2, ..., 6 represent grades A, B, C, D, F, INC }
   numberofgrades := 0;
   writeln ('Input data  frequency:');
   for letter := 1 to letters do
     begin
     read (frequency [letter]);
     write (frequency [letter]);
     numberofgrades := numberofgrades + frequency [letter];
     end; { for }
   writeln;

   for letter := 1 to letters do
     begin
     percent [letter] := 100 * (frequency [letter] / numberofgrades);
     barheight := round (percent [letter] / 5);

     { row 1 is at top of graph }
     topofbar := 21 - barheight;
     for column := 6 * letter - 5 to 6 * letter - 1 do
       begin

       { blank out part above bar }
       for row := 1 to topofbar - 1 do
         histogram [row] [column] := blank;
```

```
        { fill in bar with stars }
        for row := topofbar to nrofrows do
            histogram [row] [column] := star;
        end; { for column }

      { put blanks between bars }
      for row := 1 to nrofrows do
        histogram [row] [6 * letter] := blank;
      end; { for letter }

  writeln;
  writeln (line);
  writeln ('     Letter Grade Distribution');
  writeln;

  { print the nrofrows that are not all blank }
  for row := 1 to nrofrows do
    if histogram [row] <> allblank then
      writeln (histogram [row]);

  writeln (line);
  writeln (' A     B     C     D     F     INC');
  writeln;
  writeln ('Vertical scale:  1 line = 5%');
  writeln;
  write ('Percents: ');
  for letter := 1 to letters do
    write (percent [letter] :7:2);
  writeln;
  end.
run grades

Input data  frequency:
     5281        6003        6717        3118        2644         241


--------------------------------------------
      Letter Grade Distribution

                * * * * *
        * * * * * * * * * *
* * * * * * * * * * * * * * *
* * * * * * * * * * * * * * * * * * * *
* * * * * * * * * * * * * * * * * * * * * * * * *
* * * * * * * * * * * * * * * * * * * * * * * * *
--------------------------------------------
  A     B     C     D     F     INC

Vertical scale:  1 line = 5%

Percents:   22.00  25.01  27.98  12.99  11.01   1.00
```

The first step in plotting this histogram is to obtain a total number of grades for the college during that semester. Next, each frequency is divided by the total number of grades to obtain the proportion of the total for each letter grade, and then multiplied by 100 to obtain the percentage. In the program grades, each bar is five columns wide, with one blank between the bars. Each 5 percent of the total distribution is plotted as a bar one line high. Rounding of the computed bar heights is necessary because, in the printed output, the height of each bar must be an integer. For a different distribution, a programmer might make different decisions about the size and scale of the histogram.

Based on the same data as in the sample execution of the program grades, the higher resolution histogram in Figure 10.2 was plotted using a microcomputer. To match the resolution of screen graphics on this computer, the array, histogram, was increased in size to 160 rows by 280 columns.

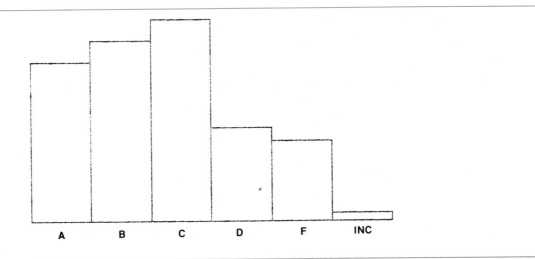

Figure 10.2 Higher resolution histogram using the same data as in the program grades.

Plotting a Graph

Many computer installations have special graph plotting equipment that can be directed by a computer. At installations that have an incremental plotter or a television-type display tube, a collection of graphics procedures is usually available written in popular computer languages. This allows a programmer to write the calculation part of a program in a general-purpose computer language and call the appropriate graphics procedure to display the answers. Besides general graphics procedures, there are also specialized graphics procedures designed for specific applications like architectural drawing, contour mapping, and so on (see Figure 10.3).

Rather than use specialized equipment, the program parabola uses the printer to plot a graph of the function $y = x^2$. Even with graphics procedure packages designed for specialized plotters, one way to draw a graph is first to locate the points on the graph, as is done in the program parabola, and then to call a graphics procedure to plot the points and draw lines between them.

```
program parabola (output);
   put blanks everywhere
   put minus signs on the x-axis
   put vertical lines on the y-axis
   put a plus sign at the origin
   for each column in the graph
      convert the column number to an x value
      calculate y = x * x
      convert y value to row number
      put an asterisk in the correct row and column in the graph
   print the graph
```

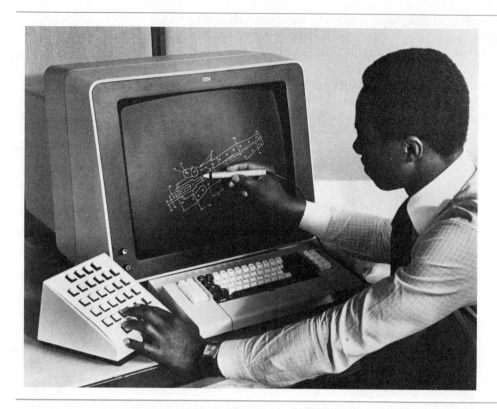

Figure 10.3 Graphic display terminals produce complex images as combinations of lines, points, and curves. Using the same generating techniques as for printer graphics, much finer detail is possible on a television-type display screen. The light pen shown may be used for graphic input by transmitting its coordinates to a computer.

Before the program parabola can be refined, it is necessary to specify in more detail what is wanted. One important detail is the selection of a range for the variables x and y. A decision is made to graph the region of the plane with both x and y coordinates between -1 and $+1$. Since the x and y coordinates include both positive and negative values, a decision is made to use both positive and negative subscripts for the array used to create the picture. Then a decision is made to use 20 columns for each unit distance in the x direction, and only 10 lines per unit distance in the y direction, because the spacing between lines is somewhat greater than that between successive characters on the same line. Thus the range of subscripts is from -20 to $+20$ for column numbers, and from -10 to $+10$ for row numbers. The program parabola can now be refined as shown.

```
program parabola (output);

   const
     rowmax = 10;
     colmax = 20;
     blank = ' ';
     star = '*';
     bar = '|';
     plus = '+';
     minus = '-';
```

```
type
  rowindex = -rowmax..rowmax;
  colindex = -colmax..colmax;

var
  row : rowindex;
  column : colindex;
  graph : array [rowindex, colindex] of char;
  x, y : real;

procedure putblankseverywhere;
  begin
  for row := -rowmax to rowmax do
    for column := -colmax to colmax do
      graph [row, column] := blank;
  end; { putblankseverywhere }

procedure putminusonxaxis;
  begin
  for column := -colmax to colmax do
    graph [0, column] := minus;
  end; { putminusonxaxis }

procedure putbarsonyaxis;
  begin
  for row := -rowmax to rowmax do
    graph [row, 0] := bar;
  end; { putbarsonyaxis }

procedure putplusatorigin;
  begin
  graph [0, 0] := plus;
  end; { putplusatorigin }

procedure putstarsoncurve;
  begin
  for column := -colmax to colmax do
    begin
    x := column / colmax;
    y := x * x;
    row := round (rowmax * y);
    if abs (row) <= rowmax then
      graph [row, column] := star;
    end; { for }
  end; { putstarsoncurve }

procedure printthegraph;
  begin
  writeln ('Graph of the function y = x * x,',
      ' -1 <= x <= 1, -1 <= y <= 1');
  writeln;
```

```
      for row := rowmax downto -rowmax do
        begin
        for column := -colmax to colmax do
          write (graph [row, column]);
        writeln;
        end; { for row }
    end; { printthegraph }

  { ····· main program ····· }
  begin
  putblankseverywhere;
  putminusonxaxis;
  putbarsonyaxis;
  putplusatorigin;
  putstarsoncurve;
  printthegraph;
  end.
run parabola
```

```
Graph of the function y = x * x, -1 <= x <= 1, -1 <= y <= 1
```

The smoothness of the graph is limited only by how closely points may be plotted. Using a microcomputer that displays 280 columns across and 192 rows vertically on a 12-inch video monitor, the authors have produced very good results (see Figure 10.4). The major changes in the program are to increase the number of columns from 41 to 280, the number of rows from 21 to 192, and to replace assignments to the array element graph [row, column] with calls to a built-in procedure that displays a dot of a specified color on the screen in that row and column. The syntax and even the name of this procedure vary from machine to machine, but all Pascal systems that support screen graphics have such a procedure.

The graphs of other functions are easily obtained by minor modifications of the program parabola. For example, the graph of the cubic equation $y = x^3$ over the same range of x and y values can be obtained merely by changing two

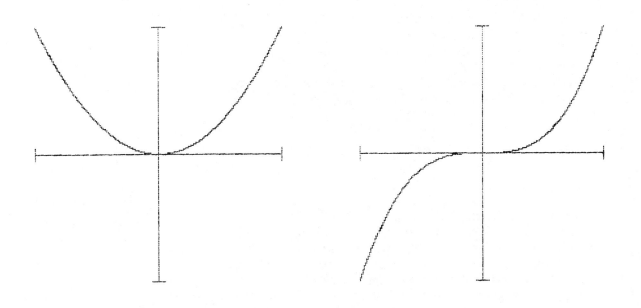

Figure 10.4 Graphs of the functions $y = x^2$ and $y = x^3$. These graphs were calculated on a grid of 191 x 191 pixels on a popular microcomputer and a dot matrix, higher resolution printer.

lines, the line that computes the y value and the line that prints the description
of the function on the output above the graph. Only the sample execution
printout of the resulting program cubic is shown, because the program itself is
so similar to the parabola. Modifications in the range of x and y values are discussed in the exercises.

```
    run cubic

    Graph of the function y = x * x * x, -1 <= x <= 1, -1 <= y <= 1
```

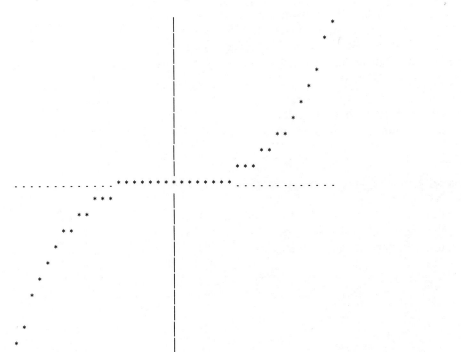

Self-Test Questions

1. How do you declare an array "picture" to be used to print a digital image 35 pixels across by 20 pixels high?
2. What does the principle of superposition mean as applied to computer graphics?
3. If a computer has a graphic display device with pixels that can be either "on" or "off", how could the following array be used to store a digital image for such a graphic output device.

```
var
    image : array [1..100, 1..100] of boolean;
```

Exercises

1. Write a program to print out a facsimile of a United States flag.
2. Write a program to accept up to 10 values for plotting in a histogram, followed by a termination signal. The program should count the number of bars, choose a scale in the vertical direction so that the largest bar is exactly 10 lines high, and plot the histogram.
3. Modify the program parabola to plot the graph of the equation $y = 2x^3 - x$ for $-1 \leqslant x \leqslant 1$ and $-1 \leqslant y \leqslant 1$.
4. Modify the program parabola to plot the graph of $y = x^2$ for $-2 \leqslant x \leqslant 2$ and $-2 \leqslant y \leqslant 2$. Be sure that the program is not confused by y values outside the region.
5. Modify the program parabola so that it uses only positive row and column numbers.
6. Write a program that accepts as input pairs of values (x, y) and plots on a graph all the pairs that precede a termination signal. For testing purposes, generate points for $x = -1, -0.95, -0.9, ..., +1$, and $y = x^2$.
7. Write a program that accepts the triple coordinates (x, y, z) of points in space and plots the points according to the following rules:

    $$\text{row} = \text{round } (4 * x - 10 * z)$$
    $$\text{column} = \text{round } (-10 * x + 20 * y)$$

    For testing purposes use the eight corners of a cube, $x = \pm 0.5$, $y = \pm 0.5$, $z = \pm 0.5$. Draw the 12 edges by hand on the plotted graph.
8. Write a program to help keep track of the solution of a 20 × 20 crossword puzzle. First, clear the 20 × 20 table of characters to all blanks. Then accept input describing a word to be entered in the puzzle. Input has the following form:

    a. Row number (for the first letter of the word)
    b. Column number (for the first letter of the word)
    c. The single character "a" meaning "across" or the single character "d" meaning "down"
    d. The word to be entered

    Print a warning if a letter in the word to be entered does not agree with the letter already in that position in the array.
9. Modify the program grades so that one asterisk is printed for each percentage point. For this case, the top row of each bar of the histogram may have from one to five asterisks, rather than always having five asterisks.

10.3   Digital Image Processing

Digital image processing consists of four major steps:

1.   Acquiring the image
2.   Digitizing the image
3.   Enhancing the image
4.   Plotting or displaying the enhanced image.

Acquisition and digitization of the image require special-purpose hardware. This section concentrates on programs for displaying and enhancing an image.

Section Preview

Visual Image Processing:

> When photographic images are digitized, each pixel is assigned a number representing the intensity of light in the image at that location.

Gray Scale Output:

> If display hardware permits, the brightness of each displayed pixel is proportional to its numerical intensity value.

Halftoning:

> If only white and black ("on" and "off") are available in the display medium, gray tones are produced by filling part of the area allocated to a pixel with black and part with white in such a way the the fraction of the total pixel area that is white (or black) is proportional to the numerical intensity value.

Image Enhancement:

> Between input of the digitized numerical intensity values and output of the final digitized image, the array of numerical intensities can be processed to enhance features of the image or to remove defects from the image.

Visual Image Processing

When equipped with special hardware for input and output, a computer can be programmed to process visual images. This includes the printing of "computer portraits" of the kind that can be found at shopping malls, science museums, and amusement parks. At the other end of the spectrum, it includes the synthesis, enhancement, and analysis of photographs transmitted back to Earth from space probes. The special hardware needed for input, a **video digitizer**, scans one frame of a television camera image and converts the light intensity at each image point in the picture to an integer that encodes the intensity. For the sake of further discussion, we assume that the digitizer encodes light intensity as an integer from 0 to 9, with 0 meaning the brightest possible image point and 9 the darkest possible image point.

Matching the input hardware, a computer used for image processing usually has a television-type **cathode ray tube (CRT)** for display and the associated circuits for converting a table of digitized light intensities into visual intensities on the screen. However, the image on a CRT is not permanent unless photographed. A second form of visual output, the printed page, is used during debugging of programs and whenever the lower cost and greater convenience of

printed output outweigh the loss in image quality. The program videoimage
uses a digitizer for input but a printer for output. Of course, if no digitizer is
available for program testing, the digitized image data can be simulated by hand
and read from another input device.

```
program videoimage (input, output);
{ initial version }
  Read a table of digitized light intensities from the video digitizer
  Convert each digitized light intensity to a printable character
      of appropriate print density
  Print the resulting image
```

The refined version of the program videoimage is broken into three procedures representing the phases of the process, the input, the conversion of
digits to characters, and the output. An echo of the input data is inserted to
make it possible to check the execution of the program.

To complete the refinement of the procedure writeimage, 10 printable
characters are chosen to represent the 10 possible digitized light intensities.
Since no print character fills more than a small fraction of the space in which it
is printed, it is not possible to obtain really dark image points in the printed
output. The following 10 printable characters form a progression from very
light to as dark as possible for a single character:

```
.   :   -   =   +   %   &   $   #   @
0   1   2   3   4   5   6   7   8   9
```

Refinement of the procedure printimage is now straightforward.

```
program videoimage (input, output);

  const
    nrofrows = 12;
    nrofcolumns = 24;
    maxintensity = 9;

  type
    rowindex = 1..nrofrows;
    colindex = 1..nrofcolumns;
    shadeindex = 0..maxintensity;

  var
    digitizedimage : array [rowindex, colindex] of shadeindex;
    printableimage : array [rowindex, colindex] of char;
    characters : array [shadeindex] of char;
    row : rowindex;
    column : colindex;

  procedure readimage;
    begin
    for row := 1 to nrofrows do
      for column := 1 to nrofcolumns do
        read (digitizedimage [row, column]);
    end; { readimage }
```

```
procedure writedigits;
  begin
  for row := 1 to nrofrows do
    begin
    for column := 1 to nrofcolumns do
      write (digitizedimage [row, column] :3);
    writeln;
    end; { for row }
  end; { writedigits }

procedure convertimage;
  begin
  for row := 1 to nrofrows do
    for column := 1 to nrofcolumns do
      printableimage [row, column] :=
        characters [digitizedimage [row, column]];
  end; { convertimage }

procedure writeimage;
  begin
  writeln;
  for row := 1 to nrofrows do
    begin
    for column := 1 to nrofcolumns do
      write (printableimage [row, column]);
    writeln;
    end; { for row }
  end; { writeimage }

{ ····· main program ····· }
begin
characters := '. : -=+%&$#@';
readimage;
writeln ('Digitized image points:');
writedigits;
convertimage;
writeimage;
end.
```

The next phase is testing the program. If a video digitizer is not available, simulated input data can be read from a more usual input device. The test data for the sample execution shown for videoimage are based on a small section of a picture of Deimos, the smaller satellite of Mars, transmitted to Earth by the Viking I space probe orbiting Mars. The region chosen shows a small circular crater about 10 kilometers in diameter, with a raised rim. The original computer-generated photograph from which the input data are derived shows the entire disk of Deimos, using approximately three times as many scan lines in the vertical direction as the sample execution does for the same region. To be seen, the printed image of the program videoimage must be far enough away that the individual print characters cannot be recognized as characters. At that distance, they appear as varying shades of white and gray. The main problems with the sample execution are the lack of a truly dark print character and the small number of points used to form the image. The crater is seen more distinctly when a larger region is shown in the same detail.

```
run videoimage
```

Digitized image points:

4	4	4	4	4	4	4	4	3	3	3	2	2	1	1	1	1	1	1	0	0	0	0	0
4	4	4	4	4	4	4	3	2	2	2	2	1	0	0	0	0	0	1	1	1	0	0	0
4	4	4	4	4	4	3	2	8	8	8	8	9	9	9	9	9	0	0	0	1	1	0	0
4	4	4	4	3	6	6	7	7	7	7	7	7	7	7	8	8	9	9	0	0	1	1	1
4	4	4	3	5	6	6	6	5	6	6	6	6	6	6	7	7	8	9	9	1	1	3	3
5	4	4	4	5	6	6	5	5	5	6	6	6	6	6	6	5	7	7	7	7	4	5	4
5	5	5	5	4	4	6	6	5	6	6	6	6	6	6	5	5	5	6	6	7	5	6	6
5	5	5	5	3	4	4	4	4	6	4	4	4	4	6	6	6	6	6	4	5	6	6	6
5	5	5	5	2	1	1	1	2	2	3	4	4	4	4	4	4	4	5	6	6	6	6	7
5	5	5	5	8	1	1	1	1	1	1	2	1	2	2	2	3	3	5	6	6	6	7	8
5	5	5	5	7	6	8	8	1	1	1	1	1	1	2	2	5	6	6	6	6	7	8	8
5	5	5	5	5	5	6	6	8	8	8	8	8	6	6	6	6	6	6	6	6	7	7	8

```
+++++++=====--:::::......
+++++++=----:........:::..
+++++++=-#####@@@@@..::..
++++=&&$$$$$$$$##@@..:::
+++=%&&&%&&&&&&$$#@@::=
%+++%&&%/%/%&&&&&&%$$$$+%+
%/%/%%+++&&%&&&&&&%/%/%&&$%&&
%/%/%%=+++++&++++&&&&&+%&&&
%/%/%%-:::--=+++++++++%&&&$
%/%/%%#:::::-:---=%&&&$#
%/%/%%$&##:::::::--%&&&&$##
%/%/%/%%&&#######&&&&&&$$##
```

Halftone Images

A more satisfactory display of the digitized image is produced using a rectangle of displayed characters for each pixel. In Figure 10.5, each of the 12×24 pixels of the image printed by the program videoimage is displayed as a rectangle of dots, 10 dots high and 5 dots across. If the numerical intensity value for a pixel is n, the fraction n/9 of the 50 possible dots is black in a random pattern. Thus, numerical intensity 0 prints as white and numerical intensity 9 prints as black. Intermediate intensities appear as gray from a distance great enough that the individual dots cannot be seen clearly.

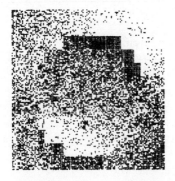 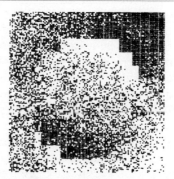

Figure 10.5 Digital image of a crater and the negative digital image of the same crater printed by a random halftone process.

This method of producing pixels that appear as varying shades of gray is **halftoning**. A satisfactory printer image halftone display can be produced by printing each pixel using a fraction of a 5 × 5 rectangle of asterisks. (*Note:* Each pixel will be rectangular and not square because each printer character occupies a rectangle and not a square.)

Image Enhancement

The processing of the video image done by the program videoimage consists of nothing more than a conversion from one form of representation to another. When a video camera and digitizer are available, this is all that is needed to print computer portraits. The subject sits before the video camera and a selected frame of the video image is digitized and printed. However, once the image is digitized, the stage is set for computer enhancement of the image to reveal details more clearly, to reduce the amount of static or snow in the image, and to perform other modifications of the image difficult or impossible to obtain photographically.

For example, details can sometimes be seen more clearly if the image is converted into a high-contrast image. What this involves is altering the digitized light intensities so that only the extreme intensities encoded as 0 and 9 are represented. The program hicontrast to do this results from adding a third procedure enhanceimage between the input and the output procedures of the program videoimage. In this procedure, all light intensities from 0 to 4 are changed to a light intensity of 0, the brightest intensity, and all light intensities from 5 to 9 are changed to a light intensity of 9, the darkest intensity.

```
program hicontrast (input, output);

   const
     nrofrows = 12;
     nrofcolumns = 24;
     maxintensity = 9;
     threshold = 4;

   type
     rowindex = 1..nrofrows;
     colindex = 1..nrofcolumns;
     shadeindex = 0..maxintensity;

   var
     digitizedimage : array [rowindex, colindex] of shadeindex;
     printableimage : array [rowindex, colindex] of char;
     characters : array [shadeindex] of char;
     row : rowindex;
     column : colindex;

   procedure readimage; ... end; { readimage }
   procedure writedigits; ... end; { writedigits }
   procedure convertimage; ... end; { convertimage }
   procedure writeimage; ... end; { writeimage }

   procedure enhanceimage;
   { changes all intensities 0..threshold to 0 }
   { changes all intensities threshold+1..maxintensity to maxintensity }
```

```
begin
for row := 1 to nrofrows do
   for column := 1 to nrofcolumns do
      if digitizedimage [row, column] <= threshold then
         digitizedimage [row, column] := 0
      else
         digitizedimage [row, column] := maxintensity;
end; { enhanceimage }
```

```
{ ----- main program ----- }
begin
characters := '.:-=+%&$#@';
readimage;
writeln ('Digitized image points:');
writedigits;
enhanceimage;
writeln;
writeln ('Modified digitized image points:');
writedigits;
convertimage;
writeimage;
end.
```

run hicontrast

Digitized image points:
```
4 4 4 4 4 4 4 4 3 3 3 2 2 1 1 1 1 1 1 0 0 0 0 0
4 4 4 4 4 4 4 3 2 2 2 2 1 0 0 0 0 0 1 1 1 0 0 0
4 4 4 4 4 4 3 2 8 8 8 8 9 9 9 9 9 0 0 0 1 1 0 0
4 4 4 4 3 6 6 7 7 7 7 7 7 7 7 8 8 9 9 0 0 1 1 1
4 4 4 3 5 6 6 6 5 6 6 6 6 6 6 7 7 8 9 9 1 1 3 3
5 4 4 4 5 6 6 5 5 5 6 6 6 6 6 6 5 7 7 7 7 4 5 4
5 5 5 5 4 4 6 6 5 6 6 6 6 6 6 5 5 5 6 6 7 5 6 6
5 5 5 5 3 4 4 4 4 6 4 4 4 4 6 6 6 6 6 4 5 6 6 6
5 5 5 5 2 1 1 1 2 2 3 4 4 4 4 4 4 4 5 6 6 6 6 7
5 5 5 5 8 1 1 1 1 1 1 2 1 2 2 2 3 3 5 6 6 6 7 8
5 5 5 5 7 6 8 8 1 1 1 1 1 1 2 2 5 6 6 6 6 7 8 8
5 5 5 5 5 5 6 6 8 8 8 8 8 6 6 6 6 6 6 7 7 8 8
```

Modified digitized image points:
```
0 0 0 0 0 0 0 0 0 0 0 0 0 0 0 0 0 0 0 0 0 0 0 0
0 0 0 0 0 0 0 0 0 0 0 0 0 0 0 0 0 0 0 0 0 0 0 0
0 0 0 0 0 0 0 0 9 9 9 9 9 9 9 9 9 0 0 0 0 0 0 0
0 0 0 0 0 9 9 9 9 9 9 9 9 9 9 9 9 9 9 0 0 0 0 0
0 0 0 0 9 9 9 9 9 9 9 9 9 9 9 9 9 9 9 9 9 0 0 0
9 0 0 0 9 9 9 9 9 9 9 9 9 9 9 9 9 9 9 9 9 0 9 0
9 9 9 9 0 0 9 9 9 9 9 9 9 9 9 9 9 9 9 9 9 9 9 9
9 9 9 9 0 0 0 0 9 0 0 0 0 0 9 9 9 9 9 0 9 9 9 9
9 9 9 9 0 0 0 0 0 0 0 0 0 0 0 0 0 0 0 9 9 9 9 9
9 9 9 9 9 0 0 0 0 0 0 0 0 0 0 0 0 0 9 9 9 9 9 9
9 9 9 9 9 9 9 9 0 0 0 0 0 0 0 0 9 9 9 9 9 9 9 9
9 9 9 9 9 9 9 9 9 9 9 9 9 9 9 9 9 9 9 9 9 9 9 9
```

```
. . . . . . . . . . . . . . . . . . . . . . .
. . . . . . . . . . . . . . . . . . . . . . .
. . . . . . . .@@@@@@@@. . . . . . .
. . . . .@@@@@@@@@@@@@. . . . .
. . . .@@@@@@@@@@@@@@@. . . .
@. . .@@@@@@@@@@@@@@@@.@.
@@@@. .@@@@@@@@@@@@@@@@@
@@@@. . . . .@. . . .@@@@@.@@@@
@@@@. . . . . . . . . . . . . .@@@@@
@@@@@. . . . . . . . . . . .@@@@@@
@@@@@@@. . . . . . . .@@@@@@@@
@@@@@@@@@@@@@@@@@@@@@@@@@
```

The data for the sample execution of hicontrast are the same data used in the sample execution of the program videoimage. In the high-contrast printout, many details are lost, but the details that remain are seen more clearly. The threshold between light and dark is critical in determining which details remain in the high-contrast printout. If, for example, instead of a threshold intensity of 4, intensities of 5 or less are considered light, and intensities of 6 or greater are considered dark, the appearance of the high-contrast printout could change considerably. It is a simple matter to program a computer to produce a high-contrast printout based on any threshold light intensity, particularly when the threshold is defined in a constant declaration. This and additional methods of image enhancement are discussed in the exercises.

Self-Test Questions

1. How is a photographic image represented in a computer?
2. How are shades of gray produced in a digital image display?
3. What advantage does the process of digitizing and displaying an image have over merely reproducing the image by photographic or electronic means?

Exercises

1. Modify the program videoimage to use a threshold of 5 for the lighter areas, (to convert any digitized intensity from 0 to 5 into an intensity of 0, and any intensity from 6 to 9 into an intensity of 9. Run the modification using the same input data used in this section with a threshold of 4.

2. Write a program to make a negative print of a video image. This means that all light intensity relationships are reversed. The brightest points in the video image are to be printed darkest, and the darkest points in the original image are to be printed lightest.

3. Simulate the effect of random interference or static in the transmission of the video picture to the computer by generating for each image point a random integer from 1 to 100. If the random integer is 96 or greater, then generate another random integer, this time from 0 to 9, and replace the actual digitized light intensity with this second random integer. Test your program using a completely uniform gray image with a digitized intensity of 4 at all points.

4. Use the static generator written and tested in Exercise 3 to put static into the picture of the crater on Deimos whose digitized intensities are given in this section.

5. Write a program that accepts as input three consecutive images of the same object, each of which has random interference noise, or static in it.

Use an array with three subscripts. Process the three images to reduce static by averaging the three values for the light intensity at each point in the image. Be sure to round the average to the nearest integer before printing.

6. Use the random noise generator written for Exercise 3 to test the program for Exercise 5.

7. Write a program that accepts three successive images of the same object and tries to reduce the random static in the images by computing a digitized light intensity at each point as follows. If two or more of the digitized intensities agree, accept that value regardless of what the other one is. If one value is more than twice as far from the other two as they are from each other, then reject that value and average the other two. If all three are relatively close, take their average, rounding to the nearest integer to obtain a valid digitized intensity.

8. Test the program for Exercise 7 using the random static generator in Exercise 3.

9. Execute the program videoimage using the following table of digitized light intensities as input data:

```
3 3 3 3 3 3 3 3 9 9 9 9 9 3 3 3 3 3 3 3 3 3 3 3
3 3 3 3 3 3 3 9 9 9 9 9 9 9 3 3 3 3 3 3 3 3 3 3
3 3 3 3 3 3 3 9 9 9 9 9 9 9 3 3 3 3 3 3 3 3 3 3
3 3 9 9 9 9 3 3 9 9 9 9 9 0 0 3 3 3 3 3 3 3 3 3
3 9 9 9 9 9 9 9 9 9 9 9 0 0 0 0 0 3 3 3 3 3 3 3
9 9 9 9 9 9 9 9 0 0 0 9 0 0 0 9 0 9 3 3 3 3 3 3
3 9 9 9 9 9 0 0 0 0 0 0 0 0 9 0 9 3 3 3 3 3 3
3 3 3 3 3 3 0 0 0 0 0 0 0 0 9 0 9 0 0 9 9 3 3
3 3 3 3 3 3 3 0 0 0 9 0 0 0 0 0 0 0 0 9 9 3 3 3
3 3 3 3 3 3 3 3 3 0 6 9 0 0 0 0 0 0 0 3 3 3 3
3 3 3 3 3 3 3 9 9 9 6 6 9 0 9 0 0 0 3 3 3 3
3 3 3 3 3 3 3 9 3 9 9 9 9 9 9 9 9 9 3 3 3 3 3 3
```

10. Modify the program videoimage so that each pixel is printed as a fraction of a 5 × 5 rectangle of asterisks. Print none of these 25 asterisks if the image intensity at that pixel is 0. Print all of these 25 asterisks if the intensity is 9 and print round (n * 25 / 9) of these asterisks if the intensity is n. You may use either random patterns of asterisks or regular patterns of asterisks within each pixel. Run this program using the data in the sample execution of the program videoimage in this section.

11. Run the program written for Exercise 10 using the input data given in Exercise 9.

10.4 Three or More Subscripts

Arrays with more than two dimensions are allowed in Pascal. There is no limit on the number of subscripts. Multidimensional arrays are quite common in scientific programming, and they also arise from time to time in general applications.

The example in this section uses a three-dimensional array. Four or more dimensional arrays occur infrequently. Just as a rectangular table with entries in each unit square of the rectangular table serves as a model for a two-dimensional array, a three-dimensional rectangular solid with entries in each unit cube of the solid serves as a model of a three-dimensional array. (See Figure 10.6.)

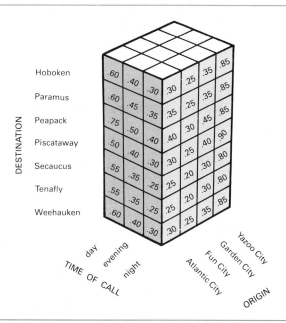

Figure 10.6 A three-dimensional table represented as a rectangular solid.

Section Preview

Multidimensional Arrays:

Arrays with three or more subscripts are permitted in Pascal.

A Three-Dimensional Telephone Rate Array

The telephone rate table in Section 10.1 has two subscripts. The row subscript of an entry in the table is a code for the destination city of the phone call, and the column subscript is a code for the time of day the call is placed. All telephone calls in the example in Section 10.1 originate from the same place, Fun City. In this section, we show how to use a three-dimensional array to generalize that example to take into account differing cities of origin of the telephone calls.

If four cities of origin, Atlantic City, Fun City, Garden City, and Yazoo City, are allowed for telephone calls, the four rate tables similar to Table 10.1 would be necessary to summarize all the applicable long distance telephone rates. Figure 10.1 shows how a 4 × 7 × 3 array of rates can be used to amalgamate these four 7 × 3 rate tables. The front slab (completely visible) gives the telephone rate table for calls originating in Atlantic City. The next slab back (only partly visible) gives the telephone rate table for calls originating in Fun City. The night rates for such calls may be seen to agree with those in Table 10.1. The third and fourth slabs give the rate table for calls originating in Garden City and Yazoo City.

Based on the analysis of the complete rate schedule as a collection or rate tables for calls originating at different cities, we might declare the complete rate array as follows:

```
const
  nroforigins = 4;
  nrofdestinations = 7;
  nrofrates = 3;

type
  ratetable = array [1..nrofdestinations, 1..nrofrates] of real;

var
  rate : array [1..nroforigins] of ratetable;
```

On the other hand, if all three subscripts in the three-dimensional array rate are considered equally important, the following declarations are appropriate:

```
const
  nroforigins = 4;
  nrofdestinations = 7;
  nrofrates = 3;

var
  rate : array [1..nroforigins,
                1..nrofdestinations,
                1..nrofrates ] of real;
```

Both of these sets of declarations declare a $4 \times 7 \times 3$ array or real values. Either one may be used. However, the subscripts always must be kept in the order that they are declared. In any reference to the array rates, for example,

```
rate [origincode, destinationcode, ratecode]
```

the first subscript always must be a city-of-origin code from 1 nroforigins, the second subscript always must be a city-of-destination code from 1 to nrofdestinations, and the third subscript always must be a time-of-day code from 1 to nrofrates.

Once the declaration of the rate array has been made properly, it is straightforward to modify the program phonecharges in Section 10.1 to handle the case of varying city of origin as well as varying city of destination. We leave this as an exercise.

Self-Test Questions

1. True/false:
    a. The following declarations for the triply-subscripted array rate may be used in place of the declarations in this section.

```
const
  nroforigins = 4;
  nrofdestinations = 7;
  nrofrates = 3;

type
  ratelisttype = array [1..nrofrates] of real;

var
  rate : array [1..nroforigins,
                1..nrofdestinations] of ratelisttype;
```

    b. Arrays with four or more subscripts are permitted in Pascal.

c.   When you declare a multidimensional array in Pascal, the subscript with the largest maximum value must be the leftmost subscript for the array.

d.   As long as you refer to every subscript variable in this section by its correct name, like destinationcode, origincode, or ratecode, the order in which the subscripts are written does not matter.

Exercises

1.   Write a program that reads input values for the elements of a 4 × 7 × 3 array of rates for long distance telephone calls like ones described in this section and then prints the array formatted into four 7 × 3 tables, one for each city of origin.

2.   Write a program that reads input values for a 4 × 7 × 3 array of rates for long distance telephone calls. It then reads coded input for city of origin, city of destination, time-of-day rate code, and duration for a telephone call between cities used in the example in this section. The program should calculate and print the charge for the call.

3.   Exercises 5—8 in Section 10.3 are based on enhancing a two-dimensinal digital image by comparing three consecutive images of the same scene. Write the declarations for an array suitable for storing the information in these three digital images.

10.5   What You Should Know

1.   An array name specifies a group of data items, and subscripts identify a particular item within the group.

2.   A subscript is sufficient to locate an item in a linear list, or one-dimensional array.

3.   Two subscripts, the row and column number, identify an item in a table, or two-dimensional array.

4.   When processing a two-dimensional array, a for-loop for the columns is often nested in a for-loop for the rows.

5.   Digital images are pictures made by selectively coloring or shading a two-dimensional array of dots. The dots are pixels.

6.   The fundamental principle in printing more complicated shapes is to decompose them into simple shapes.

7.   If the entire graphic is calculated in the computer's memory before being printed, new shapes can be superimposed over parts of pre-existing shapes. This is the method of superposition.

8.   Negative subscripts are permitted in Pascal.

9.   The graph of a function has one plotted point in each column.

10.   Until the number of points requires a change in computational strategy, the same techniques can produce high- or low-resolution digital images, depending on available computer time and output hardware.

11.   A digitized visual image may be reproduced without processing or enhancement before output.

12.   Halftoning means producing shades of gray by alternating black and white areas in suitable proportion.

13.   Examples of image enhancement include increasing contrast, making negative and false color images, and removing static and fixed imperfections of the image-acquisition apparatus.

14.   Arrays with three or more subscripts are permitted in Pascal.

RECORD STRUCTURES AND FILES 11

When information is assigned as values of variables in a Pascal program, the information is stored only temporarily. In most Pascal systems, the values of variables are lost when the execution terminates or, at the latest, when the next execution begins. Files provide a means of saving information more or less permanently between runs of a program and exchanging information between programs.

Files are organized into segments called **records**. The records of a file may be any data type, including **record data types**, described in Section 11.2. Unlike arrays, the component parts of a record data type need not all be the same type. This difference makes **record structures** a more flexible means of organizing data in a Pascal program.

In programs to create, update, and maintain a file, there is an interplay between the temporary copy of the file in main memory and the permanent copy stored in **auxiliary memory** devices like magnetic disk, magnetic tape, and bubble memory. Most programs that use a file follow the same sequence of steps. First, they read the old values from the file into main memory variables. Then they update the values from the file in main memory. Finally they save the changes by writing the updated values to a file in auxiliary memory.

11.1   Files

In most Pascal systems, when a program execution ends, the values of all variables are lost. In some interactive systems, the values can still be displayed for debugging purposes, but they are lost when the next execution begins. Files provide a way to save information between runs of a program and exchange information between programs.

Section Preview

File:

> A file is a sequence of segments called records. All the records of a file must be the same data type. The records of a file may be any data type, including record data types described in Section 11.2.

329

Built-In Procedures **Reset** and **Rewrite**:

> Before the first read from a file, the file must be positioned at its beginning by the built-in procedure reset. Before the first write to a file, the file must be erased by the built-in procedure rewrite.

Text File:

> A text file is a file of characters. The files named input and output are text files. The built-in procedures read, readln, write, and writeln work with all text files exactly as they do with the files named input and output.

Examples of File Operations:

```
program example (numberin, numberout);
  var
     numberin, numberout : file of integer;
  begin
  reset (numberin);
  rewrite (numberout);
  read (numberin, x);
  write (numberout, x);
  end.
```

File Organization

A **file** is composed of a sequence of segments called **records**. All of the records in a file must be the same data type. They may be an intrinsic data type like real, integer, or character, or a more complex data type, like an enumerated data type, an array, or a record structure type. For example, suppose that the file numberfile is declared to be a file of real values by the declaration

```
var
   numberfile : file of real;
```

Then each record of the file contains a real number.

The total number of records in a file does not have to be declared. In fact, the number of records in a file can change during during execution. A file also may be empty, in which case it has no records.

Each file used in a program, except the ones named "input" and "output", must appear in a variable declaration that indicates the data type of each record in the file.

Text Files

All of the files in this book so far have been **text** files, which means they are files whose records are single characters. The built-in procedures read and readln are nevertheless permitted to read values of types other than char from a text file. They read ahead as many characters as necessary to produce a meaningful value. The files called "input" and "output" are assumed by every program to be text files, that is, they are predeclared by the Pascal system to have the form

```
var
   input, output : file of char;
```

Similarly, the procedures write and writeln convert values like integer and real to sequences of characters for writing into a text file.

All file names used by a program must appear within the parentheses of the title line of the program.

The keyword "text" is a synonym for the phrase "file of char". Thus, a file of characters named "letterfile" might be declared as

```
var
    letterfile : text;
```

or equivalently as

```
var
    letterfile : file of char;
```

Reading From a File

The built-in procedure **reset** positions a file at its first record for reading. Thereafter, the records of the file are read in sequence. For example, the statements

```
reset (numberfile);
read (numberfile, a, b, c)
```

direct a computer to position the file of reals, numberfile, at its first record, and then to read the first three values from the file. The first value is assigned to the variable a, the second to b, and the third to c. The file numberfile is left positioned at its fourth record. The next read statement for the file will begin reading with the fourth real number in the file.

The file named "input" is reset automatically—that is, each program is executed as if it contained the statement

```
reset (input)
```

This read statement looks like the ordinary read statement

```
read (a, b, c)
```

except for an extra first argument, which is the name of the file.

The two statements

```
read (a, b, c)
```

and

```
read (input, a, b, c)
```

are considered identical, because inclusion of the default file name ("input") as a first supplied argument is optional.

Writing to a File

Information may be recorded sequentially in a file using a write statement. However, before writing to a file, a program must call the built-in procedure **rewrite** to prepare the file to receive output. The built-in procedure rewrite also positions a file at its beginning point, but it destroys the entire contents of the file in preparation for rewriting it. If there is no file with the given name, a new empty file is created. The sequence of statements

```
rewrite (numberfile);
write (numberfile, a, b, c)
```

first create a new empty file of reals named "numberfile" or erase a preexisting file of that name. Then they write the values of the variables a, b, and c as the first three records of the file. Subsequent write statements to this file will begin writing in the fourth record (unless another rewrite statement is executed in the meantime). In Pascal, it is not possible to begin writing in the middle of a file. Writing begins at the first record.

Each program is executed as if it contained the statement

```
rewrite (output)
```
Also, the two statements
```
write (a, b, c)
```
and
```
write (output, a, b, c)
```
are considered identical because inclusion of the default file name "output" as a first supplied argument is optional.

The Built-In Function Eof

The built-in function **eof** (end-of-file) returns the boolean value true if the file is positioned at the end. It returns the value false if there are still additional records in the file beyond the current position. For example the while-loop
```
reset (numberfile);
while not eof (numberfile) do
   begin
   read (numberfile, x);
   writeln ('Input data  x: ', x);
   end
```
reads and echoes all the real numbers in the file numberfile. After the last record is read, the value of the built-in function eof (numberfile) becomes true and the loop terminates.

Self-Test Questions

1.   True/false:

      a. Except for the fact that a file that is reset eventually will be read and a file that is rewritten eventually will be written to, the built-in procedures reset and rewrite are essentially the same.

      b. A program may read values only for variables of type char from a text file.

      c. The records of a file must be read in sequence.

2.   How do you declare a file whose records contain integer values?

Exercises

1.   Write a program that reads 10 numbers sequentially from a text file named "inputdata" and prints the average of the numbers.

2.   Modify the program avgofscores in Section 5.4 to accept the test scores from a text file called "scores".

3.   Assume that the sequential file named "cardfile" described in Sections 9.2 and 9.3 is a file of integers whose first record contains the number of entries in a list of credit card numbers for accounts that have been cancelled, and the remaining records of the file each contain the number of one cancelled card. Write a program that reads this file, sorts the list into increasing order, and rewrites the file with the list of cancelled credit cards in increasing order.

4.   Modify the program videoimage in Section 10.3 so that the image intensities are read from an input file named "intensities" instead of from the standard input file "input".

11.2   Record Structures

Arrays allow data to be grouped, but only if all items have the same data type. Records structures are a more flexible organization of data that does not impose this restriction.

This section treats the organization of data into hierarchical data structures and the refinement of these structures. Then it shows how to declare and use such structures in Pascal programs.

Section Preview

Record:

A record is a data structure amalgamating several component pieces of information under one heading. Unlike an array or a file, the components need not all be of the same data type.

General Form:

```
type
  recordtypename = record
    variablename : type;
    variablename : type;
        .
        .
        .
    variablename : type;
    end;
```

Example:

```
type
  statistics = record
    name : packed array [1..20] of char;
    age : 1..100;
    height, weight : real;
    shoesize : real;
    end;  { statistics }
```

Path Name:

A component of a record structure is referenced by writing the name of the record, a period, and the name of the component.

Example:

```
var
   personaldata : array [1..25] of statistics;
```

The assignment statement

```
personaldata [14] . shoesize := 5
```

assigns the value 5 to the shoesize of the 14th person in the array of statistics, personaldata. Other components of the statistics for the 14th person and statistics for the other 24 people are unchanged.

Organization of Data

A principal benefit of adopting the top-down style for constructing a program is that the resulting organization of the various programming steps is easy to understand. The organization of the data to be processed also should be easy to understand. Frequently, the organization of the data imposes certain requirements on the program steps. In many cases, designing a structure for the data is as important as designing the program itself, particularly when the program is concerned with files in auxiliary memory.

Data Structures

In order to begin with a simple example, suppose that a person decides to computerize the entries in a little black book that gives information about various acquaintances and contacts. For each person in the book, there is a name, an address, a telephone number, and sometimes a few remarks. One way of organizing the data is to have four lists, one for each type of information. However, depending on how the information is to be processed, it might be more convenient to organize the data into natural groupings, one for each person in the black book.

A **data structure** for the information in one black book entry might be organized as shown in Figure 11.1. When the owner of the black book wishes to arrange by telephone a future meeting with someone, only the person's telephone number is needed. On the other hand, to send a letter the address is needed. Different parts of the information may be needed for different purposes.

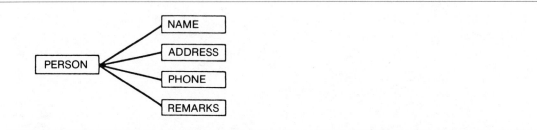

Figure 11.1 A data structure for a black book entry.

Figure 11.1 illustrates that the name of the entire structure is person and that it has four components, which are name, address, phone, and remarks. Sometimes, one or more components might be broken down into lower-level components. For instance, if the owner of the black book wanted to contact every acquaintance in a particular city, it would be helpful to have the component address broken down into lower-level components corresponding to the number, street, city, state, and postal zip code. This level of detail would enable a computer to scan the entries for city and state without having to look at the street address or zip code. For other reasons it might be convenient to subdivide each telephone number into a three-digit area code and a seven-digit local number. Figure 11.2 shows a finer structure for the same black book entry.

More detail might usefully be specified for each person's name or for the remarks. Specifying too much detail, however, makes a program less efficient than specifying the right amount. The use of the information is what determines the right amount.

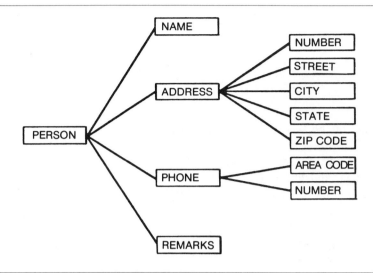

Figure 11.2 A refined data structure for a black book entry.

Refining Data Structures

The technique of **successive refinements** can be applied to the design of data structures as well as to the writing of programs. It is often a good idea to coordinate the refinement of the data structure with the refinement of the program. As more detailed steps of the program are written, the data structures used by those steps can be refined to the level of detail needed by the program.

The data structures shown in Figures 11.1 and 11.2 are called **tree structures** because of the resemblance between the subdivisions of the data structure and the branches of a tree. The tree must be visualized as lying on its side. In both figures, the box labelled "person" is the **root**. The lines between boxes are the branches. A **leaf** is a part of the structure which is not further subdivided. Thus, in Figure 11.1, the components name, address, phone, and remarks are all leaves. In Figure 11.2, the components name and remarks are still leaves, but there is further branching from the nodes address and phone, so those nodes are not leaves. The components number, street, city, state, and zip code are all leaves for the component address, and the components area code and number are leaves for the component phone. As the data structure is refined, the tree grows by acquiring new leaves.

Data Structure Declarations

In Pascal, data structures like the ones shown in Figures 11.1 and 11.2 are called **records**. The same term is used for both data structures and the components of a file, because it is often the case that the components of a file are data structures. In simple cases, the record of a file may consist of a single value, as in the examples discussed so far. A programmer communicates the form of a data structure to the computer by a record declaration. To declare the structure illustrated in Figure 11.1, the programmer writes the following data structure declaration for the type of the variable person.

```
type
  persontype = record
    name : string20;
    address : addresstype;
    phone : phonetype;
    remarks : string20;
    end; { persontype }
```

Such a declaration indicates that any variable of the type persontype consists of four components, name, address, phone, and remarks.

The type declaration for persontype is completed by making preceding declarations for the types string20, addresstype, and phonetype. If none of the components will be subdivided further, as in Figure 11.1, then the following declarations will serve:

```
type
  string20 = packed array [1..20] of char;
  string57 = packed array [1..57] of char;
  string12 = packed array [1..12] of char;

  addresstype = string57;
  phonetype = string12;
```

In order to permit immediate access to subgroupings within these components, the programmer should declare a more detailed data structure, like the one shown in Figure 11.2. This is done by writing refined declarations for the data types of the components of the type persontype, as shown below. These refined type declarations are used in the declaration of persontype and so must precede the declaration of persontype.

```
type
  string2 = packed array [1..2] of char;
  string3 = packed array [1..3] of char;
  string5 = packed array [1..5] of char;
  string6 = packed array [1..6] of char;
  string8 = packed array [1..8] of char;
  string20 = packed array [1..20] of char;

  addresstype = record
    number : string6;
    street : string20;
    city : string20;
    state : string2;
    zipcode : string5;
    end; { addresstype }

  phonetype = record
    areacode : string3;
    number : string8;  { the 4th character is a hyphen }
    end; { phonetype }

  persontype = record
    name : string20;
    address : addresstype;
    phone : phonetype;
    remarks : string20;
    end; { persontype }
```

It is certainly possible to analyze the entire address as a character string (of length 57, which includes four separator characters between the five subfields, in this example) and to pick out the number, street, city, state, and zip code as substrings of the appropriate lengths, separated by blanks or punctuation. Using the more detailed data structure saves the programmer the trouble of doing this analysis.

A record type declaration consists of the variable name, an equals sign, and the keyword "record", followed by a list of declarations of the components of the record, each of which looks like a variable declaration. The declaration is terminated by the keyword "end". Any of the components of a record may themselves be records.

A component of a record may be an array. All of the character strings in the black book entry are arrays. It is also possible to declare a variable to be an array of records, which is what we want to do, in order to be able to have all of the entries in the black book file stored in main memory at once. Thus, all programs for the black book example will use the variable person declared by

```
var
   person : array [1..100] of persontype;
```

Referencing Components of a Data Structure

A component of a data structure is referenced in a program by writing its full **path name**, which consists of all names from the root of the tree along the branch to the component. Successive names in a path are separated by a period. Any reference to a component that is part of an array must specify which element of the list or table is intended, unless the whole array is intended. For example,

```
person [13] . address . zipcode
```

is the zip code of the 13th person in the black book. Similarly, provided the variable newaddress has been declared to be of type addresstype, the statement

```
person [47] . address := newaddress
```

assigns the value of newaddress as the address of the 47th person in the black book. Assignment to a variable or component of record type is permitted as long as the right-hand side has the same type as the left-hand side.

One of the advantages of declaring a component to be a record is that one can still reference the entire record by a single name, instead of having to specify each part of the record. This is illustrated by the statement above that tells the computer to assign the entire address component newaddress to person [47] . address without having to have a separate assignment statement statement for the number, street, city, state, and zipcode components of the address.

Another example of full path name addressing for components of a data structure is the following statements that print the names and telephone numbers of all persons with area code 505.

```
{ print phone number of all persons with area code 505 }
for entry := 1 to numofpersons do
   if person [entry] . phone . areacode = '505' then
      writeln (person [entry] . name, person [entry] . phone . number);
```

Perhaps the most standard use of a little black book is to look up someone's telephone number. The instructions below tell the computer to print out the telephone number of a person whose name is the value of the variable persontobecalled. To simplify the program, a sequential search is used. The procedure readline used in this section is a modified version of the procedure of the same name in Section 6.2. The modification consists of making the name of the variable which receives the input characters a dummy argument of the procedure. This modification is left as an exercise and the procedure is not relisted here.

```
{ procedure readline borrowed from Section 6.2 }
readline (persontobecalled);
{ look in black book for person to be called }
entryposition := 1;
personfound := false;
while (entryposition <= numofpersons) and (not personfound) do
  if person [entryposition].name = persontobecalled then
    personfound := true
  else
    entryposition := entryposition + 1;
if personfound then
  writeln ('The telephone number is ',
      person [entryposition] . phone . areacode, '/',
      person [entryposition] . phone . number);
else
  writeln (persontobecalled,
      ' is not in your little electronic black book.');
```

A Data Structure for Library Information

As another example of a collection of information with a natural tree structure, a simple computerized cataloging system for a library is considered. For each book in the library, there are two kinds of data. Some of the data serves to identify the book, and the rest of it tells about the status of the copies of it owned by the library.

To identify the book, it is necessary to specify the author, the title, the publisher, the year of publication, and the Library of Congress catalogue number. In naming the publisher, it is also customary to tell the city in which the book was published. For instance, the following is a standard citation for a popular book on the oriental game of Go.

Arthur Smith,
The Game of Go, Charles E. Tuttle Company,
Rutland and Tokyo, 1956, LCN 56-12653.

The library status information is comprised of the number of copies owned by the library, the number of copies out on loan, and the number of additional copies on order. It is appropriate to make the data structure booktype shown below. The Pascal type declarations are written from the bottom up because each type must be declared above any line where it is used. The top-down tree structure is most easily seen by starting at the end with the declaration for the variable book, an array which represents the entire catalogue.

```
type
  string9 = packed array [1..9] of char;
  string30 = packed array [1..30] of char;
  publishertype = record
    company : string30;
    location : string30;
    end; { publishertype }
```

```
idtype = record
  author : string30;
  title : string30;
  publisher : publishertype;
  year : 0..1999;
  catalognumber : string9;
  end; { idtype }
copytype = record
  owned, borrowed, ordered : 0..99;
  end; { copytype }
booktype = record
  identification : idtype;
  copies : copytype;
  end; { booktype }

var
  book : array [1..numberofbooks] of booktype;
```

A Data Structure for Baseball Performance Records

A third example of a data structure is one that a baseball television announcer
or news reporter might use to organize statistics on the players. The defensive
component of a player's performance consists of the position played, the
number of fielding chances, and the number of errors committed. Different
kinds of data are kept for pitchers. The offensive component of a player's performance includes the number of times at bat, the number of hits, the number
of runs scored, and the number of runs batted in. The hits have a finer
classification as singles, doubles, triples, and home runs. The data structure
declaration shown for the type playertype might be used.

```
type
  number = 0..999;
  hitstype = record
    singles, doubles, triples, homeruns : number;
    end; { hitstype }
  idtype = record
    name, team : string20;
    end; { idtype }
  defensetype = record
    position : string20;
    fieldingchances, errorscommitted : number;
    end; { defensetype }
  battingtype = record
    timesatbat : number;
    hits : hitstype;
    walks, runsscored, runsbattedin, strikeouts : number;
    end; { battingtype }
  playertype = record
    identification : idtype;
    defensiveperformance : defensetype;
    battingperformance : battingtype;
    end; { playertype }
```

Records and Files

The records that comprise a file may have any valid Pascal type. So far, all files have had records whose types are intrinsic in Pascal. In Section 11.3, the little black book, described in this section will be saved as a file of type persontype.

Self Test Questions

1. True/false:

    a. The components of a record structure must all have the same type.
    b. Arrays are permitted as components in a record structure.
    c. The components of a record structure may be record structures.
    d. An arbitrary record type may be used for the records of a file.

2. In a typical week, 14 football games are played between teams in the National Football League (NFL). Declare a data structure suitable for storing the names of the teams and the scores in all 14 games.

Exercises

1. Write statements to print the name and telephone number of all persons in the black book with zip code 91711.

2. Assume that a program uses the data structure player declared to be an array of playertype, a type declaration given in this section, and that values have been read in for the eight players (all but the pitcher) using the statement

    ```
    for i := 1 to 8 do
      read (playerfile, player [i])
    ```

    Write a procedure to print the name of each player with the player's position and the percentage of fielding chances that have produced errors.

3. Assume that a program uses a variable book, declared to be an array of booktype, a type declared in this section, and that values have been read in for 9,437 books in the library using the statement

    ```
    for b := 1 to 9437 do
      read (bookfile, book [b])
    ```

    Write a procedure search (var there : string3) that sets there = 'yes' if the following book is in the library and sets there = 'no ' otherwise.

    > Walter S. Brainerd, Charles H. Goldberg, and Jonathan L. Gross,
    > *Fortran 77 Programming,*
    > Harper and Row, New York, 1978. LCN 78-18301.

4. Give a data structure type declaration suitable for use by the Internal Revenue Service to hold information on a taxpayer. The information should include name, address, social security number, wages reported by employers, dividends and interest paid to the taxpayer, income tax withheld, and social security contributions (FICA) withheld.

5. Design a suitable data structure type declaration for information on a college student to be used by the college registrar.

6. Using the record type declaration for Exercise 5, write statements to list all juniors with a gradepoint average of 2.8 or better.

7. Airlines accept reservations for flights up to one year in advance. Design a data structure suitable for string information associated with each reservation.

8. Design a suitable data structure for information on each flight to be made by an airline during the next year.

9.   Using the data structure for Exercise 7 or 8, write statements that tell the computer to list all the passengers on a given flight.

10.   Using the data structures for Exercise 7 or 8, write statements to determine if a given person has any reservation on any flight during the next year.

11.   Design a data structure suitable for a bank to keep the information on a checking account.

12.   Modify the procedure readline in Section 6.2 to have the name of the input line as an argument.

11.3   Creating and Updating a File

The most important use of auxiliary memory is for permanent storage of information between runs of the programs that access it. In most computer systems, storage space in main memory is too valuable to be used to retain information that might not be accessed for several hours or days. Besides, when the computer is shut down for preventive maintenance or for the night, the contents of main memory are lost. In contrast, magnetic tapes and disks retain the information recorded on them indefinitely, unless explicit user action is taken to change or erase it. Even physically removing a tape or a disk from a computer does not change the information it contains.

This section continues the discussion of the computerized little black book of information on friends and acquaintances for which a data structure was developed in Section 11.2. The procedures given here for creating and updating a black book file illustrate in miniature the procedures used for creating and updating larger files.

The point of this section is the relationship and interplay between the permanent copy of a file in auxiliary memory and the highly transient copy of the same file created in main memory during execution of a program that accesses the file.

Section Preview

Creating a File:

Creating a file consists of erasing any old version of the file using the built-in procedure rewrite, which creates an empty file.

Updating a File:

Updating a file consists of three major steps.

1.   Reading the old version of the file from auxiliary memory into variables in main memory.

2.   Changing values for the file in main memory.

3.   Writing the updated values back to the file in auxiliary memory.

With-Statement:

A with-statement allows part of the path name of a group of variables to be declared in advance, so that only the remaining part of the full path name needs to be written to distinguish between components.

Example:
```
type
  bananatype = record
    fruit, skin : integer;
    end; { bananatype }
  clump = record
    bit : boolean;
    bunch : array [1..5] of bananatype;
    end; { clump }
var
  this, that : clump;

begin
with this do
  for i := 1 to 5 do
    read (bunch [i] . fruit);
with that . bunch [3] do
  read (fruit, skin)
```

Record Assignment Statements:

If both this and that are names of record structure variables of the same type, the assignment statement

```
this := that
```

assigns to each component of the record structured variable this, the value of the corresponding component of the variable that.

Variant Record Types:

The last field in a record type declaration may have several variant possibilities, selected by a construct resembling a case-statement.

General Form:
```
record
  fieldname, fieldname, ...., : typename;
  fieldname, fieldname, ...., : typename;
  ... ;
  fieldname, fieldname, ...., : typename;
  case fieldname : typename of
    constant, constant, ..., :
      (fieldname, fieldname, ...., : typename;
       fieldname, fieldname, ...., : typename;
       ... ; );
    constant, constant, ..., :
      (fieldname, fieldname, ...., : typename;
       ... ; );
  end; { of record structure }
```

Example:
```
type
  positiontype = (hitter, pitcher);
  performancedatatype = record
    name : packed array [1..25] of char;
    case position : positiontype of
      hitter : (atbat, hits : integer;
                battingaverage : real);
```

```
        pitcher :  (inningspitched :  real;
                    earnedrunaverage  :  real);
    end;  { performancedatatype }
```

Creating a File

The first step in computerizing the little black book is to obtain file space for
the data. This consists of requisitioning a region of auxiliary memory for the
purpose and staking a claim to it. For a noncomputerized black book file, this
may be likened to buying an empty black book. In general, securing file space
is like taking a manila folder, attaching a label to it, and putting the empty
folder into a filing cabinet.

When the black book file is being read by a program, there must be a way
to determine when all of the entries have been read. Since all of the records of
the file must be the same data type, there is no simple way to put the number
of entries at the beginning of the file. We choose to use the eof (end-of-file)
built-in function discussed in Section 11.1. The program createblackbook uses
the built-in procedure rewrite to create an empty file.

```
program createblackbook (input,  output,  blackbook);

    type
      string2 = packed array [1..2] of char;
      string3 = packed array [1..3] of char;
      string5 = packed array [1..5] of char;
      string6 = packed array [1..6] of char;
      string8 = packed array [1..8] of char;
      string20 = packed array [1..20] of char;

      addresstype = record
        number : string6;
        street : string20;
        city : string20;
        state : string2;
        zipcode : string5;
        end; { addresstype }

      phonetype = record
        areacode : string3;
        number : string8;
        end; { phonetype }

      persontype = record
        name : string20;
        address : addresstype;
        phone : phonetype;
        remarks : string20;
        end; { persontype }

    var
      blackbook : file of persontype;
      answer : char;
```

```
begin
writeln ('This program will destroy any file named blackbook.');
writeln ('Do you wish to continue?');
writeln ('Enter answer:  "y" to continue, "n" to stop.');
read (answer);
if answer = 'y' then
  begin
  { create empty black book file }
  rewrite (blackbook);
  end; { if }
end.
```

Most of the lines of the program createblackbook are concerned with declaring a natural data structure for persontype. The rewrite command tells the computer to set aside space in auxiliary memory for a new file, assuming one by that name does not exist already. If a file already in the computer's auxiliary memory has the name "blackbook", then the computer removes all the information from that file and prepares to write new data into it. Therefore, it is important to know that a needed file is not being destroyed.

Putting Records Into a File on the First Updating Run

Having reserved a storage location in auxiliary memory for the black book file, the next step is to put some entries there. To conserve programming effort, the same program used to add the first entries to the empty black book file will be used later to add or delete entries. Accordingly, the program updateblackbook is written as if there already were several entries in the permanent copy of the black book file in auxiliary memory. After the program is written, it must be verified that it works equally well in the present situation, where the permanent copy of the black book file is empty.

```
program updateblackbook (input, output, blackbook);
{ initial version }

  var
    person : array [entryindex] of persontype;
    blackbook : file of persontype;
    line : string;

  begin
  readblackbook;   { from auxiliary memory }
  { requested changes are first made only in the
        main memory copy of the file }
  morechanges := true;
  while morechanges do
    begin
    write ('Enter a request: ');
    readline (line);  { reads input into variable named line }
    if line = add then
      addnewentry
    else if line = delete then
      deleteentry
    else if line = done then
      morechanges := false
```

```
   else
     writeln ('Update request must be "Add", "Delete", or "Done"');
   end; { while-loop }
writeblackbook;   { to auxiliary memory }
end.
```

Before refining the program updateblackbook, filling in missing declarations and refining the called procedures, let us see how it is supposed to work during a program execution that places the following two entries in the file. Because the number of entries is expected to remain small enough that a computer could search through them all quickly, no effort is made to put them in alphabetical order.

Otis Quattlebaum
433 Out Way
Little Rock, AR 72901
501/555-4357
Likes Mexican food

Sara Hoshizaki
1134 Squid Street
Los Alamos, NM 87544
505/555-7272
QA expert

Suppose that the program createblackbook has been run to create the empty auxiliary memory file blackbook, and that the owner of the black book finally finds the time to start putting the entries into the file. As execution of the program updateblackbook begins, the copy of the file in auxiliary memory is empty, as represented in Figure 11.3. None of the elements of the array person nor any other variable in main memory has been assigned a value.

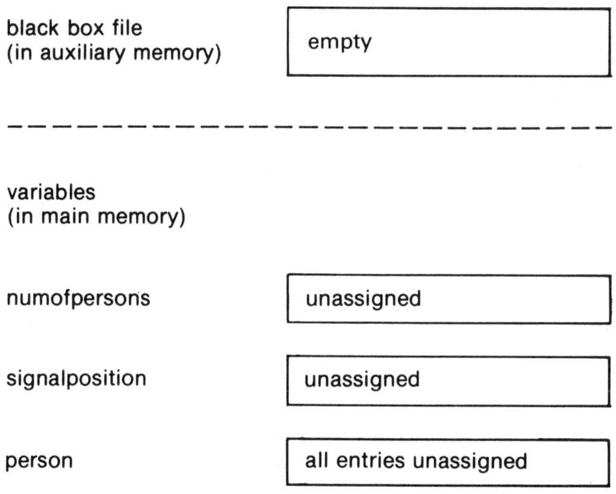

black box file
(in auxiliary memory)   empty

variables
(in main memory)

numofpersons   unassigned

signalposition   unassigned

person   all entries unassigned

Figure 11.3 The empty black book file (in auxiliary memory) and values (as yet unassigned) of the data structure person (in main memory) at the start of an execution of the program updateblackbook.

The program execution starts by faithfully copying the data in each record of the auxiliary memory file blackbook into the elements of the array person. Since the file blackbook is empty, the procedure readblackbook terminates without reading any entries and sets numofpersons to 0. Figure 11.4 illustrates this stage of the program execution.

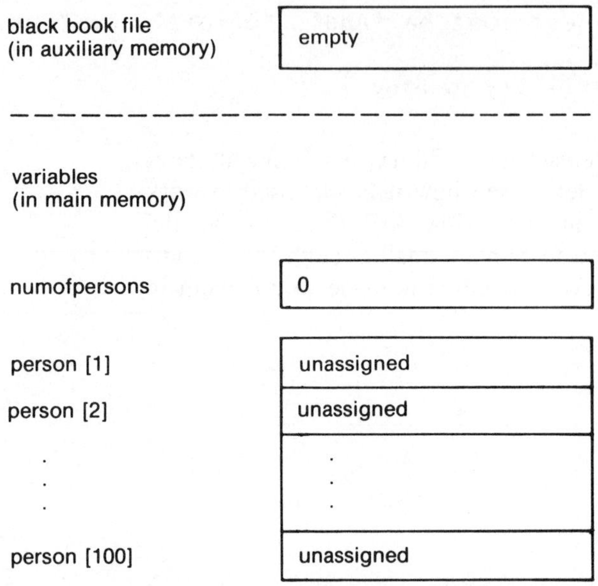

black book file
(in auxiliary memory) | empty |

- -

variables
(in main memory)

numofpersons | 0 |

person [1] | unassigned |
person [2] | unassigned |
    .   .
    .   .
    .   .
person [100] | unassigned |

Figure 11.4 The empty black book file and values of the data structure person after reading contents of the black book file from auxiliary memory into main memory.

Next, suppose that "Add" requests for Quattlebaum and Hoshizaki entries are given. Each "Add" request causes execution of the procedure addnewentry that increases the value of numofpersons by one (assuming there is any more room in the black book), and sets the value of entryposition to the first unoccupied position in the array person. Then it reads the complete data supplied for an entry and uses the data to assign values to components of the data structure person [entryposition]. What Figure 11.5 shows is that making this assignment does not change anything in the auxiliary memory file black-book. Writing new records into the permanent copy of the black book file is a program step entirely separate from organizing the data for these records in main memory. Thus, in Figure 11.5, the variable numofpersons has been changed to 2 by two executions of the procedure addnewentry.

After all intended additions to and deletions from the black book file have been entered and the request "Done" is given, a rewrite statement in the procedure writeblackbook instructs the computer to delete the contents of the auxiliary memory file blackbook in preparation for writing new entries into the file, after which the entire collection of entries is written from main memory into this permanent copy of the black book file. Repositioning the auxiliary memory file blackbook at its beginning and writing the values of person [1] and person [2] in it changes the values stored in auxiliary memory for the black book file, but does not affect the values of any of the variables in main memory. Figure 11.6 shows all these values after the last statement of the program updateblackbook is executed. Although the main memory copy of the black book file is usually erased shortly after termination of the program execution, the auxiliary memory file blackbook is retained indefinitely, so that all the information is available for future use.

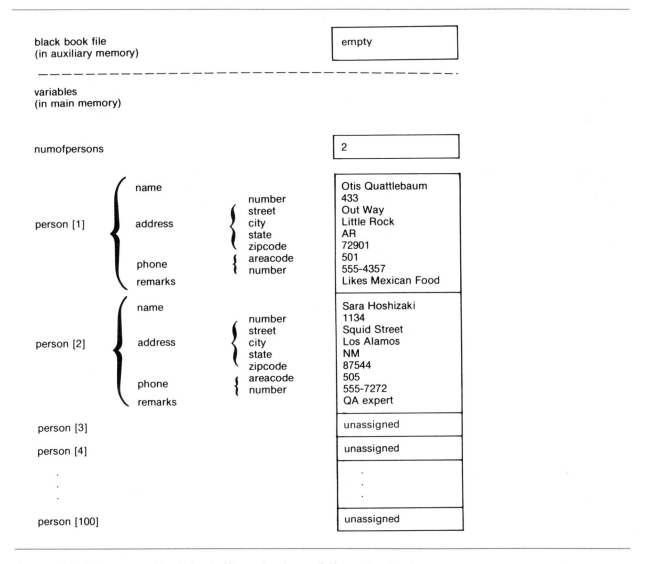

black book file
(in auxiliary memory)   empty

variables
(in main memory)

numofpersons   2

person [1]   name   Otis Quattlebaum
                  number   433
             address   street   Out Way
                       city   Little Rock
                       state   AR
                       zipcode   72901
             phone   areacode   501
                       number   555-4357
             remarks   Likes Mexican Food

person [2]   name   Sara Hoshizaki
                  number   1134
             address   street   Squid Street
                       city   Los Alamos
                       state   NM
                       zipcode   87544
             phone   areacode   505
                       number   555-7272
             remarks   QA expert

person [3]   unassigned

person [4]   unassigned

person [100]   unassigned

Figure 11.5 The empty black book file and values of the data structure person after data for the Quattlebaum and Hoshizaki entries are read.

A Second Updating Run

Suppose that the program updateblackbook is run for a second time. At the beginning of the second run, the values in the auxiliary memory file blackbook are exactly as they were at the conclusion of the first run as illustrated by Figure 11.6. The values of person in main memory, however, have been lost in the interim. Starting from this more-or-less typical status of the black book file, a second hand simulation is done in conjunction with refining the called procedures. All the main program updateblackbook needs to be fully refined is complete definitions of the called procedures and a refining of the data structure declarations.

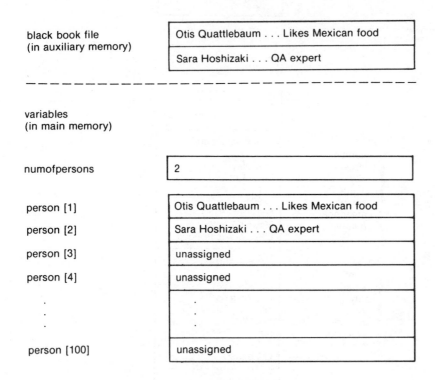

black book file
(in auxiliary memory)

| Otis Quattlebaum . . . Likes Mexican food |
| Sara Hoshizaki . . . QA expert |

variables
(in main memory)

numofpersons

| 2 |

person [1] | Otis Quattlebaum . . . Likes Mexican food |
person [2] | Sara Hoshizaki . . . QA expert |
person [3] | unassigned |
person [4] | unassigned |
. | . |
. | . |
. | . |
person [100] | unassigned |

Figure 11.6 Contents of black book file and values of person after rewriting the
auxiliary memory file. Values in main memory of person are lost after program
termination, but values in the auxiliary memory file blackbook are retained for
later use.

```
program updateblackbook (input, output, blackbook);

  const
    maxentries = 100;
    add =      'Add                 ';  { padded with blanks to length 20 }
    delete = 'Delete                ';  { because string comparisons }
    done =     'Done                ';  { require equal length strings }
    maxlength = 20;   { maximum length of string read by readline }

  type
    entryindex = 1..maxentries;
    stringindex = 1..maxlength;
    stringlength = 0..maxlength;
    string2 = packed array [1..2] of char;
    string3 = packed array [1..3] of char;
    string5 = packed array [1..5] of char;
    string6 = packed array [1..6] of char;
    string8 = packed array [1..8] of char;
    string = packed array [stringindex] of char;
    string20 = string;
```

```
      addresstype = record
        number : string6;
        street : string20;
        city : string20;
        state : string2;
        zipcode : string5;
        end; { addresstype }

      phonetype = record
        areacode : string3;
        number : string8;   { character 4 is a hyphen }
        end; { phonetype }

      persontype = record
        name : string20;
        address : addresstype;
        phone : phonetype;
        remarks : string20;
        end; { persontype }

var
  person : array [entryindex] of persontype;
  blackbook : file of persontype;
  entryposition : entryindex;
  numofpersons : 0..maxentries;
  morechanges : boolean;
  line : string;

procedure readline (var line : string); ... end; { readline }
procedure readblackbook; ... end; { readblackbook }
procedure addnewentry; ... end; { addnewentry }
procedure deleteentry; ... end; { deleteentry }
procedure writeblackbook; ... end; { writeblackbook }

begin { ----- main program ----- }
readblackbook  { from auxiliary memory }
{ requested changes are first made only in the
      main memory copy of the file }
morechanges := true;
while morechanges do
  begin
  write ('Enter a request: ');
  readline (line);
  if line = add then
    addnewentry
  else if line = delete then
    deleteentry
  else if line = done then
    morechanges := false
  else
    writeln ('Update request must be "Add", "Delete", or "Done"');
  end; { while-loop }
writeblackbook;  { to auxiliary memory }
end.
```

The procedure readblackbook directs the computer to read all the values in the black book file and assign them to elements of the array of data structures person. Reading terminates with the end of the file. After the procedure readblackbook is executed, the contents of the auxiliary memory file blackbook and the value of person in main memory are identical to what they were at the termination of execution of the previous update run, as shown in Figure 11.6.

```
procedure readblackbook;

  var
    entryposition : entryindex;
    moreentries : boolean;

  begin
  reset (blackbook);
  numofpersons := 0;
  while not eof (blackbook) and
        (numofpersons < maxentries) do
    begin
    numofpersons := numofpersons + 1;
    entryposition := numofpersons;
    read (blackbook, person [entryposition]);
    end; { while }
  end; { readblackbook }
```

Suppose the first two requests are to add entries for persons named Peggee Franklin and Carole Hicke. This causes the procedure addnewentry to be executed twice.

```
procedure addnewentry;

  var
    i : stringindex;

  begin
  if numofpersons = maxentries then
    writeln ('The black book is full.')
  else
    begin
    numofpersons := numofpersons + 1;
    entryposition := numofpersons;
    { obtain information for the new entry }
    with person [entryposition] do
      begin
      write ('Enter name: ');
      readline (name);
      write ('Enter house number: ');
      readline (line);
      for i := 1 to 6 do
        address.number [i] := line [i];
      write ('Enter street: ');
      readline (address.street);
      write ('Enter city: ');
      readline (address.city);
```

```
write ('Enter state (2 letters): ');
readline (line);
for i := 1 to 2 do
  address.state [i] := line [i];
write ('Enter zip code: ');
readline (line);
for i := 1 to 5 do
  address.zipcode [i] := line [i];
write ('Enter area code: ');
readline (line);
for i := 1 to 3 do
  phone.areacode [i] := line [i];
write ('Enter number: ');
readline (line);
for i := 1 to 8 do
  phone.number [i] := line [i];
write ('Enter remarks: ');
readline (remarks);
end; { with person [entryposition] }
end; { else }
end; { addnewentry }
```

Figure 11.7 shows the status of the auxiliary memory file blackbook and of the main memory variable person after the data are supplied for the Franklin and Hicke entries. The value of numofpersons is now 4.

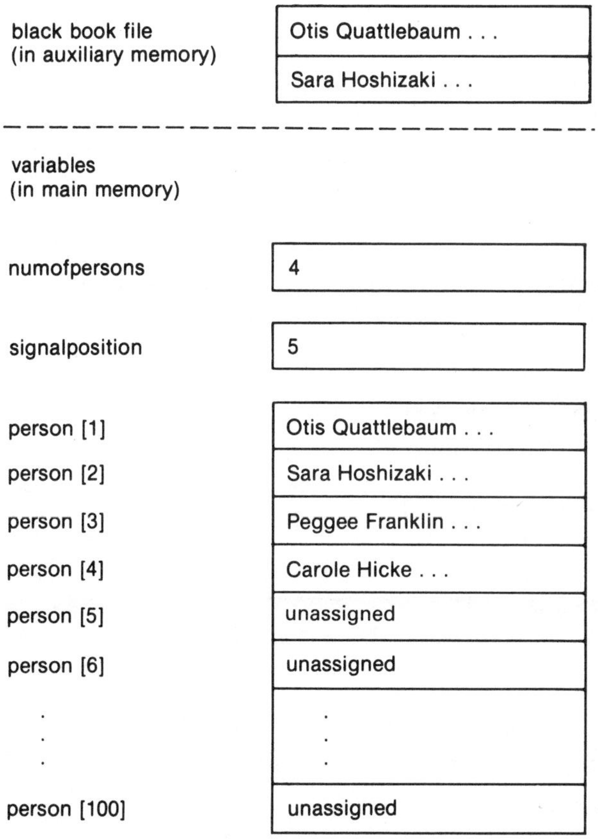

black book file (in auxiliary memory)	Otis Quattlebaum . . .
	Sara Hoshizaki . . .

variables (in main memory)

numofpersons	4
signalposition	5
person [1]	Otis Quattlebaum . . .
person [2]	Sara Hoshizaki . . .
person [3]	Peggee Franklin . . .
person [4]	Carole Hicke . . .
person [5]	unassigned
person [6]	unassigned
. . .	. . .
person [100]	unassigned

Figure 11.7 Contents of black book file and values of person after two more entries are added to the main memory copy of the file.

The With-Statement

It is something of a nuisance to have to write the full path name of a component of a record, especially when many such full path names start with the same record name. The **with-statement** allows a programmer the convenience of not repeating the initial part of a full path name. For example, all fields in the record person [entryposition] of the previous are read using a with-statement headed by

```
with person [entryposition] do
```

The scope (that is, the range of applicability) of a with-statement is the simple or compound statement that follows the keyword "do" in the heading of the with-statement. With-statements may be nested within each other.

Deleting an Entry

Suppose that the next request is to delete the entry for Sara Hoshizaki. The procedure deleteentry, which is used to remove an entry, is a little more complicated than the procedure for adding a new entry, in spite of the fact that it is shorter, because in deleting an entry it is first necessary to locate the entry to be deleted. Because the black book file is small, and because the file is not kept in alphabetical order, the procedure deleteentry uses a sequential search modelled on the program cardcheck1 in Section 9.2.

```
    procedure deleteentry;

      var
        name2delete : string20;
        entryposition : entryindex;
        namefound : boolean;

      begin
      write ('Enter name to be deleted: ');
      readline (name2delete);
      namefound := false;
      entryposition := 1;
      while (entryposition <= numofpersons) and (not namefound) do
        if person [entryposition].name = name2delete then
          namefound := true
        else
          entryposition := entryposition + 1;
      if namefound then
        begin
        { move last person to position of
            person to be deleted }
        person [entryposition] := person [numofpersons];
        numofpersons := numofpersons - 1;
        end { then }
      else
        begin
        writeln ('Cannot delete ', name2delete);
        writeln ('  It is not in the little black book');
        end; { else }
      end; { deleteentry }
```

Moving an Entire Structure in Main Memory

Once the entry to be deleted is located, there is still the problem of how to remove it. Merely obliterating (that is, blanking out) the data for Sara Hoshizaki would leave a gap at person [2] between the entries for Otis Quattlebaum and Peggee Franklin. To avoid this gap, the procedure deleteentry simply replaces the data for the entry to be deleted with the data for the last entry in the file. As shown in Figure 11.8, this results in an apparent duplication of the last person, but the duplication has no effect on the program, because the value of numofpersons is now 3, which will prevent any procedure from using the duplicate person entry.

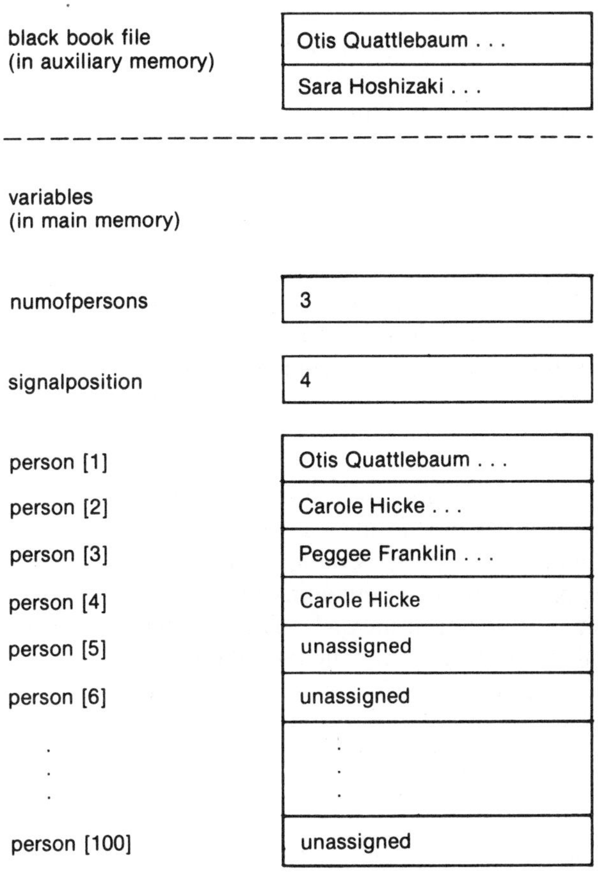

black book file (in auxiliary memory)	
	Otis Quattlebaum . . .
	Sara Hoshizaki . . .

variables (in main memory)

numofpersons	3
signalposition	4
person [1]	Otis Quattlebaum . . .
person [2]	Carole Hicke . . .
person [3]	Peggee Franklin . . .
person [4]	Carole Hicke
person [5]	unassigned
person [6]	unassigned
⋮	⋮
person [100]	unassigned

Figure 11.8 Contents of black book file and values of person after the entry for Sara Hoshizaki is deleted. The duplicate entry for Carole Hicke has no effect on the program because the value of numofpersons is 3.

Although the statement

```
person [entryposition] := person [numofpersons]
```

is an assignment statement, it is a very powerful one because each entry in the array person is a data structure. Execution of this statement causes the value of each component of the variable person [numofpersons] to be assigned as the new value of the corresponding components of the variable person [entryposition], just as if the following nine simpler assignment statements were executed.

```
person [entryposition] . name :=
   person [numofpersons] . name
person [entryposition] . address . number :=
   person [numofpersons] . address . number
person [entryposition] . address . street :=
   person [numofpersons] . address . street
person [entryposition] . address . city :=
   person [numofpersons] . address . city
person [entryposition] . address . state :=
   person [numofpersons] . address . state
person [entryposition] . address . zipcode :=
   person [numofpersons] . address . zipcode
person [entryposition] . phone . areacode :=
   person [numofpersons] . phone . areacode
person [entryposition] . phone . number :=
   person [numofpersons] . phone . number
person [entryposition] . remarks :=
   person [numofpersons] . remarks
```

Recopying from Main Memory Into Auxiliary Memory

As shown in Figure 11.8, all the changes in the black book file requested during the second simulated execution have been made only in the main memory copy of the file. The updated copy of the black book file must be recopied into auxiliary memory if the changes are to be permanent. This is exactly what happens after the request "Done" is supplied. The while-loop is exited and the procedure writeblackbook is executed.

The most recent input/output operation performed with the auxiliary memory file blackbook was to read all the records of the file. Thus the file is positioned at its endpoint, that is, after the last record. This is easily visualized if the file is stored on a reel of tape. The part of the tape containing the file has been read, and the tape is partly wound onto the take-up reel. The new file should be written starting at the beginning of the tape. Thus the tape should be rewound by a rewrite instruction before the updated version of the file is written on it by the procedure writeblackbook.

```
procedure writeblackbook;

  var
    entryposition : entryindex;

  begin
  rewrite (blackbook);
  for entryposition := 1 to numofpersons do
    write (blackbook, person [entryposition]);
  end; { writeblackbook }
```

Figure 11.9 shows that at the conclusion of the second simulated execution, the black book file in auxiliary memory contains entries for Otis Quattlebaum, Carole Hicke, and Peggee Franklin. The values of the array variable person in main memory are not changed by writing them into auxiliary memory. Main memory values are lost after program termination, but values saved in the records of the auxiliary memory file blackbook preserve all the relevant information for future use.

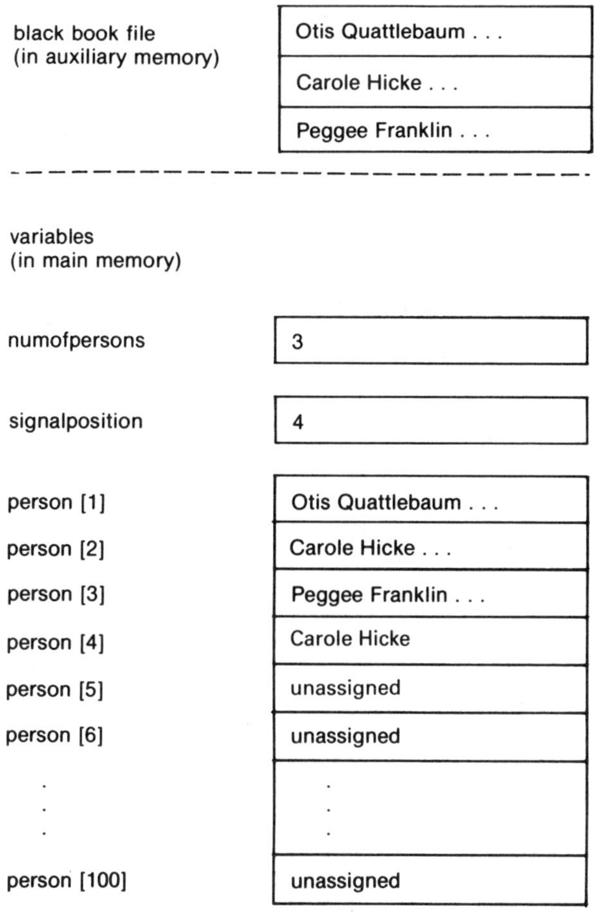

Figure 11.9 Contents of black book file and values of person after execution of the procedure writeblackbook. Values in main memory will be lost at the conclusion of the execution of updateblackbook, but values recorded in the auxiliary memory file blackbook preserve the information for future use.

A System of Programs

The programs createblackbook and updateblackbook in this section share a file blackbook in auxiliary memory and therefore may be thought of as part of a **system of programs**. Other programs of this system include the fragments in Section 11.2 to print all telephone numbers for persons in one area code, and to look up a person's telephone number. (These fragments must be furnished with data structure declarations and initialization statements, including a call to the procedure readblackbook to read the shared auxiliary memory file into main memory.) Although each program of a system of programs is technically a "main program" in the sense that it is not called by any other program, these programs must be coordinated with each other, because the values that one program writes into the shared file in auxiliary memory affect subsequent executions both of itself and of the other programs of the system.

On the other hand, the procedures readblackbook, addnewentry, deleteentry, and writeblackbook that are called by the program updateblackbook in this section form a **system of procedures**, that is, several procedures that may be called and executed during a single run of a main program. The most important difference between a system of programs and a system of procedures is that the programs of a system of programs can only pass information among themselves by writing it into one or more shared files in auxiliary memory, while the procedures of a system of procedures also can pass information by assigning it as the value of one or more variables in main memory.

Variant Record Types

It is sometimes inconvenient to require all records of a file to have the same format. For example, it might be desirable to preface the person records of the black book file with a title record giving the name of the file, the date it was last updated, and the number of entries, or it might be desirable to keep different performance statistics for pitchers than for baseball players who play other positions. An advanced Pascal feature, **variant record types**, allows the last field in a record to vary in structure.

The form of the variant part of a record resembles a case-statement, as shown in the example below, which builds on types already declared for the black book examples in this section.

```
type
   titleorperson = (titlerecord, personrecord);

mixedtype = record
   case selectionfield : titleorperson of
      titlerecord : (filename : string20;
                     date : string7;
                     numofpersons : 0..maxentries);
      personrecord : (name : string20;
                      address : addresstype;
                      phone : phonetype;
                      remarks : string20);
   end; { mixedtype }

var
   blackbook : file of mixedtype;
   person : array [entryindex] of mixedtype;
   title : mixedtype;
```

Each record of type mixedtype has a component selectionfield, called the **tag field**, whose value determines what other fields will complete the record. If the value of selectionfield is titlerecord, the remaining components of the record are filename, date, and numofpersons. properly declared and enclosed in parentheses. If the value of selectionfield is personrecord, the remaining components of the record are name, address, phone, and remarks.

The variable declarations for the black book applications may now use the type mixedtype. Blackbook is a file of mixedtype because its first record is a title record and the remaining records are person records. The variable person is an array of mixedtype, even though we intend to put only person records into it. The variable title is of mixedtype, even though we intend to read only the title record into it.

The price of variants in a record type is a tag field that appears in every record. It may be examined if desired, or ignored if the variant used in a particular record is already known. In the black book example, components such as person (37) . name and title . date would ordinarily be referenced without examining the tag field. In other applications, the mixture of record formats in the input file might be sufficiently unpredictable that the tag field must be interrogated before processing a record.

A variant record type also may have a fixed part consisting of ordinary component declarations preceding the variant part. All variants of the record would include the fixed part as well as the tag field for the variant part.

Variant parts may be nested in two ways. First, the type of a component in a variant part may itself be a record type with a variant part. Second, the last field in the parenthesized list of fields in an alternative of a variant part itself may be a variant part built using the same case construction. The names of components must all be different, even if they appear in different alternatives of a variant record type.

Self-Test Questions

1. True/false.
    a. "Creating a file" means making the file and record declarations.
    b. Every field in a record structure may be variant.
    c. A copy of each file is kept in auxiliary memory as a backup in case the main memory copy is destroyed.
    d. Variables of record structure type may be used in assignment statements.
2. What are the three main steps in updating a file?

Exercises

1. Design a data structure for records in a file on presidents of the United States. Each record must have at least the following information: name, dates of birth and death, and dates of office.
2. Write a program createpresidents that requisitions auxiliary memory space for the file of Exercise 1.
3. Write a program updatepresidents to update the file created for Exercise 2. Allowable update requests must include adding a new president, inserting a date of death, and changing dates of office.
4. For some applications, it is important that records in the file be sorted in alphabetical order or ordered by some other key such as social security number. Assume that the black book file is sorted in alphabetical order by name, that the names are written last name first, and that the file contains two records, one for "Hoshizaki, Sara", and one for "Quattlebaum, Otis", in that order.

    Modify the procedure addentry so that each new entry is inserted in alphabetical order. When the appropriate place for a new entry is found, each entry to go after the new one must be moved to the position with the next higher subscript, and this shifting must be done by moving the last person first.
5. Modify the procedure deleteentry so that, when an entry is deleted, all entries after the one deleted are moved to the next lower position in the file. If the current entries in the file are in alphabetical order, this will keep them in alphabetic order in sequential positions starting at the first record of the file.
6. Assuming that the black book file is being maintained in alphabetical order using the procedures addnewentry and deleteentry as described in Exercises 4 and 5, and that the file initially consists of records for "Hoshizaki, Sara", and "Quattlebaum, Otis", in that order, then draw figures corresponding to Figures 11.7 to 11.9 based on this starting status of the file and the following additional requests.

        Add Hicke, Carole...
        Add Franklin, Peggee...
        Delete Hoshizaki, Sara
        Done

7. Modify the program updateblackbook in this section to permit a "Change" request that modifies information for a person already listed in the black book. Use the procedures deleteentry and addnewentry that have been written already.

8. Write a program to create a data base containing information for a college registrar based on the data structure for Exercise 5 in Section 11.2.

9. Write a program to create a data base consisting of one record for each course offered by a college. To keep things manageable, assume that each course has only one section. Include information such as department, course number, number of hours credit, meeting time, and so on.

10. Using the variant record type mixedtype described at the end of this section, modify the procedures readblackbook and writeblackbook to handle a blackbook file headed by a title record containing the number of entries in the file. Also modify the procedures createblackbook and updateblackbook to process the title record properly. Do any other procedures in this section require modification because of the change in record format? Explain.

11. Ordinarily, different performance statistics are kept for pitchers than for baseball players who play other positions. Modify the data structure playertype given in Section 11.2 for keeping performance statistics on baseball players to include a variant part describing pitching performance.

11.4   What You Should Know

1. The values of variables are usually lost when execution of a program terminates.

2. Generally, disk files remain unchanged between executions.

3. A file is composed of a sequence of segments called records. All of the records in a file have the same data type, which may be an intrinsic type, like real, integer, or character, or a more complex data type, like an enumerated data type, an array, or a record structure.

4. The term "record" is used in two senses: informally, to designate the components of a file and, formally, to designate the syntactic construct that begins with the keyword "record".

5. A text file is a file of characters.

6. The standard files input and output are text files.

7. The procedures read, readln, write, and writeln operate on other text files exactly as they do on the standard files input and output.

8. The procedures reset and rewrite are executed automatically for the standard input and output files.

9. If read, readln, and eof do not specify a file, the standard input file input is implied.

10. If write and writeln do not specify a file, the standard file output is implied.

11. The built-in procedure reset positions a file at its first record for reading, after which the records of the file are read in sequence.

12. The procedure rewrite erases a file and positions it at the beginning for output. It is not possible to begin writing at the middle of a file.

13. The procedure read is used to read from a file. In standard, Pascal, the components of the file are always read in sequence.

14. The procedure write is used to write components of a file. In standard Pascal, writing is sequential.

15. The built-in function eof returns the boolean true if the file specified is positioned at its end.

16. The organization of data in the real world should be reflected in the organization of data in the program. In many cases, designing a structure for the data is as important as designing the program itself.

17. Like a program designed from the top down, data can be organized in a tree structure. Successive levels in the tree represent successive refinements in the data structure. The top level in the data structure is the root, and the components which are not further refined are leaves.

18. In Pascal, three data structures are implemented using the record structure construct.

19. A record is a data structure grouping together several component pieces of information which need not be of the same data type.

20. The components of a record structure may be of any data type, except files, and may be records themselves.

21. A component of a record structure is referenced by writing its path name, which consists of the name of the record, followed by a period and the name of the component.

22. When the component is itself a record structure, the name of the component is also a part of a path name.

23. A program to update or process a permanent file consists of three major parts:

    a. Reading the permanent copy from auxiliary memory into main memory

    b. Processing the file in main memory

    c. Writing the updated version of the file to auxiliary memory for permanence.

24. A permanent file may be accessed by many different programs.

25. The with-statement allows a programmer the convenience of not repeating the initial part of a full path name.

26. If two variables are record structures of the same type, the complete set of vaues of one may be assigned to the other in a single assignment statement.

27. The last component in a record type may vary in structure. Variant parts are declared using a construction similar to the case-statement. The tag field determines which components will appear in the variant parts of the current record.

POINTERS AND LINKED LISTS

One of the nice properties of a Pascal sequential file is that the programmer does not have to indicate a maximum size for it. However, the individual records that comprise the file tend to be difficult to access except in the original sequential order in which they were written. Insertions in the middle of a file also are difficult. On the other hand, an array must always be given a maximum size, but its elements may be accessed easily in any order the programmer desires. Insertions in the middle of an array are still time-consuming to perform, if not difficult to program.

With Pascal **pointers**, a feature discussed in this chapter, it is possible to create a structure, a **dynamic list**, that has many of the properties of an array, yet has the desirable features that no maximum size need be given, and that insertions and deletions can be made in the middle of the dynamic list without moving other items in the list.

12.1 Dynamic Data Structure Declarations

A **dynamic data structure** is one that can change its size or shape during execution. For example, a **dynamic list** permits insertions and deletions in any position in the list. Dynamic data structures are not intrinsic in Pascal, so there is more of a distinction in the section between the abstract data structure, a way of conceptually organizing data, and the concrete implementation of the abstract structures using Pascal constructs. Dynamic lists are implemented in this section as **linked lists**. Each item in the dynamic list is represented by a **node** in the linked list, containing not only the information for that item, but also a **pointer** to the node representing the next item in the dynamic list. To hold two types of information, the nodes are record structures.

Section Preview

Pointer:

> A pointer is a variable whose value is a location in the computer's memory where the value it points to is stored. Two or more pointers may point to the same location and consequently reference the same value.

361

General Form of Pointer Declaration:

```
var
    pointervariablename : ^typename;
```

Assignment Using Pointer Variables:

```
pointervariablename^ := expression of correct type;
pointervariablename := otherpointervariablename;
```

Examples:

```
var
   pointer1, pointer2 : ^integer;

begin
pointer1^ := 3 + 5;
pointer2 := pointer1;
end
```

The Pointer Constant **Nil**:

The only pointer constant is called nil. When a variable is assigned the value nil, it is not pointing to any location or value in memory.

The Built-In Procedure **New**:

If the variable p is any pointer type, execution of the procedure call

```
new (p)
```

allocates enough memory for a value of the type that p points to and assigns p to point to this place in the computer's memory. The built-in procedure new does not assign a value in the memory locations that p points to.

Dynamic List:

A dynamic list is an abstract data structure consisting of a list whose length is not fixed.

Linked List:

A linked list is a representation of a list in Pascal using record structures for nodes in the list and pointers to link each node in the list to the next node in the list.

Pointers

In Pascal, **dynamic data structures** can be implemented using a **pointer**. A pointer is a variable whose value is the location in the computer memory of a particular value. The pointer points to the value stored in that location.

A Pascal pointer variable may point to the location of a value of any Pascal type except file, including types integer, real, array of char, and record. However, once declared in a program, a pointer variable can point only to values of that one type for which it has been declared.

Declaration of Pointers

A Pascal pointer variable is declared by indicating the type of value to which it may point. For example,

```
var
    p1, p2 : ^real;
```

declares the variables p1 and p2 to be pointers to real values and

```
type
    a = array [1..9] of integer;
    pa = ^a;
```

declares pa to be a type that is a pointer to an array of integers. In a variable or type declaration the caret (^) before a type should be read as "pointer to" the type, so that p1 and p2 are declared to be "pointers to type real" and the type pa is declared to be "pointer to type a", that is, a pointer to an array of integers. Some computer output devices print the caret (^) as an upward arrow, reinforcing the interpretation that it means "pointer to something".

Use of Pointers

If p is a Pascal pointer, then p^ is the value of the object pointed to by p, that is, the value stored in the location that is the value of p. Note that this time the caret comes *after* the name of the pointer variable. For example, if p is declared to be type ^real, a pointer to a real, then

```
    p^ := 5.6
```

assigns the value 5.6 to the object pointed to by p. This object itself has no name other than p^. Similarly,

```
    write (p^)
```

will cause the computer to print the value of the object pointed to by p; this value is 5.6 in our example.

Pointers to values are similar to variables, but they have some very interesting properties that are different. In order to take advantage of these differences, it is important to keep in mind that the value of a pointer is some location in computer memory. Let us examine one of the consequences of this fact. Suppose p1 and p2 are pointers to a value of type real, declared by

```
var
    p1, p2 : ^real
```

Then suppose the following four statements are executed.

```
    p1^ := 5.6;
    p2 := p1;
    p1^ := 3.7;
    writeln (p2^)
```

What is printed? The effect of the first statement is to store the value 5.6 in the location pointed to by p1. It is convenient to picture the result of this statement by

which represents the fact that the value of p1 is a location in which the real number 5.6 is stored. That is, p1 points to the real value 5.6.

The second statement assigns to p2 the value of p1. It does not assign 5.6 as the value of p2; it assigns the location of the value 5.6 to p2. The situation now can be pictured as

Both p1 and p2 point to the same location in memory, which happens to contain the real value 5.6. Next, the real value 3.7 is stored in the location pointed to by p1. Since this is also the location pointed to by p2, both p1 and p2 now point to a location occupied by the real number 3.7. Thus the fourth statement prints the value 3.7. The situation is

Note that what happens is quite different from what would happen if p1 and p2 were real variables. The difference is that changing the value pointed to by p1 also has the effect of changing the value pointed to by p2, since in this case they both point to the same location. This property can be used very effectively in some situations.

Dynamic Lists

Suppose T is any Pascal data type other than a file. For example, T could be real, array of char, or record type. A **dynamic list** of Ts is a (possibly empty) sequence of items of type T. A dynamic list of Ts is much like an array of T except that:

a.   It has no fixed maximum length.
b.   Items in the dynamic list are not referenced using subscripts.
c.   It is not a built-in data type in Pascal.

Using Pointers to Construct Dynamic Lists

A dynamic list is a list that can grow or shrink during execution. Since dynamic list is not a built-in data type, we must construct a dynamic list out of data types that are built in. If T is any Pascal data type except file, we can represent a dynamic list of items of type T in terms of the record type node defined below.

```
type
   node = record
      info : T;
      link : ^node;
      end; { node }
```

As illustrated in the following diagram, each **node** in the dynamic list listname is a collection of memory locations containing an information (info) field of type T and a pointer field linking this node to the next node in the dynamic list. For this reason, a dynamic list also is called a **linked list**.

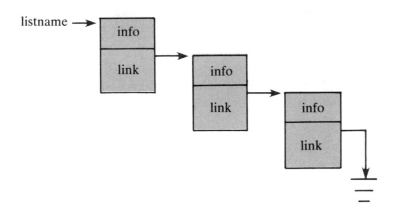

The variable listname also is of type ^node. It points to the first node in the dynamic list.

The Pointer Constant Nil

There is one constant that may be assigned to a pointer variable. It is **nil** and is used to represent the fact that the pointer isn't pointing to anything. In particular, the link field in the last node of a dynamic list has the value nil because no node follows it. An empty list is represented by assigning the value nil to the pointer variable listname.

The Built-In Procedure New

Suppose we wish to construct a dynamic list of integers containing the numbers 23, -7, and 45. First, we declare the type of the nodes in the dynamic linked list. Then we declare that the list name, listofintegers, is a variable that points to a node, the first node in the list.

```
type
  node = record
    number : integer;
    link : ^node;
    end; { node }
  listtype = ^node;

var
  listofintegers : listtype;
```

The Pascal built-in procedure **new** is used to create a new node in which to put the first integer 23. The procedure new has one argument, which must be a pointer. The procedure allocates space to store one object of the type pointed to by the pointer and sets the pointer so that it points to that location. The procedure new does not assign any values to the object pointed to by the pointer. In our case, execution of the statement

```
new (listofintegers)
```

allocates storage in memory to hold a record of type node and then assigns that location to the pointer variable listofintegers. Thus the situation may be represented by the following diagram.

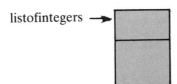

Note that the fields of the record have no values. The next task is to assign the integer 23 to the number field of the node. This is accomplished by the statement

```
listofintegers^ . number := 23
```

This may be read as "assign the value 23 to the number field of the node pointed to by listofintegers". Now the situation is

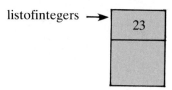

The pointer field of this first node should point to the second node containing the number -7. Of course, memory locations for the second node must first be allocated. This is accomplished by executing the statements

```
new (listofintegers^ . link);
listofintegers^ . link^ . number := -7
```

This situation is depicted by

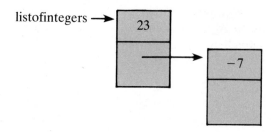

Scanning from right to left, we may read the second of these statements as "assign the value -7 to the number field of the node pointed to by the link field of the node pointed to by the variable listofintegers".

As one might readily imagine, the statements to put the third item in the list are going to become unreadably long. One solution is to introduce another variable that can point to any node.

```
var
   tempptr : ^node;
```

With this declaration, the previous two statements can be written more clearly as

```
new (tempptr);
tempptr^ . number := -7;
listofintegers^ . link := tempptr
```

after which the situation can be represented by the following diagram.

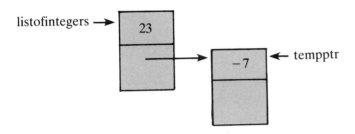

Introduction of the variable tempptr also makes it easier to add the third item to the list using a second temporary pointer tempptr2 and the statements

```
new (tempptr2);
tempptr2^ . number := 45;
tempptr^ . link := tempptr2
```

The result is this list.

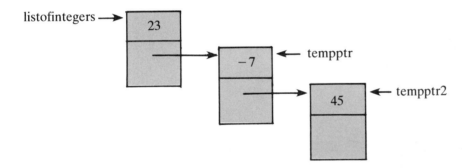

We complete the dynamic list by setting the last pointer to nil.

```
tempptr2^ . link := nil
```

This allows a program to test for a nil pointer to see when it comes to the end of the list.

Building a Linked List With a Loop

Note again that there is nothing in the declarations for a dynamic list that limits the size of the list. Integers can be added to this list until the computer runs out of storage space. To emphasize this fact, we show how to build a list of integers consisting of all the numbers in the input file up to but not including the first occurrence of some termination signal. Pascal statements needed to build this list are shown below. The resulting list is in the reverse of the order in which items are read; it is assumed that the order is not important in this example.

```
listofintegers := nil;
morenumbers := true;
while morenumbers do
    begin
    read (n);
    if n = signal then
        morenumbers := false
```

```
else
  begin
  new (newnode);
  newnode^ . number := n;
  newnode^ . link := listofintegers;
  listofintegers := newnode;
  end; { else-clause and if-statement }
end; { while morenumbers }
```

Suppose the input list consists of the numbers 23, −7, and 45, followed by the signal. After the while-loop is executed once, the situation is

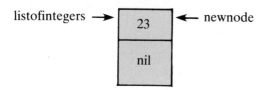

As each of the statements in the else-clause for n = −7 is executed, the resulting situation is shown.

```
new (newnode);
```

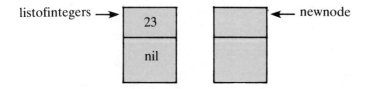

```
newnode^ . number := n;
```

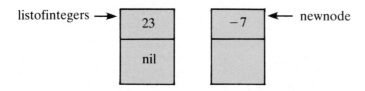

```
newnode^ . link := listofintegers;
```

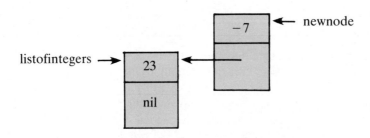

```
listofintegers := newnode;
```

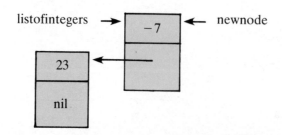

Inserting the third node for n = 45 proceeds similarly.

The order of the items in a dynamic linked list is determined solely by the array of linking pointers link. Any other order or disorder that appears in a diagram has no relevance to the program execution because the program has no knowledge of or control over which memory locations are allocated by the built-in procedure new.

Self-Test Questions

1.   Find and correct the errors in the following declarations and statements.

```
type
   integerpointer = integer^;
var
   ptr : integerpointer;

begin
ptr := 6;
end
```

2.   True/false:

a. The built-in procedure new allocates memory locations for new nodes in order of increasing memory address.
b. The pointer constant nil means the same as zero.
c. A linked list and a dynamic list are the same thing.
d. The data type node is a built-in data type.
e. The built-in procedure new must always have a supplied argument of type ^node, (i.e., pointer to node).

Exercises

1.   Write a program that reads integers until a signal is read and stores the integers in a linked list in the order they are read. That is, the first number read is first in the linked list, the second read is second in the linked list, and so on. *Hint:* Use a pointer variable that points to the last node currently in the linked list.

2.   Write a program to print the nodes of a linked list in order. Test it with the linked list formed by the program in Exercise 1 or the program in the section.

12.2   Linked Lists

An abstract data structure consists of an organization of data and a set of fundamental operations that may be performed on the structure. In this section, procedures are written for the fundamental operations of traversing a linked list and inserting new items at arbitrary positions in the list. Then the insertion operation is used to sort a list of data. As each new item is read, it is inserted in the dynamic list in a position determined by the value of its key field.

Section Preview

The Built-In Procedure **Dispose**:

The built-in procedure dispose deallocates the memory space pointed to by the pointer variable that is its argument.

Example:

```
var
    p : ^integer;

begin
new (p);
p^ := 5;
writeln (p^);
dispose (p);
end
```

Linked List Processing:

Two kinds of linked list processing are programmed in this section, **traversing** a linked list from front to back and **inserting** a node into the middle of a linked list.

Tail Recursion:

Some of the programs in this section are clearer if they use a very mild kind of recursion, called tail recursion. In tail recursion, the last statement executed in a procedure is a call to the same procedure to complete a simpler case of the same action. Because the recursive call is the last step in an execution of the procedure, tail recursion is *almost* like iteration where the procedure loops back to its first statement.

Printing a Dynamic List

The elements of a dynamic list can be printed with the help of a variable that points in turn to each of the members of the list.

```
type
  node = record
    number : integer;
    link : ^node;
    end;  { node }
  listtype = ^node;

procedure printlist (list : listtype);
{ iterative version }

  var
    p : ^node;
```

```
begin
p := list;
while (p <> nil) do
   begin
   write (p^ . number);
   p := p^ . link;
   end; { while }
end; { printlist }
```

The key step

```
p := p^ . link
```

which moves the pointer p to point to the next node in the dynamic list corresponds to the statement

```
i := i + 1
```

which might increment the subscript in a procedure to print the elements of a list stored in an array.

Tail Recursion

There is another way to look at a dynamic list. If the first element of a nonempty dynamic list is removed, what remains is still a dynamic list, although a slightly shorter one than before. This prompts a **recursive definition** of a dynamic list.

Recursive Definition of a Dynamic List:

> If *T* is any Pascal data type except file, a dynamic list of *T*s is either empty or consists of a *T* followed by a (slightly shorter) dynamic list of *T*s.

This definition of a dynamic list is **recursive** because it defines a dynamic list in terms of a dynamic list. It is not a circular definition because there is one dynamic list that is not defined in terms of another dynamic list: the empty list. All other dynamic lists ultimately are defined in terms of adding elements to an empty list.

The new definition of a dynamic list suggests a different way to print a dynamic list:

```
if the list is not empty then
   begin
   Print the first element;
   Print the rest of the list;
   end
```

The dynamic list is still a list of integers. The name of the link field has been changed in each node to restoflist to reflect its role as a pointer to the first node in the rest of the list. Its type is now listtype.

```
type
   listtype = ^node;
   node = record
      number : integer;
      restoflist : listtype;
      end;   { node }
```

```
procedure printlist (list : listtype);
{ recursive version }

  begin
  if list <> nil then
    begin
    write (list^ . number);
    printlist (list^. restoflist);
    end; { if }
  end; { printlist }
```

Except in the case where the argument of the procedure printlist is an empty list, the last statement in each execution of the procedure is a call to the procedure printlist, that is, a call from the procedure to *itself.* The supplied argument in this recursive call is a pointer to a shorter linked list, the rest of the original linked list after the number in the first node is printed.

Because the recursive call is the last statement in the procedure printlist, it behaves as if the value of the pointer, list, were set equal to the pointer list^ . restoflist and then control transferred to the if-test at the beginning of the procedure printlist. This cycle continues until after the number in the last node has been printed. At that time, the pointer variable list is assigned the value nil, the value of the restoflist field in the last node. As a result, the if-test fails and execution of the procedure readlist terminates.

A recursive call like the one in the procedure printlist is called **tail recursion** because it occurs in the last executed statement of the procedure. More general recursive procedures are discussed in Chapter 13.

Sorting With a Dynamic List

One of the special features of a dynamic list is that the programmer need not specify a maximum size for the list. Another important feature is that items may be inserted and deleted from any part of the list without moving large amounts of data. This feature will be used to construct a program that sorts a list of numbers. This program could be modified easily to sort nodes with a large amount of information in addition to the **key field** on which the nodes are being sorted. Since the nodes will *never* move about in the computer's memory, this sorting method has a great advantage over equivalent sorting methods that interchange nodes when the nodes contain a great deal of information.

The sorting procedure is quite simple. As each record is read from the input file, it is inserted into a dynamic list of integers at the appropriate place to keep the list in ascending order according to its key field. Most of the time this involves inserting each new integer between the next smaller and the next larger integers already in the list. However, this level of detail is not necessary to write the first version of the program.

```
program sortlist (input, output);

  begin
  morenumbers := true;
  listofintegers := nil;
  while morenumbers do
    begin
    read a number;
    if number = termination signal then
      morenumbers := false
```

```
    else
      insert number at correct spot in listofintegers;
    end; { while-loop }
  print listofintegers;
  end.
```

In this simple case, the items to be sorted are just integers. Thus, the appropriate declarations for the dynamic list are

```
type
  listtype = ^node;
  node = record
    number : integer;
    restoflist : listtype;
    end; { node }


var
  n : integer;
  listofintegers : listtype;
```

The essential part of this program is inserting one number at the appropriate place in the sorted list of integers. One approach is to break the process into two steps: finding the correct spot to insert the number and then inserting it. However, the recursive point of view provides an even simpler analysis. There are three cases:

1.   If the list is empty, add the new record as the only item in the list.
2.   If the new record belongs before the first record of the list, put it there.
3.   If the new record belongs anywhere after the first number in the list, insert it properly into the remainder of the list. This is a recursive call.

```
procedure insert (n : integer; var list : listtype);

  procedure putnewitemfirst;
  { This procedure is local to the procedure insert }

    var
      newitem : listtype;

    begin
    new (newitem);
    newitem^ . number := n;
    newitem^ . restoflist := list;
    list := newitem;
    end; { putnewitemfirst }

  begin
  if list = nil then
    putnewitemfirst
  else if n < list^ . number then
    putnewitemfirst
  else
    insert (list^ . restoflist);
  end; { insert }
```

The complete refined program follows.

```
program sortlist (input, output);

   const
     signal = −999;

   type
     listtype = ^node;
     node = record
       number : integer;
       restoflist : listtype;
       end; { node }

   var
     n : integer;
     listofintegers : listtype;
     morenumbers : boolean;

   procedure insert (n : integer; var list : listtype);
     ... end; { insert }

   procedure printlist (list : listtype);
     ... end; { printlist }

   begin
   morenumbers := true;
   listofintegers := nil;
   while morenumbers do
     begin
     read (n);
     writeln ('Input data  n : ', n :1);
     if n = signal then
       morenumbers := false
     else
       insert (n, listofintegers);
     end; { while-loop }

   writeln; writeln ('Sorted list:');
   printlist (listofintegers);
   writeln;
   end.
run sortlist

Input data  n : 265
Input data  n : 113
Input data  n : 467
Input data  n : 264
Input data  n : 907
Input data  n : 265
Input data  n : −999

Sorted list:
        113         264         265         265         467         907
```

The Built-In Procedure Dispose

If the program sortlist included a loop to sort many different lists, the repeated use of the procedure new eventually would use up all of the available computer memory. The built-in procedure **dispose** is used to return all storage allocated for the list to the pool of available storage at the completion of each sorting loop.

If p is a pointer variable, then the statement

```
dispose (p)
```

deallocates the memory space reserved for the node pointed to by p. The memory space is then available for other use by the program, and any values contained in the node are lost. The values of p and all other pointers to the node p^ become meaningless because the node they point to no longer exists.

The programmer-defined recursive procedure disposeall deallocates all of the nodes of a dynamic list supplied as its argument.

```
procedure disposeall (var list : listtype);

  begin
  if list <> nil then
    begin
    disposeall (list^ . restoflist);
    dispose (list);
    end; { if }
  end; { disposeall }
```

The procedure disposeall disposes of the nodes in reverse order to avoid a trap. If the first step in the procedure disposeall were to dispose of the first node in the list, then the pointer to the rest of the list would be lost and these nodes could not be disposed. Of course, a temporary pointer variable could be used to save the value of the link field before a node is disposed. A non-recursive version of the procedure based on this strategy is discussed in Exercise 4.

Self-Test Questions

1. True/false:

    a. The action of the built-in procedure dispose undoes the action of the built-in procedure new.
    b. Sorting using a dynamic linked list is faster than sorting using an array because it is easier to find the correct insertion position using a linked list.
    c. A recursive program is always more complicated and confusing than an iterative program to do the same job.

Exercises

1. Write a procedure that will merge two sorted dynamic lists.
2. Write a procedure that builds a dynamic list of integers in the same order as the input file. *Hint:* Use a pointer variable that always points to the last node of the dynamic list under construction. Test your procedure using the procedure printlist in this section.
3. Write a nonrecursive procedure to print a dynamic linked list.
4. Write a nonrecursive procedure to dispose all the nodes of a dynamic list. *Hint:* Use a temporary pointer to hold the link field of a node about to be disposed.
5. Write a recursive procedure to print a dynamic list backward, that is, last element first.

6. Write a nonrecursive procedure to print a dynamic list backward. Compare it with the recursive procedure written in Exercise 5.
7. A rough measure of the efficiency of the two sorting programs discussed in this section is the number of times the procedure insert is executed. Add a global variable count to each program and increase it by one each time the procedure insert is called. Print the value of count at the completion of the sort in order to compare the efficiencies of the sorts based on a dynamic list and a dynamic tree structure.
8. Write a nonrecursive procedure insert for use in the program sortlist to sort a dynamic list.

12.3   What You Should Know

1. A pointer is a variable whose value is the location in the computer memory of a particular value.
2. Pointers to values are similar to variables, except that two or more pointers can point to the same memory location.
3. A dynamic list is a possibly empty sequence of items with no fixed maximum length.
4. One way to implement a dynamic list is with a linked list. The nodes of a linked list consist of two parts: information and a link to the next node.
5. When a pointer variable has the value nil, it is not pointing to anything.
6. The built-in procedure new allocates space for a node of the type its argument points to.
7. The built-in procedure dispose deallocates a node.
8. In a linked list representation of a dynamic list, the list name is a pointer to the first node and each node contains a pointer to the next node. The link field in the last node has value nil.
9. The key step in traversing a linked list is changing the value of the current node pointer to the link field of the current node.
10. A linked list is printed with a pointer variable that begins by pointing to the first node and then traverses the list.
11. Sorting a dynamic list means arranging the nodes in order of the values in the key field in the node.
12. A dynamic list may be empty. If it is not empty, the part of the list that follows the first node is also a dynamic list. This is, in essence, the recursive definition of a dynamic list.
13. The recursive definition of a dynamic list engenders recursive programs to process the list.
14. A recursive call in the last executed statement of a procedure is tail recursion. The mildest form of recursion, tail recursion closely resembles iterative loops.

RECURSION 13

Many problems have solutions that can be expressed in terms of solutions to simpler problems of the same kind. For example, a nonempty list could be sorted by finding the smallest element in the list, moving it to the first position in the list, and then sorting the rest of the list.

An even better way to sort a list is to divide it into two parts on the basis of comparisons with some "middle-sized" element in the list. What results is a list of low elements and a list of high elements from the original list. Then sorting may be accomplished by sorting the low list, sorting the high list, and putting the two sorted sublists together.

In both of these examples, the solution to the original sorting problem has one or more steps which involve sorting a smaller list. Lists of length one or zero need no steps to sort, so the size reduction in either algorithm eventually reduces the problem to one so small it needs no solution. The chief advantage of the second method, called **partition sorting** is that, with anything but the worst of possible luck in the choice of the test elements, it brings the size of the lists to be sorted down to one much more quickly than the first method.

If you write a Pascal procedure to sort a list using one of these algorithms, the step or steps which require sorting a smaller list can be handled by procedure calls to the same subroutine, supplying different arguments, of course. There is no need to write a different procedure to sort the smaller list. A procedure which contains a call to itself is a recursive procedure, and the procedure call to itself is a recursive procedure call. Recursive procedures and procedure calls are discussed in Section 13.1.

A binary tree is a dynamic data structure created using two link fields in each node. Binary trees have the benefit that both search and insertion are rapid. Section 13.2 introduces binary trees and shows how to use them to sort efficiently. The major procedures in tree sorting are recursive.

13.1   Recursive Procedures and Functions

It is permissible for a procedure or function to call itself, or even for a procedure to call another procedure which calls the first one. The names and values of the arguments it supplies to itself may differ from the ones supplied in the original call. The effect of a procedure or function calling itself is as if a second copy were created and the usual substitution rules applied to the passing of arguments to the second copy.

Section Preview

Recursive Procedures:

In Pascal, a procedure may call itself. The result is as if a second copy of the procedure, complete with all local variables, is created to execute the second call. Thus, several copies of a recursive procedure may be active at the same time. Local variable references in a recursive procedure always refer to the innermost, the most recently called, copy of the recursive procedure.

Rules for Writing Recursive Procedures:

1. Although an individual recursive call may increase complexity, a sequence of calls must eventually reach simpler instances of the problem.
2. There must be nonrecursive paths through the procedure to handle the simplest cases.
3. Each possible case must reduce to one of the simplest cases in a finite number of steps of problem reduction by recursive call.

Recursive Functions:

In Pascal, functions also may call themselves. Rules 1−3 for writing recursive procedures also apply to writing recursive function programs.

Indirect Recursion:

Recursive calls need not happen in one step. For example, procedure a may call procedure b, which calls procedure c, which calls procedure a. When indirect recursion happens, one or more of the procedures must appear in a **forward declaration** to maintain the Pascal rule that anything used in Pascal program must be declared above the first place it is referenced.

Example:

```
procedure a (argument list);    { declared procedure name, }
   forward;                     { number and types of arguments }

procedure c (argument list);
   ... ;
   begin
   ... ;
   a ;
   ... ;
   end;  { procedure c }

procedure b (argument list);
   ... ;
   begin
   ... ;
```

```
        c;
        ... ;
      end;  { procedure b }

    procedure a;  { Note: no argument list here. }
      ... ;
      begin  { Declares body of procedure a. }
      ... ;
      b;
      ... ;
      end;  { procedure a }
```

Printing a List Backward

The first example of a **recursive procedure** is one to write a list backward, a task that could just as easily be accomplished without recursion. However, in its simplicity, writebackward clearly illustrates the two basic principles of recursive programming:

1. Reduction of the problem to an instance of the problem that is simpler in some sense

2. A direct, nonrecursive path through the procedure to handle the simplest cases

```
procedure writebackward (list : listtype;
                         sizeoflist : listsizetype);

  begin
  if sizeoflist > 0 then
    begin
    write (list [sizeoflist]);
    writebackward (list, sizeoflist - 1);
    end;  { if }
  end;  { writebackward }
```

The idea of the procedure writebackward could be described simply as follows:

```
if the list isn't empty then
  begin
  Write the last element of the list and then;
  Write the rest of the list backward;
  end
```

If the list is empty, there is nothing to be done.

The driver program testbackward uses the procedure readlist from Section 8.1 to provide a list as input for the procedure writebackward to write backward.

```
program testbackward (input, output);

  const
    maxlistsize = 100;
    signal = -1;

  type
    listdatatype = integer;
    listindex = 1..maxlistsize;
    listtype = array [listindex] of listdatatype;
    listsizetype = 0.. maxlistsize;
```

```
var
  inputlist : listtype;
  numberofentries : listsizetype;

procedure readlist (var list : listtype;
                        maxlistsize : listsizetype;
                        signal : listdatatype;
                        var numberofelements : listsizetype);
  ... end; { readlist }

procedure writebackward (list : listtype;
                            sizeoflist : listsizetype);

  begin
  if sizeoflist > 0 then
    begin
    write (list [sizeoflist]);
    writebackward (list, sizeoflist − 1);
    end; { if }
  end; { writebackward }

begin
readlist (inputlist, maxlistsize, signal, numberofentries);
write ('Reversed list: ');
writebackward (inputlist, numberofentries);
writeln;
end.

run testbackward

Input data  datum:        2
Input data  datum:        3
Input data  datum:        5
Input data  datum:        7
Input data  datum:       11
Input data  datum:       -1
Reversed list:     11   7   5   3   2
```

A Recursive Exponentiation Function

A second example shows how a simple **recurrence relation** is implemented as a **recursive function**. In mathematics, nonnegative integral powers of a number are defined by the following recurrence relations.

$$x^0 = 1$$

$$x^n = x \times x^{n-1} \text{ for } n > 1$$

The recursive function simplepower implements this recursive relation exactly. A preliminary test prevents function evaluations for negative powers which would never reduce to the nonrecursive path in this simple version of the function. See Exercise 1 for ways to treat negative powers.

```
function simplepower (x : real; n : integer) : real;

  begin
  if n <= 0 then
    simplepower := 1
  else
    simplepower := x * simplepower (x, n - 1);
  end; { simplepower }
```

The function program features a nonrecursive assignment

```
simplepower := 1
```

in case the power n = 0 and a recursive assignment

```
simplepower := x * simplepower (x, n - 1)
```

for higher powers. All function evaluations for nonnegative integral powers reduce in a finite number of steps (in fact, exactly n steps) to the nonrecursive case, x to the zero power = 1, so that recursion ultimately ends. For pedagogical purposes, writeln statements are inserted at the beginning and end of the recursive function simplepower to trace the execution sequence.

```
program testsimplepower (output);

  function simplepower (x : real; n : integer) : real;

    begin
    writeln ('Entering simplepower to compute ',
        x :11, ' to the power ', n :1);
    if n <= 0 then
      simplepower := 1
    else
      simplepower := x * simplepower (x, n - 1);
    writeln ('Leaving simplepower evaluation of ',
        x :11, ' to the power ', n :1);
    end; { simplepower }

  begin
  writeln (simplepower (2, 10) :11);
  end.

run testsimplepower

Entering simplepower to compute    2.000e+00 to the power 10
Entering simplepower to compute    2.000e+00 to the power 9
Entering simplepower to compute    2.000e+00 to the power 8
Entering simplepower to compute    2.000e+00 to the power 7
Entering simplepower to compute    2.000e+00 to the power 6
Entering simplepower to compute    2.000e+00 to the power 5
Entering simplepower to compute    2.000e+00 to the power 4
Entering simplepower to compute    2.000e+00 to the power 3
Entering simplepower to compute    2.000e+00 to the power 2
Entering simplepower to compute    2.000e+00 to the power 1
Entering simplepower to compute    2.000e+00 to the power 0
Leaving simplepower evaluation of  2.000e+00 to the power 0
Leaving simplepower evaluation of  2.000e+00 to the power 1
Leaving simplepower evaluation of  2.000e+00 to the power 2
Leaving simplepower evaluation of  2.000e+00 to the power 3
Leaving simplepower evaluation of  2.000e+00 to the power 4
Leaving simplepower evaluation of  2.000e+00 to the power 5
```

```
Leaving simplepower evaluation of    2.000e+00 to the power 6
Leaving simplepower evaluation of    2.000e+00 to the power 7
Leaving simplepower evaluation of    2.000e+00 to the power 8
Leaving simplepower evaluation of    2.000e+00 to the power 9
Leaving simplepower evaluation of    2.000e+00 to the power 10
    1.024e+03
```

Recursion As Top-Down Programming

The recursive function program simplepower in this section and the nonrecursive function program intpower in Section 8.3 both calculate a number raised to a nonnegative integral power by repeated multiplication. However, there is a significant difference in approach evident in the program listings. The nonrecursive function intpower uses a for-loop to calculate x to the power zero, which is 1, x to the first power, which is x, x to the second power, x to the third power, and so on until x to the power n is calculated. This is bottom-up programming.

In contrast, the recursive function program simplepower addresses the stated task, calculating x to the power n, and describes how to do this task in terms of the simpler task of calculating x raised to the power n — 1. It so happens that the simpler task may be accomplished by the same function program, which is what makes this example recursive, but the principle of writing a program to handle the highest-level task and letting the details take care of themselves later is a perfect example of top-down programming.

A More Efficient Power Function

Repeated multiplication is not the most efficient method for raising a number to a nonnegative power. For example, raising 2 to the 16th power requires 15 multiplications to obtain the answer 65,536. On the other hand, repeated squaring can produce the answer with 4 multiplications: 2 squared is 4; 4 squared is 16; 16 squared is 256; and 256 squared is the answer 65,536.

In general, any number raised to an even power may be calculated as the square of that number raised to half the power. Odd powers may be obtained by one additional multiplication.

The recursive function program power, shown below with a driver program testpower, implements the recurrence relationships. Recall that n div 2 is the integer part of the quotient n/2, and that odd (n) is true if n is odd and false if n is even.

```
program testpower (input, output);

  var p : real;

  function power (x : real; n : integer) : real;
    begin
    writeln ('Entering function power to calculate ',
        x :11, ' raised to the power ', n :1);
    if n <= 0 then
      power := 1
    else if odd (n) then
      power := x * sqr (power (x, n div 2))
    else
      power := sqr (power (x, n div 2));
```

```
    writeln ('Leaving function power to calculate ',
       x :11, ' raised to the power ', n :1);
    end; { function power }

  begin
  p := power (2, 10);
  writeln ('2 to the 10th power = ', p :11);
  p := power (1.181543, 63);
  writeln ('The population of NJ in 2590 will be ',
     6066782.0 * p :11);
  end.
run testpower
```

```
Entering function power to calculate    2.000e+00 raised to the power 10
Entering function power to calculate    2.000e+00 raised to the power 5
Entering function power to calculate    2.000e+00 raised to the power 2
Entering function power to calculate    2.000e+00 raised to the power 1
Entering function power to calculate    2.000e+00 raised to the power 0
Leaving function power to calculate    2.000e+00 raised to the power 0
Leaving function power to calculate    2.000e+00 raised to the power 1
Leaving function power to calculate    2.000e+00 raised to the power 2
Leaving function power to calculate    2.000e+00 raised to the power 5
Leaving function power to calculate    2.000e+00 raised to the power 10
2 to the 10th power =    1.024e+03
Entering function power to calculate    1.182e+00 raised to the power 63
Entering function power to calculate    1.182e+00 raised to the power 31
Entering function power to calculate    1.182e+00 raised to the power 15
Entering function power to calculate    1.182e+00 raised to the power 7
Entering function power to calculate    1.182e+00 raised to the power 3
Entering function power to calculate    1.182e+00 raised to the power 1
Entering function power to calculate    1.182e+00 raised to the power 0
Leaving function power to calculate    1.182e+00 raised to the power 0
Leaving function power to calculate    1.182e+00 raised to the power 1
Leaving function power to calculate    1.182e+00 raised to the power 3
Leaving function power to calculate    1.182e+00 raised to the power 7
Leaving function power to calculate    1.182e+00 raised to the power 15
Leaving function power to calculate    1.182e+00 raised to the power 31
Leaving function power to calculate    1.182e+00 raised to the power 63
The population of NJ in 2590 will be    2.225e+11
```

In the first example, 2^{10} is to be calculated as the square of 2^5. A second copy of the function program power is created and delegated the task of calculating 2^5. The second copy of power decides that 2^5 will be calculated as 2 times the square of 2 to the power (5 div 2) $= 2 \times (2^{5 \text{ div } 2})^2 = 2 \times (2^2)^2$. A third copy of power is created to calculate 2 raised to the power 2. The third copy decided that 2^2 is the square of 2 raised to the power 1 and creates a fourth copy of power to calculate 2^1. The fourth copy decides to calculate $2^1 = 2 \times (2^0)^2$ and creates a fifth copy to calculate 2^0. The fifth copy has more immediate success, assigning a value of 1 to power and returning this value to the fourth copy which squares it and multiplies by 2 to get the value 2 for 2^1. This value 2 is returned to the third copy which squares it to get the value 4 for 2^2 to return to the second copy. The second copy squares 4 and multiplies the result by 2 to get the value 32 for 2^5. The value 32 is returned to the first copy where it is squared to get the final answer 1024, which is returned to the calling program testpower for printing.

The Towers of Hanoi

According to legend, there is a temple in Hanoi which contains a ritual apparatus consisting of 3 posts and 64 gold disks of graduated size that fit on the posts. When the temple was built, all 64 gold disks were placed on the first post with the largest on the bottom and the smallest on the top as shown schematically in Figure 13.1. It is the sole occupation of the priests of the temple to move all the gold disks systematically until all 64 gold disks are on the third post, at which time the world will come to an end.

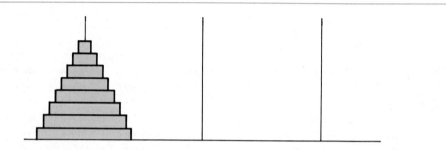

Figure 13.1 The towers of Hanoi.

There are only two rules that must be followed:

1. Disks must be moved from post to post one at a time.
2. A larger disk may never rest on top of a smaller disk on the same post.

A smaller version of this apparatus with only eight disks made of plastic is sold as a recreational puzzle. The sequence of moves necessary to solve the simpler puzzle is not obvious and often takes hours to figure out. We propose to write a simple recursive procedure hanoi to print complete directions for moving any number of disks from one post to another. It is extremely difficult to write a nonrecursive procedure to print these directions.

The recursive procedure hanoi is based on the following top-down analysis of the problem. Suppose n disks are to be moved from a starting post to a final post. Because the largest of these n disks can never rest on a smaller disk, at the time the largest disk is moved, all $n - 1$ smaller disks must be stacked on the free middle post as shown in Figure 13.2.

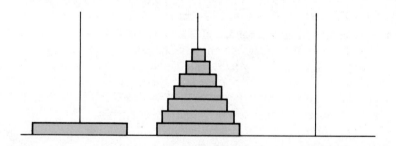

Figure 13.2 Locations of the disks when the largest disk is to be moved.

For the number of disks $n > 1$, the algorithm has 3 steps.

1. Legally move the top $n - 1$ disks from the starting post to the free post.
2. Move the largest disk from the starting post to the final post.
3. Legally move the $n - 1$ disks from the free post to the final post.

The middle step involves printing a single move instruction. The first and third steps represent simpler instances of the same problem, simpler in this case because fewer disks must be moved. The first and third steps therefore may be handled by recursive procedure calls. In case $n = 1$, only the second step should be executed, and this provides a nonrecursive path through the procedure for the simplest case. The Pascal procedure hanoi, its test program testhanoi, and a sample execution output for 4 disks is shown.

```
program testhanoi (input, output);

   type
     smallnumber = 0..64;
     postnumber = 1..3;

   var
     numberofdisks : smallnumber;

   procedure hanoi (numberofdisks : smallnumber;
                     startingpost, goalpost : postnumber);

      const
        allposts = 6;

      var
        freepost : postnumber;

      begin
      freepost := allposts - startingpost - goalpost;
      if numberofdisks > 1 then
         hanoi (numberofdisks - 1, startingpost, freepost);
      writeln ('Move disk ', numberofdisks :1,
              ' from post ', startingpost :1,
              ' to post ', goalpost :1);
      if numberofdisks > 1 then
         hanoi (numberofdisks - 1, freepost, goalpost);
      end; { hanoi }

   begin
   read (numberofdisks);
   writeln ('Input data  numberofdisks: ', numberofdisks :1);
   writeln;
   hanoi (numberofdisks, 1, 3);
   end.
run testhanoi

Input data  numberofdisks: 4

Move disk 1 from post 1 to post 2
Move disk 2 from post 1 to post 3
Move disk 1 from post 2 to post 3
Move disk 3 from post 1 to post 2
Move disk 1 from post 3 to post 1
Move disk 2 from post 3 to post 2
Move disk 1 from post 1 to post 2
Move disk 4 from post 1 to post 3
Move disk 1 from post 2 to post 3
```

```
Move disk 2 from post 2 to post 1
Move disk 1 from post 3 to post 1
Move disk 3 from post 2 to post 3
Move disk 1 from post 1 to post 2
Move disk 2 from post 1 to post 3
Move disk 1 from post 2 to post 3
```

Dangers of Recursive Programming

The power of recursive programming brings with it two entirely new types of dangers, exponential execution time and infinite recursive descent. For example, each call to the recursive procedure hanoi specifying a number of disks $n > 1$ generates two recursive calls to hanoi at the next level to move $n - 1$ disks. Thus when the testing program testhanoi executes 1 call to hanoi to move 4 disks, the procedure hanoi executes 2 recursive calls, each to move 3 disks. These calls produce 4 recursive calls, each to move 2 disks, which in turn produce 8 recursive calls, each to move 1 disk. These last calls produce no further recursion.

The total number of calls to the recursive procedure hanoi produced by one call of it in the main program for moving 4 disks is

$$1 + 2 + 4 + 8 = 15 = 2^4 - 1$$

Looking at examples with different numbers of disks, it is not hard to convince yourself that, in general, one main program call to hanoi for n disks produces exactly $2^n - 1$ total calls to hanoi. The mathematically inclined may wish to prove this by induction. The number of total calls is approximately 2^n, where n is the number of disks. This is the meaning of **exponential execution time**: the number of steps in an execution is approximately proportional to 2 raised to the power that is one of the supplied arguments. The danger of exponential execution time is that 2 raised to a power increases exceedingly rapidly, so that procedures that work rapidly for small values of their arguments may take a very long time to execute for only slightly larger values of their arguments. It is left as an exercise to calculate how long it would take to move all 64 disks, and how many recursive calls and pages of output the procedure hanoi would use to print the directions.

The recursive procedure hanoi cannot be blamed for producing exponential execution time. Exponential execution time is inherent in the Towers of Hanoi problem because the expected number of lines of output, one for each call to the procedure hanoi, is itself exponential. Thus no program could print the expected output in less than 2^n steps because the number of lines of output is just one less than that number.

Fibonacci Numbers

In the next example, exponential execution time is not inherent, but is introduced by careless use of recursion. The Fibonacci sequence

$$1, 1, 2, 3, 5, 8, 13, 21, 34, ...,$$

arises in such diverse applications as the number of petals in a daisy, the maximum time it takes to recognize a sequence of characters, and the most pleasing proportions for a rectangle, the "golden section" of Renaissance artists and mathematicians. It is defined by the relations

$$f(1) = 1$$

$$f(2) = 1$$

$$f(n) = f(n-1) + f(n-2) \quad \text{for } n > 2$$

Starting with the third term, each Fibonacci number is the sum of the two previous Fibonacci numbers. Naive incorporation of this recurrence relation in a recursive function program

```
function fibonacci (n : integer) : integer;
  begin
  if n <= 2 then
     fibonacci := 1
  else
     fibonacci := fibonacci (n - 1) + fibonacci (n - 2);
  end; { fibonacci }
```

produces an exponential execution time disaster for moderately large n. Like the recursive procedure hanoi, each call to the function fibonacci produces two recursive calls to fibonacci, one to calculate fibonacci (n − 1) and one to calculate fibonacci (n − 2). Table 13.1 shows the first 20 Fibonacci numbers and the number of recursive calls to the function fibonacci to calculate them. Taking the last two ratios $13529/8361 = 1.618...$ and $8361/5167 = 1.6180339...$, it is clear that the number of recursive calls does not quite double each time, but more than doubles each two times.

Table 13.1   Fibonacci numbers f_n and number of recursive calls c_n to calculate them.

n	f_n	c_n	n	f_n	c_n
1	1	1	11	89	177
2	1	1	12	144	287
3	2	3	13	233	465
4	3	5	14	377	465
5	5	9	15	610	1219
6	8	15	16	987	1973
7	13	25	17	1597	3193
8	21	41	18	2584	5167
9	34	67	19	4181	8361
10	55	109	20	6765	13529

On the other hand, a simple for loop to calculate Fibonacci numbers

```
f [1] := 1;
f [2] := 1;
for i := 3 to n do
   f [i] := f [i - 1] + f [i - 2];
```

requires only n − 2 additions, but requires instead an array with at least n elements. (This poses something of a problem in Pascal since each array must be declared to be a fixed size.) Exponential execution time is clearly not inherent in the calculation of Fibonacci numbers. See Exercise 6 for ways to write a recursive program to calculate Fibonacci numbers without exponential execution time.

An even worse execution time disaster happens in the next program. The factorial function (denoted $n!$ in mathematics) is defined by the recurrence relations

$$0! = 1$$

$$n! = n \times (n - 1)! \quad \text{for } n > 0$$

In an effort to trace the various levels of recursive calls, a writeln statement is inserted in the recursive function program factorial to print the answer before returning from a successful execution of the function program.

```
program testfactorial (output);

   function factorial (n : integer) : integer;
     begin
     if n <= 0 then
       factorial := 1
     else
       factorial := n * factorial (n - 1);
     writeln ('Completion of factorial execution-- ',
          n :1, '! = ', factorial (n) :1);
     end; { factorial }


   begin
   writeln ('3! = ', factorial (3) :1);
   end.
```

The writeln statement disguises a recursive call from within factorial to itself with the same value for the dummy argument n. This recursive call is not for a simpler instance of the same problem; it is for the same instance of the same problem. Thus one level of recursion follows another indefinitely without any simplification of the problem leading to a nonrecursive path through the function.

This execution time disaster, called **infinite recursive descent**. may be guarded against by carefully checking that there is at least one nonrecursive path through a procedure or function, and that each recursive call that does appear in the procedure or function supplies changed values for the dummy arguments in such a way that, after a finite number of nested recursive calls, a nonrecursive path is taken.

Indirect Recursion, The Forward Declaration

When a procedure or function calls itself, the process is called **direct recursion**. It is also possible for the path to the recursive call to be more roundabout. A first procedure could call a second procedure, which calls a third procedure, and so on, until finally one of the called procedures calls the first procedure. Such a circle of calls is called **indirect recursion**. Although no procedure in the circle calls itself directly, the execution is still recursive because the first copy of the first procedure is still active when the last procedure in the circle calls it again.

A circle of indirectly recursive procedures causes a problem with the general Pascal rule that any variable, type, procedure, etc., used in a program must be declared in a line of the program that comes earlier than the line in which it is used. Strict adherence to this rule is not possible when a program contains a circle of indirectly recursive procedures. No procedure of the circle could come first, because each one calls some other procedure of the circle. The **forward declaration**, used in the next example, exempts indirectly recursive procedures from the general rule on a technicality.

The problem considered next is how to write a program to recognize whether its input is a simple algebraic sum similar to the following examples.

A
A+B
X+Y+Z
P+Q+A+B+C+X+Y+Z

This task is a greatly simplified version of what a compiler must do to recognize and translate algebraic expressions, or what a natural language processor must do to understand a sentence.

All valid sums to be recognized start with a letter. The rest of the sum could be empty, as in the first example, or nonempty, as in the remaining examples. If the rest of the sum is nonempty, it starts with a plus sign (+), followed by a sequence of characters that look exactly like a valid sum.

The two principal functions in the program to perform the task will be

```
function sumfound (position : stringindex) : boolean;
```

and

```
function restofstringok (position : stringindex) : boolean;
```

The function sumfound will start looking in the position in the input string specified by its argument. If the input string is a sum expression, it will find a letter and then evaluate restofstringok to determine if the rest of the string is an algebraic sum expression. The function restofstringok usually will find a plus sign and then evaluate the function sumfound. The pair of functions, sumfound and restofstringok, exhibit indirect recursion. They call each other. The nonrecursive exit from this circle of recursive calls happens when the rest of the sum expression sought by restofstringok is empty.

```
program recognizesums (input, output);
{ tests whether a character string is
  a valid algebraic sum expression }

  type
    stringindex = 1..80;
    string80 = packed array [stringindex] of char;

  var
    inputline : string80;

  procedure readline (var line : string80);
  { adapted from Section 7.2 }
    const
      blank = ' ';
    var
      position : stringindex;

    begin
    for position := 1 to 80 do
      line [position] := blank;
    position := 1;
    writeln;
    write ('Input data: ');
```

```
      while (not eoln) and (position < 80) do
        begin
        read (line [position]);
        write (line [position]);  { echo }
        position := position + 1;
        end;  { loop }
     readln;
     writeln;
     end;  { readline }

function letterfound (c : char) : boolean;
   begin
   letterfound := ('A' <= c) and (c <= 'Z');
   end;  { letterfound }
```

{ The following forward declaration predeclares
  the function checkrestofstring }
```
function restofstringok (position : stringindex) : boolean;
   forward;
```

```
function sumfound (position : stringindex) : boolean;

   begin
   if letterfound (inputline [position]) then
     sumfound := restofstringok (position + 1)
   else
     sumfound := false;
   end;  { sumfound }
```

```
function restofstringok;
```
{ Note: The argument list is omitted here because
  there was a forward declaration above. }

```
   const
     blank = ' ';
     plus = '+';

   begin
   if inputline [position] = blank then
     restofstringok := true
   else if inputline [position] = plus then
     restofstringok := sumfound (position + 1)
   else
     restofstringok := false;
   end;  { restofstringok }

{ ********* main program ********* }
begin
while not eof do
  begin
  readline (inputline);
  if sumfound (1) then
    writeln ('The input is a well-formed algebraic sum.')
```

```
    else
       writeln ('The input is not an algebraic sum expression.');
    end;  { while-loop }
  end.
```

run recognizesums

Input data: A+B+C
The input is a well-formed algebraic sum.

Input data: +B+C
The input is not an algebraic sum expression.

Input data: Q
The input is a well-formed algebraic sum.

Input data: X+Y+Z+
The input is not an algebraic sum expression.

Input data: 436
The input is not an algebraic sum expression.
The forward declaration

```
function restofstringok (position) : boolean;
    forward;
```

predeclares the function restofstringok to meet the requirements of Pascal sequencing. The reason Pascal has the rule about declaring procedures before they are referenced is to make it easier to write a compiler for Pascal, especially for a computer with limited memory. The forward declaration tells the compiler the name of the procedure and the names and types of its arguments. This is all the information a compiler needs to compile code for the procedure calls to the function restofstringok.

Throughout this book, we have emphasized that programmers should be considerate of the needs of the eventual user of the program. Even at the expense of extra effort in the design and implementation, a program should be made user-friendly because the user has to live with the result long after the programmer has moved to other projects. Designers of compilers and computer languages have the same obligation to their users. Languages and compilers should be designed for programming, not compiler writers. The forward declaration violates this principle.

Self-Test Questions

1. True/false:

   a. Recursive procedures are always more efficient than nonrecursive procedures to do the same thing.

   b. A genuine directly recursive procedure has no nonrecursive paths through the procedure.

   c. The average number of recursive calls per execution of a recursive procedure always should be less than two to prevent exponential execution time disasters.

   d. A procedure must always be declared above the first place in the program where it is called by another procedure. Explain your answer.

   e. Recursive calls must always be for simpler instances of the same problem.

Exercises

1. The recurrence relations

    $$x^0 = 1$$

    $$x^n = x \times x^{n-1} \quad \text{for } n > 0$$

    $$x^n = \frac{x^{n+1}}{x} \quad \text{for } n < 0 \text{ and } x \neq 0$$

    define x^n for all integers n. Modify the function program simplepower to calculate x to the nth power for any integer power n.
2. What execution time problems could develop if the test for n < 0 were removed from the function program simplepower? Explain.
3. Modify the function program power to handle negative powers also.
4. Axiomatic developments of the nonnegative integers define addition recursively by the relations

    $$a + 0 = a \quad \text{for all } a$$

    $$a + b = succ \, (a + pred \, (b)) \quad \text{forall } a, \text{ andfor } b > 0$$

    Write a recursive function sum (a, b) based on these recurrence relations and test it on the sum $5 + 3$.
5. In axiomatic developments of the nonnegative integers, multiplication is defined by the recurrence relations

    $$a \times 0 = 0$$

    $$a \times b = a + a \times pred \, (b) \quad \text{for } b > 0$$

    Write a recursive function program product (a, b) based on these relations. Use the recursive function sum written in Exercise 4 to do the addition. Test your program with the product 5×3.
6. Define a Fibonacci sequence as any sequence of numbers satisfying the recurrence relation

    $$f_n = f_{n-1} = f_{n-2}$$

    The usual Fibonacci sequence, 1, 1, 2, 3, 5, 8, ..., is specified by the additional conditions that $f_1 = f_2 = 1$. Other Fibonacci sequences, for example 1, 3, 4, 7, 11, ..., are generated by other starting values. Define a Fibonacci triple (a, b, n) as a first term, a second term and a number of terms in a Fibonacci sequence and the value $v\,(a, b, n)$ of a Fibonacci triple as the value of the nth term f_n in the Fibonacci sequence starting with $f_1 = a$ and $f_2 = b$. Values of Fibonacci triples satisfy the recurrence relations

    $$v\,(a, b, 1) = a$$

    $$v\,(a, b, 2) = b$$

    $$v\,(a, b, n) = v\,(b, a + b, n - 1) \quad \text{for } n > 2$$

    Write a recursive function program to calculate the nth term in the usual Fibonacci sequence based on these relations.

7. In the recursive program for Fibonacci numbers written in Exercise 6, how many calls are necessary to calculate f_{10}, f_{20}, f_n?

8. For positive integers a and b, the greatest common divisor of a and b satisfies the following recurrence relationship.

$$gcd\ (a, b) = b \quad \text{if } a \text{ mod } b = 0$$

$$gcd\ (a, b) = gcd\ (b, a \text{ mod } b) \quad \text{if } a \text{ mod } b \neq 0$$

Write a recursive function program gcd (a, b) using these recurrences. Test the program by finding gcd (24, 36), gcd (16, 13), gcd (17, 119), and gcd (177, 228).

9. Modify the function factorial so that the value computed by the function is printed correctly just prior to leaving the function.

10. (Very difficult) Write a program to print instructions for the Towers of Hanoi without using recursion. It is not fair if you fake recursion using the advanced data structure technique of stacks or using level of recursive call subscripts on variables.

13.2 Binary Trees

More complicated dynamic data structures can be built using more than one pointer per node. To conclude this chapter, we will consider briefly a structure that is one of the simplest ones except for dynamic lists.

Section Preview

Binary Tree:

A dynamic data structure in which each node has two link fields, a left link and a right link.

Root:

The one node in the tree from which every other node may be reached is called the root of the tree.

Left Subtree, Right Subtree:

The left subtree of a given node in a binary tree is the tree whose root is the left link of the given node. The right subtree has the right link of the given node as root.

Leaf:

A leaf is a node with nil left link and right link pointers.

Recursive Tree Traversing Procedures:

Since both the left subtree and the right subtree of a node are trees, recursive procedures are well-suited to *traversing*, that is, visiting and processing information, in every node of a tree.

Program for Tree Traversal (Infix Order):

```
procedure traverse (tree : treetype);
  begin
  Process left subtree;
  Process root node;
  Process right subtree;
  end
```

Trees

Using the recursive approach, if T is a Pascal data type, then a binary tree of Ts is either empty or it is a node containing a T and links to two binary trees of Ts. The first node of a binary tree is called the **root**, and the two subtrees linked to that node are called the **left subtree** and the **right subtree** of the binary tree. More general tree structures do not restrict the number of subtrees to two.

One common use of trees in computer science is to represent expressions of a computer program. For example the Pascal expression (a + b) * (c + d) can be represented by the tree

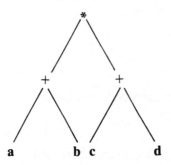

The root of this tree is the node containing the multiplication operator (*). Its two subtrees correspond to the two expressions (a + b) and (c + d) that are multiplied to form the complete expression. Each of the two subtrees is itself a binary tree with a plus sign (+) in the root node and only one node in each subtree.

The term "leaf" is applied to a node with only empty subtrees. In this example, the nodes containing a, b, c, and d are leaves.

This tree would be implemented in Pascal using records consisting of a one-character operator (+, *, a, b, c, d in the example) and two pointers, one to the first operand (the left subtree) and one to the second operand (the right subtree). The type statements

```
type
   binarytreetype = ^node;
   node = record
      operator : char;
      leftsubtree, rightsubtree : binarytreetype;
      end; { node }
```

define a record organization suitable for constructing binary trees. In terms of this record structure, a more detailed picture of the tree above would be

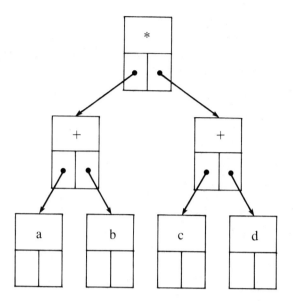

Sorting Using a Tree Structure

It is possible to use a tree to create an even more efficient program to sort a file. Suppose a file of integers contains the numbers 265, 113, 467, 264, 907, and 265. When the first number is read from the input file, a tree is created containing only one node, which contains the number.

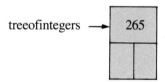

When the next number is read, it is compared with the first. If it is less than the first number, it is placed as a node in the left subtree; if it is greater than or equal to the first number, it is placed in the right subtree. In our case, 113 < 265, so a node containing 113 is created and the left pointer of the node containing 265 is set to point to it.

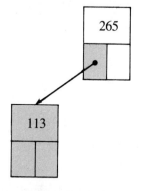

The next number is 467, so it is placed in the right subtree of 265.

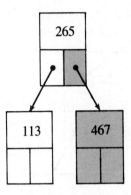

The next number is 264, so it is to be placed in the left subtree of 265. It is then compared with 113, the occupant of the top of the left subtree. Since 264 > 113, it is placed in the right subtree of the one with 113 at the top yielding

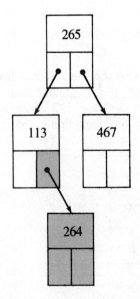

The next number 907 is larger than 265, so it is compared with 467 and put in the right subtree of the node containing 467.

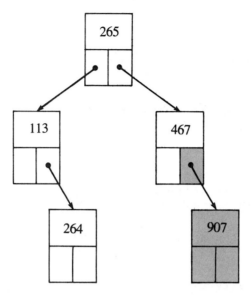

The final number 265 is equal to the number in the root node. An insertion position is therefore sought in the right subtree of the root. Since 265 < 467, it is put to the left of 467. Notice that the two nodes with key 265 are not even adjacent, nor is the node with key 264 adjacent to either node with key 265. This doesn't matter.

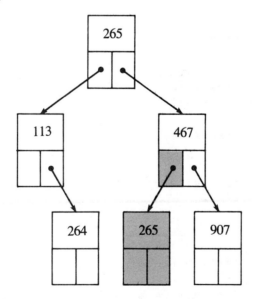

Printing the Tree in Order

Once the tree has been constructed, it is necessary to write out the numbers in the tree in the correct order. The correct order is to print all the numbers in the left subtree in order, then print the number in the top node, then print all the numbers in the right subtree in order. This procedure works because in the whole tree and in each subtree, all numbers in the left subtree are less than the number at the top and all numbers in the right subtree are larger than or equal to the number at the top. This procedure just described is, of course, recursive. Both the insert procedure and the print procedure are contained in the complete version of the program sortnumbers below. The output from the program is not shown because it is identical to the output from the previous program.

```
program sortnumbers (input, output);

  const
    signal = -999;

  type
    binarytreetype = ^node;
    node = record
      number : integer;
      leftsubtree, rightsubtree : binarytreetype;
      end; { node }

  var
    n : integer;
    treeofintegers : binarytreetype;
    morenumbers : boolean;

  procedure insert (var tree : binarytreetype);

    var
      newitem : binarytreetype;

    begin
    if tree = nil then
      begin
      new (newitem);
      newitem^ . number := n;
      newitem^ . leftsubtree := nil;
      newitem^ . rightsubtree := nil;
      tree := newitem;
      end { if }
    else if n < tree^ . number then
      insert (tree^ . leftsubtree)
    else
      insert (tree^ . rightsubtree);
    end; { insert }

  procedure printtree (tree : binarytreetype);

    begin
    if tree <> nil then
      begin
      printtree (tree^ . leftsubtree);
      write (tree^ . number);
      printtree (tree^. rightsubtree);
      end; { if }
    end; { printtree }

  begin { main program }
  morenumbers := true;
  treeofintegers := nil;
  while morenumbers do
    begin
    read (n);
    writeln ('Input data  n : ', n :1);
```

```
      if n = signal then
        morenumbers := false
      else
        insert (treeofintegers);
      end; { while-loop }

   writeln; writeln ('Sorted list:');
   printtree (treeofintegers);
   writeln;
   end.
```

Both for debugging purposes and to understand the sequence of procedure calls in a recursive program such as this, it is desirable to insert write statements into the principal recursive procedures to trace the execution. Inserting the following if-statement at the beginning of the procedure insert gives a good picture of what happens in that procedure.

```
   if tree = nil then
     writeln ('found insertion place for ', n :1)
   else if n < tree^ . number then
     writeln ('look to the left of ', tree^ . number :1)
   else
     writeln ('look to the right of ', tree^ . number :1);
```

If even further prettying of the output is desired, an integer variable depth may be introduced to keep track of the current depth of recursive call, that is, the number of simultaneous executions of the procedure insert started but not yet completed. Each output line then can start with a number of dots proportional to the current depth of recursive call. Additional statements are

```
   var
     depth : 0..999;
```

in the main heading,

```
   depth := 0;
```

at the beginning of the main program,

```
   var
     i : 0..999;
```

in the procedure insert,

```
   depth := depth + 1;
   for i := 1 to depth do
     write ('..');
```

before the added if statement at the beginning of the procedure insert, and

```
   depth := depth - 1;
```

just before the end of the procedure insert. The resulting output is interpreted easily.

```
   run sortnumbers

   Input data  n : 265
   ..found insertion place for 265
   Input data  n : 113
   ..look to the left of 265
   ....found insertion place for 113
   Input data  n : 467
   ..look to the right of 265
   ....found insertion place for 467
```

```
Input data  n : 264
..look to the left of 265
....look to the right of 113
......found insertion place for 264
Input data  n : 907
..look to the right of 265
....look to the right of 467
......found insertion place for 907
Input data  n : 265
..look to the right of 265
....look to the left of 467
......found insertion place for 265
Input data  n : -999

Sorted list:
        113        264        265        265        467        907
```

Suggested Readings

Donald E. Knuth. "Information Structures". In *Fundamental Algorithms*, Vol. 1. *The Art of Computer Programming*. Reading, Mass.: Addison-Wesley, 1968.

Donald E. Knuth. "Algorithms". *Scientific American,* Vol. 236 (1977): 63-80.

Niklaus Wirth. *Algorithms + Data Structures = Programs.* Englewood Cliffs, N. J.: Prentice-Hall, 1976.

Self-Test Questions

1. True/false:

    a. A tree always has a root and leaves.
    b. In a binary tree, the left and right subtrees of a given node are always binary trees.
    c. The average number of comparisons it takes to locate the correct insertion position in a binary tree is proportional to the number of nodes in the tree.
    d. The recursive procedure to print the nodes of a binary tree in order is much simpler and clearer than any nonrecursive procedure that could be written to do the same thing.

Exercises

1. Modify the tree sorting program in this section to count the number of compari - sons the program makes while sorting. Print the number of comparisons for tree sorting random lists of length 64, 128, 256, and 512. Based on your output, how does the efficiency of tree sorting compare with the efficiency of the sorting methods in Section 9.3?
2. Write a program to search an ordered binary tree, such as the one constructed in this section, to see if the information field in a node in the tree matches informa- tion supplied as input.

13.3   What You Should Know

1. It is permissible for a procedure or function to call itself, or even for a procedure to call another procedure which calls the first one.
2. When a procedure calls itself, it is as if a second copy of the procedure, complete with all local variables, is created to handle the new call. Thus several copies of a recursion procedure may be executing simultaneously.
3. The two basic principles of recursive programming are:

    a.   Reduction of the problem to an instance of the problem that is simpler in some sense
    b.   A direct, nonrecursive path through the procedure to handle the simplest cases

4. In top-down programming, the top-level procedure is designed without concern for how the lower-level procedures will be implemented. The same is true in writing recursive procedures. In fact, since the lower-level procedure is the same as the higher-level procedure, the lower-level details are automatically taken care of in writing the higher-level details.
5. Exponential execution time means that the number of steps in an execution is approximately proportional to 2 raised to the power that is one of the supplied arguments.
6. Exponential execution time should be expected when the average number of recursive calls per execution of the recursive procedure exceeds 1.
7. Infinite recursive descent is a sequence of recursive calls that never reaches one of the simplest non-recursive cases. New copies of the recursive procedure are spawned until the computer runs out of memory. No copy is ever exited.
8. Direct recursion is when a procedure or function calls itself.
9. Indirect recursion is when one procedure calls a second procedure, and that second either directly or indirectly calls the first one.
10. A forward declaration allows the procedure name and the types of the dummy arguments to be declared without the body of the procedure. It is used in the declaration of indirectly recursive procedures to satisfy Pascal rules.
11. A binary tree consists of a distinguished node, the root, and links to two subtrees, the left subtree and the right subtree. A binary tree may also be empty.
12. A leaf is a node with only empty subtrees.
13. A tree is sorted when, in the whole tree and in each subtree, all numbers in the left subtree are less than the numbers in the root node and all numbers in the right subtree are larger than or equal to the numbers in the root node.
14. A nonempty tree is printed in order by printing its information in its left subtree, then the information in its root node, then the information in its right subtree. The first and third of these steps are recursive.

ADDITIONAL FEATURES OF PASCAL 14

Pascal has several less commonly used features that deserve mention. Although we have not had the occasion to use them in this book, some of them are very nice features, and no treatment of the language Pascal would be complete without them.

Alone among major computer programming languages, Pascal has a **set data type** and a **set membership operator**. Variables and constants of set type have as their values sets of value chosen from a scalar base type. The set membership operator **in** determines whether a given scalar value is a member of a set of values.

Finally, in Section 14.2, the infamous **goto-statement** is discussed. This completes the survey of Pascal.

14.1   Set Data Type, Set Membership

The set data type is unusual in that values of set types are not individual elements, but collections of elements of another type, the base type. If you think of a list containing all elements of the base type, a set is specified by checking off precisely those elements which are included. Some efficient implementations of set data types use methods which are not very different from this.

Section Preview

Set Data Type:

General Form:

    type
       set type = set of *base type*;
    var
       variable name : set of *base type*;

403

Examples:
```
type
  lettercollection = set of 'a'..'z';
var
  wordjumble : lettercollection;
  smallprimes : set of 1..20;
```
The **base type** from which members of the sets are chosen may be any scalar (i.e., ordered) type except real. However, in the name of implementation efficiency, Pascal systems may restrict the size of the base type.

Set Constructors:

General Forms:

[] { the empty set }
[*expression, expression, ..., expression*]
[*expression..expression, ..., expression..expression*]

Examples:
```
empty := [];
workday := [mon, tue, wed, thu, fri];
compositenumbers := [4, 6, 8..10, 12, 14..16, 18, 20];
vowels := ['a', 'e', 'i', 'o', 'u'];
```

Set Operators:

+   union
*   intersection
—   set difference, i.e., members in the first set but not in the second set

Relational Operators:

=   < >   set equality or inequality
<=   >=   subset or superset inclusion
in   set membership

Set Variables and Types

Pascal allows the value of a variable to be a **set** or collection of elements of a fixed **base type**. This is a feature found in very few major programming languages. For example, the following declaration defines the variable alphabet to be a set of characters.

```
var
  alphabet : set of char;
```

The permissible values of alphabet are not single characters, but collections of characters. The type char is called the base type of the set type. In theory, the base type may be any scalar (i.e., ordered) type except real. However, in practice, Pascal systems are permitted to place upper bounds on the number of elements in a base type to take advantage of certain extremely efficient implementations of the set operations that work best with small base types. In some Pascal systems, even the full base type char, with 128 or 256 elements, is considered too large.

Set types may be given names using type declarations. For example, the declarations

```
type
  charactercollection = set of char;
  day = (sun, mon, tue, wed, thu, fri, sat);
  daycollection = set of day;
var
  punctuationmarks : charactercollection;
  sleeplatedays : daycollection;
```

declare set types charactercollection and daycollection, and set variables punctuationmarks and sleeplatedays.

Set Constants

One of the more reasonable values we could assign to the set variable alphabet is the set of uppercase letters.

```
alphabet := ['A'..'Z']
```

Set constants are constructed by listing their members between square brackets ([]). The members may be listed either as a range of values, as shown above, or individually, as in

```
vowels := ['A', 'E', 'I', 'O', 'U']
```

or by a combination of these two methods, as in

```
numbercharacters := ['0'..'9', '.', '+', '-', 'E']
```

The **empty set** is a special set that has no members in it. There can be an empty set of any base type. The empty set is denoted by listing no members between the opening and closing brackets.

```
empty := []
```

Set Operations

There are three binary operations by which sets of the same base type may be combined to form other sets. They are

1.   **Union**, denoted by a + b, the set of values of the base type that belong to at least one of the sets a or b.
2.   **Intersection**, denoted by a * b, the set of values of the base type that belong to both of the sets a and b.
3.   **Relative complement**, denoted by a — b, the set of values of the base type that belong to the set a, but not to the set b.

Thus, the set expressions below evaluate as shown.

```
['a', 'e', 'i', 'o', 'u'] + ['a'..'e'] = ['a'..'e', 'i', 'o', 'u']
['a', 'e', 'i', 'o', 'u'] * ['a'..'e'] = ['a', 'e']
['a', 'e', 'i', 'o', 'u'] - ['a'..'e'] = ['i', 'o', 'u']
```

The set operations are used to construct more complex set values. For example, in some applications, a reasonable value for alphabet is

```
alphabet := ['a'..'z'] + ['A'..'Z']
```

The Set Membership Operator In

The **set membership operator in** tests whether a value of the base type is a member of a set of the base type. For example, the following if-test determines whether the current value of the character variable c is an uppercase or lowercase letter.

```
if c in alphabet then ...
```

The set membership operator often provides a much more natural and clear way to test for membership in a set. Alternative methods, like

```
if (('a' <= c) and (c <= 'z')) or (('A' <= c) and (c <= 'Z')) then ...
```

are clumsier. Compare the equivalent tests:

```
if c in vowels then ...
if (c = 'a') or (c = 'e') or (c = 'i') or
   (c = 'o') or (c = 'u') then ...
```

Set Comparisons

The standard comparison operators, equality (=) and inequality (<>), make sense for set values. Two sets are equal if they have exactly the same members. Otherwise, they are unequal.

The comparison operator written "<=" is permitted, and means "is a subset of". We say that

```
a <= b
```

is true if every member of the set a is also a member of the set b. The relation a <= b also is called set inclusion.

The comparison operator written ">=" is also permitted and means set inclusion in the opposite direction. The relation

```
a >= b
```

is true if and only if b <= a is true. In other words, a >= b is true if and only if each member of the set b is also a member of the set a.

The comparison operators written "<" and ">" are not permitted between values of set type.

An Example

The program countvowels below counts how many vowels appear in an input line. It also tests to determine whether all five vowels appear at least once.

```
program countvowels (input, output);
{ counts vowels in the input
  and sees if all 5 vowels appear at least once }

   type
      alphabetic =  set of 'a'..'z';
   var
      vowels, lettersused, alphabet : alphabetic;
      count : 0..100;
      c : char;

   begin
   alphabet := ['a'..'z'];
   vowels := ['a', 'e', 'i', 'o', 'u'];
   lettersused := [];
   count := 0;
   while not eoln do
      begin
      read (c);
      write (c);
```

```
if c in alphabet then
    lettersused := lettersused + [c];
if c in vowels then
    count := count + 1;
end; { while-loop }
writeln;
writeln ('contains ', count :1, ' vowels.');
if vowels <= lettersused then
    writeln ('All five vowels were used.');
end.

run countvowels

beware the frumious bandersnatch.
contains 11 vowels.
All five vowels were used.
```

Self-Test Questions

1. True/false:

    a. Set data types and enumerated data types are almost the same.
    b. An enumerated data type can be the base type for a set type.
    c. All six comparison operators are permitted between set values.

Exercises

1. Write a program that converts every lowercase letter in a string supplied as input into the corresponding capital letter.
2. Write a program to examine text and determine the ratio of the number of letters from the first half of the alphabet to the number of letters from the second half of the alphabet.

14.2   The Goto-Statement and Structured Programming

In this section, we discuss the infamous **goto-statement**. The goto-statement is a gun without a safety catch. It is easy to shoot yourself in the foot with a goto-statement, and programmers have been shooting themselves in the foot with it since the beginning of computer programming.

Nevertheless, carefully used within the framework of structured programming concepts, sometimes it can make a program clearer when using a programming language that does not have a complete set of control constructs. For example, in Pascal there is no direct way to exit a loop in the middle, and a goto-statement can be used for this purpose, as we will illustrate in this section.

Early computer programming languages and most ancient and modern machine languages make extensive use of the goto-statement or its equivalent.

> **Section Preview**
>
> The **Goto-Statement**:
>
> > Execution of a goto-statement tells the computer that the next statement is to execute is the one with the label specified in the goto-statement.

General Form:

> goto *label*

Examples:

```
goto 19;
goto 9999;
```

Label:

Any Pascal statement in a program may be given an integer of up to four digits as a label. Except for a label that is intended as the target of a goto-statement, there is little reason to attach a label to a statement.

General Form:

> *label* : *statement*

Examples:

```
19 : count := i − 1;
9999 : writeln ('Execution of the loop is complete.')
```

Label Declarations:

In any block, label declarations precede the constant (const) declarations.

General Form:

> label
>   *label*, *label*, ...; *label*;

Examples:

```
label
  19; 9999;
```

Scope of a Label:

A label is known throughout the block in which it is declared, including within blocks nested within the block of declaration. A label may be the target of a goto-statement placed anywhere in the scope of its declaration. However, using a goto-statement to branch into a procedure, function, or loop structure from outside is not permitted. *Warning:* Indiscriminant placement of labels and goto-statements is such a bad programming practice that many programmers avoid the goto-statement as a matter of principle. Structured programming was invented partly to avoid this kind of chaos.

Use of the Goto-Statement

A while-loop has its exit test at the top, and a repeat-until-loop has its exit test at the bottom. One problem facing a Pascal programmer is what to do when the natural place to exit a loop is the middle of the loop body.

For example, consider the program calculateaveragegoto (calculate average using goto) that reads a list of numbers terminated by a signal value and calculates their average.

```
program calculateaveragegoto (input, output);
{ uses goto-statement to exit the main loop }

  label
    19;
  const
    maxlistsize = 100;
    signal = -999.0;
  var
    index : 1..100;
    count : 0..100;
    number, sum : real;

  begin
  sum := 0;
  count := 0;
  for index := 1 to maxlistsize do
  { or exit early when signal is read }
    begin
    read (number);
    writeln ('Input data  number: ', number :1:2);
    if number = signal then
      goto 19;   { exit the loop }
    count := index;
    sum := sum + number;
    end;   { for-loop }

  19: writeln ('There were ', count :1, ' numbers.');
  if count > 0 then
    writeln ('Their average is ' , sum / count :1:2);
  end.   { program calculateaveragegoto }
run calculateavggoto

Input data  number:   13.90
Input data  number:   44.13
Input data  number:   18.37
Input data  number:  -999.00
There were 3 numbers.
Their average is  25.47
```

First we explain the new syntactic features in this program. Then we discuss the merits of its structure.

Any unsigned integer (limited to a maximum of 9999 in some Pascal systems) may be used as a statement **label**. This means that any statement in a Pascal program may be prefixed with an unsigned integer to label or identify it. Unlike other programming languages that make extensive use of labels, like assembler languages, the choice of labels in Pascal is very primitive.

Only one statement in the program calculateaveragegoto is labelled. The label, 19, appears on the first statement following the for-loop. This statement is labelled to identify it as the next statement to be executed when a signal entry has been detected in the input data.

Labels are declared in much the same way as constants, types, and variables. In this program the label 19 is declared by the label declaration

```
label
  19;
```

Label declarations appear in a program or procedure above the constant (const) declarations.

The scope of applicability of a label declaration follows the same rules as the scope of applicability of a constant or variable declaration. A label is known throughout the **block** in which it is declared. If the same label is declared in two or more nested blocks, the declaration and label in the innermost block are in effect within that block. The primitive and relatively uninformative nature of labels in Pascal discourages their use for any purpose other than as the target of a goto-statement.

A goto-statement is a simple statement that tells the computer to "go to" a specific labelled statement in the program for its next instruction. For example, the goto-statement

```
goto 19
```

tells the computer to execute the statement labelled 19 next. Thereafter, the execution sequence proceeds normally.

Merits of the Goto-Statement

The reason a goto-statement was used to exit the loop in the program calculateaveragegoto is that the need to exit the loop can be discovered by the computer only after the signal data item is read, and it must be discovered before the signal item is added to the sum. Consider the alternative way of writing this process as without using a goto-statement. A while-loop must now be used because the number of times the loop will be executed cannot be computed in advance. Instead, the boolean variable moredata controls the execution of the loop.

```
program calculateaverageflag (input, output);
{ uses goto-statement to exit the main loop }

  const
    maxlistsize = 100;
    signal = -999.0;
  var
    count : 0..100;
    number, sum : real;
    moredata : boolean;

  begin
  sum := 0;
  count : = 0;
  moredata := true;
  while moredata and (count < maxlistsize) do
    begin
    read (number);
    writeln ('Input data number: ', number :1:2);
    if number = signal then
      moredata := false
    else
      begin
      count := count + 1;
      sum := sum + number;
      end;
  end;  { while-loop }
```

```
writeln ('There were ', count :1, ' numbers.');
if count > 0 then
   writeln ('Their average is ' , sum / count :1:2);
end.   { program calculateaverageflag }
```

The programs are almost exactly the same length. However, the main body of the loop must be nested within the else-clause of the test that determines whether a signal has been read. This probably makes the program somewhat less clear.

In the program calculateaverageflag, the use of a goto-statement has been exchanged for the device of **flag setting**, a practice with an equally checkered history. The goto-statement in the program calculateaveragegoto is direct and unambiguous. It transfers control to precisely the same statement that would be executed next upon normal exit from the for-loop.

In structured programming, it is desirable to have sections of program with one entrance and one exit. The loop in the program calculateaveragegoto has one entrance, but it has two exits, side and bottom. However, both exits go to the same place, so we have not used a goto-statement to write unstructured code. We have used a goto-statement to write clear code for a well-structured loop.

Some programming languages have introduced an "exit" statement for precisely the purpose we have used the goto-statement—to exit from the middle of a loop to the first statement following the loop.

Both of these programs are more complicated than they would be if the loop were terminated by coming to the end of the file rather than looking for a signal value. In this case, neither a goto-statement nor a flag is needed.

```
program calculateaverageeof (input, output);
{ uses end of file to exit the main loop }

   const
     maxlistsize = 100;
   var
     count : 0..100;
     number, sum : real;

   begin
   sum := 0;
   count := 0;
   while (not eof) and (count < maxlistsize) do
     begin
     readln (number);
     writeln ('Input data  number: ', number :1:2);
     count := count + 1;
     sum := sum + number;
     end;   { for-loop }

   writeln ('There were ', count :1, ' numbers.');
   if count > 0 then
      writeln ('Their average is ' , sum /count :1:2);
   end.   { program calculateaverageeof }
```

Misuses of the Goto-Statement

Syntactically, the target label of a goto-statement and the goto-statement with the target label must both be within the scope of the same label declaration. Using a goto-statement to branch into a procedure, function, or loop structure from outside is not permitted. Branching out of a procedure, function, or loop structure is permitted.

The following abuses of the goto-statement are legal, but should be avoided because they are bad programming practices, resulting in programs that are very difficult to understand.

1. Do not transfer from the middle of a loop to a place other than the "normal" exit of the loop.
2. Do not use a goto-statement to exit from a procedure or function. In extraordinary circumstances, such as an unrecoverable error condition, dramatic action may be required. An unconditional transfer to the error handling routine often is much clearer than setting an error flag and trying to unwind all levels of procedure calls.
3. Do not create a loop by using a goto-statement to branch back to the top statement of the loop for the next iteration. Use for-, while-, or repeat-until to form the loop.
4. Do not use goto-statements to create a program whose flowchart looks like a freeway map of Los Angeles.

The goto-statement has a very bad reputation, and when it is used poorly, it is easy to see why its reputation is well deserved. However, after a programmer has developed a structured style of programming without using the goto-statement, it may be used sparingly and carefully to enhance the clarity of some algorithms. There are even some advanced algorithms whose structure is so complex that it cannot be expressed naturally with the other Pascal constructs. For these, the goto-statement is necessary, or at least more desirable.

We do not reject the goto-statement dogmatically because of its history of abuse. We prefer to judge each instance on the clarity of the resulting program. Most of the time, but not all of the time, we wind up avoiding the goto-statement.

Self-Test Questions

1. True/false:

   a. Any valid variable name is also a valid label.
   b. Labels must be declared.
   c. It is impossible to write "structured" programs using goto-statements.
   d. It is a good programming practice to use goto-statements to exit from loops and procedures.

14.3 What You Should Know

1. Pascal allows the value of a variable to be a set or collection of elements of a fixed base type.
2. Set constants are constructed by listing their members between square brackets. Subranges are permitted in the list.
3. The empty set is a set that has no members.
4. There are three set operations: union, intersection, and relative complement.
5. The set membership operator "in" tests whether a value of the base type is a member of a set of the base type.
6. There are four set comparison operators: equality ($=$), inequality ($<>$), subset ($<=$), and superset ($>=$).

7. Set data types differ from enumerated data types in that a value of set type is a collection of elements, while a value of enumerated types is an individual element.
8. The goto-statement tells the computer to execute a specified statement next.
9. A label is an integer used to identify a statement that is the target of a goto-statement.
10. Labels must be declared.
11. In structured programming, it is desirable to have sections of programs with one entrance and one exit.
12. The goto-statement can sometimes be used to improve the readability of a program without upsetting its structure.
13. A goto should never be used to branch into a procedure, function, or loop structure.
14. In exceptional circumstances like error conditions, when dramatic action is necessary, a goto may be used to branch out of a procedure or function.
15. Sometimes, it is clearer to use a goto to exit directly from the middle of the loop than it is to set a flag. The flag is used to prevent the rest of the loop from doing its normal processing so that the exit test can be reached.
16. A goto-statement should not be used to create a loop.

PASCAL RESERVED WORDS A

and	downto	if	or	then
array	else	in	packed	to
begin	end	label	procedure	type
case	file	mod	program	until
const	for	nil	record	var
div	function	not	repeat	while
do	goto	of	set	with

1. ⟨PROGRAM⟩:

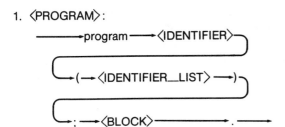

2. ⟨BLOCK⟩:

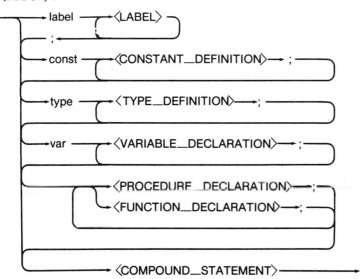

3. ⟨CONSTANT_DEFINITION⟩:

——⟨IDENTIFIER⟩——→ = —→⟨CONSTANT⟩——→

4. ⟨TYPE_DEFINITION⟩:

→⟨IDENTIFIER⟩→ = →⟨TYPE_DENOTER⟩→

5. ⟨TYPE_DENOTER⟩:

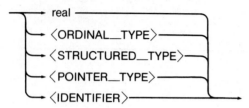

6. ⟨ORDINAL_TYPE⟩:

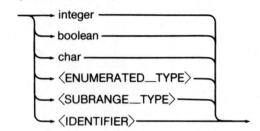

7. ⟨ENUMERATED_TYPE⟩:

──────→ (──→⟨IDENTIFIER_LIST⟩→) ────→.

8. ⟨SUBRANGE_TYPE⟩:

→⟨CONSTANT⟩──→.. →⟨CONSTANT⟩→

9. ⟨STRUCTURED_TYPE⟩:

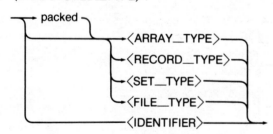

10. ⟨ARRAY_TYPE⟩:

──→ array ──→[─┬─⟨ORDINAL_TYPE⟩*─┐
                └─⟨TYPE_DENOTER⟩─┘
                └─] → of →⟨TYPE_DENOTER⟩──→

*except integer

11. 〈RECORD_TYPE〉:

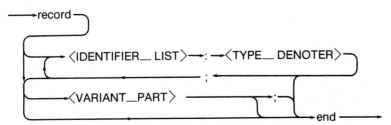

12. 〈SET_TYPE〉:

────set of 〈ORDINAL_TYPE〉* ────────→

*except integer

13. 〈FILE_TYPE〉:

──────→ file of ──→〈TYPE_ DENOTER〉──────→

14. 〈POINTER_TYPE〉:

15. 〈VARIABLE_ DECLARATION〉:

──→〈IDENTIFIER_ LIST〉──→: ──→〈TYPE_ DENOTER〉──→

16. 〈PROCEDURE_ DECLARATION〉:

──→〈PROCEDURE_ HEADING〉──→ ; ──→〈BLOCK〉────────→

17. 〈PROCEDURE_ HEADING〉:

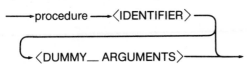

18. 〈FUNCTION_ DECLARATION〉:

──→〈FUNCTION_ HEADING〉──→; ──→〈BLOCK〉──→

19. 〈FUNCTION_ HEADING〉:

20. ⟨DUMMY_ARGUMENTS⟩:

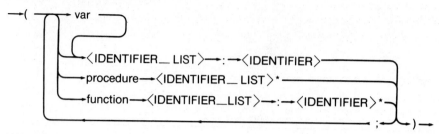

*Allows functions and procedures to be passed
 as arguments.

21. ⟨COMPOUND_STATEMENT⟩:

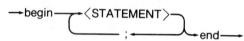

22. ⟨STATEMENT⟩

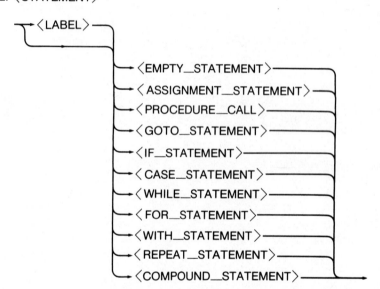

23. ⟨EMPTY_STATEMENT⟩:

24. ⟨ASSIGNMENT_STATEMENT⟩:

→⟨VARIABLE_REFERENCE⟩→:=→⟨EXPRESSION⟩→

25. ⟨PROCEDURE_CALL⟩:

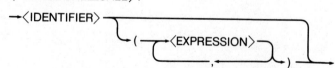

26. ⟨GOTO_STATEMENT⟩:

27. ⟨IF_STATEMENT⟩:

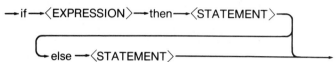

28. ⟨CASE_STATEMENT⟩:

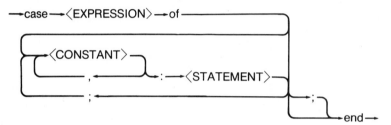

29. ⟨WHILE_STATEMENT⟩:

30. ⟨FOR_STATEMENT⟩:

31. ⟨WITH_STATEMENT⟩:

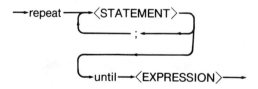

32. ⟨REPEAT_STATEMENT⟩:

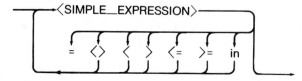

33. ⟨EXPRESSION⟩:

34. ⟨SIMPLE_EXPRESSION⟩:

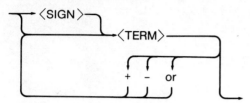

35. ⟨TERM⟩:

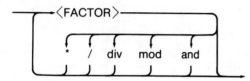

36. ⟨FACTOR⟩:

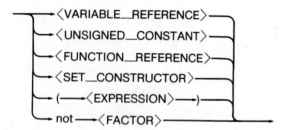

37. ⟨VARIABLE_REFERENCE⟩:

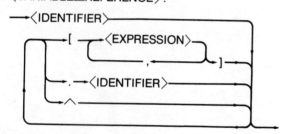

38. ⟨UNSIGNED_CONSTANT⟩:

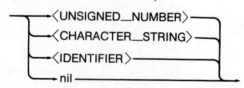

39. ⟨FUNCTION_REFERENCE⟩:

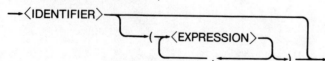

40. ⟨SET__CONSTRUCTOR⟩ :

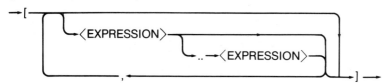

41. ⟨IDENTIFIER__LIST⟩ :

42.   ⟨IDENTIFIER⟩ :

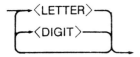

43. ⟨CONSTANT⟩ :

44. ⟨UNSIGNED__NUMBER⟩ :

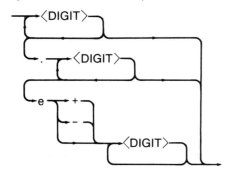

45. ⟨CHARACTER__STRING⟩ :

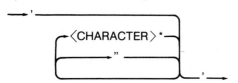

*The set of allowed characters is processor-dependent;
 it does not include an apostrophe (').

46. ⟨LABEL⟩:

47. ⟨LETTER⟩:

48. ⟨SIGN⟩:

49. ⟨DIGIT⟩:

PASCAL REFERENCE GUIDE

PROGRAM

program program name (file name 1, file name 2, . . . , file name n;

  const

    constant name 1 = constant 1;

    constant name 2 = constant 2;

    . . . ;

  type

    type name 1 = type 1;

    type name 2 = type 2;

    . . . ;

  var

    variable name 1.1, variable name 1.2, . . . , variable name 1.n1 : type 1;

    variable name 2.1, variable name 2.2, . . . , variable name 2.n2 : type 2;

    . . . ;

  procedure procedure name 1 (dummy argument declaration 1.1; . . .);

    . . . **end**; { procedure name 1 }

  . . . ;

  function function name 1 (dummy arg. decl. 1.1; . . .): result type name;

    . . . **end**; {function name 1}

  . . . ;

  begin main program

  statement 1;

  statement 2;

      .

      .

      .

  statement n

  end. {program name}

*Note: All file names except "input" and "output" must be declared as variable names (**var**). With only one other exception (recursive type definitions using pointer variables), all names must be declared in earlier lines than they are referenced.*

NAME

A name consists of a letter followed by any number of letters or digits (no blanks).

Note: All Pascal identifiers (i.e., program names, file names, constant names, type names, procedure names, etc.) have this form.

CONSTANT

  unsigned number

  ± unsigned number

  constant name

  ± constant name

  'xyz . . . w'

TYPE
  Simple Type
    Enumerated Type
      (element name 1, element name 2, . . . , element name n)
    Subrange Type
      constant 1 . . constant 2
    Named Type
      type name
  Pointer Type
    ^type name
  Structured Type
    Array Type
      array [simple type 1, simple type 2, . . . , simple type n] **of** type
    Record Type
      record
        field name 1.1, field name 1.2, . . . : type 1;
        field name 2.1, field name 2.2, . . . : type 2;
        . . . ;
        case field name : type name **of**
          constant 1.1, constant 1.2, . . . : (field name & type list 1);
          constant 2.1, constant 2.2, . . . : (field name & type list 2);
          . . . ;
        end   { record name }
    File Type
      file of type
    Set Type
      set of type name
      set of constant 1 . . constant 2
      set of (element name 1, element name 2, . . . , element name n)
    Packed Type
      packed array type
      packed record type
      packed file type
      packed set type

Notes:
1) Either the variant part (following **case***) or the fixed part (preceding* **case***) of a record type may be omitted.*
2) The base type for a set type must be finite and unstructured. Pascal implementations are permitted to further restrict the size of the base type in the interest of efficient implementation.
3) Packed types are implementation dependent.

PROCEDURE AND FUNCTION DEFINITIONS
  Procedure Declaration
    procedure procedure name (variable name 1.1.1, . . . : type name 1.1;
                    . . . ;
                    var variable name 2.1.1, . . . : type name 2.1;
                    . . . ;
                    function function name 3.1.1, . . . : type name 3.1;
                    . . . ;
                    procedure procedure name 4.1.1, . . . ;
                    . . .);
      const
        . . . ;
      type
        . . . ;
      var
        . . . ;

```
      procedure or function declaration 1;
      ... ;
      begin
      statement 1;
      statement 2;
          .
          .
          .
      statement n
      end;  { procedure name }
```

Note: There are four kinds of dummy arguments, "by value" parameters that cannot return a value to the calling program, variable (var) parameters that can return values, and function and procedure dummy arguments whose corresponding supplied arguments are function or procedure names (some restrictions apply). Dummy arguments of all kinds may be mixed in any order.

Function Declaration

```
      function function name (dummy arg. & type list): result type name;
      const
          ... ;
      type
          ... ;
      var
          ... ;
      procedure of function declaration 1;
      ... ;
      begin
      statement 1;
      statement 2;
          .
          .
          .
      statement n
      end;  {function name}
```

Notes:
1) Each execution path should have one function value assignment statement of the form

function name: = expression

2) Dummy argument declarations for a function follow same rules as dummy argument declarations for a procedure.

STATEMENT

Assignment Statement

variable : − expression

Restrictions:
1) The type of the expression must be assignable to the type of the variable. Usually they are identical types or have a base type/subrange type relationship. Integer expression values are assignable to real variables.
2) Arithmetic, boolean, and set variables allow unrestricted expressions of assignable type.
3) Character string, pointer, and record variables allow only simple expressions (i.e., variables, constants, or constant names) of the corresponding types.
4) Function value assignments follow the rules for the result type.

Conditional Statement

```
      1) if boolean condition then
           statement
      2) if boolean condition then
           statement 1
         else
           statement 2
```

*Caution: A semicolon after **then** or **else** implies that the then-clause or else-clause consists of an empty statement. A semicolon between statement 1 and **else** is a syntax error.*

Compound Statement
    begin
    statement 1;
    statement 2;

       .
       .
       .

    statement n
    end
Comment
    { text of comment }
Note: May be placed anywhere a blank is permitted.

  Empty statement

Note: The empty statement has no characters at all. It explains why a semicolon may immediately precede **end** *in a compound statement—statement n, the last statement, is empty.*

  For Statement
      1) **for** variable name : = expression 1 **to** expression 2 **do**
        statement
      2) **for** variable name : = expression 1 **downto** expression 2 **do**
        statement
While Statement
    while boolean condition **do**
      statement
Note: The while-condition is tested immediately before each execution of the statement. If the while-condition is initially false, the statement will not be executed at all. If some assignment within the statement causes the while-condition to become false, the current execution of the statement is still completed normally, and the while-condition is tested for an exit before the next execution of the statement begins.

  Repeat-Until Statement
    repeat
      statement 1;
      statement 2;

       .
       .
       .

      statement n
    until boolean condition
Note: The until-condition is tested only upon completion of statement n. Normal exit from a repeat-until-loop cannot occur before one complete execution of the statement sequence.

  Case Statement
    case expression **of**
      constant 1.1, constant 1.2, . . . :
        statement 1;
      constant 2.1, constant 2.2 . . . :
        statement 2;
      . . . ;
      constant n.1, constant n.2, . . . :
        statement n;
    end   { case statement }
With Statement
    with record variable 1, record variable 2, . . . **do**
      statement
Note: Permits abbreviated names instead of full path names for subfields of the indicated record variables.

Procedure Call
>   1) procedure name
>   2) procedure name (supplied arg. 1, supplied arg. 2, . . .)

*Note: Supplied arguments are expressions with the type of the corresponding dummy arguments. For a variable (**var**) dummy argument, the supplied argument must be a variable. Procedure or function dummy arguments require procedure or function names as supplied arguments.*

EXPRESSION

Arithmetic Expression
>   1) unsigned number
>   ± unsigned number
>   arithmetic constant name
>   ± arithmetic constant name
>   arithmetic variable
>   arithmetic function name (supplied argument 1, . . .)
>   2) Combinations of arithmetic expressions using
>   + − * /
>   div   mod   (integer types only)
>   (   )

Boolean Expression, Boolean Condition
>   1) true
>   false
>   boolean variable
>   boolean function name (supplied argument 1, . . .)
>   2) Combinations of boolean expressions using
>   **or   and   not**
>   (   )
>   3) expression 1   comparison operator   expression 2

Expression Type	Comparison Operators
arithmetic	< > = <= >= <>
boolean	all 6 (false < true)
set	= <> <= >= (set inclusion)
character string	all 6 (must be same length and type)
pointer	= <>
record	none
array, file	none except character strings

>   4) element expression **in** set expression

Note: The type of the element expression must be the same as the base type of the set expression.

Set Expression
>   1) [   ]   (the empty set)
>   [expression 1, expression 2, . . . , expression n]
>   [expression 1.1 . . expression 1.2, exp. 2.1 . . . exp. 2.2, . . .]
>   [list of mixed element and subrange expressions]
>   2) Combinations of set expressions using
>   +   (set union)
>   *   (set intersection)
>   −   (relative complement)
>   (   )

Character String Expression
>   character string constant: 'char 1   char 2 . . . char n'
>   character string constant name
>   character string variable: Has declared type
>   **packed array** [simple type] **of char**
>   where
>   simple type = (element name 1, . . . , element name n)
>   or constant 1 . . constant 2
>   or type name of previously defined simple type

Pointer Expression
   nil
   pointer variable name
   record variable . pointer field name
Record Expression
   record variable

VARIABLE

variable name
array variable [expression 1, expression 2, . . . , expression n]
record variable . field variable name
file variable ^   (references the "file buffer" which contains the next
                   "unread" component—usually a record—in the file.)
pointer variable ^   (has type that pointer variable points to.)

BUILT-IN PROCEDURES

Input/Output
   1) **read** (variable name 1, variable name 2, . . . , variable name n)
   2) **read** (file name, variable name 1, variable name 2, . . . , variable name n)
Note: When the file name is omitted, the standard file "input" is implied.

   3) **write** (item 1, item 2, . . . , item n)
   4) **write** (file name, item 1, item 2, . . . , item n)
     where
       item = expression
             expression : field width
             real expression : field width : number of decimal places
Note: When the file name is omitted, the standard file "output" is implied.

   5) **reset** (file name)
     (positions file at start for reading)
   6) **rewrite** (file name)
     (erases file and positions file at start for writing)
Input/Output For Text Files Only
   1) **readln**
   2) **readln** (file name)
   3) **readln** (file name, variable name 1, variable name 2, . . . variable name n)
*Note: **readln** passes over next end of line character after reading.*

   4) **writeln**
   5) **writeln** (file name)
   6) **writeln** (file name, item 1, item 2, . . . , item n)
*Note: **writeln** writes an end of line character after other items.*

File Buffer Procedures (not used in this book)
   1) **get** (file name)
*Note: **get** advances the file one component and assigns the values found there to the file buffer
file name ^.*

   2) **put** (file name)
*Note: **put** appends the current contents of the file buffer (i.e., file name ^) to file as next
component. File name ^ is the name of the file buffer, a variable with the same type as the base
type of the file.*

Dynamic Allocation Procedures
   1) **new** (pointer variable name)
*Note: **new** allocates storage for a node of the type pointed to by the pointer variable, and sets
the pointer variable to point to this node.*

   2) **dispose** (pointer variable name)
*Note: **dispose** releases storage for the node pointed to.*

Appendix

PREDECLARED IDENTIFIERS D

Constants:

maxint   true   false

Types:

boolean   char   integer   real   text

Variables:

input   output

Functions:

abs	eof	odd	round	sqrt
arctan	eoln	ord	sin	succ
chr	exp	pred	sqr	trunc
cos	ln			

Procedures:

get	page	readln	rewrite	write
new	put	reset	unpack	writeln
pack	read	dispose		

THE VOCABULARY

absolute value The size of a number, disregarding its sign. For positive numbers and zero, the absolute value is the number itself. For negative numbers, the sign is changed. The built-in function abs finds absolute values.

actual parameter The value, variable, or expression supplied to replace a dummy parameter in a procedure or function call.

address The number by which a specific cell in the computer's memory is located.

algorithm An unambiguous set of instructions or steps that produce an answer or halt after a finite number of steps.

alternative computational procedures Sequences of program steps, only one of which is to be executed each time. The decision is made on the basis of a computed test.

argument A supplied or dummy variable used to communicate values between a calling program and a procedure or function. Arguments appear in parentheses after the procedure or function name.

arithmetic comparison An expression formed by comparing two arithmetic expressions using one of the comparison operator $<$, $>$, $=$, $<=$, $>=$ and $<>$.

arithmetic expression An algebraic expression composed of numeric variables, constants, and functions, arithmetic operators, and parentheses.

array A subscripted variable. An array with one subscript is a sequence of values of the same type. An array with two subscripts is a table of values of the same type.

ASCII American Standard Code for Information Interchange. A 128-character code for representing characters in computer-readable form.

assignment operator The symbols ":=" used to separate the variable on the left in an assignment from the expression whose value is to be assigned to it:

assignment statement A Pascal statement which directs the computer to evaluate an expression and assign the result as the new value of a variable.

automatic operation The ability of a computer to operate as much as possible without human direction or assistance.

auxiliary memory The slower access, higher capacity parts of a computer's memeory such as magnetic disk and tape. Data written to auxiliary memory tends to be saved more or less permanently between runs.

base type   The ordered type from which the members of values (collections) of a set type are chosen.

batch execution   A mode of program execution in which all the input data is stored in files before the execution begins. In large computer systems, batching also means the system automatically collecting a number of jobs in the same computer language to run together.

binary computer   A computer that does its internal arithmetic using a binary number system.

binary number system   A number system using powers of 2 to determine place values.

binary search   A search strategy that eliminates half of the remaining candidates for the location of a value by testing against the middle value of those remaining. Repeated halving quickly reduces the search to one possible candidate.

binary tree   A dynamic data structure in which each node has two link fields, a left link and a right link.

bit   A binary digit, 0 or 1.

body of a loop   The repeated part of a loop.

boolean   An intrinsic data type that has only two possible values: true and false. The type boolean is named after the mathematical logician George Boole.

boolean expression   An expression whose value is either true or false.

boolean operator   One of the logical connectives "and", "or" and "not", used to construct compound boolean expressions.

boolean variable   A variable of type boolean. The only values a boolean variable may have are true and false.

buffer   A holding area where input/output data are stored temporarily, pending transfer. Input data are generally read into an input buffer and then transferred to other variables. Output data are often collected in an output buffer until enough data is accumulated to write.

bug   A mistake in a program.

built-in functions   Functions supplied with the Pascal system.

call   To direct the computer to execute a procedure or function.

case statement   A decision statement in which alternative courses of action are chosen on the basis of the value of a selector variable or expression. Cases are described by listing the possible values of the selector.

cathode ray tube, CRT   A television-type display screen.

character   An intrinsic type in Pascal (denoted char), whose values may be any one computer-representable character.

character constant   A sequence of characters enclosed in apostrophes.

character string   A sequence of computer-representable characters.

character string variable   A packed array of characters.

collating sequence   The ordinal sequence of all the computer-representable characters. The two most widely used collating sequences are based on the 128-character ASCII character set and the 256-character EBCDIC character set.

column   The second subscript in a table (doubly subscripted variable).

columns indicator   A formatting command that specifies the number of columns to be used to print a value.

comment   A remark inserted in the program listing by placing it between braces ({}). comments have no effect on program execution, but they can improve the readability of a program.

compiler   A program that translates a higher-level language like Pascal into a computer's machine language for execution.

compound condition   A boolean condition formed by connecting simpler boolean conditions with the boolean operators "and" and "or".

compound statement A Pascal statement formed by sandwiching a sequence of statements between the keywords begin and end. A compound statement may be used anywhere Pascal syntax permits a statement.

computer A general purpose machine for processing data automatically under control of a stored program.

computer program A set directions telling a computer which sequence of operations to perform.

computer programming Writing computer programs.

computer terminal A device for communicating with a computer. It usually has a keyboard for typing, circuits for transmitting typed information to a computer as input, a screen or typing element for display, and circuits for receiving output from a computer and displaying the output.

computer-assisted instruction A flexible learning experience, presented to the student by means of a computer.

constant A named or unnamed value that cannot change during the execution of a program.

constant declarations Sections of a Pascal program, headed by the keyword const, in which the values of constants are declared.

creating a file Erasing the previous contents of the file, if any, and writing a file in the correct form with no data in it.

data structure An organization of data.

data transfer Moving data from one place to another in a computer.

debugging Locating and removing errors from a program.

debugging trace A trace of program execution for the purpose of locating bugs in a program.

decimals indicator A formatting command used to specify the number of decimal places to be printed. Use of a decimals indicator also directs the computer to print the value using positional notation.

decision A place in a computer program where the computer selects one of several alternative steps in its program to execute next.

declaration A nonexecutable statement (or statements) that specify information needed later in the program such as the value of a constant, the type of a variable, or the steps of a procedure.

default A value, type, or declaration that is supplied automatically by the system without the programmer having to specify it.

descending for statement A for statement using the keyword downto. The for variable decreases each iteration in a descending for loop.

deterministic simulation A simulation in which the algorithms for predicting future values of the simulated quantities involve no elements of chance.

digital computer graphics Digital images produced by computer.

digital image A picture made by selectively coloring or shading a two-dimensional array of dots called pixels.

direct recursion When a procedure or function calls itself.

dispose A built-in procedure that releases the memory space previously allocated for a node in a dynamic data structure.

div the integer quotient operator.

divide and conquer A general strategy for attacking problems that yields many very efficient algorithms. In divide and conquer, a problem is broken up into two nearly equal subproblems, and each of these subproblems is broken up into two nearly equal subproblems. In this way, the complexity of the subproblems remaining to be solved reduces rapidly.

documentation Material that explains, describes, annotates, clarifies, or elucidates the nature of the problem, the plan for its solution, the organization of the modules in the solution, the details of the solution, or which describes how to use the program, when to use the program, etc.; any supporting material that accompanies a program.

dummy argument An argument listed in the heading of a procedure or function declaration. The same as a dummy parameter.

dummy parameter A parameter listed in the heading of a procedure or function declaration.

dynamic data structure A data structure that can change its size or shape during execution of a program.

dynamic list A data structure consisting of a list whose length is not fixed. Insertions lengthen a dynamic list and deletions shorten it.

EBCDIC Extended Binary Coded Decimal Interchange Code. A 256-character code for representing characters in computer-readable form.

echo of input data After input data are read, the values are usually echoed to the screen or printer to verify what values were read and whether they were read correctly.

else-ambiguity The problem of deciding to which nested if statement an else-clause belongs. The answer is that it belongs to the nearest if statement not yet completed.

else-clause The part of an if statement that is executed if the boolean condition is false. The else-clause is optional.

else-if construction A program structure formed by nesting one if statement in the else-clause of the preceeding if statement.

empty set The value of set type consisting of no memebers of the base type.

empty statement A statement consisting of no characters at all. Its primary use is to allow semicolons to appear where Pascal syntax would otherwise forbid them.

endless loop A loop that never terminates. See infinite loop.

enumerated data type A programmer-defined data type, defined by enumerating (listing) the possible values in the type.

eof A built-in function that detects the end of data in an input file.

eoln A built-in function that detects an end-of-line character sequence in a text file.

exit test A test in a loop to determine whether the loop body should be repeated or whether the loop should be exited.

explicit arguments The arguments or parameters listed in the heading of a procedure or function declaration. Implicit arguments are values that help determine the outcome of a procedure or function call, but which the procedure or function accesses as the values of global variables.

exponential execution time The number of steps or procedure calls in an execution is approximately proportional to two raised to a power that is an input parameter of the problem.

exponential notation A form of scientific notation useful in writing very large or very small numbers. The value is multiplied by a power of ten (written after the character "e"). for example, 2.3e6 is 2.3×10^6, which is 2,300,000.

external documentation Documentation not in the program listing.

file A sequence of values or records, usually stored on an auxiliary memory device such as magnetic disk.

flag A boolean value that will be tested later in the program execution.

flag setting A programming technique in which a boolean value is set at one place in a program and tested at another (sometimes far removed) place in the program.

for loop A for statement.

for loop heading The part of the for statement that specifies what values the for-variable will take on in successive iterations of the loop body.

for statement A loop statement in which the for-variable takes on successive values either increasing or decreasing by one.

for variable The variable whose values are controlled by the for loop heading.

forward declaration A Pascal statement that declares the name and argument list of a procedure or function without supplying details of the procedure or function body. Forward declarations are a technical device to allow declaring indirectly recursive procedures or functions without formally violating the Pascal rule that procedures should be declared in the program listing above where they are called.

function A construct similar to a procedure that may have dummy parameters, but also returns a single value as the function value.

function value assignment A statement like an assignment statement that assigns the value to be returned by the function.

garbage in, garbage out A computer science aphorism meaning that if the input data or algorithm are unreliable, the output also will be unreliable, even if it is neatly printed to seven decimal places.

generalized for loop A construct like a for loop, but with arbitrary starting value, stopping value, and step size for the for-variable. In Pascal, a generalized for loop must be refined to a while or repeat-until loop.

global variable A variable that is referenced by the same name throughout the program because it is declared in the variable section of the main program.

goto statement A statement in Pascal that directs the computer to change its execution sequence so that a specific labelled statement is executed next. The goto statement was much abused in the early days of computer programming and acquired a reputation as a statement to avoid if you want to write clear programs. Once a clear, structured programming style is established, situations can be found where a goto statement improves the clarity of a a program.

gray scale A choice of display intensities to correspond to each digitized pixel intensity.

half-toning A technique for producing the effect of intermediate gray shades by combining suitable patterns of black and white image elements. Half-toning can also produce pastel shades by combining suitable patterns of dots of highly saturated primary colors.

hand simulation A debugging technique in which you put yourself in the role of the computer and perform by hand the steps which the computer is directed to perform by its program.

hard copy Printed output.

histogram A bar graph showing the frequency of occurrence of each of the categories.

if statement The most general-purpose decision statement in Pascal. If the condition is true, the then-clause is executed; otherwise the else-clause is executed.

image enhancement Once an image is digitized, it can be processed by computer to improve, enhance, or modify the image before it is displayed.

in The set membership operator in Pascal.

increment The amount a variable is increased in each iteration of a loop.

incrementation Increasing the value of a variable.

index A subscript.

index variable A variable that appears as a subscript in an array reference.

indirect addressing A flexible way to access memory cells in which the value in one memory cell determines which memory cell will be read from or stored into.

indirect recursion When procedures call each other recursively in a cycle of recursive procedures or functions.

infinite loop A loop that never terminates. See endless loop.

initialization Assigning starting values to variables at the beginning of a program, loop, or procedure execution.

input All operations supplying a computer with information.

input The name of the standard default input file in Pascal.

input buffer An area in memory into which input data is read in preparation to moving it to its intended destination.

input prompt A message sent to the user before an interactive input operation telling what kind of input is expected.

insertion in a list Adding additional nodes or values to a list, possibly in the middle of the list. if the list is stored as an array, insertion in the middle requires moving subsequent entries down one position. If the list is stored as a linked list, a small number of pointers are changed, and no data is moved at all.

integer An intrinisic type in Pascal whose values are whole numbers not exceeding maxint in absolute value.

integer constant A number written without a decimal point.

interactive When the computer responds relatively quickly to user requests.

interactive dialogue A conversational mode of communication between a user and a computer during interactive execution of a program.

interactive editing Preparing or changing a program or data file using an interactive program. Most Pascal systems now provide an interactive editor.

interactive execution Execution of a program while the user is at a computer terminal. The user may receive output on the terminal screen or printer, and may enter input data for the program execution during the execution.

internal documentation Documentation that appears in the program listing for the benefit of programmers who will later read the program to modify it, verify its correctness, or fix a bug.

intersection A binary operation on set type values, denoted a * b. The set of values of the base type that belong to both sets a and b.

iteration Repetition of a loop.

key field That field in a record that is sorted upon, that is, the field in the records of a sorted list that is in increasing or decreasing order.

keyword A word or abbreviation that has a precise intrinsic meaning in the syntax of a programming language.

label An unsigned integer that precedes and identifies a statement as the target of a goto statement.

leaf A node in a tree structure that is not further subdivided.

leaf A node in a binary tree with nil left and right link pointers.

left subtree That part of a binary tree whose root is the left link of the given node.

lexicographic order The order of words in a dictionary, alphabetic order.

linear list A one-dimensional array.

link A field in a node that points to another node in the dynamic data structure.

linked list A representation of a dynamic list using record structures for nodes in the list and pointers to link each node in the list to the next node in the list.

list A one-dimensional array, an array with one subscript.

local variable A variable that is declared in a procedure or function. A local variable may be referenced within the procedure in which it is declared or in any subprocedure, but it is unknown outside that procedure or function. Local variables help prevent side effects of a procedure or function.

localization of variables Declaring variables locally in the procedures that use them to prevent side effects.

loop A sequence of program steps that may be executed more than once during a single execution of the program.

loop control variable A variable that appears in the exit/repetition test of a loop.

machine language A representation of the set of basic operations a computer is capable of performing.

magnetic disk A medium for storing data in computer-readable form on rotating disks coated with magnetizable iron oxide. Disks range in size from small, flexible "floppy" disks to large fixed disk packs storing billions of bytes of data.

magnetic tape A medium for sequentially storing relatively large quantities of data in computer-readable form. Although maximum read/write speeds are high, information in random parts of the reel are hard to access quickly.

main memory The main collection of high-speed, high cost memory cells in a computer. Data in main memory is not usually saved between runs.

manual A set of directions for using a program or computer system.

mathematical model A scaled-down representation of a real situation using numerical values and equations or algorithms that specify how the values change.

memory The capacity of a computer to retain information and to recall that information later.

memory cell An individual unit of the computer's main memory.

mod The remainder operator in integer division.

modular subprocess A part of the total algorithm that is reasonably self-contained, easily described, and which is a meaningful conceptual unit to the designer and reader of the program.

module A coherent set of instructions that serve a specific and well-defined purpose in the solution of a problem.

multi-level search A search strategy in which the elements of an ordered list are organized into several hierarchical levels of groupings. First, the correct highest-level grouping is located, then the correct next-level grouping, and so forth, until finally, the lowest level is searched to find the item.

nested if statements The then-clause or else-clause of one if statement contains or is another if statement.

nesting When one program structure is wholly contained within another structure. Procedure declarations, if statements, and loop statements are often nested.

new A built-in procedure that allocates memory for a new node in a dynamic data structure.

nil The only pointer constant. A pointer of nil points to no location in the computer's memory.

node The fundamental unit from which dynamic data structures are built. A node is usually declared to be a record structure containing information fields and one or more pointer fields called links.

number In Pascal, a real or integer constant.

operating system A program that controls the flow of information through the computer and schedules the use of the computer's hardware components. Usually the operating system is the first program run when the computer is turned on, and it then schedules all subsequent requests for computer use.

ord A built-in function whose value is the position of its argument in an ordered data type.

output All operations in which a computer transmits information to another device.

output The name of the standard output file in Pascal.

output buffer An area in the computer's memory into which data is transferred in preparation to writing it as output.

packed array An array whose internal representation is designed to minimize the amount of memory required. Character strings are usually stored as packed arrays of characters.

parameter A variable used to communicate between a calling program and a procedure or function.

parity Whether a number is even or odd. The built-in function odd is true if the parity of a number is odd.

partition sorting A sorting strategy in which a list is divided into "low" and "high" sublists, and each sublist is sorted by the same procedure. Typical of divide and conquer strategies, partition sorting is very efficient. The well-known algorithm, quicksort, uses a partition sorting strategy.

path name The name of a component in a hierarchical data structure, formed by writing the root name, followed by a period, followed by the name of the first level subdivision, followed by a period and a more detailed subdivision name, continuing until the component is completely specified.

pixel An individual picture element or dot in a digital image.

pointer A value that points to the location of other values. In most Pascal implementations, the value of a pointer is an address in main memory. However, the Pascal programmer can usually neither print nor assign this address, except by specifying what the pointer points to. Two or more pointers can point to the same location.

pointer variable A variable whose value is a location in the computer's memory where the value it points to is stored.

positional notation The usual decimal notation for numbers in which the position of a digit relative to the decimal point determines its value.

pred A built-in function whose value is the previous element in an ordered data type. The predecessor of the first element in an ordered data type is not defined.

printer graphics Digital images produced using printable characters of differing densities to display the pixels.

procedure A part of a program that is executed only when a statement in another part of the program calls for its execution.

procedure call A statement invoking the execution of a procedure. In Pascal, a procedure call consists of the name of the procedure and a list of its supplied arguments.

procedure declaration The part of a program that specifies in detail the steps a procedure will perform.

program A set of directions telling a computer which sequence of operations to perform.

program heading The first line of a Pascal program giving the program name and information about the files used in the program.

program listing A printed or displayed copy of a program.

program memory In some programmable calculators, program steps are stored in different memory cells than data. In most computers, memory is used interchangeably for program steps or data.

programmable A device is programmable if sequences of its basic operations can be selected in advance for automatic execution.

pseudorandom numbers A sequence of numbers generated according to an algorithm that are extremely unpredictable (except by simulating the algorithm). Adequate pseudorandom number sequences share many properties with random numbers including the correct distribution, mean and standard deviation of values, and negligible correlations between successive values.

punchcard A rectangle of cardboard in which information can be stored in computer-readable form by punching holes in appropriate positions. Invented in its present form by Herman Hollerith to tabulate census data, it was once the primary means of preparing input data for computers.

railroad syntax chart A syntax chart in a form that resembles the tracks of a railroad switching yard. Syntactically correct Pascal constructs are constructed by following the tracks. Backing up is not permitted.

read statement A Pascal statement that directs the computer to accept input from a file and assign the values it reads to variables in the program. Officially, read is a built-in procedure and not a statement, but there is little practical difference.

reading Programmers usually speak of a computer reading all input, regardless of the source of the input.

readln statement A Pascal statement that reads input data in the same fashion as the read statement. After reading is completed, it directs the computer to skip to the beginning of a new line. Officially, readln is a built-in procedure and not a statement.

real An intrinsic type in Pascal, whose values include numbers with and without fractional or decimal part.

real constant A number written with a decimal point, and possibly with a power of ten written after the character "e".

recall To retrieve information from a computer's memory. Recall is more often used to describe this operation on a hand calculator.

record A data structure consisting of values grouped together using the keyword record. The components of a record need not all be the same type.

record One of the components of a file.

record assignment statement If the left side and right side of an assignment statement are both records structures of the same type, the assignment statement is valid and assigns each component of one data structure to the corresponding component of the other data structure.

record structure A composite data type constructed using the Pascal record construct.

recurrence relation An equation that defines the value of a recursively defined function in terms of its value for other (usually smaller or simpler) values of its arguments.

recursive definition A definition that refers to a construct of the same kind as part of the definition.

recursive function a function that calls itself, either directly or indirectly.

recursive procedure A procedure that calls itself, either directly or indirectly.

reference parameter, by reference parameter A dummy parameter declared as variable (var). No memory space is reserved for a by reference parameter; the memory space reserved for the corresponding actual parameter is used for the values.

refine To replace a step in a problem solution with the same step described in greater detail.

refinement of a program A new version of the program in which one or more steps have been described in greater detail.

relative complement A binary operation on set types, denoted a − b. the set of values of the base type that belong to set a, but not to set b.

repeat-until loop A repeat-until statement.

repeat-until statement A loop statement with the exit test at the bottom of the loop body.

reset A built-in procedure that positions a file at its beginning in preparation for writing to the file.

rewrite A built-in procedure that erases a file and positions it at the beginning in preparation for writing to the file.

right subtree That part of a binary tree whose root is the right link of the given node.

root The primary, or most accessible, node in a tree. The one node in a tree from which all other nodes may be reached.

round Built-in function whose value is the integer nearest to a real value.

roundoff, roundoff error Differences, usually small, between an exact answer and a computed answer. Roundoff occurs in type real quantities when the fixed number of significant digits is not sufficient to retain the exact answer.

row The first subscript in a doubly subscripted variable (table).

running a program Making the computer execute the steps of a program.

scalar data type An ordered data type.

scheduling algorithm The rules by which an operating system decides when a request for program execution or a request for an editing operation or a request for any other computer use will be carried out.

scope of a declaration The set of lines in a program listing to which a particular declaration applies.

self-documenting A variable name or program or procedure is self-documenting if its meaning is clear without additional explanation.

sequential search A search strategy in which the elements of a list are tested, one at a time, in sequence, to locate a given item.

set data type A programmer-defined data type whose values are sets (collections) of values from a specified scalar (ordered) base type. Many Pascal systems restrict the maximum size of the base type.

set membership operator Denoted by "in" in Pascal, the set membership operator tests whether a value of the base type is a member of a set of objects of that base type.

side effect A peripheral effect of one procedure or function on another, unrelated to the well-defined task of the offending procedure.

signed number A number, possibly preceded by a plus sign or minus sign.

snapshot A debugging printout showing the instantaneous values of a group of related variables in a program.

sorting Arranging a list of data in order.

square The built-in function sqr finds the product of a number with itself.

square root A number whose square is the given number. The built-in function sqrt finds the computer-representable number closest to the square root of its argument.

store To save information in a computer's memory.

structured programming A style of programming that includes writing programs with clear and readable structure, top-down program design, using procedures to clarify the organization of the program, and using standard loop constructs and sections of code with one entrance and one exit.

subrange type A programmer-defined data type that is a subrange of an intrinsic or programmer-defined ordered (scalar) data type.

subscript A value in brackets in an array reference that specifies which element of the array is intended.

subscripted variable An array.

succ A built-in function whose value is the next element in an ordered data type. The successor of the last value in an ordered type is not defined.

successive refinement The process of adding detail to the steps in a problem solution. If a refined step is still not described in executable Pascal statements, it is refined again. Successive stages of refinement continue until each step is executable.

superposition A technique for forming a complex digital image by super-imposing simple shapes.

supplied argument The value, variable, or expression written in a procedure or function call to replace the corresponding dummy argument.

syntax The precise grammar of a computer language.

syntax chart A way of depicting correct Pascal syntax. Any complete path from the beginning to the end of a syntax chart represents a syntactically correct Pascal construct.

system of procedure A collection of procedures that are part of the same execution. The procedures in a system of procedures may share data both through argument passing and through values saved in one of the common files.

system of programs A collection of programs that share information written to or read from one or more common files.

table An array with two subscripts, a two-dimensional array.

tail recursion A single recursive call that occurs as the last executed statement of a procedure. Since no further statements of the procedure remain to be executed upon return from this recursive call, the tail recursion can be rewritten as a loop, but usually not as clearly.

termination signal An input data value that is recognized by the program as indicating that no more data (of the current kind) will follow.

text file A file of characters, similar in structure to the standard files input and output.

then-clause The part of an if statement that is executed if the boolean condition is true.

time sharing When many users share a central computer, a time sharing operating system schedules requests in such a way as to make each user feel that there are no other users on the system.

top-down program design A method of analyzing problems in which the solution is attempted first at the highest possible conceptual level, in terms closest to the problem statement. Then, details are added to each step of the proposed solution until the result is an executable program.

tracing Monitoring the progress of a program execution by means of frequent printouts showing which step is being executed. Tracing also may include printing the values of key variables at each step.

traversing a linked list Processing or examining the nodes in a linked list in sequence, starting with the first node and proceeding by following the link fields to successive nodes in the list until the last node in the list (with link field nil) is processed.

traversing a tree Visiting or processing information in every node of a tree. There are several natural orders in which to traverse a binary tree: (1) infix order in which the left subtree is visited first, then the root, and then the right subtree, (2) prefix order in which the root is visited before either subtree, and (3) postfix order in which both subtrees are visited completely before the root is visited.

tree sorting Sorting a list by placing the entries in a binary tree. Because there are rapid tree insertion and tree traversal algorithms, tree sorting is a very efficient method.

tree structure A hierarchical data structure. Finer and finer subdivisions of the data correspond to branching of the tree.

truncation the operation of removing the fractional part of a real number to get the integer part. The built-in function trunc finds the integer part of a real quantity.

two-level search A searching strategy that involves looking first for the correct page and then searching the correct page for the given entry.

type A description of the kind of values a variable will have.

union a binary operation on set types, denoted a + b. The set of values of the base type that belong to at least one of the sets a or b.

updating a file Reading the contents of a file, making changes, and saving the new version of the file.

value argument, value parameter A dummy parameter that can receive an initial value from the calling program, but which cannot return a value to the calling program. Changes in a value parameter do not affect the corresponding actual parameter.

variable A construct in a Pascal program that refers to one or more related values that can change during the execution of the program.

variable declarations Sections of a Pascal program, headed by the keyword var, in which the types of variables are declared.

variable name A name used in Pascal to refer to one or more memory locations. The name usually describes what the values represent.

variant record types The last field in a record type declaration may be a variant part, formed using a construction similar to a case statement.

video digitizer A device for digitizing frames of television pictures.

visual image processing When an optical image is digitized by assigning to each pixel a number representing the intensity of light in the image at that point, the image may be processed by computer and then displayed.

while loop A while statement.

while statement A loop statement in which the exit test is at the head of the loop body.

with statement A statement that can predeclare part of the full path names of components of a data structure. Formed using a construction similar to a case statement.

writing Programmers usually speak of writing all output, regardless of whether the output is transmitted to printer, screen, plotter, or magnetic disk.

write statement A Pascal statement that writes values to an output device.

writeln statement A Pascal statement that writes values to an output device and than skips to the beginning of a new line.

ANSWERS TO SELF-TEST QUESTIONS

Chapter 1

Section 1.1

Please bear in mind that many of these answers are matters of interpretation and legitimate differences of opinion can exist.

1. Automatic, accepts input, sends output, saves data, programmable (but has a very limited repertoire of basic operations), and decides when to turn on the radio. It does not perform arithmetic, move data, access memory flexibly, or store its program in the same cells as data.
2. Same as 1. Digital doesn't matter.
3. A simple 4-operation hand calculator can perform arithmetic, accept input, and display output.
4. A programmable hand calculator usually has all 10 attributes of a computer, although some may lack flexible memory access (indirect addressing). A programmable hand calculator is usually a computer, although its input, output, and memory are often severly limited.
5. Babbage's Analytical Engine was missing flexible memory access and stored program. The program was stored on card, but not in the same memory cells that could hold data.
6. All! A computer is a computer.
7. A player piano definitely is automatic and sends output to the listener's ears. It is a matter of opinion whether the piano roll that determines the music it plays is input or a program.
8. A record player is automatic, accepts records as input, produces sound as output. It can be programmed by means of a record to produce any reasonable sounds, but it probably cannot be programmed to do every reasonable sequence of movements of the tone arm.
9. An automatic speed control mechanism is automatic, accepts input about speed, sends output control impulses to the engine, and has so few meaningful sequences of operations that it probably passes the programmability test almost by default.
10. A Jacquard loom is automatic, programmable, and sends the output (the woven cloth) to the user. It probably accepts no input except its program.

Chapter 2

Section 2.1

1-2.

Correct	program division (output);
Correct	begin
Wrong, parentheses are required	writeln (243 / 11);
Wrong, a period is required at the end of a program	end.

3-4.

Wrong, semicolon required	program multiplication (output);
Wrong, no period, optional semicolon is OK	begin
Correct	writeln (1 * 2 * 3 * 4 * 5);
Wrong, period at end of program, not semicolon	end.

5. No. A *compound statement* is a group of statements beginning with the keyword begin and ending with the keyword end.
6. run   or   run *programname*
7. a. True.
    b. False, * is the symbol for multiplication.
    c. False, Pascal has no symbol for raising to a power.

Section 2.2

1. a. True.
    b. True.
    c. True, the value assigned to a constant determines its type.
    d. False, a constant cannot appear on the left side in an assignment statement.
2. All are valid expect phone# (invalid character), real (reserved word), and 4gotton (starts with a digit).
3. x: valid.
    n: valid.
    equalsign: invalid, replace colon with equal sign.
    number: invalid, integer is a type, not a constant.
    baseofnaturallogarithms: invalid, replace colon with equal sign.
4. x: invalid, need a type, not a value.
    n: valid.
    letter: invalid, the Pascal keyword is "char", not "character".
    number: invalid, variable declarations use colon, not equal sign.
    e: valid.
5. Valid.
    Invalid, assignment operator is :=.
    Invalid, expression is on the left.
    Valid.

Section 2.3

1. b2.500   bbbb6.3
2. Largest: 9999.999, smallest: −999.999
3. 6 columns: 1000.0   (The columns indicator specifies the *minimum* number of columns, not the maximum number of columns.)
4. |0.33333|

Section 2.4

1.   round (x / 0.1) * 0.1   or   round (x * 10) * 0.1
2.   123 / 10 = 12.3 is larger than 123 div 10 = 12.
3.   They are equal when x / y is an integer.
4.
    6
    5.3
    16 (sqr is the squaring function)
    −123
    123.456
    1.1 (sqrt is the square root function)

5.   Two consecutive calls to the built-in procedure write will produce both sets of output values on the same line (assuming they fit), while two consecutive calls to the procedure writeln will put each set of output values on a different line.

Section 2.5

1.   a. False.
      b. False, they may be in any computer-readable form.
      c. True.
      d. False.
      e. False, on a microcomputer serving one user at a time, editing and execution are interactive, but no timesharing is necessary.
      f. True.
      g. False, not as "batch" is used in this book.
2.   a. True.
      b. Doubtful.
      c. True.
      d. True, and very important!
      e. True.
      f. Your authors do, for batch programs.

Chapter 3

Section 3.1

1.   a. False, first you should make a high-level breakdown into major areas.
      b. True.
      c. False, many problems have no best solution.

Section 3.2

1.   The Pascal compiler enables a computer to refine a Pascal program directly into machine language, so that the computer can understand the instructions directly and execute them. Refer back to Chapter 1 if you want to review what machine language is.
2.   a. True.
      b. False, remember that in the vacation example, you had to refine the details of where you were going and what you were doing before you could refine the details of making reservations or packing your luggage.

Section 3.3

1. a. True, computer programs are supposed to be perfect. Testing part of a program means making sure that no part of it has any flaws at all.
    b. False, comments are used to explain whatever in your program is not self-explanatory. Throwing them into a program that is already self-explanatory without them tends to clutter the program and make it harder to read. The program should be designed to be clear without many comments. (But don't be afraid to use comments when they are needed.)
    c. Partly true; another reason to modularize is to facilitate testing and debugging.

Chapter 4

Section 4.1

1-2.

a.   Correct.
b.   Correct.
c.   Incorrect. The compound statement starting at "begin" should have an end-statement before the "else" and not at the end of the if-statement. The correct form is:

```
if x = y then
   begin
   writeln (x);
   z := x;
   end
else
   z := 5;
```

d.   Correct. Always sets x to 6.
e.   Correct.
f.   Incorrect. The semicolon before "else" shouldn't be there.

```
if a >= 0 then b := a
else b := -a;
```

g.   Meaningless. Omit the semicolon after "then".

```
if you = me then
   we := 'yes'
```

h.   Incorrect. The equality comparison operator is "=", not ":=".

```
if x + 1 = y - 1 then
   begin
   z := x;
   writeln (y - 1);
   end
```

Section 4.2

1.a.
```
case code of
     1:   x := 1;
     2, 3, 4:
        begin
        x := 1;
```

```
        y := 1;
      end;      { semicolon required between statement and next case }
    5, 6:  y := 1;
    7:   z := 1
    end           { a case-statement ends with "end" }
```

b.
```
  case digit of
    1, 3, 7:  writeln ('Case 1');
    2, 4, 6:  writeln ('Case 2');
    5, 8:     writeln ('Case 3');
    9, 0:     writeln ('Bad data');
    { There is no else clause in case }
    end   { end missing again }
```

c.
```
  case compasspoint of
    'N', 'S':  writeln ('vertical');
    'E', 'W':  writeln ('horizontal');
    end
```

This case-statement is correct. Although a semicolon usually separates the cases, the last semicolon before "end" is permissible because an empty case is presumed to follow it.

2.
```
  case letter of
    'a','e','i','o','u':  writeln ('vowel');
    'b','c','d','f','g','h','j','k','l','m',
    'n','p','q','r','s','t','v','w','x','y','z':
        writeln ('consonant');
    end
```

3.
```
  if (letter = 'a') or (letter = 'e') or (letter ='i')
                    or (letter = 'o') or (letter ='u') then
    writeln ('vowel')
  else
    writeln ('consonant')
```

An even simpler test is possible using the set membership operator introduced in Section 14.1. You know enough to read Chpater 14 now.

```
  if letter in ['a','e','i','o','u'] then
    writeln ('vowel')
  else
    writeln ('consonant')
```

Section 4.3

	45	75	95
1.	no output	Input data x = 75 is high	Input data x = 95 is very high
2.	no output	Input data x = 75 is high	Input data x = 95 is very high
3.	no output	Input data x = 75 is high	Input data x = 95 is very high
4.	Input data x = 45 is high	Input data x = 75 is high	Input data x = 95 is very high

The semicolon after "else" completes the nearest if-statement (testing $x > 90$). This appears to leave the then-clause of the $x > 50$ if-statement with two statements, an if-statement and a compound statement. The first of these, the inner if-statement, is the then-clause of the outer if-statement. The improved statement forms the third statement of the body of the program. It is always executed, regardless of the input value.

5. Syntax error: the semicolon after "end" completes both if-statements leaving the "else" dangling without an active "if".

6. Input data x = 45 is high; Input data x = 75 is high; Input data x = 95 is very high. Note that the semicolon after "then" terminates the then-clause of the x > 50 if-statement with a null statement as the entire then-clause. Thus nothing is done either way the test comes out, and the x > 90 if-statement and test are done in any event.

Section 4.4

1. Both are valid. The first declares signal to be a character string of length 4; the second declares bee to be a single character.

2. The declaration of firstname is invalid; the range of subscripts is missing. The declaration of signal is valid.

3. a. Valid, if see has type char.
    b. Valid, if word is declared a character string of length 9.
    c. Invalid, lengths are both 3, but a constant must not appear on the left.

4. a. Valid and true.
    b. Invalid, different lengths.
    c. Invalid, you can't compare a character string and a number.
    d. Invalid, both are character string, but of different lengths.
    e. Valid, true if the EBCDIC collating sequence is being used and false if the ASCII collating sequence is being used.
    f. Valid and true.

Chapter 5

Section 5.1

1-2. a. n loop: correct.
    b. x loop: incorrect, missing "do".
    c. year loop: syntactically correct, only the last value read is still available.
    d. n loop: correct, end of line means nothing in Pascal.
    e. n loop: correct, but semicolon after "do" makes the loop body empty.
    f. count loop: correct. Don't let the semicolon after "score" fool you.
    g. time loop: correct. A compound statement doesn't have to have many statements as part of it.

3.

n	product
undefined	1
2	2
3	6
4	24

4.   1   3   5   7   9 11 13 15 17 19

Section 5.2

1-2. a. No problems. n = 10.
    b. No syntax errors; however, body of while-loop is empty. Moreover, it is executed no times. Final value of n = 0, since n := n − 1 is executed once.
    c. No syntax problems. However, need initialization, say n := 1. Then the final value of n = 10.

d. No syntax errors. Datavalue not initialized. If this is fixed, segment ends with datavalue = 0.

e. No syntax errors. However, write (inchar) is not part of the loop. Either add "begin" and "end" or change indentation. At end, inchar = first character not "x".

f. Errors. The roles of until and repeat are interchanged. Also until clause should not have keyword "do". When these errors are fixed, loop ends with inchar = '.'.

3. There is never just one way to write a program. Here is one. There are others.

```
count := 1
n := count * 13;
while n < 100 do
   begin
   count := count + 1;
   n := count * 13;
   end; { while-loop }
writeln (n :1, ' is the first multiple of 13');
writeln ('that exceeds 100');
```

4. The simplest way is to execute the repeat-until-loop only if times > 0.

```
read (times);
count := 0;
if times > 0 then
   repeat
      writeln ('Hello');
      count := count + 1;
   until count = times
```

Section 5.3

1. signal: valid, if signal is a character string of length 4.
   bee: valid, if bee is of type char.
2. firstname: invalid, missing range of subscripts.
   signal: valid.
   vector: invalid. You can't have a *packed* array of reals.
3. valid, if bee has type char.
   valid, if word is declared a character string of length 9.
4. 20 characters.
5. 11 reals.

Section 5.4

1. The old value of the variable sum is increased by 1 to get a value, which is then assigned as the new value of the variable sum.
2. a. sum = 1 + 1 + 1 + 1 + 1 + 1 + 1 + 1 + 1 + 1 + 1 = 10
   b. sum = 1 + 2 + 3 + 4 = 10
   c. sum = 1*1 + 2*2 + 3*3 + 4*4 = 1 + 4 + 9 + 16 = 30
   d. sum = 5 + 4 + 3 + 2 + 1 = 15
3.

n	product
undefined	1
2	2
3	6
4	24

4.   a. Syntax is correct; end-of-line means nothing in Pascal.
      b. Semicolon after "do" makes the loop body empty. Most Pascal com-
      pilers will not flag this mistake, because it is syntactically correct, though
      meaningless.
      c. Syntax is correct; don't let the semicolon after "score" fool you. Cal-
      culates the sum of n test scores read from input. The variable sum needs
      initialization.
      d. Syntax is correct; a compound statement doesn't have to have more
      than one statement as part of it. There is no sum calculated.

Section 5.5

1.   The output looks like this:

```
run bug1

n = 1       sum = 1
n = 2       sum = 2
n = 3       sum = 3
n = 4       sum = 4
n = 5       sum = 5
Final sum = 5
```

The final answer is wrong, so there is clearly a bug. The first line of output is correct, that is, the sum should be 1 when only one number is
added. The second line is wrong. The sum should be $1 + 2 = 3$, but it
is only 2. The wrong amount seems to be added to the sum on the
second iteration of the for-loop. The reason that the correct amount was
added the first time, but the incorrect amount was added the second time,
is clear. The statement

```
sum := sum + 1
```

is wrong. It should be

```
sum := sum + n
```

to add a different amount each time. With this statement corrected and
the program rerun, the output looks like this:

```
run bug1

n = 1       sum = 1
n = 2       sum = 3
n = 3       sum = 6
n = 4       sum = 10
n = 5       sum = 15
Final sum = 15
```

Perhaps we should consider renaming the program.

Chapter 6

Section 6.1

1.   You write its name as a statement in the program.
2.   It goes below the constant and variable declarations, but before the com-
      pound statement that forms the body of the main program.

3. a. False. Any number of calls is permitted.
    b. False. So far, using the same names is the only way of passing information to or receiving information back from a programmer-defined procedure.
    c. True.
    d. True, and very important.
    e. True.

Section 6.2

1. We know exactly what the output should look like.
2. It is a reasonably self-contained, easily described, and meaningful conceptual unit to the designer of the program.
3. a. False, the planning that precedes it represents more real progress.
    b. True.

Section 6.3

1. There are several advantages. First, the use of the return key to end lines of input is standard practice and most people familiar with computers, or even with typewriters, are already used to it. Second, if another character is reserved as the termination character, it cannot be used as a valid character within the character input. Third, many of the nonstandard extensions of Pascal to include variable-length character string input use return as their termination signal, so why teach users a signal that is special only to your program?
2. A buffer is a temporary area where input data is stored, preparatory to moving it to ints intended destination. An output buffer is a temporary area where data is moved from its usual location preparatory to writing it to an output device.
4. On some systems, if the line of input has not yet been transmitted to the computer by pressing the return or enter key, the mistake can be corrected by backspacing over it. If the mistake has been transmitted, the easiest thing to do is to terminate the current grade report by typing "No more courses" to the next request for a course title and starting over again for that student. Since no summary totals are being kept by this program and each grade report is processed independently of any other grade report, no harm is done.

Section 6.4

1. A procedure declaration must precede any call to that procedure. As a result, the main program usually comes last, the procedures it calls come before it, the procedures they call come before them, etc.
2. Internal documentation, external documentation, and a manual for use. Internal documentation includes self-explanatory variable names and comments. External documentation describes the problem and the algorithms for its solution. The manual for users describes how to use the program to a nonprogrammer.
3. You should test a program until you are sure that it will perform correctly with any valid combination of input data. Test cases should be designed to exercise every single branch and alternative in the instruction sequence.

Chapter 7

Section 7.1

1. The program will examine up to 10 integers. Each nonzero integer is counted after it is read, so the final value of count will be the number of nonzero integers read before the first zero, or ten if no zero was found.
2. If the input data to a program is "garbage" (wrong or inaccurate), we must expect the output of the program to be "garbage" in the same sense. Similarly, if the algorithm is wrong or inaccurate, the output will be garbage.
3. A model is made simpler than the original to make it easier to understand and easier to solve or simulate in a reasonable amount of time. The danger is that the behavior of an oversimplified model will not resemble the behavior of the original situation sufficiently well. The predictions of the simulation may then be correct for the model, but not for the original.

Section 7.2

1. Eoln is true when the next character to be read is an end-of-line character.
2. a. False, this while-loop continues whenever *condition1* and *condition2* are both true.
    b. True, both conditions false is the only case in which (*condition1* or *condition2*) is false.

Section 7.3

1. Initialization, repetition/exit test, loop body, and loop control variable modification.
2. One possible answer is: if all the loop control variables are read from input data in the body of the loop.
3. A for-loop is the preferred loop construct when the problem naturally has a variable that takes on values in a counting sequence, either increasing of decreasing, and the number of repetitions of the loop body is known before the loop is entered.
4. These more general loop constructs are not only preferable, but nearly essential in all other circumstances. Not matter how hard you try, a for-loop cannot be used if the number of iterations is not known before the loop is entered. While- and repeat-until-loops also are necessary in Pascal when a loop has multiple exit conditions.
5. The loop body is the statement executed repeatedly. The initialization, increment, and test steps all are contained in the for-loop heading. The initialization of the loop control variable, the **for-variable**, is contained in the first expression following the assignment operator (:=). The test is whether the for-variable has exceeded the value of the expression following the keyword "to". The increment is +1 if the keyword "to" is used, and −1 if the keyword "downto" is used. The incrementing step takes place *after* each iteration of the loop. The testing takes place before each iteration of the loop, so that no iterations is a possibility.

Section 7.4

1.
```
x := 10;
while x <= 20 do
  begin
  writeln (x);
  x := x + 0.1;
  end  { while-loop }
```

2. This while-loop is equivalent to the non-Pascal generalized for-loop

```
for x := 100 to 1 in steps of −1/3 do
  writeln (x);
```

It prints reasonable approximations to the numbers, 100, 99 2/3, 99 1/3, 99, 98 2/3, ..., 1 1/3, 1.

Section 7.5

1. All five are important debugging aids. However, inserting a write state-ment to print the loop control variables (and other relevant variables that might affect loop termination) in the body of the loop is a technique par-ticularly well-suited to finding out why a loop failed to terminate.
2. Execution of the write statement embedded in the loop can be made con-ditional on an if-test. For example, the write statement could be done every tenth or hundredth iteration, or the write statement could be exe-cuted only for the first ten and the last ten expected iterations.

Section 7.6

1. There are two reasons. If the step size (or other change in a loop control variable) is real, the roundoff error might make the equality test fail, and if the step size is greater than one, the values of the loop control variable might skip over the upper limit without reaching it exactly.
2. It is safe to use an equality test at the upper limit if all values are small integers and the step size is one or minus one.

Section 7.7

1.
```
type
  game = (tic, tac, toe);
```

2. a. ord (wed) = 3, because the lowest value of ord is ord (sun) = 0.
   b. pred (thu) = wed
   c. succ (sat) is an error! Enumerated data types are not circular. Since ord (sat) = 6, it could only be followed by a value with ord = 7, which the enumerated data type day does not have.

3. It tells the computer to print the four temperatures, temperature [wed], temperature [thu], temperature [fri], temperature [sat] on the same line of output.

Chapter 8

Section 8.1

1. a. False.
    b. True for var arguments. The same or an assignable type for non-var arguments.
    c. True, to a value dummy argument.
    d. True, but if you don't declare the variable in the procedure, it will be a global variable and not a local variable.
2. A local variable may be changed without affecting a variable that happens to have the same name in a different part of the program.
3. Dummy arguments are called by value if the value of the corresponding supplied argument is not supposed to be changed by the procedure. A dummy argument is called by reference (var) if it is supposed to be changed by the procedure.

Section 8.2

1. a. False. You should test all of the essentially different possible paths of execution using test data specially designed to exercise each alternative.
    b. False. Hand simulation means tracing the values by hand, not by computer.
    c. False. If the bug seems to be in the loop, you want the snapshot taken at selected times during the loop execution.
    d. True.
2. Computer tracing lets the computer do all the tedious work. Doing the same work by hand, you will sooner or later make a mistake. Also, when hand simulating, people tend to read and simulate what they *think* the program says. The computer executes what the program actually says.
3. You don't get the same insight into how the program should work when the computer traces as when you think about it while hand simulating. Also, if you are not too careful in selecting what and where to snapshot, you could wind up with enormous quantities of output tracing uninteresting parts of the program which do not have a bug.

Section 8.3

1. They differ in two ways. A function returns one value to the calling program; a procedure can return any number of values. A procedure is called by writing its name as a statement in the program; a function is called by using it in an expression.
2. a. True, function parameters are just like procedure parameters.
    b. True.
    c. False, the last value assigned is the value returned. It is good programming style to assing the function value only once in each execution of a function.

Chapter 9

Section 9.1

1.
```
var
   profit : array [1..100] of real;
```

2.
```
var
   name : packed array [1..30] of char;
```

3. In Pascal, an array must have fixed declared size, so the maximum antici- pated length of the list is declared as the array size. A separate variable, perhaps called "actualupperbound", is used to keep track of how may items are really in the list and to control processing of the list.

4. a. False. Any integer may be the lower bound.

b. False. Any order scalar type is permitted including char, enumerated data types, and their subranges.

c. True.

d. False. An array usually is used, but if the entire list does not have to be in the computer's memory at one time, the program can be written without using an array.

e. False. A while-loop can do anything a for-loop can do. However, when the exact range of subscripts is known, a for-loop is a convenient and natural way to program writing and reading the values in an array.

f. True! If subscripts could not vary, there would be little point in using arrays.

Section 9.2

1. a. False, the main advantage is faster completion of the search in case the objective is not in the list. Humans ordinarily would not read the com- puter data base.

b. False, sorting takes so much time that it would be inefficient to sort the entire list just to seek one object. However, if you will repeatedly seek objects in the same list, the one-time price of sorting might be worth the cost.

c. False, not always. Suppose that the objective is in the list, but that it appears toward the end of the sorted sequence. An example might be the name Zeke Zebra. Nearly every entry must be searched to locate Zeke Zebra in a sorted list; however, on the average, only half of the entries must be searched to find Zeke Zebra in an unordered list. If you answered "true", you probably were thinking of seeking an objective not in the list, for which searching an ordered list is always faster.

2. It is a second source of input data, different from the input file, which is being used to enter the card number to be verified.

Section 9.3

1. a. False, the entire point of this section is the study of more efficient ways to search ordered lists.

b. True, how else would you search an unordered list? All of the methods given in this section depend on the order for their efficiency.

c. True, up to the point where there are so many levels that some levels have only one item in the search at that level.

d. True, All the examples had gaps.

     e. False, a binary search program is shorter and simpler than all but the least efficient sequential search program.

     f. False, Binary search widens its lead as the lists grow larger. For example, a list of 1,000,000 entries can be binary searched in 21 comparisons, less than the average number of comparisons for a four-level search of 100,000 entries.

2.   To search 10,000 entries, a two-level search does two sequential searches, each of length 100 entries. Divide the 10,000 entries into 100 "page lists" of 100 entries each and one additional list consisting of the last entry on each "page". A two-level search on a 10,000 entry list can be performed in a computer with a little more memory than 100 entries by searching the "page index" of length 100 to determine the correct page and then searching that page. For greater efficiency, a binary search could be used on both the "page index" and the page in which the entry is to be found.

Section 9.4

1.   a. True.

     b. If you count only the number of comparisons, the answer is false. This sorting method uses exactly the same number of comparisons no matter what the order of the input list. However, the innermost loop will execute slightly faster because the if-conditions will never be true and the then-clause will never be executed with a sorted input list. Hence, from this point of view, the answer is true.

     c. True.

2.   In sort2, convert the procedure findnextsmallest to a procedure findnextlargest by changing less than (<) to greater than (>) in the if-test. Some variable names also should be changed to reflect the changed roles.

Chapter 10

Section 10.1

1.
```
var
   puzzle : array [1..20, 1..20] of char;
```

2.   The following output is produced:

```
run example

Input data  a:
 9 7
 2 5
Table b:
 9 7
 2 5
```

The program reads four values into a table a and copies these values to table b. Both tables are printed.

Section 10.2

1. The simplest way is

   ```
   var
     picture : array [1..35, 1..20] of char;
   ```

2. The principle of superposition means to form an image by first storing one shape in an array, then replacing part of the stored image with other shapes, building the digital image by superimposing several shapes. Finally, when all shapes have had their effect on the array, the array is printed or displayed.

3. Since the pixels for such a device can be either "on" or "off", we can use the value of the array element image [row, column] to record whether the pixel in a given row and column is "on". The boolean value true means it is on and the boolean value false means it is off.

Section 10.3

1. The intensity of the light is sampled at regularly spaced points in the image and the numerical intensities obtained in the fashion are stored in an array.

2. If the display hardware can handle a scale of intensities at each displayed dot, gray may be produced this way. If only "on" and "off" (white and black) are possible, intermediate grays are produced by turning on a suitable fraction of the dots.

3. When the digitized image is available as input to a computer program, the image may not only be reproduced but also enhanced. Contrast may be improved, static may be removed, and permanent distortions and malfunctions of the image-acquiring apparatus may be corrected, to name a few of the possibilities.

Section 10.4

1. a. True, the array rate still has the same three ranges of subscript values in the same order.
   b. True.
   c. False, the range of values of the subscripts has nothing to do with the order of subscripts. You, as programmer, may declare any subscript first.
   d. False, when an array reference occurs in an instruction to be executed, its subscript expressions are evaluated to produce numerical values before they are used. Using meaningful subscript names in the wrong subscript position cannot reference the correct array element because only the sequence of evaluated subscript expression values is used to locate an element in an array. You must keep the subscripts in the declared order. If you don't, you risk subscript-out-of-bounds errors, or worse yet, incorrect array elements used in the calculation.

Chapter 11

Section 11.1

1. a. False, the procedure rewrite erases the file as well as positioning at the
    first record.
    b. False, the built-in procedures read and readln also will read values for
    other intrinsic data types. They can read a sequence of characters from
    the file and convert the sequence to the proper data type.
    c. True.
2.  ```
    var
       integerfile : file of integer;
    ```

Section 11.2

1. a. False, if they all have the same type, you might as well use an array.
    b. True.
    c. True, this permits further refinement of the data structure.
    d. True, this is one of the important uses of record types.
2. There are many possible solutions. The following one does the job.
    ```
    type
       nametype = packed array [1..20] of char;
       gamedatatype = record
          teamname : array [1..2] of nametype;
          score : array [1..2] of integer;
          end;  { gamedatatype }
       var
          weeksresults : array [1..14] of gamedatatype;
    ```

Section 11.3

1. a. False, it also means executing a rewrite statement for the file.
    b. False, only the last field may be variant.
    c. False is the better answer. The true situation is that the copy on auxi-
    liary memory is kept because the main memory copy *will* be destroyed.
    d. True, provided that the variable on the left of the assignment operator
    (:=) is the same type as the variable on the right of the assignment
    operator.
2. The main steps are:
    a. Reading the old values from the file in auxiliary memory into variables
    in main memory.
    b. Changing the values in main memory.
    c. Writing the changed values from main memory to the file to save them
    permanently.
    ```

Chapter 12

Section 12.1

1. The correct statements are

```
type
  integerpointer = ^integer;   { The caret comes first. }
var
  ptr : integerpointer;

begin         { Since ptr is a pointer to integers, }
ptr^ := 6;    { the value it points to is an integer, }
end           { not the location pointed to. }
```

2. a. False, it is possible that in some Pascal systems, some of the time, memory locations for new nodes might be allocated sequentially, but the Pascal programmer should not know this and certainly should not attempt to use it. Space for new nodes could be allocated anywhere in memory and, in most Pascal systems, the programmer and program cannot even find out where new nodes are located.
   b. False, zero is not a valid value for a pointer variable. It is an integer.
   c. False, a dynamic list is an abstract data structure. A linked list is one way to implement the abstract structure using Pascal features.
   d. False, it is programmer-defined.
   e. False, the supplied argument to the built-in procedure new may be any pointer type except pointer to a file.

Section 12.2

1. a. True.
   b. False, assuming equivalent sorting algorithms, the advantage of a linked list is that for nodes with a great deal of information in them, it is faster to change two link fields than it is to swap two nodes as one might have to do using an array of nodes.
   c. False, the examples in this section are clearer with tail recursion.

Chapter 13

Section 13.1

1. a. False, compare the recursive and nonrecursive programs to calculate Fibonacci numbers, for example.
   b. False, if there are no nonrecursive paths to treat the simplest case or cases, the procedure is guaranteed to produce an infinite recursive descent execution-time disaster.
   c. False, in fact, recursive procedures with only one recursive call usually can be written just as well as iterative procedures without recursion. The real benefit of recursion usually makes its appearance when there are two or more recursive calls per execution of a recursive procedure.
   d. True is the better answer if your explanation mentions the general Pascal rule to this effect and if you consider a forward declaration as declaring the procedure. False is the correct answer if you mention that

the body of the declaration of at least one of the procedures involved in indirect recursion cannot help but appear after the call to that procedure.

e. False, not every call must be for a simpler instance. All that matters is that is gets simpler eventually.

Section 13.2

1.   a. True.
     b. True.
     c. False, the number of comparisons is at most the maximum height of the tree. If the tree is at all balanced, the height of the tree is approximately $\log_2 n$, where n is the number of nodes. The height is much smaller than the number of nodes.
     d. True, if you don't believe it, try to write a clearer procedure without using recursion.

Chapter 14

Section 14.1

1.   a. False, a value of set type is a collection of elements, while a value of enumerated type is an individual element.
     b. True, certainly. An enumerated data type is a small, ordered type.
     c. False, the comparison operators "<" and ">" are not permitted.

Section 14.2

1.   a. False, labels are unsigned integers.
     b. True, label declarations precede constant declarations.
     c. False, what is true is that is is possible to write extremely unstructured programs using goto-statements.
     d. False, it is very rarely a good practice to use a goto-statement to exit from a procedure. Only seldom is it a good practice to use a goto-statement to exit from a loop. Even then, great care should be taken that the goto-statement transfers control to the same place as a "normal" exit of the loop.

INDEX